Towards a British Natyam

DANCE AND PERFORMANCE STUDIES

General Editors:
Helena Wulff, *Stockholm University*, and **Jonathan Skinner**, *University of Surrey*

Advisory Board:
Alexandra Carter, Marion Kant, Tim Scholl

In all cultures, and across time, people have danced. Mesmerizing performers and spectators alike, dance creates spaces for meaningful expressions that are held back in daily life. Grounded in ethnography, this series explores dance and bodily movement in cultural contexts at the juncture of history, ritual and performance, including musical, in an interconnected world.

Recent volumes:

Volume 16
Towards a British Natyam: Creating a British Classical Indian Dance Tradition
Magdalen Gorringe

Volume 15
Perspectives in Motion: Engaging the Visual in Dance and Music
Edited by Kendra Stepputat and Brian Diettrich

Volume 14
24 Bars to Kill: Hip Hop, Aspiraton, and Japan's Social Margins
Andrew B. Armstrong

Volume 13
Lullabies and Battle Cries: Music, Identity and Emotion among Republican Parading Bands in Northern Ireland
Jaime Rollins

Volume 12
Singing Ideas: Performance, Politics and Oral Poetry
Tríona Ní Shíocháin

Volume 11
Staging Citizenship: Roma, Performance and Belonging in EU Romania
Ioana Szeman

Volume 10
Collaborative Intimacies in Music and Dance: Anthropologies of Sound and Movement
Edited by Evangelos Chrysagis and Panas Karampampas

Volume 9
Languid Bodies, Grounded Stances: The Curving Pathway of Neoclassical Odissi Dance
Nandini Sikand

Volume 8
Choreographies of Landscape: Signs of Performance in Yosemite National Park
Sally Ann Ness

Volume 7
In Search of Legitimacy: How Outsiders Become Part of an Afro-Brazilian Capoeira Tradition
Lauren Miller Griffith

For a full volume listing, please see the series page on our website:
https://berghahnbooks.com/series/dance-and-performance-studies

Towards a British Natyam
Creating a British Classical Indian Dance Tradition

Magdalen Gorringe

berghahn
NEW YORK · OXFORD
www.berghahnbooks.com

First published in 2025 by
Berghahn Books
www.berghahnbooks.com

© 2025 Magdalen Gorringe

All rights reserved. Except for the quotation of short passages
for the purposes of criticism and review, no part of this book
may be reproduced in any form or by any means, electronic or
mechanical, including photocopying, recording, or any information
storage and retrieval system now known or to be invented,
without written permission of the publisher.

Library of Congress Cataloging-in-Publication Data

A C.I.P. cataloging record is available from the Library of Congress

Library of Congress Cataloging in Publication Control Number: 2024033544

British Library Cataloguing in Publication Data

A catalogue record for this book is available from the British Library

ISBN 978-1-80539-849-3 hardback
ISBN 978-1-80539-850-9 epub
ISBN 978-1-80539-851-6 web pdf

https://doi.org/10.3167/9781805398493

For all those who have worked towards a 'British Natyam'.
Past, present and to come.

கற்றது கை மண் அளவு. கல்லாதது உலகளவு
Kattradhu kai mann alavu. Kallaadhadhu ulugalavu

What I know, is the size of a fistful of earth.
What I don't, the expanse of the spinning globe.

—Avvaiyaar *(Translated from Tamil, with thanks to Geetha Sridhar)*

Contents

List of Illustrations	viii
Acknowledgements	x
Introduction. Flourishing or Fragile? The Contradictory Context of Classical Indian Dance Forms in Britain	1
1. Context: *BBC Young Dancer* and the Professionalization of South Asian Dance in Britain: A Snapshot of the Sector and Its Place within British Dance	33
2. Professionalism: Of Work, Love and Money: Living to Dance – or Dancing to Live? What It Means to Be a 'Professional' Classical Indian Dancer in Britain	79
3. Learning: Migration, Identity, and Making Professional Dancers	118
4. Livelihood, Learning, Embodiment: 'Technical Habitus', Classical Indian Dance Forms and the Limits of the 'Versatile Dancer'	160
5. Legitimacy: Professionalizing Classical Indian Dance in Britain and Entering the 'National Cultural Canon'	193
Conclusion. Part of the 'British DNA'?	235
Appendix 1. List of Judges and Mentors Engaged for *BBC Young Dancer*	246
Appendix 2. Table of South Asian Dance Tuition in British HE Institutions	250
Appendix 3. Table of Members of the South Asian Dance Alliance	254
Appendix 4. Project Interlocutors	260
References	262
Index	287

Illustrations

Figures

0.1. Akshay Prakash presenting a moment of *abhinaya* in *Shivoham*. 2018. © Dinesh Mahathevan. — 5

1.1. Jaina Modasia performing a *chakar* in *In Akbar's Palace*, one of the pieces she performed as part of the South Asian category finals, *BBC Young Dancer*, 2017. © BBC Photo Archive. — 54

1.2. Shree Savani, the winner of the 2019 *BBC Young Dancer* South Asian dance category final, performs *Maa* (Shree Savani and Dimple Chauhan, 2019) with her dance partner Shreya Vadnerkar. 2019. © BBC Photo Archive. — 72

2.1. Students of the Bharatiya Vidya Bhavan in a production of the *Kadiragama Kuruvanji* bharatanatyam dance drama. Bhavan, London. 2018 © Dinesh Mahathevan. — 80

3.1. A bharatanatyam class taking place in the Dance Xchange studios, Birmingham. 2018 © Magdalen Gorringe. — 119

3.2. Prakash Yadagudde teaches a bharatanatyam class in the Hathi Hall of the Bharatiya Vidya Bhavan, West Kensington, London. 2023. © Magdalen Gorringe. — 120

3.3. Odissi dancer Katie Ryan in an *abhinaya*-based dance piece. © Simon Richardson. — 138

4.1. Dancers in Akademi's *Paradiso* on the rooftop of the Royal Festival Hall, London. 2017 © Simon Richardson. — 187

5.1. A bharatanatyam (or kuchipudi?) dancer on page twenty-eight of the British passport (designed in 2015). © Magdalen Gorringe. — 198

5.2. Natya Project dancers in rehearsal, Birmingham 2018. © Simon Richardson. — 221

5.3. Amina Khayyam Dance Company (a new NPO in 2023) in *Bird* (Amina Khayyam, 2023). Dancers R-L: Abirami Eswar, Jane Chan, Jalpa Vala, Selene Travaglia © Simon Richardson. 229

5.4. Seeta Patel Dance Company (another new NPO in 2023) in rehearsal for Patel's interpretation of *The Rite of Spring*. © Simon Richardson. 230

6.1. The author and Kalidasan Chandrasegaram in Akademi's, *Coming of Age,* London 2000 Photo © Ali Zaidi. Thanks also to Akademi. 236

6.2. The Natya Project at the Midlands Arts Centre, Birmingham, performing in front of a mural by the black British photographer Vanley Burke, 2018. An illustration of the multiple narratives that interweave in contemporary Britain. © Magdalen Gorringe. 239

Tables

5.1. Top ten funded dance NPOs (2018–22), including dance companies and agencies. © Magdalen Gorringe. 196

5.2. Top ten funded dance NPOs (2023–26), including dance companies and agencies. © Magdalen Gorringe. 196

5.3. Top ten funded dance company NPOs (2018–22). © Magdalen Gorringe. 200

5.4. Top ten funded dance company NPOs (2023–26). © Magdalen Gorringe. 201

5.5. National dance agency funding, 2018–22. © Magdalen Gorringe. 216

5.6. Funding for NPO members of the South Asian Dance Alliance (SADA), 2018–22. © Magdalen Gorringe. 216

5.7. National dance agency funding, 2023–26. © Magdalen Gorringe. 217

5.8. Funding for NPO members of the South Asian Dance Alliance (SADA), 2023–26. © Magdalen Gorringe. 217

5.9. South Asian dance NPOs, 2018–22. © Magdalen Gorringe. 228

5.10. South Asian dance NPOs, 2023–26. © Magdalen Gorringe. 228

Appendix 2.1. 'Chart'-ing the courses teaching South Asian dance in Britain – a Table of South Asian Dance Tuition in British HE Institutions © Magdalen Gorringe. 251

Appendix 3.1. Table of Members of the South Asian Dance Alliance, UK. © Magdalen Gorringe. 255

Acknowledgements

The most enjoyable part of any piece of writing must surely be writing the acknowledgements. So enjoyable in fact that I have composed these in my head many times when the actual work of the book has seemed a lot more difficult and a lot less compelling. A work of this nature inevitably draws on the generosity and the forbearance of many – and it is my pleasure to acknowledge these many people here.

First and foremost, my thanks go to all those who have found time to speak to me and share their knowledge and expertise, their hopes, dreams and fears for the development of South Asian dance in Britain. These people are too many to list individually here, though a list of all the people I interviewed can be found in the appendices. Many more people have contributed than this list suggests. If I have done my work well, this book will belong as much to the sector as it does to me. I thank you all.

The research for this book was made possible thanks to a Vice-Chancellor's Scholarship from the University of Roehampton, and took shape under the generous and patient guidance of my PhD Director of Studies Ann R. David and co-supervisors Avanthi Meduri and Alexandra Kolb. Andrée Grau, my first co-supervisor, died prematurely in 2017. Her warmth, her humour and her cheerful exhortations to 'Courage!' have remained with me nonetheless. I hope this work carries with it some of her passion and compassion. Special thanks to Ann for endless kindness in helping me navigate the at times daunting process of getting a manuscript ready for publication. The text has benefitted from the careful reading and insightful suggestions of Joe Kelleher and Prarthana Purkayastha.

Mira Kaushik is owed special thanks for getting me into this in the first place. She called me up, told me to apply to do the PhD and brushed aside my fears of not being able to do it. The resulting work may not be what she had envisioned when she suggested I take it on, but I hope she forgives me and enjoys it anyway.

Thanks to my guru, Prakash Yadagudde, and all those who have guided me in bharatanatyam over the years – Udipi Laxminarayan, Mavin Khoo, Leela Samson, Geetha Sridhar, Stella Subbiah, Shakuntala, and Mira Balchandran Gokul. Thanks to Bisakha and Sanjeevini for moral support.

My dad Tim has been the recipient of many tearful phone calls attesting to the impossibility of writing and has painstakingly read and commented on every chapter. My brother Hugo has read and commented on articles and abstracts and has found time to discuss Bourdieu and social theory despite his heavy workload.

My dad Tim and stepmum Gill, my sister Iona, Jaya, Ramani, Loga, Claudia and Arul have all helped hugely with childcare – especially when the boys were younger, and I was travelling for fieldwork. Helen Lucas has provided both sanity and sanctuary in the form of a place to stay in London. Thanks to Rebecca Homan. Thanks and apologies in equal measure to Rosie, Jonaki, Ashufta, Arti, Lucia, Kate, Claire, Sonia, Emma, Alfy and Mai who, together with all those named above, have provided coffee, counsel and company. I'm sorry my mum Carol (1946–2004) didn't get a chance to see this. She would have approved of the amount of tea that fuelled it.

Finally, to the beloved and infuriating men who centre my life – my husband Shivaji and sons Ishaan and Kiran – for putting up with sharing their home with a book. Especially as I know Kiran would have rather shared the house with a baby. Or a dog.

Introduction

Flourishing or Fragile? The Contradictory Context of Classical Indian Dance Forms in Britain

9 May 2015 saw the Grand Final of the first ever series of the televised competition *BBC Young Dancer*, held at Sadler's Wells theatre in London. A show loosely modelled on *BBC Young Musician*, launched in 1978, it aimed to discover 'the UK's most gifted and dedicated dancers aged 16–21 in four categories: Ballet, Contemporary, Hip Hop and South Asian Dance' (BBC 2023).[1] For this final, the winners from each category, together with two 'wildcards', performed in front of a 'judging panel made up of some of the biggest names from the dance world' (ibid.).

The choice of categories was inevitably contentious, but for the world of South Asian dance,[2] to be one of only four categories chosen by the British Broadcasting Corporation (BBC)[3] to represent British dance was momentous. Mira Kaushik, former director (1989–2019) of Akademi in London, an organization committed to the promotion of South Asian dance in Britain,[4] felt that it was 'the best news for the position of South Asian dance in this country' (Kaushik 2017a). The selection of South Asian dance was all the more significant thanks to the framing of the show, as a serious event with strong and realistic links to the dance profession – unlike more spectacular or celebrity-driven dance talent shows like *The Greatest Dancer* or *So You Think You Can Dance*. *Young Dancer* self-consciously considered 'throughout the process . . . what the professional life of a dancer is like', because 'these young people will hopefully enter the professional world in a year or two' (Hackett 2015). This alignment with 'the professional world' is partly what made the inclusion of South Asian dance as a category both so important and so gratifying. To quote Kaushik again,

> All this time South Asian dance has been perceived to be a community activity. In this context, where it is put alongside ballet, contemporary

dance and other forms where professionals are working and in a field where professionals are aspiring to create professionals, the inclusion of South Asian dance is big and good news. (Kaushik 2017a)

While this competition effectively elevates South Asian dance to a status comparable to that of ballet or Euro-American[5] contemporary dance, a very brief exploration betrays a different story. In 2015, while all ten of the contemporary and ballet finalists were either enrolled in or about to commence specialist full-time training courses in their respective dance forms and had their sights on a professional dance career,[6] the position of the South Asian dancers was much more equivocal. Of the five finalists, only one, Vidya Patel, was clear about pursuing dance as a career. Of the others, one was studying physiotherapy,[7] one was studying sports science while hoping to 'pursue [dance] further', a third was studying civil engineering and a fourth was studying for A levels and went on to take up a degree in dentistry.[8] The situation for the second round of the competition in 2017 was very similar.[9] Again, all the contemporary and ballet dancers were engaged in or about to embark on full-time professional training. Of the South Asian dancers, two were enrolled in medical school and hoped to combine a career as a dancer with a career as a medic. The remaining three aspired to a career in dance, but their pathway to achieving this was far from clear.

There is still no vocational training school available for classical Indian dance forms in Britain (see Chapter 3) despite efforts to create one, meaning that while the 2015 South Asian dance category winner Vidya Patel expressed a desire to pursue a 'dance degree', she was not able to pursue a degree in her own style, kathak (at least in Britain), because there was no such course available.[10] The *Young Dancer* 2017 category winner Shyam Dattani likewise voiced his intention to take a vocational qualification and train full-time. A year later he had enrolled in a Business Management degree, working overtime to maintain his dance practice while studying for his degree.[11]

Even if such a course were to exist, in terms of subsequent employment opportunities, there remain very few companies in Britain that are able to offer dancers who have trained in classical Indian dance forms regular paid work. Shobana Jeyasingh's and Akram Khan's dance companies continue to be referenced as providing such opportunities.[12] However, while Jeyasingh's earlier work was rooted in and explored the vocabulary of bharatanatyam (the dance form in which she herself trained), her choreographic interests have taken her work away from a focused exploration of this form, and the company now employs predominantly Euro-American contemporary dance-trained practitioners.[13] Khan's work has a more explicit connection to kathak, the first dance form in which he was trained. His website describes the company as 'embracing an artistic vision that both respects and challenges the Indian kathak form and contemporary dance' (Akram Khan Company 2019). In practice, however, most of his dancers are again primarily Euro-American contemporary dance-trained. In fact, in 2019, there were only three companies that could be argued to represent classical Indian dance forms operating within the comparative security of being Arts Council National Portfolio Organizations (NPOs), a significance I discuss at greater length below.[14] Two of these, Leicester Dance Theatre (whose artistic director is the kathak dancer Aakash Odedra) and Sonia Sabri Company, frequently tour solo shows, thereby limiting the need to employ more dancers, and Odedra's first ensemble piece, *#JeSuis* (2018), used exclusively Euro-American contemporary dance-trained practitioners. The third company, Balbir Singh Dance Company, like Khan's, has a dual focus on kathak and contemporary dance and again uses at least as many Euro-American contemporary as classically Indian-trained dancers. Thus, while for Euro-American contemporary-trained and ballet dancers, excellence in the competition can lead to career opportunities (2017 competition winner Nafisah Baba, for example, was subsequently offered a role as guest artist in Phoenix Dance Company's production of the *Windrush*, Sharon Watson, 2018), such opportunities are limited for classical Indian dance practitioners because of the lack of training schools or dance companies to offer them. Kathak dancer Vidya Patel has had continuous employment since her success in the *Young Dancer* competition highlighted above, but a significant part of this employment has been as a guest kathak artist for Euro-American contemporary dance companies or as a kathak dancer within contemporary dance works. While South Asian dance has benefitted from the profile and the kudos of being an equal fourth professional dance category alongside ballet, contemporary dance and hip-hop, the reality behind the dancers sharing the stage space in the finale is one of very different levels of opportunity, infrastructure, visibility and acceptance.

As I argue throughout this book, the story of the emerging professionalization of South Asian dance, or of classical Indian dance forms in Britain, is one in which contradictions such as those seen with *BBC Young Dancer* are pervasive. South Asian dance is sufficiently significant to have been selected as one of only four categories chosen to represent British dance and yet there is no vocational training school in classical Indian dance forms for the young dancers it showcases. The dance forms have received considerable mainstream recognition – Akram Khan, a choreographer whose roots are in the classical Indian dance style kathak, is considered one of Britain's 'leading triumvirate of choreographers' (Jennings 2015);[15] in 2006, the classical bharatanatyam artist, teacher and choreographer Nina Rajarani won the Place Prize, 'Europe's most prestigious award for choreography' (Lim 2006) for a piece rooted 'completely in bharatanatyam and Carnatic music' (Manch UK 2020c: 32:47); and a growing number of members of the South Asian dance world have been honoured for their contribution to dance in Britain.[16] And yet there remain very few companies to offer young dancers employment.

Given this status quo, it is perhaps hardly surprising that although hundreds of students each year attend classes in classical Indian dance forms (see Chapter 3) and undertake examinations held either by the Imperial Society of Teachers of Dancing (ISTD) or by their own institutions, there remain very few who take up dance as a career. A lack of vocational training means that companies that might be interested in employing South Asian dancers struggle to find dancers trained to a high standard due to lack of supply.[17] Younger students who might consider taking up a course in South Asian dance are put off by the lack of obvious career progression due to the small number of companies, and therefore the apparent lack of demand. The sector is thus caught up in the archetypal 'vicious circle'.

In this way, despite the high profile of sector members and the influence the sector has undoubtedly had on the wider world of British dance, South Asian dance in Britain remains in many ways a fragile and tentative entity. Almost fifty years after researcher and arts policy advisor Naseem Khan[18] wrote her influential book *The Arts Britain Ignores* in 1976 (a work that highlighted the vast array of cultural activity that took place in Britain, unfunded and largely unacknowledged),[19] and despite the Arts Council's explicit commitment to cultural diversity for over thirty years,[20] many classical Indian dancers still feel that classical Indian dance is 'not what is wanted in the UK' (cited in Gorringe, Jarrett-Macauley and Srivastava 2018: 35). This book has at its heart these contradictions – the tension between a sector that apparently flourishes but still feels ignored; between the numbers of children up and down the country who flock to attend classical Indian dance classes and the handful who go on to make it a career; between the perception of some that 'British dance is defined by its diversity' (Wayne McGregor on *BBC Young Dancer* 2019) and the perception of others, as evidenced by the dancers cited above, that Britain's dance culture remains essentially homogeneous.

The Challenges of Professionalization

The key questions that drive this book are what it takes to make a viable working life as a performing dance artist – and whether it is possible to do so in Britain today as a practitioner of an Indian classical dance form. In a world that increasingly demands what choreographer and dance scholar Susan Leigh Foster calls the 'hired body', or one that 'does not display its skills as a collage of discrete styles, but rather homogenizes all styles beneath a sleek, impenetrable surface' (Foster 1997: 255), what does this mean for any dancer, but particularly for the practitioner of classical Indian dance? Is it possible for practitioners of these forms to find a niche in the world of British professional dance on their own terms, without being reshaped within the hungry eclecticism of Euro-American contemporary dance? More fundamentally, is professionalization necessarily a desirable outcome? This question is especially pertinent when professionalization involving engaging with the wider world of professional British dance arguably imposes as many constraints as it offers advantages.

As an illustration, take *Shivoham* (lit. 'I am Shiva'), choreographed by Akshay Prakash and Prakash Yadagudde in 2017, a solo bharatanatyam recital performed at the Bharatiya Vidya Bhavan (the Institute for Indian Culture based in West Kensington, London)[21] in July 2017 to a packed auditorium. The audience members were overwhelmingly of South Asian heritage (I was one of fewer than ten audience members of non-South Asian heritage in an audience of about three hundred; fieldwork notes, July 2017).[22] Several in the audience displayed the depth of their connection to, and knowledge of, the codes and conventions governing bharatanatyam by keeping the *talam* (time or measure in Carnatic music) with their right hands; others shook their heads or 'tutted' in appreciation.[23] The artists in the meantime were evidently likewise enjoying themselves. Performing for an audience that they knew would have a basic level of competence with their art forms' conventions and codes allowed them to take the space to play with their forms. The *mridangist* (mridangam player M. Balachander) excelled in conjuring percussion accompaniments to Prakash's *abhinaya* (briefly, expressive dance)[24] – the stumbling walk of an old man; a swarm of bees; the sudden and incandescent anger of Shiva. Dancer and percussionist riffed with each other – throwing each other suggestions to be run with or discarded in that moment. Watching the performance therefore involved the thrill not only of strong technique and narrative, but of risk. These performers were figuratively throwing each other juggling balls. Would they keep them up in the air, or would one drop? The context of the Bhavan permitted such play and improvisation, leading to a forty-five-minute *varnam* (literally figure/shape/colour – the longest and

Figure 0.1. Akshay Prakash presenting a moment of abhinaya *in Shivoham. 2018. © Dinesh Mahathevan.*

most challenging piece of the bharatanatyam repertoire, interspersing bursts of abstract dance with an extended exploration of the emotional state of the character portrayed – and something performers confess to avoiding for inexperienced audiences).[25] What would happen to this playfulness and invention if the piece had to tour in theatres less flexible on time frame? What is the impact on the improvisation that is the creative heart of the *varnam* when one needs to honour technicians' contracts for a specific time period or consider an audience mindful of parking meters or the time of their last train home?

The performance of *Shivoham* started late. Equally, several of the audience members arrived 'late'. Would a prompt start have breached the implicit contract between the performers and the audience established for this particular event? There were long speeches during the interval, which from one perspective could be considered 'unprofessional'. From another perspective, however, these speeches that customarily honour the performers (including the musicians) and their lineage (by naming their gurus or teachers) are fulfilling an important aspect of expected etiquette. To not have them could be seen as equivalent to failing to present a cast list – or in other words, could be construed as highly 'unprofessional'. If 'professionalization' is not to mean adherence to a culturally arbitrary set of rules, it is clearly vital to establish what in fact it does mean, which will allow a better understanding of whether or not it is important.

Critical to the development of any art form is, of course, the provision for training – and how classical Indian dancers in Britain are trained is a further central concern in this book. In 2003, dance scholar Christopher Bannerman commented, echoing the findings of the Leverhulme-funded *South Asian Dance in Britain* report (Grau 2001), that

> Of course, there are barriers to the continued development of South Asian dance in Britain. One of these is the lack of a school for professional training and, as a result of this, the lack of a clear pathway of professional opportunity. This will continue to be an inhibiting factor until proper provision, mirroring that available for ballet and contemporary dance, is established. (Bannerman 2003)

The following year, a memorandum submitted to the British Parliament by the South Asian Dance Alliance (SADAA),[26] as part of the sixth report by the Department for Culture, Media and Sport, made this point a parliamentary concern, noting 'A serious barrier to the continued development of South Asian dance in Britain is the lack of a school for professional training and, as a result of this, the lack of a clear pathway of professional opportunity' (Select Committee on Culture Media and Sport 2004).

Indeed, the issue was highlighted far earlier. Naseem Khan wrote in her 1976 report that 'A school of Indian classical music and dance could have many advantages, not least of providing a recognised standard of tuition . . . a central institute . . . would be able to train teachers, set standards and act as a focus of interest for Indian music and dance' (Khan 1976: 64). Even in 1976, Khan observed that 'people in the field have talked *for years* of the value of a well-run, demanding and disciplined music and dance school that could provide a high standard of tuition' (ibid., my emphasis). I discuss the attempts that have been made to achieve this and how the shape of training impacts the shape of the professional sector.

Through a discussion of this specific case study of classical Indian dance forms in Britain, I consider wider questions about what it means to professionalize, and what it means to professionalize an art form. This question is complicated by the positioning of the arts within what the sociologist and philosopher Pierre Bourdieu calls the 'reversed economy', or a field that places value on (at least the apparent) disinterestedness in and independence from economic market constraints – a context particularly relevant for classical Indian dance (see Chapter 2). I consider the environment required for an art form to develop successfully as a profession, how professional practice adapts across national boundaries and how far art forms are tied to or transcend a particular national identity. This in turn feeds into further-reaching discussions about migration and identity, about universalism and particularism in art forms and about the endeavour to resist cultural homogenization while avoiding separatism. While the focus of this book is unapologetically the British context, I hope that the discussions of the professionalization of an art form, the relation of the arts to national identity and the importance of representation will speak to the context of the arts beyond this small island.

The Arts Britain Still Ignores?

This is the title of a 2018 article written by director, actor and theatre scholar Jerri Daboo – in this case considering the continued gaps in diverse representation in British theatre forty years on from Khan's report (Daboo 2018). In it she asks, 'There have been advances made in the visibility of BAME [Black, Asian and minority ethnic] practitioners across the theatre sector since 1976, and yet how much has really changed? Are we still repeating the same issues that Naseem Khan raised forty years ago?' (ibid.: 6).

Within dance likewise, this was a question that interviewees raised throughout my research. Despite the talent in the sector, the energy of the agencies, the commitment of teachers and the (overall) good intentions of the Arts Council,[27] how much has really changed?

It is easy to point fingers, and many in the sector do so. The lack of progress is attributed to Asian parents and their unwillingness to support a child's choice to pursue a career in the arts (Courtney Consulting 2020 37); to the fractious relationship with the dance agencies, accused of pursuing their own agendas at the expense of a vision for the wider sector (ibid.: 80, 81); to the lack of commitment among dancers, accused of a sense of entitlement and a lack of preparedness for hard work (ibid.: 104); and to the Arts Council and the marginalization of classical in favour of 'innovative' dance work (Kedhar 2020; Courtney Consulting 2020: 85).[28]

There may be an element of truth in each of these accusations or explanations, but none of them represents the whole story. In 2016, I attended a major sector conference, Navadisha 2016, organized by Sampad Arts in partnership with New Dimensions Arts Management. At this conference I experienced both the excitements and the frustrations of a sector that has come so far and has so much to offer, and yet in some ways remains stuck with the same challenges and questions it faced when it made its first steps to anchor itself in Britain. How do we ensure high-quality training – and who determines what this is? How do we produce work with a sufficient appeal to tour widely and sustain the costs and demands of touring without compromising the artistic and aesthetic integrity of our forms? As I shared in the highs and lows of the conference, immersed in common exhilaration and indignation, a part of me wondered whether if the sector could only have access to more information – to the stories of the journeys of other dance forms, of the wider narrative of migration and diaspora; if it could remember so much that seemed forgotten of even relatively recent battles and victories; if it could understand the way it has been positioned by the history of colonialism and therefore the narrative of power in which it is placed (Thobani 2017; Purkayastha 2017b) – could this provide some sort of self-understanding to give it the clarity and the determination to move forward?

It was and remains a lofty ambition, and yet this is my hope. This is because my interest in this field, in its thriving and surviving, is not only academic, but also personal. I address this below, considering my personal investments in the field as part of a broader consideration of my methodology. First, however, I situate the following discussion by giving a broad overview of the early history of Indian dance forms in Britain and explaining the context of funding for the arts in Britain, including the role of the Arts Council.

A (Very) Brief History of Indian Dance Forms in Britain

The first recorded performance of 'Indian dance' in Britain was by a troupe of hereditary dancers (*devadasis*, or as they were called in Europe, *bayadères*),[29] who made their British debut at the Adelphi Theatre in London on 1 October 1838. They had initially been brought to Europe by the French impresario E.C. Tardivel, and were leased from Tardivel for £5,000 by the then manager of the Adelphi, Frederick Yates (Bor 2007: 55).[30] In both London and Paris, they performed in major theatres, were celebrated by royalty, the press and the artistic cognoscenti, and were well looked after and accommodated and comparatively competitively paid.[31]

Yet in spite of the interest from the great and the good, as well as the largely positive attention from the press, the Adelphi performances appear to have benefitted largely from their status as a curiosity, rather than indicating any deeper audience interest and engagement. For a contemporary critic, though he felt that the performance of the *bayadères* had been the 'most interesting he ever saw', nonetheless,

> We suspect that there is something in the performance not entirely consistent with our English tastes and feelings . . . The interesting dancers themselves may attract notice – the curious tattoo of their hands, their jewels and dress . . . but 9 out of 10 think nothing at all of the dances . . . and they can't tell what to make of it. (*Brighton Herald*, 19 January 1838, cited in Bor 2007: 65)

As a consequence, for almost a century after this, 'there is little evidence in Britain of performances of Indian dance by Indian dancers' (David 2005b: 30).[32] Dancer and scholar Anusha Kedhar draws attention to archival records showing that a performing troupe from Bombay was contracted in November 1867 for three months by two brothers from Manchester to perform in Egypt, Malta, France and England (Kedhar 2011: 8). There were also the displays of dancers at Imperial Exhibitions such as the *Empire of India and Ceylon Exhibition* held at Earl's Court, London in 1886 and the Franco-British Exhibition in 1908 at White City, among others (see Purkayastha 2019), where the displays had resonances of the Roman imperial displays of the captured conquered. There is, however, no sustained interest in and engagement with Indian dance in the manner that may have been expected from 'Oriental' fascination of the time. Thus, musician and musicologist Joep Bor comments wryly, 'Clearly it was not the real Orient that appealed to audiences in nineteenth century Europe, but an imaginary Orient: a world composed of sylphs, nymphs, shades and other supernatural beings' (Bor 2007: 66).

Indeed, the only reason for the invitation to the hereditary dancers in 1838 had been the Western European preoccupation with 'the Orient', present since at least the seventeenth century. The 'exotic' foreigner, of uncertain geographical provenance, was tremendously popular in Western entertainment through much of the eighteenth, nineteenth and into the twentieth century, with the *bayadère* in particular cropping up as a recurrent figure (Grau 2011). This enchantment was one that remained among American and Western European audiences into the beginning of the twentieth century, with the same preference for an 'imagined' rather than actual representation of difference. As literary theorist and dance historian Elizabeth Kendall claims of the American dancer Ruth St. Denis, who gained her reputation through her portrayal of 'Oriental Dances', 'It was to Ruth's advantage that she wasn't Indian or trained by Indians; the audience preferred her to be American, like their home brand of Orientalia' (Kendall 1979: 78, cited in Shay 2008: 60).

The first Indian performer to present 'Indian' dance in the West after the hereditary dancers initially did nothing to discourage such Orientalist fantasies, but rather, with a degree of panache, charm and talent, exploited them – in a similar model to Ruth St. Denis. This was Uday Shankar (older brother of the sitarist Ravi Shankar), who, being male, educated and middle-class, could not have come from a more different background than his precursors. Shankar had been sent to London from India to continue his training as a visual artist at the Royal College of Art. His decision to pursue a career in dance rather than in visual arts was largely thanks to the prima ballerina Anna Pavlova, who wanted to include some Indian-themed dances in her repertory. Shankar was introduced to her as an enthusiast – and the resulting collaboration led to Shankar choreographing two Indian-themed dances, *Krishna and Radha* and *A Hindu Wedding* (Mackrell 2013), which premiered in Covent Garden in 1923 and went on to tour America (Shankar also performed in the first piece). The experience with Pavlova was enough to convince Shankar to swap art for dance, and he set off to Paris to try and make his living as a dancer. As he had no classical training and little more than his recollections of watching Rajasthani folk dances as a child to guide him (Abrahams 2007), there does not appear to have been a great deal to distinguish Shankar's early choreographies from those of the white purveyors of Orientalia, other than his masculinity and brown skin. Shankar did subsequently take time to train in different forms of Indian dance and music so as to root his performances in a firmer basis of technique rather than, as in his earlier years, simply playing to the 'popular European imaginary of the Empire' (Purkayastha 2012: 75). Nonetheless, it took the dancer Ram Gopal's arrival in London in 1939 to finally bring the discipline and idioms of Indian dance forms to the British stage for the first time since the hereditary dancers in 1838.

Gopal made his London debut in the West End's Aldwych Theatre and appears to have taken the capital by storm. In her monograph on Gopal (in which her meticulous research is enhanced by her personal friendship with Ram in his latter years), dance anthropologist Ann R. David notes that for his shows, there were 'queues outside the door' of the Aldwych, along with a sign saying 'House Full' (the Aldwych seats an audience of twelve hundred). The two-week run had to be extended to four to 'accommodate the audiences flocking to see him dance' (David 2024: 49). For South Asian dancers in Britain today, Gopal's standing is legendary – and it is he, rather than Shankar, or the dancers Amani or Sundaram of a hundred years earlier, who is usually credited with first putting classical Indian dance on the British radar.[33] There are a number of factors that contribute to his near-mythic status. Long-limbed, with distinctive half-Burmese, half-Indian features, often clad for his performances in a short skirt-like costume, bejewelled and frequently with an ornate headdress or even wings, Gopal had a larger than life quality that comes across even through faded black and white images from the 1930s and 1940s.[34] Together with this was his phenomenal success as a performer, which was at a level that South Asian dance practitioners in the UK today can only dream of, including the sell-out success in London's prestigious West End theatres described above. In a documentary on Gopal, David observes, 'Indian dance in a West End stage for two weeks would be unheard of now'. Kaushik comments similarly, 'Ram arrived and had up to six months' worth of shows at venues like Aldwych', pointing out that today's South Asian dancers have 'not yet reached [the] West End'.[35] In addition, unlike several other classical Indian dancer artists who performed in Britain at a similar time – Mrinalini Sarabhai (1949), Shanta Rao (1964) and Balasaraswati (who performed to packed houses and audiences, including Merce Cunningham and Margot Fonteyn at the Edinburgh Festival in 1963) – Gopal was the first to make Britain his home (Uday Shankar did so, but only briefly, as his time in Europe was spent primarily in Paris).

Gopal's career bridged a period of critical change in Britain, in particular in relation to perceptions of 'distant lands', the 'foreign' and the 'exotic'. When Gopal first started touring in the late 1930s, it was in the context of a continuing fascination with Orientalia. Gopal's tremendous popularity must be understood against this context. Prior to Indian independence, there is also, as David (2001: 20) observes, a suggestion of 'colonialist pride in the display of cultural wealth' in his enthusiastic reception. When Queen Mary invited him to tea, there was certainly a sense of her celebrating the 'jewel in the crown' (ibid.).

By the time of the end of Gopal's career in the 1960s, the social context in Britain had changed dramatically. Britain was no longer an empire. The Empire had been replaced by the Commonwealth – and the 1948 Nationality Act ruled that all citizens of countries within the British Commonwealth were also 'all full British subjects', entitled to settle in Britain (Marwick 2003: 132). Indeed, immigration and settlement of workers from outside of Britain was actively encouraged by the British government in the late 1940s and early 1950s to combat the acute labour shortage that Britain faced after the war, and was followed by immigration of 'British subjects' from the West Indies, India and Pakistan. Then, in the late 1960s and early 1970s, the Africanization policies of Kenya, Uganda and Tanzania, seeking to establish African sovereignty after independence from Britain, led to the enforced migration of large numbers of East African Asians. For Indian dance forms, this migration was galvanizing – as Naseem Khan (1997: 26) puts it, here 'almost overnight' was a new audience for the forms, a new demand for training and classes. It was the 1970s that really saw the emergence of the groups that later turned into the institutions that form the focus of this book. The Bharatiya Vidya Bhavan in London was founded in 1972, acquiring and moving to its present premises in a disused church in West Kensington in 1978. Akademi (then the Academy of Indian Dance) was formed in 1979 (see Appendix 3).

While the presence in India of Britain's East India Company and subsequent imperial rule meant that there had been an exchange of populations between India and Britain since the beginning of the seventeenth century (Visram 2002; Fisher, Lahiri and Thandi 2007), immigration after the Second World War was on a much larger scale. Kedhar (2020: 6) explains, 'from 1948 to 1981, migration from South Asia to Britain within thirty years surpassed anything seen in the previous three hundred years, increasing from forty-three thousand in 1951 to approximately one million in 1981'. Suddenly 'race' was an issue in Britain, as it was already in other parts of the world. The 'Lure of the East' was not so easy to sustain in the face of the reality of people from the 'East', who, far from fulfilling their roles as figures of improbable opulence and mystique, set about on the necessary grind of earning a living, as owners of corner shops or labourers in textile mills. In August 1958, in what social historian Arthur Marwick (2003: 163) describes as a 'landmark' indicating the 'point of change between the post-war age of consensus and the new age of cultural change', violent race riots broke out in Notting Hill in West London.[36] Ten years later, in 1968, the Midlands-based member of parliament Enoch Powell made his now infamous 'rivers of blood' speech, in which he predicted grave consequences if immigration was allowed to continue (see Chapter 3). Against this backdrop, while in the post-war London of the late 1940s and 1950s, David (2024: 120) records a 'fresh readiness' among audiences 'to respond to artistic creations from abroad', and Gopal continued to perform successfully until the mid-1960s, there was now a whole other context to the performance of Indian dance. Such performances no longer necessarily evoked the lavish spirituality of a distant land, but came accompanied also by associations with race riots and the realities of a rapidly changing world. The 'exotic dancer' had become the 'ethnic dancer'. A new phase in the history of South Asian dance in Britain had begun. The dancers seeking to make their way in this book carry with them this legacy – the legacy of the 'Other' as fantasy, together with the 'Other' as threat; of Indian dance forms as holding the promise of an Oriental escape, while containing also the threat of a potentially overwhelming 'foreignness'. As I discuss, the need to navigate these two equally undesirable frames of representation necessarily shapes the way young dancers practising these forms enter their working lives.

The Patron State – the Context of Arts Funding in Britain

The period following the Second World War also saw a dramatic change to Britain's sociopolitical structures through the foundation of a comprehensive system of social insurance 'from the cradle to the grave', including the formation of Britain's National Health Service and commitments to comprehensive education, social security and social housing. The same period also saw the foundation of the Arts Council, an arms-length governmental body that has played a critical role in funding the arts in Britain since its foundation by Royal Charter in 1946.

Initially the Arts Council of Great Britain, it arose out of the Council for Encouragement of Music and Arts (CEMA) set up as an emergency measure to keep the arts alive and support morale during the war (Heilbrun 1984). The great economist John Maynard Keynes was instrumental in its creation, and in ensuring its status as an institution funded and guided by, and yet independent of, the state.[37] Since its foundation, the Arts Council has gone through a number of restructurings and transformations, notably changing from the Arts Council of Great Britain to the Arts Council of England in 1994 (renamed Arts Council England in 2003), with the accompanying formation of the Scottish Arts Council and the Arts Council of Wales.[38] In 1994, the Arts Council also acquired responsibility as one of the distributors for the National Lottery Good Cause funding (initially only for capital investment in construction, infrastructure and film production, but in 1996 extending this remit to investment in 'human capital', enabling the current National Lottery Projects funding discussed below).

The Arts Council started out with four administrative departments: Drama, Music, Literature and Visual Arts, with dance managed by a Dance Advisory subcommittee to the Music Panel. The Arts Council only created a separate dance department with its own director and a full panel in 1979/80, reflecting 'a burgeoning enthusiasm which has characterised the dance scene over the last few years' together with a 'demand for dance classes [that] has never been higher' (Arts Council of Great Britain 1980: 29). A few years later in 1984, Akademi (then Academy of Indian Dance) made their first (and successful) submission to the Arts Council for funding for a full-length Indian dance production, *The Adventures of Mowgli* (V.P. Dhananjayan, Pratap Pawar, Priya Pawar, 1984).[39]

Arts Council funding remains vital to the arts sector in Britain today, along with ticket sales, commercial sponsorship, donations and grants from trusts and foundations, and local public investment through local authorities (though this has been considerably reduced since 2010).[40] The Arts Council now falls under the remit of the Department for Culture, Media and Sport (DCMS), distributing money received from DCMS as Grant in Aid, as well as distributing National Lottery funds. It operates a range of funding programmes, including a funding stream for capital projects. For the purposes of this book, the most pertinent funding stream is its portfolio investment, whereby organizations that are properly constituted and that help to serve the Arts Council's aims can apply to be in the 'national portfolio' as a 'National Portfolio Organization' (NPO),[41] receiving regular annual funding for three to four years, and potentially longer if they are successful in successive portfolio rounds. For individual practitioners a key funding stream is National Lottery Projects Grants (NLPG, or Grants for the Arts until 2018), a funding stream open to organizations and individuals for which individuals need only be over 18, living in England and in possession of a bank account to apply for grants for discrete projects for anything between £1000 and over £100,000.[42] The role of the Arts Council is key to the following discussion, not least in the way that its portfolio of organizations can be seen as a kind of cultural canon (see Chapter 5).

I turn now to outlining the broader theoretical framing of this book, in particular addressing the centrality I assign to the thinking of French philosopher Pierre Bourdieu.

The Theoretical Framework: Squaring Decolonization with Bourdieu

This book, as discussed above, is about dancers and their work – how they prepare themselves for work, how they find work and importantly, how their work is valued. As such, it focuses less on the specific dance pieces that a dancer might perform and more on why they decide to perform what they do; less on individual dance companies and more on why it is that certain dancers and dance companies receive more attention than others; on why within the broader landscape of dance in Britain, certain companies thrive while others languish.

My work falls therefore across the areas of dance studies, cultural studies and sociology, and draws on scholarship in all three areas. As is indicated by the brief history of Indian dance forms in Britain above, in considering the representation and reception of art forms originating from a former colony (India) within the context of a formerly colonizing power (Britain), I have swiftly and inevitably come up against the continued power imbalances that are the legacy of colonization. The book is therefore also necessarily situated within the growing discourse around decolonization and the journeys that countries and peoples make to shake off the structures and conditioning imposed by colonial rule. Indeed, while my discussion of 'professionalization' takes its starting point from sociologists of profession (Wilensky 1964; Brante 1988; Ackroyd 2016; Evetts 2013, 2014), it soon becomes evident, as I point to above, that when discussing the professionalization of South Asian dance forms in Britain, what is important is not so much *what* might be considered professional but *who* determines what this is. A significant factor in both facilitating and recognizing the 'professionalization' of South Asian dance forms rests, I argue, not so much on anything the sector itself can or should do, but on the need for the wider British dance (and cultural) sector to recognize that there are 'many professionalisms', rather than accepting as unarguable the understanding assigned to the term by Euro-American former colonial powers.

My work has also become increasingly rooted, in ways I did not anticipate, in the sociology of Pierre Bourdieu (1930–2002). Since, not to put too fine a point on it, the theoretical model of a dead white man may not seem an obvious starting point from which to theorize South Asian dance in Britain, I will briefly explain both why I found myself drawn to his thinking and why I feel it provides a helpful and appropriate framing. Though Bourdieu himself resisted biography, his work is nonetheless usefully contextualized by reference to his personal circumstances. While he rose to the highest echelons of French academia, he was raised in a small French peasant village by a postal worker father who never completed his schooling and a mother who left school at 16 (Friedman 2016a). He never forgot his origins and within his acquired sphere of academic privilege battled with a sense of unease all his life (ibid.). This apparent poster boy of meritocracy perceived all too clearly what he understood as the fallacies of this ideology, and the philosophical underpinning provided it by rational action theory (RAT), briefly, a philosophy that privileges the ability of the individual agent to make sovereign choices about their life on the basis of rational analysis.[43]

For Bourdieu a serious problem with RAT was its ahistoricism. As he put it, 'this narrow, economist conception of the "rationality" of practices ignores the individual and collective history of agents through which the structures of preference that inhabit them are constituted' (Bourdieu and Wacquant 1992: 123). In other words, there are systems and structures beyond the individual that shape our thought processes and limit our existence as 'free agents', which prevent us from neatly analysing and ordaining our lives as if following an abstract set of mathematical principles. There is also the presence of other agents with whom we must negotiate to attain status or power. Bourdieu vehemently resisted philosopher Jean-Paul Sartre's notion of the 'original project', which he read as 'this sort of free and conscious act of self-creation whereby a creator assigns to himself his life's designs' (ibid.: 133). His sociology is premised therefore on a profound recognition of the structural limitations on an individual's choice and ability for self-fulfilment. Against the meritocratic conviction that 'the best will make it', and despite his own phenomenal success in this respect, Bourdieu reminds us again and again of the limits of unconscious, unacknowledged and unspoken structures of domination that seat themselves insidiously (or, to build on Foster's (2009: 7) wordplay, in(sinew)ously) in our very musculature. Yet this recognition is not a counsel of despair. On the contrary, Bourdieu's repeated summons to reflexivity urge us to examine our unexamined thoughts and practices as a way of contesting a dominant culture, which, though tending to inertia, remains a 'site of struggle', a state of 'no more than a temporary equilibrium' (Bourdieu 1990: 141). If we recognize the systemic patterns that limit us, we are more likely to be able to challenge and transcend them. To use contemporary terminology, one could say that Bourdieu is urging us to be 'woke'.

Bourdieu's commitment to the use of his theoretical concepts as tools, evolving in response to their use (Bourdieu and Wacquant 1992), has meant that they possess a malleability that allows their use in ways that he himself did not envisage (Thatcher et al. 2016). The now ubiquitous spread of his concepts of 'social' and 'cultural capital', for example, in itself points to their value and to how, whatever the limitations of his framework, it remains 'enormously good for thinking with' (Jenkins, cited in Wainwright et al. 2006: 553). His constant probing into structures of domination, particularly those so 'rooted in our collective unconscious that we no longer even see [them]' and 'so in tune with our expectations that [they] become hard to challenge' (Bourdieu 1998), has meant that I have found his theoretical tools of great help in the attempt to radically 'unmask and deconstruct the western hegemony' in the field of the humanities and other disciplines (Mbembe 2010), an unmasking that is so necessary for decolonization. His emphasis on embodiment, meanwhile, through his concepts of *habitus* and *hexis* (see Chapter 4), makes him especially useful when considering the embodied art of dance. While Bourdieu's own work did not focus much attention on issues of race and ethnicity, giving greater attention to questions of class (1984) and gender (2001), as sociologist Derron Wallace (2016: 38) remarks, despite this, 'his concepts have long been used to interpret the outcomes of racial, ethnic and class minorities'. Thus, 'perhaps he has more to say on issues of race and ethnicity than we give him credit for'.[44] The twin focus in his work on the use of his theoretical tools as, firstly, inherently malleable and intended to be adapted to circumstance and, secondly, a means to reveal structures of domination is in part why they have been used so productively by more recent theorists such as Sara Ahmed (2007), Ghassan Hage (2000) and Wallace (2016). These writers bring his concepts into the twenty-first century and into the work of decolonization and the recognition of the violence inherent in colonialism's 'laws of race' (Mbembe 2010). As the focus of this book moves from the tensions within the concept of professionalism associated with class and income to the related yet distinct tensions associated with ethnicity and race, my work draws more on Bourdieu as reflected and refracted through these more recent thinkers.

Methodology: Ethnography, Auto-Ethnography and Self-Consciousness

The research for the specific purposes of this book took place primarily between 2016 and 2020. It draws on interviews with fifty-one dance artists and arts administrators in the sector, and the attendance of forty-nine live performances across England, in theatres, temples, community centres and town squares, as well as many more online.[45] I have taken part in sector conferences (Navadisha 2016), round table meetings and discussions, and have attended classes both in person and latterly (during the Covid-19 pandemic) over Zoom. I have largely taken the role of a 'participant observer' (Becker and Geer 1957; Whyte 1979; Jackson 1983), a research practice by which the researcher gathers material as much by participating in activities in the field (e.g. taking part in discussions, participating in classes) as by gathering material as a researcher positioned outside the field. Such 'performing as a way of knowing' is particularly important in acknowledging that 'not all knowledge is verbally based, and that people use kinaesthetic as well as intellectual intelligence to process information' (Grau 2001: 35). It recognizes that an embodied experience of a dance form allows for a richer ethnography (David 2013b). It is also important in accessing the unedited and sometimes more authentic views of people in the field gleaned through gossip, hearsay and informal conversations (Lancaster 1994; Hamera 2011; Kedhar 2011). This intensive period of research builds on a much longer-standing relationship with classical Indian dance forms in Britain developed over more than thirty years. In this way my ethnography also takes the character of what dance ethnographer Peter Harrop (2013: 3) calls 'long ethnography', meaning the acquired understanding of a field over an extended period of time.

My relationship with classical Indian dance, specifically bharatanatyam, began when I was 7. My father's work placement in the temple town of Madurai in Tamil Nadu,[46] South India, meant an end to the ballet classes I had been taking in Birmingham in Britain – leaving my parents looking for the nearest available equivalent. This, they were told, was bharatanatyam – and since that time, this has been my dance form. By the time I returned to Britain as a teenager, I had embraced bharatanatyam, Tamil and Madurai to the extent that clinging to bharatanatyam was a way of holding on to a place I had not wanted to leave. I therefore spent several years stubbornly trekking from my home in Oxford to the Bhavan in West Kensington (referenced above) every weekend to practise my *adavus* (basic movement units/steps within bharatanatyam) with my guru, Prakash Yadagudde. My first job after university was as Education Officer for Akademi, under the leadership of Mira Kaushik. I then worked as a research assistant for Andrée Grau on the Leverhulme-funded project on South Asian dance in Britain[47] before returning to Akademi as Dance Development Officer, working with Kaushik to produce, among other things, the conferences South Asian Aesthetics – Unwrapped (2002) and Negotiating Natyam (2005). I combined this with working variously as a dancer, dance animateur[48] and dance teacher in London, Exeter and Birmingham, including a stint as Education Officer (and briefly apprentice dancer) for Shobana Jeyasingh Dance Company and a memorable summer spent working on *Images in Varnam* (2001) with Mavin Khoo Dance.

In many ways, therefore, this story of the changing fortunes of working as a classical Indian dancer in Britain is inextricably intertwined with my own personal story. I have known some of those interviewed, both personally and professionally, for over thirty years. I met one of my interviewees, my teacher at the Bhavan, Prakash Yadagudde, when I was 16 – and another, Bisakha Sarker, as a 14-year-old in Oxford, participating in a dance performance on Tagore. I have known Amina Khayyam since my early twenties, when we both attended classes at the Bhavan (she in kathak) and worked together on combining kathak with bharatanatyam, fuelled by her particularly potent brand of ginger chai. Shane Shambhu has been a friend since, along with the dancer Jasmine Simhalan, we toured the country's backwaters in a rickety minivan for the rural touring scheme Live Music Now! At one time or another I have worked, both as dancer and as writer or administrator, for all three of the organizations that formed the core of the aforementioned 'South Asian Dance Alliance' (Akademi, Sampad and Kadam, South Asian arts organizations based in London, Birmingham and Luton respectively).

My long-standing embodiment of bharatanatyam means that the daily ache in my knees reminds me of the toll that intensive training can take on the body, especially when undertaken on hard floors or in insufficiently heated rooms. I relate all too closely with the battle to motivate oneself to practise, alone and in the confined space of one's living room because there is no available group class. Similarly, the humiliation and frustration of being assessed on one's deficit – judged for what you cannot perform rather than credited for what you can (see Chapters 4 and 5) – is something I relate to from personal experience.

While in this way an insider to the field, I have at the same time always been positioned as somewhat apart – because I am white, and because I have two white, London-born parents who had never heard of bharatanatyam before I started learning it. My engagement in bharatanatyam and fluency in spoken Tamil as a blonde, blue-eyed child earned me entirely unmerited attention while growing up in Madurai, and the status of something of a curiosity. My technical lapses were sometimes overlooked due to my sheer novelty, and the most banal Tamil conversation was sufficient at times to earn myself and my siblings extra fizzy drinks (at that time Limca or Thums Up) in restaurants. On one occasion, after my return to Britain, I was given £1 by a stranger of South Asian heritage because I had spent the bus journey singing my old school songs to myself (which were variously in Hindi, Bengali, Sanskrit, Tamil and English). My engagement in bharatanatyam has therefore always been accompanied by a certain self-consciousness, and an awareness of myself as 'Other'. In this way, even before I placed a deliberate distance between myself and the field by looking at it as an ethnographer, I have always been an 'insider-outsider'.

Of course, as cultural anthropologist and novelist Kirin Narayan (1993) eloquently reminds us, the character of 'insideness' and 'outsideness' is as subject to variation as any other form of identity, such that the ethnographer, as with the subjects of their field of study, exists in a permanent dance of alienation and belonging, of 'insideness', of 'outsideness' – and primarily, of 'shaking it all about-ness'. Where I felt my 'outsideness' on the grounds of my 'whiteness', many of my (brown) interviewees revealed their equally complex relationship to the cultures and subcultures of the practice of classical Indian dance forms – speaking of times they felt accepted, and times they felt 'Othered' on account of their gender, their sexuality, their Britishness, their Indianness, their 'being from a different part of India-ness', their economic background, their religion, their lack of religion. Akram Khan has spoken of feeling like an 'outsider' on account of being 'Bangladeshi',[49] while Nina Rajarani describes a sequence of levels of acceptance almost like a stack of Russian dolls.[50] Having said this, the visible and non-negotiable epidermal difference of my skin colour marks a more substantive difference between my experience and that of many of my fellow practitioners – because of the very societal white-centredness that this book explores.

As discussed in Chapter 3, dancers of classical Indian dance forms in Britain overwhelmingly have a South Asian heritage – and are brown-skinned. Without wishing to reduce to a white–brown binary the multiplicity of narratives that unite and distinguish individuals' experiences of the world, it is nonetheless the case that as a white bharatanatyam dancer, I have not had to contend with the day-to-day racism of being told to 'go home' or being asked where I am 'really' from.[51] My experience has been marked by sometimes extravagant delight at my (unremarkable) accomplishments from some (particularly Tamil) communities, and by sometimes extravagant disappointment at my white skin from some (particularly white) audiences. During a season I spent performing in an Indian restaurant as part of the Edinburgh Festival (1999), I was told both 'to colour my skin with teabags' and that 'I danced very well', but that 'it was a shame I was white'. My own response has inevitably varied by context. There have been times when I have shamelessly basked in unwarranted attention, and many times when I have wholeheartedly wished to be shorter, dark-haired and brown-skinned – to be less conspicuous, to 'fit in'.

Where my experience aligns with that of many of my interviewees is in the discrimination I have faced because of the codes and conventions of my artform: through embodying the dance form that a school will bring in for the students to learn about 'India', but not book as a regular after-school activity; through the assumption that anyone who is a dancer 'must be able to do the splits'; through the refusal to see that the reinterpretation of a *padam* (a lyrical, often slow expressive piece, in which the dancer explores a character's emotions) about a woman spying on the love affairs of her neighbour can have as much contemporary relevance as a dance piece about risk in the modern world.

Through this 'long ethnography', my research draws both on deliberately recorded field notes and formal interviews, together with years' worth of less formal 'head notes' (Sanjek 1990; Grau 1999): lived experience, snippets of conversation and friends' realities. Just as inevitably, this has presented me with both the 'gains and losses' (Hastrup 1995: 157) of the participant observer. The role has often allowed me 'privileged' access to the field (ibid.) and has supplied me with a real passion to understand it better. At the same time, there have certainly been occasions when I have been reticent to ask questions that I know touch upon sensitivities within the field, such as which caste an artist might belong to, or how much they might charge for a performance. There has also been the risk of exploiting or misusing information gained from participants in the vulnerable informality of day-to-day exchange rather than from the clearly signalled formality of an interview, and there have been times when I have almost forgotten myself and my role and had to suppress the urge to dispute an (in my view) particularly ill-judged opinion.

The best I can say is that in recognizing these shortcomings, I have attempted to overcome them. As all data is incomplete, and all data in being presented is interpreted, there seems to be no perfect way out of this conundrum of being an 'insider-outsider', compassionate yet critical, searching for belonging while seeking to remain separate. As the social anthropologist Kate Fox (2004) observes, it is now almost a requisite part of any ethnography that the ethnographer prefaces their work with a penitent disclaimer emphasizing the limitations and unavoidable subjectivity of their work. I can only echo her wry conclusion that 'while participant observation has its limitations, this rather uneasy combination of involvement and detachment is the best method we have for exploring cultures, so it will have to do' (ibid.: 4). Having said this, I attempt to mitigate some of my implicit bias by ensuring that my interviewees come from a range of contexts in the field – independent dance artists, representatives of institutions, young artists still learning their art forms and established artists secure in their position. Information gained formally from interviews, from curated or recorded conversations, is balanced by information gained informally by standing around in theatre lobbies, in changing rooms for dance classes and in late-night conversations in hotel rooms.[52]

A proper understanding of where we are demands at the very least a broad knowledge of our history. Along with ethnographic research, therefore, a part of my research has been historic, and there are points at which my ethnographic interviews have crossed into the arena of oral history. What were classes in classical Indian dance forms in Britain like in the 1960s and 1970s? What was the audience response to specific performances? What were the primary motivations behind a certain (historic) decision? In making sense of the now, this work moves back and forth between history and ethnography, the past and the present. The third point of this triangulation is theory – or those different lenses that can help make sense of data in different ways. These lenses are taken, as discussed above, from sociology, in particular Bourdieu, as well as from theories of decolonization.

I highlight some of the specific boundaries and limitations of my research below. Before that, however, I address the perennially vexed topic of the label 'South Asian dance' (David 2005a; Meduri 2008a, 2008b) and the equally unsatisfactory collective term 'classical Indian dance'.

'South Asian' or 'Classical Indian' Dance Forms?

> 'South Asian Dance – what the fuck is that?'
> —Akram Khan, Navadisha 2016

This was a question Akram Khan pondered in his keynote address at Navadisha 2016. As he makes clear, 'South Asian dance' is not a term with a self-evident meaning – and it is one that many within the sector have been and remain unhappy with. Despite this, throughout this work I refer variously to both 'South Asian dance' forms and 'classical Indian dance' forms, the justification being that in doing so, I follow the model of the sector itself. The London-based organization Akademi is 'Akademi – South Asian Dance in the UK'. The Birmingham organization Sampad champions 'South Asian Arts and Heritage'. An invitation was sent out in 2018 by Dance Hub Birmingham asking for tenders to research the feasibility of a 'South Asian dance' degree. The competition *BBC Young Dancer* had as one of its dance categories 'South Asian dance'. The phrase 'classical Indian dance', though slightly less prominently used, is nonetheless well recognized. Notably, the relevant dance faculty of the ISTD is now called the Classical Indian Dance Faculty (CIDF), changing from the name 'South Asian Dance Faculty' in 2002 (see David 2013a). The Liverpool-based arts organization Milapfest advertises its summer school, Dance India, as offering a 'renowned intensive training programme in Indian classical dance', not South Asian dance (Milapfest n.d.a.). The Bharatiya Vidya Bhavan is the home of 'Indian classical arts' (Bhavan n.d.).

Pragmatically, 'South Asian dance' is the term used in Britain, by those within and outside the 'South Asian dance' sector, to refer to the range of dance forms originating from the Indian subcontinent (which includes India, Bangladesh, Sri Lanka, Pakistan and Nepal), including folk dance forms, bollywood dance and other forms not considered 'classical'. Emerging from the US State Department, based on a bureaucrat's term used to refer to post-partition India and its neighbours (Khilnani 2003; Meduri 2008a), this unpoetic phrase (Khilnani, cited in Meduri 2008a) crossed into academia and thence into the British arts establishment, adopted by dancers and arts officers in Britain in the late 1980s (Grau 2004). For a while, dancers and institutions within the sector seized upon the term almost with a sense of defiance (see for example Meduri 2008a, 2008b on Akademi's decision to change its name, mentioned above) in that the more geographically vague term 'South Asian' seemed to offer space for exploration beyond the sometimes stifling constraints of 'Indian' dance. More recently practitioners and institutions have, with equal determination, rejected the term, proud instead to champion the specificities and parameters of being 'classical' and 'Indian'.

The label 'classical Indian', however, as suggested by the need to escape 'stifling', brings with it its own challenges (Lopez y Royo 2003; Purkayastha 2017b). The specificity of 'India' can be seen to exclude countries such as Pakistan, Bangladesh and Sri Lanka, where the classical dance forms, particularly, in the case of Pakistan, kathak, have also emerged and evolved. At the same time the term obscures the regional provenance of the separate forms within the vast reach of the Indian subcontinent. Meanwhile, the term 'classical' is an uneasy adoption of a European term, which 'needs to be divested of its total Eurocentric bias' before providing a 'more fruitful avenue of understanding' (Jeyasingh 2010: 182). Though often presented as equivalent, the indigenous categories *margi* and *desi* clearly do not fully translate to 'classical' and 'folk' in the loaded sense that both these terms have within Euro-American dance studies, carrying with them the idea of 'high' and 'low' art.[53] The importance of being labelled a 'classical dance form' in itself was politically driven and only arose as an issue for Indian dance forms 'as part of the movement to reinscribe Indian dance forms in modern artistic practice and give them a status, equivalent to that of classical ballet in the West' (Lopez y Royo 2003: 156).

In relation to both these collective terms, for several practitioners, the very label 'dance' is unhelpful. As dance anthropologist Adrienne Kaeppler (1999: 13) has argued, 'traditionally in many societies there was no category comparable to the Western concept [of dance]' (see also David 2014; Meduri 2019). For many practitioners the line between what in Euro-American terms are 'dance' and 'drama' is, in Indian performance art forms, so blurred as to make the division unhelpful. These performance forms could or should as readily be considered 'drama' as 'dance' by a Euro-American classification, both labels fitting the forms as well (or as inadequately). Bringing these points together, dancer and scholar Anurima Banerji (2021b) succinctly argues that 'the phrase "Indian Classical Dance" is a misleading misnomer, given that it is not "Indian", but regional and transnational in character; not "classical", but a confluence of ritual, folk, court, and concert forms; and not "dance", but interdisciplinary performance.'

There is an increasing recognition of the justice of this argument, and an increasing frustration within the sector at the need for a collective label at all, accompanied by a desire for dance forms to be referred to by their individual names of kathak, kathakali, kuchipudi and so on, thereby avoiding the connotations and constraints of imperfect labels.[54] The lack of a critical mass of practitioners however means that for many initiatives and institutions (e.g. the Centre for Advance Training (CAT)[55] training schemes, the ISTD, *BBC Young Dancer* or even the dance agencies), it is simply not viable to treat each style entirely independently, economically or infrastructurally. To attain the visibility, or at times the economic subsidy, that attaches to such initiatives, therefore, disparate and often very different dance forms (such as kathak and bharatanatyam) make at times uneasy alliances to make sure that their presence counts. In this respect, the sector shares a dilemma faced by the Association for Dance of the African Diaspora (ADAD). Needing a more generic signifier than the individual names of a panoply of dance styles, both South Asian and African diaspora dance forms in Britain have settled for labels they are less than happy with, which nonetheless help to situate them within the broader field of British dance.

Which imperfect 'collective' might be preferable has long been a subject of discussion – and the question as to which label is politically and aesthetically most apt has been debated by the sector for over twenty years, without conclusion. In 2004, Akademi organized a symposium to discuss what might be meant by 'South Asianness' (No Man's Land – Exploring South Asianness), and several of those present expressed their dissatisfaction with the label (Meduri 2008b), a dissatisfaction still felt today, as Khan's opening question makes clear.

For the moment, while recognizing the problems with both labels, I meet the sector where it is and swap between names, following the lead of the artist or organization discussed, for example when discussing the 'South Asian dance' category in *BBC Young Dancer*, or Akademi's 'South Asian Dance in the UK'. The term I use more consistently is 'classical Indian dance' – for two main reasons. Firstly, my work looks primarily at bharatanatyam and kathak – and to a lesser extent odissi and kuchipudi – all forms (however unsatisfactorily) counted among the now eight dance forms commonly labelled 'classical' dances of India.[56] Secondly, in considering these forms, my focus is on their 'classical' technique, even when this technique is used within a (Euro-American) contemporary dance context. Using the term 'classical Indian dance forms' retains this focus. As others have observed, the term 'South Asian dance' has latterly been increasingly understood to refer particularly to that hybridized form that constitutes 'South Asian contemporary dance' (Thobani 2017; Kedhar 2020). While I use the term, I acknowledge its several limitations and challenges, so clearly articulated by Banerji. Wherever I am referring more specifically to a discrete form, such as bharatanatyam or kathak, I use these specific names. A possible collective noun, avoiding culturally inappropriate and geographically tethering terminology, could, I suggest, be 'Natyam' (Sanskrit for 'dance/drama'). I touch on this possibility in Chapter 5. For the moment, however, I adhere to the labels the sector has adopted for itself.

Boundaries and Limitations

Before outlining the contents of the book, a note about what it is not about. As mentioned above, the focus of this book is on the so-called 'classical' dance forms. Thus, while bollywood and bhangra, among other forms, have an increasingly significant role within Britain, it is beyond the scope of this project to consider these forms. Of the 'classical' forms, while both odissi and kuchipudi have a growing presence in Britain, they have not yet been incorporated into the institutions of, for example, Yuva Gati (the South Asian strand of the CAT scheme) or the ISTD. This has meant that, although I consider odissi and kuchipudi, my engagement with these forms has been limited, and my research has inevitably engaged more with bharatanatyam and kathak than other forms.

In analysing work as a dancer, while appreciating the importance of work as a teacher, dance movement therapist or dance animateur, my focus has been on performance. This is because an important part of professionalization is necessarily 'how dances come to be seen' (Lepecki et al. 2004), and more importantly, 'what dances come to be seen'. Performance dictates training, so has an inevitable impact on the role of teaching. Thus, while not diminishing the critical role of the dance animateur, and the all-important role of the teacher, the particular focus of this work has been on the dancer as professional *performer*.

Finally, it is important to note that the focus of this work on a few select classical dance forms reflects the pattern by which these dance forms have come to stand in for Indian dance heritage at the expense of multiple subaltern, Dalit and minoritarian[57] dance knowledges. Where classical Indian dance forms are marginalized by the white-centred structures and aesthetics of contemporary Britain, these dance forms are themselves the instrument of marginalization in dominating the representation of what it means to be Indian or of Indian heritage – both within India and in the diaspora. This domination, as my book touches upon, is intimately related to the transfer within India in the early twentieth century of the practice of 'classical dance forms' to the high-caste and the well-heeled. This process, the gender and sexuality scholar Shefali Chandra (2020: 1195) suggests, was one of 're: colonization' – by which Brahmanism was 'rendered according to the mandate of whiteness: universal and transparent'. Where this book argues for the decolonization of the British canon through the making of space for the aesthetics and artistic narratives of Indian classical dance forms, the fuller work of decolonization must look also to confront this pattern of 're: colonization', both in the context of India and the diaspora (Prakash 2019; Chandra 2020; Banerji 2021a).

Chapter Outline

I start by 'setting the scene' and providing the context for the book through a closer consideration of the place of South Asian dance within *BBC Young Dancer*. I then turn to a detailed examination of what is meant by 'professionalism' and 'professionalization'. This is succeeded by chapters broadly centred around each of the three key features of professionalism I identify: learning, livelihood and legitimacy.

Chapter 1 ('Context') sets the context for the book by presenting a snapshot of the place of South Asian dance in Britain by analogy with the place of the South Asian dance category in the competition *BBC Young Dancer*. Drawing on the critique of televised competitions within dance and cultural studies (Penman 1993; Morris 2008; Redden 2008, 2010; Weisbrod 2010, 2014; Elswit 2012; Dodds and Hooper 2014; Foster 2014), I consider how far the *Young Dancer* competition avoids the susceptibility of other televised competitions to spectacularized conformity. I argue that several of the challenges evinced by the position of the South Asian dance category within the *Young Dancer* competition apply equally to the position of South Asian dance within the broader field of British dance. These include the paradox of high achievement and a high profile resting on a fragile infrastructure and the limited awareness of the specific artistic narratives of South Asian dance forms within a wider audience. Efforts at equal representation, I argue, can only go so far while the legacy of colonialism in ideologies that deny coevalness (Fabian 2014) and subscribe to the 'rhetoric of modernity' (Mignolo 2007) remains unchallenged in our cultural sphere.

Chapter 2 ('Professionalism') unpicks the vexed question of 'professionalism'. A topic acknowledged as contentious at the best of times – hence sociologist Thomas Brante's statement, 'Perhaps it is not an overstatement to say that there are almost as many theories of professions as there are scholars of professions'

(1988: 126) – it is further complicated in the context of the arts, and yet further in the context of South Asian dance (in Britain). I acknowledge the increasing scrutiny of the concept owing to its disciplinarian force (Fournier 1999; Evetts 2013) and return to the question Bourdieu raised in 1992, which is how far this Anglo-American, culturally laden value should be abandoned in favour of a concept less prescriptive. In this light, I propose a reading of 'professionalism' in line with the Tamil concept of *virutti*,[58] meaning a 'way of life', 'conduct' or 'behaviour', 'employment', 'business', 'devoted service' or 'means of livelihood' (Agarathi n.d.), leading me to propose three core features of professionalism: learning (or excellence), livelihood, and license (or legitimacy).

Chapter 3 ('Learning') takes a sociohistorical approach, looking at how classical Indian dancers are trained in Britain today and the institutions involved in providing such training. I focus on the Classical Indian Dance Faculty (CIDF) of the Imperial Society for Teachers of Dancing (ISTD), the South Asian-focused Centre for Advanced Training (CAT), Yuva Gati and the failed attempt to establish a BA in Contemporary Dance with a South Asian dance strand at London Contemporary Dance School (LCDS). Starting with a historical reflection on how hereditary dancers were trained and considered to attain proficiency, I then look at some of the early efforts to establish classical Indian dance classes in Britain. I argue that similarly to the situation in the United States (Srinivasan 2012), British cultural policy from the 1970s led to a repositioning of classical dance forms from being ones with a universal appeal to being 'minority arts' for a 'minority' people. This framing reinforced the ways in which the dance forms were used by migrant communities as a form of 'cultural long-distance nationalism' (Wong 2010). Such positioning, I argue, has had long-term repercussions in terms of circumscribing the available pool both of potential performers and potential audiences for classical Indian dance in Britain. This has had a knock-on impact on standards of dance due to the lack of demand for classical work, and hence a lack of a critical mass of candidates to make a vocational training school for the dance forms a viable entity.

In Chapter 4 ('Livelihood, Learning, Embodiment'), I address two related questions. The first is how far the technique of a professional dancer is influenced by the context within which they live. What happens when the cultural contexts in which the dancer lives are mismatched or non-aligned with the cultural context in which their dance technique was formed? The second is what the professional demand for the versatile dancer means for the performance of dance technique, particularly of techniques that do not form part of the dominant dance discourse – such as classical Indian dance forms in Britain. How far can the versatile dancer embody distinctive dance techniques without being co-opted into that 'wonderfully unifying and legitimizing aesthetic category of "contemporary dance" (really meaning Euro-American modern/contemporary dance)' (Chatterjea 2013: 10)? This chapter deals therefore with livelihood insofar as it highlights the constraints placed on dancers (and their techniques) by the need to meet a particular market demand. In considering these questions, I use Bourdieu's concept of habitus (as extended by Wainwright, Williams and Turner 2006, 2007). Contrary to dance anthropologist Brenda Farnell (2000) and to Foster (2009), I argue that this concept is too useful for the theorization of dance technique to be abandoned.

Chapter 5 ('Legitimacy') looks at the role played in 'professionalization' by 'consecration' (Bourdieu 1991) or legitimacy, in particular through absorption into the 'national cultural canon'. While, as I discuss, there are multiple factors that have contributed to the failure to form a professional field for the pursuit of classical Indian dance forms in Britain, this chapter argues that their position will remain precarious until they are considered more integral to national cultural capital. Following Australian anthropologist Ghassan Hage's argument in his book *White Nation* (2000), I propose that these dance forms need to be perceived more as what Britain *is* than as what it *has*. To achieve this, I suggest, will first necessitate a decolonization of national cultural capital and the cultural canon by means of unsuturing (Yancy 2017) or delinking (Quijano 2007) from a canon and an aesthetics dominated by 'white' (Anglo-European) values. This will then permit a true broadening of the 'horizon of expectations' (Mignolo 2007) and a shift from 'multiculturalism' to 'pluriversality', allowing for the development of a 'British Natyam'.

Notes

1. The competition has now changed to be open to dancers of any genre. See afterword to Chapter 1.
2. I use both 'classical Indian dance forms' and 'South Asian dance' as collective terms to refer to the dance styles of (primarily) bharatanatyam and kathak, but also odissi and kuchipudi. I recognize the multiple problems with these labels, which I discuss at greater length later in the introduction. My use of these terms does not signify agreement, but, as I explain below, as far as possible follows current usage by the sector.
3. The BBC was established in 1922 by Royal Charter. While the broadcasting dominance of the BBC has been increasingly threatened in recent years by the explosion of broadcasters in the form of Netflix, YouTube, Amazon and Apple to name a few, the BBC retains an institutional and symbolic status meaning that its programming choices remain significant (See Chapter 1).
4. Akademi is the only organization exclusively devoted to promoting South Asian dance in Britain. There are several other organizations promoting South Asian arts, but they promote both music and dance, or dance as one of several South Asian art forms.
5. I thank dance artist Jane Chan for highlighting to me the importance of using this term rather than cementing the binaries of 'East' and 'West'.
6. The career intentions and experience of all dance artists in the competition can be found on the BBC website. For the 2015 dance artists, see: https://www.bbc.co.uk/programmes/profiles/3tRg7qMclgMJ0ZY4HBrjQQS/2015-dance artists (retrieved 3 July 2024).
7. This dance artist, Anaya Bolar, has subsequently decided to take up dance professionally.

8. See 'Jaina Modasia', https://www.bbc.co.uk/programmes/profiles/3y0fSYWMHyg8hgry Zk5n552/jaina-modasia (retrieved 3 July 2024); 'Sivani Balachandran', https://www.bbc.co.uk/programmes/profiles/fj5tZY8kFSv2w7gbbqK4qw/sivani-balachandran (retrieved 3 July 2024); Ranjan, personal communication, April 2018.
9. Information on the 2017 dance artists is available here: https://www.bbc.co.uk/programmes/profiles/4BGhz5dvR804r5hPK10tzZq/2017-dance artists (retrieved 3 July 2024).
10. It should be noted however that she has worked continuously and very successfully as a professional dance artist since this point even without such additional training, featuring in works choreographed by Richard Alston (*An Italian in Madrid*, 2016), Gary Clarke and Shobana Jeyasingh, and in commissions by Akademi and Sampad. In Akademi's contemporary dance production *The Troth* (2018) (choreographed by contemporary dance choreographer Gary Clarke) Patel was one of two classical Indian dance-trained performers.
11. Shyam Dattani, personal communication, 6 March 2019. Shyam has, however, subsequently gone on to a successful career as a dancer working extensively with Akademi and companies such as Nina Rajarani's Srishti, Urja Thakore's Pagrav and Amina Khayyam Dance.
12. At Navadisha 2016, for example, a member of Arts Council England (ACE) put forward these companies as options when I raised with them the problem of employment opportunities for South Asian dancers (field notes, 20 May 2016).
13. In the company's description of its work, there is no reference to a particular interest in South Asian dance forms. Rather, the company self-defines as 'restless, inquisitive and intrepid', taking its inspiration from 'the complexities and contradictions of the world around us' (Shobana Jeyasingh Dance n.d.). It is difficult to see what more Shobana Jeyasingh needs to do to show that, while she may draw on bharatanatyam when her exploration takes that direction (for example, she used bharatanatyam and odissi dance artist Sooraj Subramaniam in works such as *Material Men* (2015), *Material Men Redux* (2017) and *Bayadère – The Ninth Life* (2017)), this is no longer her primary interest.
14. These are Leicester Dance Theatre (LDT), also known as Aakash Odedra Company; Sonia Sabri Company; and Balbir Singh Dance Company. LDT emphasizes its specialism in 'South Asian dance' (Aakash Odedra Company n.d.). Sabri's company self-defines as 'presenting Kathak dance in a contemporary context' (Sonia Sabri Company n.d.). Balbir Singh's company, like Khan's, emphasizes a focus on two dance forms – kathak and contemporary and an 'interest in exploring the creative potential of synthesising the two forms' (Balbir Singh Dance n.d.). There are many more companies that work with classical Indian dance forms (particularly bharatanatyam and kathak), including Urja Desai Thakore's Pagrav, Nina Rajarani's Srishti, Amina Khayyam Dance Company, Seeta Patel Dance and Kamala Devam Dance Company. In 2019, all these companies continued to operate within the precarity of project-based funding, though a number have since joined the portfolio. Indeed, the number of organizations with NPO status representing classical Indian dance more than doubled for the 2023–26 portfolio. See afterword to Chapter 5.
15. This characterization of Khan as a top British choreographer is widely accepted – he is referred to elsewhere as Britain's most famous choreographer and is listed as one of four named artists and companies 'in demand on a global level' in the Arts Council report

Dance Mapping (Burns and Harrison 2009: 378). The others are contemporary choreographers Wayne McGregor and Hofesh Shechter along with DV8 Physical theatre.

16. These have been Queen's honours, somewhat ironically awarding the recipients varying degrees of authority in relation to the British Empire (Order of the British Empire, Member of the British Empire, Commander of the British Empire and British Empire Medal). Recipients include Ram Gopal, Nilima Devi, Shobana Jeyasingh, Mira Kaushik, Akram Khan, Naseem Khan, Nina Rajarani, Piali Ray, Bisakha Sarker, Sunita Golvala, Geetha Upadhyaya, Sujata Banerjee, Pratap Pawar, Pushkala Gopal, Vikas Kumar, Chitra Sundaram, Anand Bhatt and Aakash Odedra.

17. Jeyasingh observed back in 1993 that 'One of the greatest challenges I face every year is recruiting dance artists' (Jeyasingh in Brinson 1993: 56). In 2021, the situation has shifted, but not so very much. Dance artist and choreographer Amina Khayyam comments: 'As I start to make a transition from performing to "choreography", I find myself in a dilemma. I have at least five years of work ahead, and the issue for me is that I haven't been able to find dancers that are a good fit for my work. Though dancers are trained well in kathak, yet they are not versatile and are too hung up on their training and relationship with their "Gurus"' (Khayyam, personal communication, 21 May 2021). Dance artist and choreographer Seeta Patel feels similarly. For her, it is not only a question of the calibre of dance artists, but of their availability to commit to a touring project – 'there are good dancers coming up . . . but without availability to work in the way I need – i.e., 8 consecutive weeks' (Patel, personal communication, 2019). Tellingly, for her 2019 ensemble production of *The Rite of Spring*, four of the six dance artists in the ensemble were recruited from outside Britain. Seeta Patel Dance's 2023 tour of *The Rite of Spring* featured twelve dancers and was performed live to accompaniment by the Bournemouth Symphony Orchestra – a first for bharatanatyam in Britain. The piece was very well received with 4-star reviews, and advertising for the piece broadcast on billboards at Piccadilly Circus in the heart of London. Hearteningly, three of the twelve dancers (Aishani Ghosh, Shree Savani and Adhya Shastry) were born and primarily trained in the UK.

18. Naseem Khan worked for a number of years for the Arts Council, acting as Head of Diversity from 1996 to 2003.

19. This report was jointly funded by the Arts Council of Great Britain, the Gulbenkian Foundation and the Commission for Racial Equality.

20. In the same year that she published her report, Naseem Khan set up the Minority Arts Advisory Service (MAAS), which advised artists and arts organizations (including the Arts Council) to help improve the representation of ethnic minority arts in Britain. MAAS closed in 1994, shortly after which the Arts Council formed its own diversity department, of which Khan was head between 1996 and 2003.

21. The Bharatiya Vidya Bhavan in London was established in 1972, moving to its current premises in 1978. It is one of 110 Bharatiya Vidya Bhavan centres worldwide, 105 of which are in India (Bhavan n.d.). The Bharatiya Vidya Bhavan was founded as an educational trust by politician and activist K.M. Munshi in Gujarat, India in 1938.

22. The Mountbatten Hall, the main theatre space of the Bhavan, has a capacity of 294.

23. Whereas in the Anglo-European context shaking one's head and 'tutting' connotes disapproval, in the Indian context shaking one's head and a particular pattern of 'tutting' can often signal intense enjoyment or appreciation. These are just a couple of examples of the contingency of embodied language, which I discuss further in Chapter 4.

24. The Sanskrit word *abhinaya*, made up of the prefix *abhi* (to, towards), together with the verb root *nii* (to guide, conduct, lead, direct), means literally 'to lead towards' or 'to convey'. It is the word used within the Sanskrit compendium on drama, the *Natyashastra* (200 BCE–200 CE), to refer to the expressive aspect of dance and drama and is a central element in the performance of Indian classical dance forms.
25. The bharatanatyam dance artist Uma Venkataraman, for example, tends to choose shorter pieces for performances in Britain ('I try not to do a single piece that is longer than say fifteen minutes') on the basis that 'audiences may not necessarily be prepared for sitting through a forty-five-minute *varnam* – they might be uncomfortable' (Venkataraman 2018). In adopting this approach Venkataraman adopts the same strategy as that employed by artists such as Ram Gopal and Uday Shankar in the 1930s and 1940s. To make his performances more accessible to Euro-American audiences, Gopal 'prune[d] the traditional dances of all repetitive movement' (Gopal 1957: 55). See David (2001) for more on Gopal's approach.
26. An alliance formed 'to provide a visionary development path for South Asian dance in the UK and internationally, through a programme of strategic initiatives' (Akademi n.d.b.). It was launched through an Arts Council development initiative (see end note 27 below). See Appendix 3 for full details of SADAA's current membership.
27. Whatever the impact of Arts Council initiatives, as I discuss later, it can hardly be accused of not trying to make a difference. Naseem Khan's 1979 report for example was partly funded by the Arts Council; and the Arts Council initiated a three-year development strategy for South Asian dance in 1987/88 (Arts Council of Great Britain 1988: 10) at the same time as launching a further three-year plan that included a focus on South Asian dance in education (ibid.). There was another three-year initiative (Chaturang, focused on the north-west of England) in 1997 in which year it also commissioned a significant review of South Asian dance in England leading to a further national three-year initiative focused on South Asian dance development (Arts Council England 2000). This initiative saw £303,000 distributed among four organisations (Aditi, Akademi, Kadam and Sampad) between 1999 and 2002 (though Aditi closed in 2001). It was this development programme that led to the launch of SADAA, initially with these four organisations as core members. More recently the Arts Council commissioned the South Asian Dance and Music Mapping Study (Courtney Consulting 2020), designed to consider how the sector might be best supported. It was Arts Council funding that enabled the initial research that led both to the creation of the Classical Indian Dance Faculty of the ISTD and to the short-lived BA in South Asian and Contemporary Dance Forms at London Contemporary Dance School (see Chapter 3 and Appendix 2). In 2018, South Asian dance forms were explicitly named as a priority in Arts Council corporate strategy. I qualify my reference to 'goodwill' because of the constraints that restrict any policy based on 'goodwill' without attention to systemic change. The 1987/88 development strategy, for example, though well intended, was damaging in its focus on the development of the South Asian dance artist as a 'professional' in precisely the way this book contests – by reference to a very specific notion of professionalism that encouraged an embrace of the norms of Euro-American contemporary dance (see Kedhar 2020, particularly Chapter 1).
28. This last factor can be seen as being particularly influential, as I discuss later.
29. *Devadasi* (literally translated from Sanskrit as 'female servant of god') was one of the names used for the hereditary dancers employed in temples and courts across India (who

were however known by different names) from at least the sixteenth to the early twentieth century. The term *bayadère* comes from 'the Portuguese *bailador*, from *baila*, to dance, whence comes the term *bayadère* (Port. *bailadeira*) for temple-dancing girls' (Puri 2014: 223).
30. The UK inflation calculator gives this as equivalent to almost £700,000 in 2024.
31. Gautier reports that the contract between the *bayadères* and Tardivel was for eighteen months, during which time each performer was entitled to ten rupees a day together with a lump sum, once at the beginning and once at the end of the engagement, of five hundred rupees each (Guest1992). It is difficult to give an exact equivalent of how much this would equate to today, but inflation calculators suggest that the purchasing power of ten rupees in 1850 would be about £300 today (as a comparator, the Equity minimum day rate for a performer working outside of London in 2023/24 is £116.34). As an example of their being looked after, they were taken to the theatre to see a production of *Le Dieu et la bayadère* laid on especially for them – apparently, they were unimpressed (Bor 2007: 58).
32. To arrive at this conclusion, Ann. R. David 'examined and analysed all available editions from 1910–2000 of the two prominent dance magazines published during this period, *The Dancing Times* and *Ballet* magazine, for reviews pertaining to Indian dance or interpretive "oriental" dance. This was the conclusion drawn from the little evidence available' (David 2005b: 57 n. 5).
33. This was the view of dance historian Cyril Beaumont, who wrote in a programme note for Gopal's 1956 season, 'It was Ram Gopal, through his initial London recitals in 1939 who first opened our eyes to the various styles and rich vocabulary of Indian dance' (cited in David 2024: 50).
34. As David (2010b: 2) points out, his personal beauty was a large part of his appeal – and led to a number of scopophiliac reviews of his work.
35. Quotations from David and Kaushik taken from SADAA (2016).
36. In this case, the tension was focused on West Indians rather than Asians. However, Marwick's point about the shift in attitudes remains apposite.
37. How far an organization funded by and ultimately responsible to government can be genuinely independent has been much debated, most notably by the sociologist (and one time Arts Council vice-chair) Raymond Williams (1979), who argued that while it is at arm's length, the arm is still attached to, and controlled by, the body, and felt a better description of the relationship would be 'at wrist's length'. Nonetheless, the principle of the separation of the Arts Council and thereby its intended insulation from party politics is important.
38. When I refer to the Arts Council throughout this book, this can be understood to refer to the Arts Council of Great Britain prior to 1994 and to the Arts Council of England after this.
39. Previous successful funding applications to the Arts Council had been made both by the Academy of Indian Dance and other classical Indian dance artists. For example, the kathak dancer Alpana Sengupta was given an award in 1977 as part of the small-scale touring scheme (Arts Council 1978). *The Adventures of Mowgli* was the first full-scale Indian dance piece to be funded (Arts Council 1985).
40. See the report from the Creative Industries Policy and Evidence Centre, 'A New Deal for Arts Funding in England?' (Pec: 2023).

41. Until 2012, these organizations were called 'Regularly Funded Organizations' or RFOs.
42. For the 2023–26 portfolio, 990 organizations receive a share of £446 million each year. It should be emphasized that while Project Grant funding is deliberately designed to be as open access as possible, this does make it an extremely competitive programme.
43. Also known as rational choice theory.
44. Derron Wallace, interviewed on *Thinking Allowed: A Special Programme on Pierre Bourdieu*, BBC Radio 4, June 2019, https://www.bbc.co.uk/programmes/b07gg1kb (retrieved 3 July 2024). I am indebted to Wallace and all the contributors to the excellent volume *Bourdieu: The Next Generation* (2016) in helping me to grapple with and reach a deeper understanding of Bourdieu.
45. A list of all interviewees happy to be named can be found in Appendix 4.
46. My father went to India with a mission organization, USPG (or the United Society for the Propagation of the Gospel), and worked within a theological college, Tamil Nadu Theological Seminary (TTS), which promoted liberation theology and sought actively to disentangle Christianity from Eurocentrism. My earliest bharatanatyam performances were in the TTS chapel, to a Tamil Easter song composed by the campus's resident musician, Swamikannu, in the Carnatic music tradition.
47. This resulted in the report *South Asian Dance in Britain – Negotiating Cultural Identity through Dance* (Grau 2001).
48. 'Dance animateurs' are skilled dance artists who encourage public participation in dance. The dance animateur movement really took off in Britian in the early 1980s in response to another 1976 report on the arts, in this case by Lord Redcliffe-Maud, emphasizing the importance of public participation in the arts. This led to a period of local authority (local government) and Arts Council of Great Britain funding for dance animateur roles. The animateur movement also played a critical role in the blossoming of 'community dance' in Britain. Community dance in the British context refers to dance practised with a focus on social engagement rather than the art market, led by principles of group creativity and participation.
49. 'When I went to Kathak Kendra [India's national institute for training in and developing kathak, based in New Delhi] I would always hear whispers that "he's Bangladeshi . . . he's not real" – almost like I'm not from the family, not from the lineage of the great masters' (Talk with Akram Khan as part of Darbar, Lilian Bayliss Studio, Sadler's Wells, London, 11 November 2017).
50. 'So, there is that mindset that the best dancers come from India. Then if it's bharatanatyam, it has to be South India – so I am not someone who lives in India, nor am I South Indian – nor do I have an artistic family background' (Rajarani 2018).
51. I have, however, been with my (brown) husband when he has been called a 'terrorist' and a 'Paki' and taunted with an extremely poor simulation of *adimi* (the sliding side-to-side neck movement of bharatanatyam). This taunt was all the more ironic considering that of the two of us, *adimi* is indisputably more part of my embodied repertoire than my husband's.
52. I was very aware even before I started writing this book of the all-important voices of my interviewees – and of how, where the book might contribute anything at all, it would be through the shared wisdom and experiences of these artists and cultural leaders. For this reason, I asked all my interviewees for permission to use their names in the publication – in part to ensure I gave credit where credit is due. Where the material used is

sensitive, sources have been anonymized. The majority of the fieldwork for this book was conducted as part of research at the University of Roehampton and adhered to the ethical standards specified by the university.
53. They do suggest different levels of formalization, with *margam* translating to 'of the route or pathway', and *desi* to 'vernacular' or 'provincial'. *Desi* also translates as 'seen', supporting the commonly held belief that *margi* forms relate to texts such as the *Natyashastra* or *Abhinaya Darpana*, while *desi* forms are passed down without such written codification.
54. Shane Shambhu, personal communication, February 2024.
55. A government-funded dance training scheme. See Chapter 3 and *passim*.
56. The others being mohiniattam, kathakali, manipuri and sattriya.
57. Dalit, meaning 'crushed' or 'broken', is the self-appointed name for people formerly known as untouchables, a people so othered that they are considered to lie outside the fourfold caste classification system as set out in the Hindu religious texts such as the Laws of Manu.
58. I am indebted to Avanthi Meduri for urging me to look more closely at this Tamil concept and its relationship to 'professionalism'.

Chapter 1

Context: *BBC Young Dancer* and the Professionalization of South Asian Dance in Britain
A Snapshot of the Sector and Its Place within British Dance

Introduction

On 23 January 2017, in a studio theatre within the glass-walled modernist building that forms the international arts centre the Lowry in Manchester, the young bharatanatyam dancer Akshay Prakash performed a short section of an *abhinaya*-based dance on the Hindu god Anjaneya, or Hanuman, and his relationship with Lord Rama. Cheeks and chest puffed out, and alternating impressive crouches and leaps with a sedate and dignified gait, Prakash swapped between the role of the strong ruler of the monkey army (Hanuman), and, with his left arm raised, his left hand in *shikara* (a hand gesture in which the fist is closed, but the thumb raised, like a thumbs up) and his right hand by his side in *kapitha* (a hand gesture in which the fist is closed and the index finger curled around the thumb), symbolized the bow that only the Lord Rama could string (Yadagudde 2017b). While there can hardly have been more than a hundred audience members in the theatre in Manchester, and many of these were friends and family of the performers, Prakash's piece, and those following it, were filmed, edited and (interspersed with footage of the competitors in training and going about their everyday life) broadcast to an audience of approximately 189,000 people on prime-time Friday night TV,[1] with many more watching it on catch-up.[2] This was the final for the South Asian dance category of *BBC Young Dancer* 2017 – only the second round of the competition, launched by the BBC in 2015.

As noted in the introduction, the inclusion of the South Asian dance category in this competition proved a significant boost for the sector, both in terms of mainstream recognition and providing high-profile performance opportunities for young dancers. It was widely welcomed, both by organizations and by individual artists. Thus, as previously cited, Akademi's Mira Kaushik was pleased by the decision; Prakash Yadagudde, resident bharatanatyam teacher at the Bharatiya Vidya Bhavan (and father of Akshay Prakash), felt it was 'an encouragement to the youngsters' (Yadagudde 2017a); and Piali Ray, Director of Sampad, an organization committed to promoting South Asian arts and heritage in Birmingham, acknowledged that there had been reservations about the competition, but felt that overall, 'it has been good. It has been a huge profile raiser and has created a lot of excitement, and an environment of ambition within students and parents' (Ray 2017b).

Yet as I discuss in the introduction, while the inclusion of South Asian dance as a category was significant – an equal fourth among three other dance styles – this inclusion also brought into focus the manifold ways in which South Asian dance was and clearly is not an 'equal fourth'.[3] This disparity remains evident in the revised format of the competition, which this time was open to 'anyone aged 16–24 whose passion is dance' (BBC 2022a). The range of dance styles brought together, including bharatanatyam, ballet, contemporary dance and clog dance, boast very different levels of resources. While the career path of most dancers is marked by precarity (see Chapter 2), the training and career opportunities for talented and passionate young classical Indian dancers are yet more limited than those for their ballet and contemporary dance-trained peers. *BBC Young Dancer*, therefore, at once emphasizes the distance South Asian dance forms have come in this country (in making up one of only four original categories) while highlighting the distance they have yet to travel. The specific case study of the place of South Asian dance in this competition, both in its original and revised formats, can be seen as a microcosm that reveals, on a smaller scale, many of the wider issues that impact on the place of South Asian dance forms in the world of British dance. These include the need to understand an art form within the parameters of its own narrative and the deep-seated hegemony of a Euro-American aesthetic ideal within the field of British dance. This televised competition, with its specific performance requirements, also highlights some of the tensions that beset any dancer practising dance as a profession – how to balance expertise with accessibility, to balance experimentation with financial viability, and to make an impact when the audience may have no understanding of the conventions of one's art form. I return to these themes throughout this book. Most importantly, the hope, commitment and talent showcased in a competition focused on young Britain-based dancers, who 'will hopefully enter the professional world in a year or two' (Hackett 2015), underlines what is at stake in discussing how South Asian dancers and their dance forms take their place in the world of professional British dance. It therefore seems an appropriate place to begin.

In this chapter, I focus primarily on the *Young Dancer* competition as it was first introduced, with four categories of dance, and the winner from each category going forward to the finals. After providing a brief introduction to the competition and explaining its rubric, I go on to contextualize it within the broader debates associated with dance competitions and televised dance, and reflect on how its production team has sought to position it in relation both to these shows and to the wider world of British dance. I then look specifically at the inclusion of a South Asian dance category, highlighting some of the benefits this has brought to the South Asian dance profession in Britain, along with some of the problems that its inclusion has brought into focus. In 2022, after the bulk of the research for this book was complete, and after just three iterations of the programme (2015, 2017 and 2019), the BBC released the fourth series of the competition (delayed due to the Covid-19 pandemic), with a format significantly altered by the new artistic director, Emma Gladstone (1960–2024; former contemporary dancer; Artistic Director and Chief Executive of Dance Umbrella 2013–21; Artistic Director of Sadler's Wells 2005–13).[4] I conclude the chapter by reflecting on these changes and what they mean for South Asian dance, and by considering what this competition tells us about the context within which the South Asian dance profession in Britain is striving to develop.

What is *BBC Young Dancer*?

BBC Young Dancer (or simply *Young Dancer*) is a biannual competition launched in 2015, based loosely on the model of *BBC Young Musician*, which was established in 1978. As Jane Hackett,[5] former Director of Creative Learning at Sadler's Wells[6] and the dance consultant for the original format of the programme, explains, the BBC had been thinking about a dance equivalent to *Young Musician* for some time and had initially attempted to impose the same framework they had used for music on dance. Deciding that this approach was not working, they asked Sadler's Wells for advice, and Alistair Spalding, the Artistic Director of Sadler's, seconded Hackett to work with them on the programme's development (Hackett 2017).

The rubric of the competition as first broadcast was straightforward, and consisted of three competitive performance rounds (two of which were broadcast), as well as a preliminary round based not on live performance, but on video submissions. It was and remains open to dancers aged between 16 and 21 who 'must not, nor should ever have been employed on a professional full-time contract as a dancer' (*Young Dancer*, entry brochure, 2017).[7] To enter, dancers in each of the categories from across the country were invited to send in a short video, showing themselves performing two contrasting solos with a total duration of no more than six minutes.[8] These videos were assessed by judges,[9] who, as with each of the subsequent rounds, were figures with established experience, expertise and standing in the dance fields represented by the categories. The judges marked all dancers across all categories according to the following criteria: 'technique; artistry and interpretation, including musicality; performance quality; distinctive movement style/individuality, with an additional criterion for partner work being communication and interaction/combined virtuosity' (ibid.). These judges put twenty dancers from each category forward to the first live performance round. In this round (the Second Round), which was filmed, but not necessarily broadcast, each of the twenty dancers again performed two solos (each between one minute thirty and four minutes in duration), on the basis of which a fresh expert panel selected five dancers to participate in the category finals. For the category finals, which were broadcast on BBC Four, the dancers prepared two solos and 'a pas de deux/duet that demonstrates partnering skills' (ibid.), 'repeating at least one solo from the Second Round'. Again, each of the dances was between one minute thirty seconds and four minutes in duration. The finalists from each category, together with one 'wildcard', then competed against each other in the Grand Final, which took place in a renowned theatre with an established connection to dance performance[10] 'in front of an audience and a panel of internationally renowned dance professionals' (ibid.) and was filmed for broadcast on BBC Two. They performed one solo and one duet (both of which could be the same as in a previous round, but need not be), which together should not last more than nine minutes. In addition, they each performed a new solo created especially for them for the competition by a professional choreographer. The judging panel for the Grand Final featured expert representatives from each of the dance categories.

Before considering what the selection of South Asian dance as one of the four categories, as well as the way it was framed within the original competition, said about the South Asian dance sector in Britain and its positioning within the wider British cultural scene, it is helpful to consider some of the issues raised in broader discussions related to competition dance, and particularly, televised competition dance. These discussions, as I indicate above, though intensified in the context of a televised competition, nonetheless raise some of the broader issues and challenges facing dancers entering the professional world.

The Televised Dance Competition – the Context of *Young Dancer*

In recent years, as the professional ballet dancer and now scholar Geraldine Morris points out, there has been a 'proliferation of ballet competitions' (Morris 2008: 39). And not only of ballet competitions. Among the features of twenty-first-century Britain has been the introduction of a plethora of televised dance competitions: *Strictly Come Dancing* (2004) (*Strictly*);[11] *Strictly Dance Fever* (2005); *Got to Dance* (2009); *Move Like Michael Jackson* (2009); *So You Think You Can Dance* (2010) (*So You Think*); *BBC Young Dancer* (2015); and *Flirty Dancing* (2019).[12] Admittedly, not all of these have lasted very long,[13] but the very fact of their emergence indicates a growth of interest in this format – and *Strictly Come Dancing* is hugely popular, attracting 13.1 million viewers for its final in 2016 (Press Association 2016). This undoubtedly forms part of a wider trend of increasing popularity for other competition-based reality TV shows such as *The Great British Bake-Off* and *Britain's Got Talent* (Redden 2008).

In terms of the dance community itself, dance competitions can serve as occasions to bring different sections of the dance world together (or even, as I will show in the case of *Young Dancer*, sections of several dance worlds). They can provide motivation to competitors and a goal to work towards where other performance opportunities may not be forthcoming. They offer a chance to see and be seen, to network and to assess the performance of oneself and others (Marion 2008).

For the audience outside the dance community, competitions provide a format that is inherently accessible. In a wider discussion of competitive reality TV shows, cultural and media theorist Guy Redden observes that 'Entertainment value is easily driven by questions of who will win and who will lose, with what costs and results' (Redden 2008: 134). The reward for such accessibility, as illustrated above, is phenomenal viewing figures: 636,000 people watched the *Young Dancer* Grand Final in 2017 (by transmission), with a further 55,000 on the BBC's streaming service, iPlayer; 189,000 watched the South Asian dance category final.[14] As a consequence, as dance scholar Alexis Weisbrod points out, many different dance styles make their way into people's homes, giving the audience a greater sense of familiarity with dance and 'empowering audience members to dialogue with and about the practice in greater detail or possibly for the first time' (Weisbrod 2014: 320).

In the televised competitions, this accessibility is reinforced by the human detail provided in the shows. *Young Dancer* follows a standard trope of such programmes, in what performance studies scholar Kate Elswit (2012: 136) terms an 'extended choreography', intersecting the dancers' performances with clips from their everyday life, their rehearsals and interviews with them and their teachers about their feelings and hopes. Dance writer and producer Robert Penman (1993: 114) has noted that 'Documentaries about dance and dancers, are often successful because they take the viewer backstage to meet artists on human terms' – and certainly, over a quarter of a century later, viewing figures would seem to bear him out.

Competition Dance: Aesthetics or Artistry?

While competitions can offer positive experiences for both the dance community and the audience, the format of the competition, which gives a competitor a very short period of time in which to make an impact and impress the judges (the four minute maximum for the *Young Dancer* solos is comparatively generous), can tempt a dancer to use that time to display their most spectacular physical feats or to pull out their favourite 'tricks'. The result can be that the performance is dominated by, as Morris (2008: 45) observes of the Prix de Lausanne,[15] 'high extensions and big, split-jumps . . . to the detriment of light and shade, articulate footwork and flexible upper bodies'. For the judges, likewise, a short clip of a performer makes it easier to assess the visually striking qualities of technique rather than the more nuanced and complex qualities of artistry (discussed below). In this way the competition format is almost inevitably weighted in favour of technical virtuosity and the spectacular rather than interpretation and depth – a weighting that can only be addressed by the deliberate choice of the competitor or the deliberate intervention on the part of the competition organizers.

This tendency is only reinforced in the context of a television show. Popular dance scholar Laura Robinson argues that 'virtuosic displays of athleticism are linked with the tight temporal framework of the T.V. competition, as the performers must engage and impress the judges and audiences in under 2 minutes, requiring an intensity and compression of choreography' (Robinson 2014: 314). The result can be a slide towards what dance philosopher Anna Pakes describes as the 'easy consumability or aesthetic surface of dance practice' (Pakes 2001: 249), or in Weisbrod's (2014: 325) terms, the privileging of 'entertainment and popular culture over visionary or experimental art practice'.

Morris draws on the philosophy of aestheticians Graham McFee (2005) and David Best (1982) to support her reservations about the current ethos of the ballet competitions she studies, and to explain why she agrees with the highly respected teacher of Cecchetti ballet Richard Glasstone that 'Artistic excellence has little to do with virtuosity and nothing at all to do with gymnastic stunts' (Glasstone, cited in Morris 2008: 49). Both Best and McFee agree that while aesthetics deal with mere appearance – with what you can see – art relates to a deliberate and intelligent act of design. This act is situated within a broader history of such acts of design, or within a specific 'historical narrative' (Carroll 2001: 84),[16] which you cannot see. Thus, while you might consider both a sunset and the photograph of that same sunset to be beautiful, only the photograph would count as art – as only here has a person 'captured' the scene in such a way as to frame (however successfully) elements of contrast and balance. In order then to properly appreciate this photograph, it would need to be understood within the context of the history of landscape photography. Similarly, it is the awareness of this narrative that distinguishes as art an image taken by a photographer rather than a snapshot you might have taken on holiday. Art, then, as opposed to the aesthetic, is about much more than immediately meets the eye. As an illustration, Best (1982: 361) describes watching a performance of bharatanatyam dancer Ram Gopal, observing that 'I was quite captivated by the exhilarating and exquisite quality of his movements' (i.e. the immediate sensual or aesthetic qualities), 'yet I was unable to appreciate his dance artistically since I could not understand it'. Lacking a knowledge of bharatanatyam's narrative – its traditions and history – Best must content himself with a superficial aesthetic satisfaction, rather than with the informed appreciation of an aficionado of the art form (or in the language of Indian aesthetic theory, of a *rasika*). In dance terms, to follow Morris, this means that while a high level of technical competence deriving from 'flexibility, strength, physical control' (2008: 43) will make an excellent technician, more than this is demanded for an artistic rendition of choreography. Here, interpretative choices need to be made in relation to (though not necessarily in accord with) the dancer's knowledge of the narrative of her art form. For example, Morris (2008: 49) explains that in interpreting the choreography of Frederick Ashton, to be true to Ashton's vision, the dancer would need to appreciate that 'sharpness and motion are of greater significance than balanced shape'. Without such attention to the interpretation and the artistic narrative, Morris holds, the 'distinction between dancer and gymnast will disappear' (ibid.).

Weisbrod makes a related point, contrasting the 'normative' discipline of technique with the potentially 'transgressive' qualities of interpretation and artistry. She draws on cultural theorists Randy Martin and Toby Miller (1999), who examine the centrality of sport in American life. Sport is easily accommodated, she writes, because it privileges

> The Foucauldian bodily experience of power wherein the body is disciplined by training, regimented by rules and overseen through visible and non/invisible subjects. Directly opposite sport experience is the less controllable practice of art ... Rather than maintaining normative behaviors as if being constantly policed, the artistic body is often transgressive, pushing the standards of customary representations. (Weisbrod 2010: 46)

Her contention is that 'Competition, by structuring dance as sport, diminishes or entirely removes the artistic element, in particular those that often situate it outside normative social practices' (ibid.).

While the argument of Best and McFee about art and its 'narrative' is compelling, it is not always easy to separate the aesthetic from the artistic – especially in the case of music and dance. Morris interviewed Mavis Staines, then artistic president of the Prix de Lausanne, who felt that for ballet, artistry cannot be separated from technique, and that 'separating the two is potentially destructive' (Staines, quoted in Morris 2008: 43). Morris concedes that 'she may well have a point, since it is necessary for professional students to have achieved a high level of technical competence' (ibid.). A dancer could be very well informed about the stylistic preferences of different choreographers, and about the history and development of ballet (ballet's narrative), and yet lack the strength or physical control to execute the choreography as required. A dancer is not an academic. Indeed, in order to flout the rules of good technique to portray a choreographic (or musical) style, the dancer must arguably be in absolute command of her technique (she *could* execute the movements to a prescribed standard, but she *chooses* not to). Morris's concern rather is that 'in the profession having a good technique does not always mean having flexibility, strength and physical control, on the contrary it can mean mastery of the vocabulary of classical dance according to prescribed instructions' (ibid.). Her objection is to the disciplinarian quality of technique – or what Weisbrod terms its normative rather than transgressive qualities.[17] Competition dance, then, can be perceived as weighted to privilege spectacle over nuance, technique over interpretation. In this way, for Weisbrod, competition dance is inherently conservative.

Competition Dance: Popular Art, 'High' Art and 'Consumer Culture'

It is telling that in Weisbrod's discussion of *So You Think* she laments that in the format of the competition, 'the performance and training of these contemporary bodies centralises *entertainment* and *popular culture* over visionary or experimental artistic practice' (Weisbrod 2014: 325, my emphasis). Here she aligns herself with the orthodoxy of cultural theory, which is that the former (entertainment, the popular, 'low' art) is inferior to the latter (visionary artistic practice), and according to which the two are perceived as mutually exclusive.

Dance scholar Sherril Dodds, in her study of popular dance, *Dancing on the Canon*, situates her ethnography with a clear and detailed summary of the debates within cultural theory about 'high' and 'low', 'folk' and 'classical' art. She shows how in these discussions, 'high' art emerges as 'profound' and concerned with 'transcendence' while 'low' art is focused on 'entertainment' and 'exists for commercial gain' (Dodds 2011: 43). 'High' art is viewed as 'independent of the market and produced for its own sake, unlike mass or popular art which is driven by capitalist production' (ibid.: 90).

Dodds outlines the argument often raised in critique of 'popular' art – which is that the homogeneous and formulaic nature of much popular, commercially successful culture lends itself to unquestioning, passive consumption, meaning that the audience is arguably left vulnerable to manipulation by the producers, creators or managers of this product. Dodds's critique of this view, supported by three detailed ethnographic studies, is that it is both patronizing and reductive. The effect of dance, she points out (and I would argue, the effect of all art), cannot be measured in terms of the piece of art alone but must be understood in terms of how its audience engages with it. I might watch the piece by the Britain-based Israeli contemporary dance choreographer Hofesh Shechter, *Political Mother* (2010), and be totally gripped and disturbed by the visual references to prisoners of the Nazi concentration camps, or I might sit in the theatre more preoccupied by whether I have enough food in the fridge for my sons' packed lunches and whether I need to stop by the grocery shop on my way home. As Stuart Hall (1973) taught us, the impact of a piece of art is not predetermined by the artwork itself but must be forged together with the response of its audience – a response that will vary from person to person (it is impacted, in dance scholar Priya Srinivasan's (2009: 53) terms, by the 'unruly [or the 'ruly'] spectator'). In Dodds's studies, each of the communities she looks at engages with the different 'popular' dance forms in ways that enable them to subvert and question their day-to-day experience. Engagement in these dance forms provides participants from each group studied with an 'imagined community' (Dodds 2011: 157), opportunity to 'play' (ibid.: 204–5) and a great deal of 'pleasure' (or joy) (ibid.: 123–24 and *passim*).

Dodds's study is an important corrective to the frequent denigration of popular culture and her emphasis on the importance of 'pleasure' and 'play' is well made. The suspicion of 'entertainment' and 'escapism' shown by some cultural theorists can assume a puritanical dimension that makes one fear a Cromwellian cancellation of Christmas.[18] Writing in the 1970s, sociologist Richard Dyer argued that the 'larger-than-life spectacle' of the televised talent contest 'constituted the aesthetics of escape for alienated workers' (Redden 2010: 132), offering momentary respite from 'necessity and scarcity' (Dyer, cited in ibid.). As an occasional bit of escapism, can such programmes as *Strictly* or *So You Think* not help refresh and restore us to better deal with the challenges of life? Or, without the utilitarian justification, can they not simply provide fun (pleasure)?

Equally, Weisbrod is critical of *So You Think*'s propensity to turn 'dancing bodies' into 'commodities for consumption' by 'mainstream and popular culture'. Within cultural theory, the assessment of art as 'commercial' has been typically pejorative (see Frow 1996; Dodds 2011). And yet, as literary and cultural studies scholar John Frow argues, following aesthetician Sandor Radnoti (1981), 'in reality all cultural production is dependent on the market' (Frow 1996: 19). Within a capitalist economy, all culture, high or low, is to a greater or lesser extent a consumed commodity. To make a crass point, where the art is not consumed, the artist is unable to consume (food, drink or other cultural products), unless they have an income provided by some other means (independent wealth or state or other patronage, or through working in other capacities to supplement their lack of earnings from their art).[19] Indeed, the rhetoric around 'high' art and the disdain for the idea of the motivation of financial gain (explained by Pierre Bourdieu (1983) in terms of the 'reversed economy', whereby accumulation of symbolic capital assumes a greater importance than material reward) undoubtedly contributes to the embarrassment and reluctance dancers show in talking about money and in asking for financial recognition of their labour – asking for decent pay (see Chapter 2).

There is certainly an argument here for increased state patronage for the arts, or for the more radical but increasingly popular suggestion of a universal basic income (as I discuss in the conclusion). England is fortunate for the moment to have the Arts Council, with an open funding programme, as I explain in the introduction, offering the possibility of funding for individuals and small organizations. Without this, it is not clear what the artist is supposed to do apart from market their art (thereby making it a commodity), or, as the nineteenth-century French poet and journalist Theophile Gautier is supposed to have observed of his contemporary countryman, novelist Gustave Flaubert, to have 'the wit to come into the world with money'.[20] There is absolutely nothing romantic about living in a garret (or about sofa surfing, which is the contemporary equivalent for many dancers). In this light, dancers in *So You Think* or *Young Dancer* – all of whom choose to enter these competitions voluntarily – are doing no more than using their talent and hard-won skills to try and ensure themselves a better future (and in so doing providing the audience with some enjoyable entertainment).[21] Under this interpretation, some of the objections to *So You Think* and other talent shows (voiced by Weisbrod and Redden among others) could be construed as arising from a misplaced academic snobbery and reluctance to have a good time, together with an unhelpfully idealistic vision of art created without thought of financial gain.[22]

And yet, while Dodds's work is an important reminder of the variety of 'popular dance', as well as the variety of responses to it, it is interesting that each of the dance forms she chooses to illustrate 'popular dance' comes from a community that could hardly be considered 'mainstream'. Dodds clearly distinguishes the burlesque striptease she studies, for example, from the striptease marketed by such corporate or 'mainstream' venues as Stringfellow's Cabaret of Angels or the Spearmint Rhino Gentleman's Club (Dodds 2011: 111). In each of the examples she uses, she describes how the opportunity for fantasy and escape is shaped by participants to allow them a creative response to real-life exclusions and inequalities. None of the dance forms she describes is commercially driven.[23] While, as discussed above, it is naïve to think that art in contemporary Britain can escape some degree of commodification, what is perhaps important is the extent to which being a commodity has been the dominant ideology shaping the work, and the extent to which this has meant abandoning artistic (and often moral) integrity. To build on one of Dodds's examples, burlesque striptease is an art form. The Cabaret of Angels (which makes no concessions to the demands of artistry or to avoiding exploitation of dancers) is not. The problem (*pace* Weisbrod) is not with popular art, or with entertainment, or with making money – but is a matter of intention and degree. Which ideology – that of art or commerce – is dominant in shaping the product?

This is not always an easy question to determine, and (given that the commodity value for something that disclaims its artistic or cultural status is likely to fall) is unlikely to be answered honestly. Theologian Timothy Gorringe (following cultural theorists Stuart Hall and Paddy Whannel) quotes the television pianist Liberace, who confessed, 'My whole trick is to keep the tune well out front. If I play Tchaikovsky, I play his melodies and skip his spiritual struggles. Naturally I condense. I have to know just how many notes my audience will stand for' (Liberace, cited in Gorringe 2004: 55). What are Liberace's priorities here? Are they box office returns? In this case his overriding concern could be argued to be commercial, making his primary role that of businessman rather than artist. Is his priority audience engagement and accessibility? Does his desire for accessibility compromise his artistic integrity? Tchaikovsky's (possibly uncomfortable) struggles, represented in the more complex passages that lend depth to his work, are omitted, while the aesthetically pleasing (if superficial) tune is kept 'out front', for just as 'many notes' as his 'audience will stand'. What Liberace is describing could, I suggest, be likened to 'fast art', being a little like fast food (and related to but distinct from cultural anthropologist Grant McCracken's (2009) definition of fast culture) – easy to consume, low on nutrients and roughage, often cheap and addictively tasty, fine as a treat, but liable to lead to obesity if not otherwise part of a balanced diet. This is not so much because the work is 'popular', but because it is comfortable and, to return to Weisbrod's critique, essentially conformist.

The question is whether Liberace's decisions are driven primarily by a concern for the accessibility of the piece of music as a work of art or by its viability as a product (commodity) to be consumed. Is the overriding principle determining the shape of his music art or commerce? This question of what constitutes the 'overriding ideology' was one of philosopher and sociologist Theodore Adorno's key gripes with what he terms 'the culture industry'. He accepts that some degree of cultural commodification is hard to escape. He concedes that 'ever since these cultural forms first began to earn a living for their creators as commodities in the marketplace, they had already possessed something of this quality [the quality of commodification]' (Adorno 1975: 13). The distinction comes when a cultural product's identity as an artwork becomes subsumed by its purpose as a commodity. Thus, he continues, 'But then they sought after profit only indirectly, over and above their autonomous essence. New on the part of the culture industry *is the direct and undisguised primacy of a precisely and thoroughly calculated efficacy* in its most typical products' (ibid., my emphasis). From this perspective, none of the examples of popular art that Dodds describes could be said to belong properly to the 'culture industry'. Her distance from Adorno is perhaps not as great as it might initially seem.

The entity to be wary of, then, is not 'popular art', but 'fast art', or art as 'industry'. In his 1975 essay 'Culture Industry Reconsidered', Adorno highlights two key dangers with culture as 'industry'. The first is its 'scaffolding of rigidly conservative basic categories' (1975: 13), which means that the industry 'standardizes' culture: 'what parades as progress in the culture industry, as the incessantly new which it offers up, remains the disguise for an eternal sameness' (ibid.: 14). The second is that in this standardization of product, it encourages a standardization, or a conformity, among its audience. Controlled by 'the most powerful interests . . . the consensus which it propagates strengthens blind, opaque authority' (ibid.: 17), impeding 'the development of autonomous, independent individuals who judge and decide consciously for themselves' (ibid.: 19). Thus, the discussion returns to the dangers of passive consumption and vulnerability to media manipulation.

Televised Competitions, Standardization and the Contempt for the Ordinary

Building on Adorno, media theorist Neil Postman's seminal study of the influence of television on Euro-American culture, *Amusing Ourselves to Death* (2007), drew on Aldous Huxley's novel *Brave New World*, where the soma-drugged[24] workers repeat to themselves, 'I'm so glad I'm a Beta [as opposed to a harder-working Alpha] . . . I'm really awfully glad I'm a Beta, because I don't work so hard' (Huxley 1979: 33). Huxley was critiquing a Fordist model of labour, where people were required to work as efficient units of a machine during working hours, and Postman's point is that TV (the modern-day opium of the people) acts like soma to reconcile workers in the Fordist machine to their inferior and routine status, creating a feeling of well-being that exchanges an induced feeling of euphoria for rights to civil action.

In a 2014 essay, dancer and scholar Susan Leigh Foster draws attention to the post-Fordist model of labour, one she labels the Toyotaist model (based on the Toyota car company) (Foster 2014). While Fordist model employees leave work behind at the end of the working day, the Toyotaist model demands a greater level of engagement, such that 'employees do not leave work and come home, but instead continue to work at some level non-stop' (ibid.: 2). Performance studies scholars Annelies van Assche, Katherina Pewny and Rudi Laermans (2019: 139) point out that increasingly such work 'without boundaries' has become the norm – 'ubiquitous and hegemonic'. While it appears to promise greater freedom (flexible working) due to the loss of constraints around where and when work can take place, the flip side is that post-Fordist 'transnational and project-based labour' has 'eroded the difference between work and private life' (ibid.). Furthermore, the nature of work has shifted such that as performance theoretician Bojana Kunst (2015: 31) argues, a critical aspect of today's professional life is the performative – 'we work by means of our affective, intimate, communicational and human powers'. In this context, 'the performer becomes the ideal virtuoso worker of contemporary capitalism'. Along these lines, Foster contends that on *So You Think*, it is not only dancers' bodies that are displayed as commodities for the viewing public, but their very selves – their personal lives, their struggles in rehearsal, their hopes and dreams. The labour portrayed on these shows is passionate, all-consuming and intense. It is also precarious, with the performers' labour constantly overshadowed by the threat of being voted off the show. To complete the replication of conditions of work within the gig economy, the competitions combine the Toyotaist model of round-the-clock labour with, as Redden (2008: 139) argues, the values of a meritocracy that boasts 'equality of opportunity amid inequality of reward'. Evidently, in every competition where one will win, others must lose.

Beneath the veneer of entertainment, such reality TV talent competitions are, Redden argues (following a similar line to Adorno), deeply pedagogic, and are exploitative and damaging to both competitors and audience. They are not so much about talent as about escape. They recognize the talent of 'ordinary folk', but only as a vehicle towards a new life (more glamorous, less ordinary) (Redden 2008, 2010). Being ordinary is a condition to be left behind. So great is the allure of this reward (the escape from the ordinary) that despite the 'work of being watched' (Andrejevic 2004, cited in Redden 2010), despite gruelling mental and physical demands confronted in front of millions of viewers, despite the high chance of failure, there remains a constant supply of competitors willing to be exploited on the gamble of making it big. The lessons taught are 'don't be a nobody' and 'keep working to make it'. Thus, the labour of the competitor is exploited while the audience is taught the lesson of discontent – which will in turn ensure that they keep labouring. The economic reality of such a meritocracy, as Redden points out, is entrenched inequality, as the 'desired few' are rewarded ever more handsomely (and their individual irreplaceability underlined), while the 'undesired many' have their contracts cut, their wages frozen and are treated with the contempt of 'disposability'.[25]

The Huxleyan workers under the Toyotaist model would not be content with being Betas, but would feel the need to strive and labour ceaselessly to be Alphas, lured by the fairytale appeal of the Alpha world. Soma, the sedative, has been replaced by a stimulant; drug-induced contentment replaced by drug-induced discontent. In this context 'escapism' assumes a whole new significance. The goal of this escapism is not to shut down after the struggles of day-to-day life for a short while, returning to them refreshed and better able to deal with them (with perhaps even a creative approach to tackling them). The goal of this escapism is, Redden (2008: 141) argues, one of 'rupture'. The individual crosses over to the elite from the ranks of the 'meritless majority' (ibid.). In this way, the genius of the talent show, Redden (2010: 139) shows, is that it enables those invested in the media to 'render an image of social life that legitimates their material interests, and simultaneously those of any organisation that dreams of an endless supply of workers who will work passionately for ever diminishing returns, with security traded for the chance of making it – while loving it'. It is the capitalist's wet dream.

Dance Competitions and Manufactured Identity

Weisbrod (2010), in her detailed analysis of *So You Think*, points to another insidious harm lying beneath the glitz of competitive entertainment, which is the role the programme plays in shaping and reinforcing stereotypical images. The format of the dance competition lends itself to simplistic representations, which can be used to shape or manipulate audience perceptions. The same appeal to the spectacular and the superficial aesthetic – what I shall call (following the idea of the 'soundbite'), the 'vision-bite' – that makes it so marketable a commodity also lends itself well to the creation and perpetuation of myth and stereotype.

Dance ethnologist Anca Giurchescu (2001: 116) draws attention to the 'network of institutions and a system of competitions named *Cantarea Romaniei* (Song to Romania)' that 'was given the task to select, construct and disseminate these symbols – symbols that were meant to build an idyllic image that would hide a reality full of deep contradictions'. It is not only in the context of a totalitarian state that such selective representation is harnessed to manufacture an idealized and simplistic rallying point for cultural identity. Irish step dance competitions organized by the Gaelic League performed a similar function for Irish culture (Wulff 2007), while in Indian folk dance competitions held at American universities, 'Prize-winning teams are those that score high points in both skill and traditionality. Performances posit their existence as authentic representations of Punjabi culture' (Chacko and Menon 2013: 106). Similarly, David (2014: 30) notes the 'reifying of tradition' and the emphasis on a supposed 'authenticity' that marks the success of teams competing in *raas* and *garba* (Gujarati folk dance) contests in Britain. Each of these portrayals of culture conveys a caricature, a cartoon image constructed from cherry-picked features that skates over complexity. As with Liberace's rendition of Tchaikovsky, the Romania, the Ireland or the Punjab of these competitions is portrayed with the 'melody' (an idealized depiction of an authorized version of identity) out front, without the difficult complications of 'spiritual struggles.'.

In the televised competition, the cartoon impressions provided by such 'vision-bites' of dance are further reinforced by the 'extended choreography' of the commentary of the judges and the selection of the rehearsal and 'backstage' material. Weisbrod shows how on *So You Think*, the training histories of the dancing bodies presented are simplified in order to project a stereotype of the 'raw untrained hip hop dancer' in contrast to the 'classically technical contemporary dancer', thereby sustaining 'a paradigm of race that has an extensive history in American culture, which ensures that these bodies fit into an established system of discipline and racial discourse' (Weisbrod 2014: 330). The intensification of the contrast between categories of competitor serves to intensify the spectacle of the show, while precisely this intensification of spectacle serves to reinforce and underline established racial prejudices rather than disrupt or question them. Yet more perniciously, the judges' rhetoric around the 'raw, untrained body' thereby 'invisibilizes the labour' (ibid.) of young, black men already struggling to combat a widely held American stereotype of black male laziness and disaffection.

At the same time as minimizing the labour that goes into the technical mastery of hip-hop, the programme adds insult to injury by presenting hip-hop on mainstream TV in a manner calculated to emasculate its transgressive and radicalizing potential, making it safe for placid consumption by viewers at home.[26] Furthermore, as dance scholars Dodds and Colleen Hooper (2014: 105) argue in their illuminating critique of *So You Think*, for all its alleged diversity, ultimately the competitors who succeed must 'be re-trained in the choreography round according to the judges' Euro-American dance standards paradigm'. In order 'to progress in the competition', the competitor 'needs to conform' (ibid.: 106). The discussion returns to the point raised at the beginning – the propensity of the dance competition to uniformity, discipline and the normative.

To summarize the preceding discussion, the dance competition is a format that, while offering benefits, is fraught with aesthetic and ethical concerns, concerns intensified when the competition is televised following the tropes of the increasingly pervasive reality TV show. A format biased to privilege spectacle over artistry, it is predisposed towards the stifling of the transgressive and the experimental and facilitates the manipulation of 'vision-bites' to reinforce stereotypes and impose conformity. Within the context of the reality TV show, the inherently 'meritocratic' format of the competition is linked to a Toyotaist model of 'surveilled affective labour' (Redden 2010) to peddle a social model of elitism whereby the talented and 'strong actually do what they can and the weak suffer what they must' (Varoufakis 2017: 19, citing Thucydides). The benefits of bringing together sections of the dance world and accessibility and entertainment for an audience seem small rewards for so great a price.

BBC Young Dancer – Breaking the TV Competition Mould?

In this light, it is small wonder that the response of Judith Mackrell, dance writer for the *Guardian* newspaper, to the announcement of the launch of *Young Dancer* was somewhat muted. Rather wearily she asked, 'Does the dance world need another competition?' (Mackrell 2014). Yet she conceded (of the original format) that *Young Dancer* was a competition that had been thought through 'with unusual care' (ibid.). It was also widely welcomed across the British world of dance, and as I show at the beginning of the chapter, specifically by the world of South Asian dance. The enthusiasm with which it has been greeted by practitioners together with its strong links to the world of professional British dance mean that it is not a competition that can be easily dismissed. How far has it succeeded in avoiding the exploitative and manipulative qualities found in other televised talent contests? How far has it enabled the BBC to fulfil its aim to 'support the arts and . . . develop new talent'? (BBC 2023).

From the outset, *Young Dancer* was modelled on the form of the talent competition *Young Musician*,[27] in which the emphasis is more on the art form than on the potential life change for the competitor. Granted, lives are changed as a result of the exposure provided by the competition, but these changes come across as an acceleration of the consequences of high levels of discipline and talent, whereby other competitors will also succeed (albeit in the longer term), rather than as the somewhat arbitrary 'rupture' whereby gaining the crown in a single TV series marks the divide between extraordinary success and fame and the return to odd jobs and oblivion. The application pack for the 2017 programme took care to point out that the competition is 'not just about winning', emphasizing that it is an enriching experience in itself, and that 'most importantly of all, the competition brings the opportunity to meet and work alongside other young people with a passion for dance' (*Young Dancer*, entry brochure, 2017). Similarly, Redden (2008: 135) observes of the competitive TV shows of the 1960s and 1970s that 'The older talent shows focused mostly on the moments of performance and their assessment by judges' and this remains the case, I believe, with *Young Dancer*. There are clips of the competitors in rehearsal, as well as clips providing some context in terms of their everyday life outside the competition, but the majority of the programme focuses on the performance pieces themselves and the judges' commentary.[28]

The self-conscious commitment to artistry (regardless of how successful the endeavour) both contributes to, and is reinforced by, the show's deliberate alignment with the wider world of professional dance in Britain. The show considered throughout the process of its construction 'what the professional life of a dancer is like' (Hackett 2015). *Young Dancer* comes highly supported and endorsed by artistic heavyweights from across the British dance world. So much so that attending the 2017 Grand Final felt like being present at a Who's Who of British dance, with professionals supporting the performance as judges, commentators or audience members including dancer-choreographers Richard Alston, Shobana Jeyasingh, Jasmin Vardimon, Matthew Bourne and Nahid Siddiqui, Sadler's Wells director Alistair Spalding, former Chief Executive of the Place[29] Kenneth Tharp and former prima ballerina Darcey Bussell.

A commitment to training and expertise is highlighted in that the interest of the show is not so much in a talented and charismatic individual who might win over hearts and minds through charm and untutored pluck (though charisma, charm and pluck inevitably play their part). Rather, the programme's stated interest is in young dancers who have spent 'hours and hours practising and perfecting what they are doing' and then use their techniques 'to express something new that's relevant to everyone today' (Hackett 2015). Charisma matters, but only on the basis that, as the show's commentators and judges reiterate throughout, 'technique is a given'. Importantly, these dancers then use their acquired technique to creatively respond to and interpret their environment. Obviously 'given technique' means different things in the context of different dance styles – and the presence of specialist mentors and judges for each category is designed to accommodate this.[30]

To facilitate this commitment to interpretation beyond technique, in contrast to programmes like *So You Think*, in *Young Dancer* dancers compete only in the dance style in which they are trained, rather than doing their best in a range of styles they have barely come across before. The familiarity they have with the style they perform permits them more scope for interpretation rooted in established technique. This exploration is supported by time spent with appointed mentors. The presence in the final of pieces choreographed for category contestants by 'some of the UK's leading choreographers' (BBC 2017b: 1) (choreographers who, in contrast to those on *So You Think*, are themselves trained in the competitors' respective dance styles) can be argued to again reinforce the development of interpretation rather than spectacle. After all, as Anusha Kedhar (2020: 153) argues, it is particularly in the absence of those 'familiar with the nuances of Indian classical dance' that 'dance that is seen as risky, fast, athletic, and virtuosic stands in as a marker of good dancing' so that 'subtlety is often sacrificed for spectacle'. At the same time, *Young Dancer* (somewhat paradoxically) sets down rules that encourage the transgression of norms as a part of the competition, in the sense that for each category, one of the two solos performed in the final is specified in a manner calculated to take participants out of their comfort zone. I use the term 'transgression' here not to suggest the radical subversion of social conventions, but in the less dramatic yet still important sense as used by Weisbrod, of encouraging the experimental – or of stretching the boundaries of the canon. For ballet, for example, while one solo should be 'classical technique', the other should show 'neo-classical or contemporary ballet' (Young Dancer entry brochure, 2017). For the South Asian category, the second solo 'could show a more contemporary style and/or could show movement vocabulary from another South Asian dance form'. The distinction between this extension of the canon and performance based on learning a new technique is that the core of the performance remains rooted in known vocabulary (though the suggestions for South Asian dance are problematic, as I discuss below).

The restriction of competitors to known technique, the commitment to mentoring and the emphasis on developing the form by moving it 'in a different direction' all serve, I suggest, to counterbalance the pull of competitive dance towards the spectacular, and to encourage competitors to go beyond simply the 'aesthetic' or surface appeal. This is reinforced by the criteria for and manner of assessment, which is done by panels of judges with expertise in each of the categories represented, and which takes account of, as mentioned above, 'artistry and interpretation, including musicality; performance quality; [and] distinctive movement style/individuality', as well as 'technique' (*Young Dancer*, entry brochure, 2017).

It was in part the desire for an artistic rather than merely aesthetic assessment (to return to Best and McFee's understanding of these terms) of the competitors by both judges (and, as far as possible, on the basis of information provided within the programme, by the audience) that informed the difficult decision of the original competition to restrict the number of dance categories featured to four, and within the South Asian dance category, to restrict the dance styles represented to two. Making these decisions was a tough call, and inevitably, the BBC received 'a lot of letters from musical theatre and other groups contesting the category selection' (Hackett 2017). The final decision was based on a combination of factors, including the popularity of the forms in terms of the numbers of people engaged in them, the fact that 'each style has a very rigorous and detailed technique' and the presence of, as discussed above, a 'highly skilled set of dancers taking the form in a different direction' (ibid.).

Disappointing as it was for dance forms not chosen, the limit was imposed because Hackett felt that it would allow both the BBC and the viewing public to gain a deeper understanding of each form presented (Hackett 2017), making for a more enriched experience of the show. The limit enabled judgement by specialists (established dancers, choreographers and researchers) from each category chosen, each one conversant with the 'narrative' framing an individual performance. In Hackett's words, 'We didn't want the competition to be a repeat of *Britain's Got Talent* so we needed forms that would have clear criteria upon which to make a judgement – so that the decision wouldn't just be a question of personal preference' (ibid.).

How far 'clear' or absolute 'criteria' of judgement are ever possible, and how far personal preference can genuinely be avoided, are debates beyond the scope of this chapter. However, knowledge of the 'narrative' of an art form allows for an informed assessment and guards against mistaken judgements made about the dance forms 'because inappropriate assumptions about the art are imported' (from other narratives) (McFee 2005: 369). The same reasoning led to the restriction of the South Asian dance category to bharatanatyam and kathak, a decision that has caused disappointment that forms such as odissi and kuchipudi were not included. Thus, in the original format, the South Asian dance category was able to have on the judging panel a specialist in each form, bharatanatyam and kathak. For Hackett, to accommodate further forms would simply not have been practical.[31] This is a straightforward prioritizing of depth over breadth.

In the same vein, this limit allowed for the provision of a significant level of information and education about each form featured. True to the mission statement of BBC founder John Reith, *Young Dancer* aimed and apparently still aims not only to entertain but also to 'inform' and 'educate'. The 2015 South Asian category final included short introductions to the forms from Akram Khan (kathak) and Seeta Patel (bharatanatyam), and the website for the first three iterations featured links to more information about all the categories featured, including South Asian dance. This information provided a basic sketch of the 'narrative' of the different dance styles, allowing the viewing public (at least to some extent) an artistic alongside an aesthetic appreciation of the dance forms. As the editors of the South Asian arts website *Finding Lila* noted, 'When else would you hear *abhinaya* being discussed on Friday night TV?' (Somasundaram and Basu 2015).

The balance between accessibility, artistry and expertise is weighted (both in the original and the revised format) so that in contrast to *So You Think* or *Britain's Got Talent*,[32] where arguably the professionals step into the domain of the general public, with *BBC Young Dancer*, the public is invited in to witness the expert workings of the privileged sphere of the professional. Endorsing this view,

Hanna Weibye (2015), writing for the specialist arts website *The Arts Desk*, commended the competition for being 'remarkably gimmick free' and 'light years away from the razzmatazz, sparkling scoreboards and celebrity judge in-fighting of the BBC 1 show [*Strictly Come Dancing*]'. Kenneth Tharp, then Chief Executive of the London-based dance centre (and home to London Contemporary Dance School) the Place, agreed, writing in a blog on the competition, 'I remember watching the very first contemporary solo and what struck me immediately from the first 30 seconds was that the quality of the performance and that of the choreography was not the kind of wham-bam razzmatazz showpiece you might expect from a competition piece' (Tharp 2016). *Young Dancer*, then, works hard to present what the eighteenth-century champion of ballet professionalism Louis de Cahusac would consider 'real dance' as opposed to 'a means to achieve hollow effects' (Cahusac, cited in Weickmann 2007: 53). How far does it succeed in avoiding the other dangers of competition dance discussed – those of projecting a 'vision-bite' of stereotyped identity, and of implicit validation of a meritocratic social model? These are crucial questions, intimately connected to the question of what inclusion in the competition means for South Asian dance. I will therefore return now to the discussion of these questions, before concluding with a consideration of the new format and a more general reflection on the competition's position in relation to these broader issues.

The competition has, as indicated above, been felt to be significant for the sector. In the discussion below, I highlight three key ways in which the sector has benefitted, which I identify as building profile and networks, dialogic representation and institutional endorsement. I then go on to consider areas of the programme that are more problematic.

Building Profile and Networks

> This is the biggest outreach project that could ever happen.
> —Jane Hackett, 2017

The most obvious benefit of *Young Dancer* for South Asian dance is the impact it has had on the visibility of the sector to three different groups: the wider public, the dance world and, perhaps most surprisingly given its comparatively small size, the South Asian dance sector itself. Appearing on prime-time television, and then available on catch-up, within a framework designed to have a broad appeal, the programme has brought South Asian dance forms to more people in Britain than ever before. Tharp celebrated this achievement when he blogged (along the same lines as Weisbrod's comments on the more positive aspects of *So You Think* cited above):

> I witnessed many comments [by people] on social media . . . and what their comments had in common was that watching a full hour of classi-

cal Indian dance on TV had clearly been a huge eye opener. Many were thrilled and surprised at the combined beauty of the music, dance, performances, and costumes . . . What the BBC Young Dancer did alongside show-casing and inspiring young talent was to allow huge numbers of people to enjoy a whole range of dance they might not otherwise have seen. (Tharp 2016)

Hackett (2017) agrees: 'There is actually very little known about South Asian dance forms outside the immediate dance world – and we have had a lot of feedback from people on Facebook for example saying, '*I had no idea that South Asian dance had that much in it*' (my emphasis).

Profile in itself could be unhelpful if the way in which South Asian dance was portrayed fed into stereotype (as I discuss below), or otherwise cultivated an impression of South Asian dance as somehow inferior to, or less nuanced than, Euro-American dance forms. It is therefore noteworthy that the Facebook commentator Hackett refers to above is left with a greater appreciation of the complexity of South Asian dance forms. This is in contrast to *So You Think* where, as Weisbrod (2010) shows, the labour and expertise that goes into hip-hop is diminished in favour of the image of the 'raw' and 'untrained' dancer. Clearly the effort to provide background and information to supply a 'narrative' context to the work that facilitates artistic appreciation has had an effect in this instance.

As well as the broader public, the programme has been instrumental in educating dancers across dance styles about other forms and encouraging 'cross-form' collaboration. For example, South Asian dance category finalist Akshay Prakash described how 'there were two contemporary dancers performing in the duets [at the category final] – and I was very impressed – because I never watch contemporary or ballet, but I was interested with the way they have control of their body and it kind of pushed me . . . to want to reach that kind of level. It kind of motivated me' (Prakash 2017).

While watching the South Asian category finals for *Young Dancer* 2017 in Manchester, I found myself sitting among the contemporary dance category finalists, none of whom had seen more than snippets of classical Indian dance forms before. As a result, to quote Hackett (2017) again, 'already there have been a number of collaborations that have come out of *Young Dancer* 2015 that would never have happened without it . . . the collaboration between Connor[33] and Vidya for example, or between Richard Alston and Vidya.[34] These are all incredibly enriching collaborations.'

Finally, the competition has facilitated connections between the participants across the very different spheres that make up the South Asian dance sector within Britain. As Ann R. David shows through her ethnographic work among the British Tamil community, 'Young people studying Bharatanatyam in one of the weekend Tamil schools were unaware of the names of prominent London professional Bharatanatyam dancers and were not encouraged to see performances; Leicester kathak and Bollywood dance teachers were uninformed of the London Tamil dance scene' (David 2010c: 90).

Akshay Prakash spoke of how *BBC Young Dancer* opened his world and gave him a sense of pride and confidence in just how widespread bharatanatyam is in Britain.

> What [the] BBC and the production gave me is a life lesson at the same time... I kind of kept myself confined – in a sense I never really explored out... A lot of dancers and teachers came to the competitions and since then I have been keeping in touch with some of them and talking about productions here and there – it's been very interesting... the fact that in the UK when it comes to Indian culture – it's not just confined to Bhavan – it feels really, really good to see and hear that bharatanatyam is expanding in the UK. (Prakash 2017)

The isolation of dance worlds is not one-way. At the performance of a dance drama at the Bhavan featuring twenty-four committed and talented young bharatanatyam dancers (including Prakash), there were no representatives from other South Asian dance or arts organizations present.[35] Against this background of fragmentation, *Young Dancer* has brought together members from across these dance worlds – and beyond. An online Tamil journal covered *Young Dancer* 2017, drawing attention to the participation of Anjelli Wignakumar and Piriyanga Kesavan: 'Congratulations to the talented young Tamils for representing our art on the world stage' (Thamarai 2017). In *Young Dancer*, the BBC has produced a programme that is invested in by parties as diverse and distinct as London Contemporary Dance School and Harrow Tamil School. This is a clear illustration of anthropologist and ballroom dancer Jonathan Marion's (2008) point (raised earlier) about the value of competitions in bringing together different sectors of the dance world.

Dialogic Representation

Scholars of decolonization (Fischer-Lichte et al. 2014; Hall 1999; Mbembe 2010; Said 1995; Tshimanga 2009) rightly interrogate the representation of art forms, in an attempt to reveal and dismantle Western hegemony in the field of humanities and other disciplines (Mbembe 2010). As all representation is mediated, and decisions are inevitably made from the context of an ideological framework, the presentation of art forms originating from a former colony (India) by the mainstream media of the formerly colonizing power (Britain) is bound to be a sensitive area. In addition, as discussed above, competitions are susceptible to the use of the 'vision-bite', or stereotype – projecting an image of what a culture *should be*, while glossing over its complexity and 'spiritual struggles'.

Figure 1.1. Jaina Modasia performing a chakar in In Akbar's Palace, *one of the pieces she performed as part of the South Asian category finals,* BBC Young Dancer, 2017. © *BBC Photo Archive.*

In presenting 'South Asian dance', on the one hand lie the dangers of Orientalism (Said 1995), now well-rehearsed, whereby artistic and cultural forms from outside the Western cultural establishment are presented as 'static, frozen, fixed eternally' (ibid.: 208). On the other hand lie the dangers of assimilation, whereby these art forms are valued most when 'sufficiently processed to meet the western palate' (Sporton 2004: 88) – so processed that they can no longer be said to display the distinctive technical and aesthetic vocabularies characteristic of these dance styles. Kedhar (2020: 4) puts it vividly: 'Like other racialized dancing "acrobats" who balance performing ethnic particularity and cultural assimilation, the British South Asian dancer must also walk a tightrope between sameness and difference.' How does one avoid the presentation of Asian classical dance forms in 'concert halls and festivals in the west' whereby, as dance scholar Anthony Shay (2008: 167) articulates, 'over a century since the appearance of Asian dance in world exhibitions, [Western] audiences search for meaning and truth in "ancient" and "timeless" traditions of dance and music they feel [are] lacking in their own lives'? Counter to this is the question voiced by an audience member at the Academy of Indian Dance debate 'Traditions on the Move' back in 1993, and echoed repeatedly since then in a variety of contexts, which is that with innovation, is there a line where 'work stops being Indian dance' (Tucker 1993: 2)? Where is the line between innovation within a technique and the creation of a new technique?

Clearly this question stands across dance forms, though the reality of dominant economic and cultural power structures makes more likely the assimilation of non-Euro-American art forms in Britain into a dominant cultural framework. The problem is well summarized by Akram Khan, who commented in an interview for *BBC Young Dancer* 2015 that he felt South Asian dance was at a 'critical time' in which it was necessary to ensure that 'on the one hand . . . South Asian dance [is] still protected in a sense of its form', while on the other, artists are allowed to 'find a way to experiment . . . by taking aspects of South Asian dance to a more contemporary place' (BBC 2015).

The cultural anthropologist Dwight Conquergood in his essay 'Performing as a Moral Act' (2013), poses a related question about the performance of non-Euro-American art forms in a Euro-American context. How do we find our way out of this 'moral morass and ethical minefield of performative plunder, superficial silliness, curiosity seeking and nihilism'? His solution is to suggest a model of 'Dialogical Performance . . . a kind of performance that resists conclusions . . . more than a definite position, this dialogical stance is situated in BETWEEN competing ideologies. It is more like a hyphen than a period' (ibid.: 75).

My contention is that *BBC Young Dancer*, in its original format, allowed for such dialogic performance, granting space for classical together with more contemporary interpretations of South Asian dance. As an illustration, for the 2017 category finals, bharatanatyam dancer Anaya Bolar started with a conventionally classical rendition of an *abhinaya*-based solo depicting a story from the *Mahabharata* about Draupadi being unrobed by the deceitful Duryodhana but saved from shame by the intervention of Lord Krishna. With her duet, choreographed by dance artist and choreographer Subhash Viman Gorania, she explored the potential of bharatanatyam in relating to another dance style, as she and her ballet-trained partner Kaine Ward played with moving along, under and over a rope, positioned now on the floor, now held between them. Dialoguing between the conventional and the experimental, the normative and the (mildly) transgressive, these young dancers displayed their mastery of the 'grammar' and 'architecture' of the dance form (Samson, cited in David 2005a: 7), as well as their ability and imagination in putting that grammar to new uses. Similarly, kathak dancer Jaina Modasia presented first a compelling *nritta* or abstract dance piece, *In Akbar's Palace* (Sujata Banerjee, 2017), highlighting the rapid footwork and dramatic turns of classical kathak. Her duet, with contemporary dancer Peter Camilleri, combined kathak with partner work, including lifts and weight exchange with her partner that took her work well beyond the boundaries of classical kathak, which is conventionally a solo art form, and where even when performing together, there would not normally be any physical contact between performers. This piece was, I felt, problematic in several ways (and I discuss these below), but it nevertheless demonstrated an attempt to push the boundaries of the form. For her final solo, she presented *Krishna*, an engaging kathak rendition of the South Indian Kannada song 'Krishna Nee Begane Baro', an established piece within the bharatanatyam repertoire, but not commonly rendered in kathak. The original *Young Dancer* facilitated and encouraged such dialogic representation, steering between, and thereby avoiding, both essentialist and assimilationist ideologies. There is a further discussion to be had about what is defined as normative, and what transgressive, and in what context, and I address this later. For the moment, it is important to acknowledge that the programme as originally conceived avoided oversimplification and embraced complexity by encouraging a broad representation of the dance forms.

Institutional Endorsement

The most significant benefit to the sector (as well as potential hazard, as I discuss below) is arguably its implicit endorsement, by inclusion as a competition category, by the BBC. Whatever the criticisms of the BBC, and it has received its fair share of these, it remains undoubtedly an iconic institution. It is, as journalist Charlotte Higgins puts it,

> An institution at the heart of Britain. The BBC defines and expresses Britishness – to those who live in the UK and to the rest of the world. The BBC . . . is the most powerful institution of them all, for as well as informing, educating and entertaining, it permeates and reflects our existences and infiltrates our imaginations. (Higgins 2015: xi)

When such an institution presents four categories to represent dance in Britain, and South Asian dance is one of these categories, it is, to agree with Kaushik (2017a), 'big and good news'. It is also a tribute to the amount of work put in by artists, individuals and agencies over the past forty or so years to work to establish the sector and secure its standing in relation to the 'mainstream'. Defying the challenges that I discuss throughout this book, the South Asian dance sector in Britain continues to produce fresh, individual dance voices that reimagine both classical and contemporary South Asian work. Thus, when Hackett went looking for forms with a critical mass of participants as well as 'a highly skilled set of dancers taking the form in a different direction', South Asian dance was ready as a contender. Despite understandable reservations about representation on mainstream media, its inclusion by the BBC is important because, as Andrée Grau points out, institutions are typified by historicity, coercive power and moral authority, where by moral authority she means

> That institutions have a claim to the right of legitimacy. They are established, recognised as such and in the example of the arts they have helped in the creation of aesthetic canons, the yardsticks by which the arts are evaluated. (Grau 2001: 29)

The BBC, founded in 1925, has an indisputable historicity and an acquired moral authority, which in turn lends it a coercive power, defined by Grau as the possession of norms that we must follow 'whether we agree with them or not' if we wish to collaborate with these institutions (ibid.). In this context, it is pertinent to note the observation on the Britain-based South Asian arts blog *Finding Lila* that 'Many of those who watched it felt that it was . . . the *first time that South Asian dance had been presented on an equal footing with ballet, hip hop and contemporary dance on mainstream TV*' (Somasundaram and Basu 2015, my emphasis).

While it is debatable whether this is the first time the BBC has presented South Asian dance 'on an equal footing' (the BBC commission of Jeyasingh's *Duets with Automobiles* in 1993, for example, as part of a series of commissioned pieces of dance for film, is surely another case of 'equal presentation'), it is certainly significant that this is how the competition has been perceived by parts of the South Asian dance community. Many in the sector (including Jeyasingh herself) do not consider Jeyasingh's or Akram Khan's work representative of 'South Asian' dance forms, and it is difficult to think of another programme that has profiled classical bharatanatyam and kathak alongside other dance styles in this way. This is important because, as policy advisor Bhikhu Parekh wrote in 2000, 'Notions of cultural value, belonging and worth are defined and fixed by decisions we make about what is or is not culture and how we are represented (or not) by cultural institutions' (Parekh and Runnymede Trust 2000: 159); or again, 'It is essential if people are to have a sense of belonging to society as a whole that they should not feel alienated or marginalised by public bodies' (ibid.: 49).

The positioning and choices of institutions – particularly of influential and symbolic institutions such as the BBC – are hugely significant in shaping perceptions of ourselves and others as to our place and value within a wider cultural framework. The extent of this significance can be seen in the fuller commentary on this decision made by members of the sector, extracts of which I used to open this discussion. Kaushik, for example, believes that the competition has lifted South Asian dance out of the realms of being a 'community activity'.

> I think it's the best news for the position of South Asian dance in this country because all this time South Asian dance has been perceived to be a community activity. In this context, where it is put alongside ballet, contemporary dance and other forms, where professionals are working and in a field where professionals are aspiring to create professionals, the inclusion of South Asian dance is big and good news. (Kaushik 2017a)

For Mira Balchandran-Gokul, the programme reinforces the British presence of South Asian dance as art: 'I think it's brilliant because you are seeing it not just as a cultural form, you are seeing it along [with] all the different dance forms' (Balchandran-Gokul 2017).

Such equal positioning, together with the use of terms such as *abhinaya* from within the Indian aesthetic tradition, is also important because it marks an attempt, as the semiotician and literary theorist Walter Mignolo (2007) articulates, to expand the 'space of experience' and the 'horizon of expectations' of viewers, reminding them of the world's 'pluriversality', and of the existence of multiple aesthetic codes and multiple dance canons.

In addition, then, to being a programme with a level of artistic integrity several notches above that of other televised competitions, the programme works hard to avoid the pitfalls of stereotyping and presents South Asian dance forms with respect and nuance, with an invocation of aesthetic standards from classical Indian dance that should at least alert the attentive viewer to a plurality of cosmologies.

Tempting as it is to leave this analysis of *BBC Young Dancer* here on a high, it would be both unhelpful and dishonest to stop here. In the following section, I will discuss three problems or gaps, both within the sector and in terms of its wider positioning within the world of British dance, that *BBC Young Dancer* brings starkly to light. These are: the fragmentation of the world of South Asian dance (already touched upon above); the lack of a broader infrastructure to support the sector; and finally, issues with understanding, legibility and cultural translation. Underneath and related to all of these lies the question of how we understand ourselves as communities, what we value – and how we want to live. Such questions are unavoidable in any discussion of cultural representation – especially when discussing today the bright talent of tomorrow.

South Asian Dance – a Divided Sector?

Divisions and factions within the South Asian dance sector in Britain have long been a subject of lament. Abha Adams, the first director of the South Asian dance umbrella organization ADiTi, which was founded in 1989 and folded in 2001, felt that the organization's greatest challenge was 'to bring together what was perceived to be a divided dance community' (Adams, cited in Grau 2001: 43). More than twenty years later, at the Moving On conference led by the Centre for Indian Classical Dance in Leicester, Paul Russ, then director of the Nottingham-based dance agency Dance 4, spoke of the 'many competing levels of expectations, and largely unspoken issues of personality and agenda of control' that were 'putting the brakes on development' (Menski 2011). One respondent in the 2020 Arts Council South Asian dance mapping report echoed this, remarking damningly, 'The organizations are so competitive with each other. That's a real problem. I haven't seen any solid collaboration in this country that goes outside of their boundaries' (Courtney Consulting 2020: 96). Given this background it is not surprising that one of the challenges Hackett faced in helping to draw together the South Asian dance category was that 'as a sector, it is not as unified as it could be . . . there are a lot of people working on their own on their own little islands... Perhaps there isn't the kind of support for each other that would be of overall benefit to the entire sector' (Hackett 2017). There are many possible reasons for these divisions, which I touch on throughout the book. Fundamentally, as Hackett observes, 'to some extent this happens whenever a sector is poorly resourced and supported, so that people are competing for the same small pool of resources' (ibid.). This observation brings us to the second set of problems highlighted by the competition.

The South Asian Dance Profession – 'Mind the Gap!'

In her review of *Young Dancer* 2015, dance critic Ismene Brown points out, 'There's a muddle here as there is no level playing field for ballet, South Asian, contemporary and street dance' (Brown 2015). This is, of course, absolutely right. Looking at the steps of the career ladder, for South Asian dance in Britain, there is no institution providing full-time vocational training; there are no apprentice schemes or 'postgraduate-style' companies for newly trained dancers; and most importantly of all, there are hardly any dance companies to which to apply for a job (Ramphal and Alake 2010; Gorringe et al. 2018; Meduri 2020). As I show in the introduction, these gaps have not passed unnoticed. I discuss in Chapter 3 the many attempts to address these gaps over the years, together with possible reasons for their failure. Suffice it to say for now that the only vocational training available for South Asian dancers in Britain today is through 'portfolio' training arranged through their teacher, or guru, and the best chance of employment is through forming your own company. As Akram Khan said at Navadisha 2016, 'there just isn't enough access to long-term serious classical training, and the many opportunities needed, to make a full-time career as a classical [South Asian] artist today' (Khan, in Gibson 2016: 25–26).

With such gaps in progression routes, it is only to be expected that, in marked contrast to ballet and contemporary contestants, all of whom are engaged in full-time vocational training, this is true of only two of the South Asian dance category finalists. And yet, much as many in the sector would love to dance full-time, it is difficult to make this choice when the options for employment seem so scarce. Hard as life is for contemporary and ballet dancers, with many condemned after years of intensive training to a soul-destroying procession of highly competitive auditions, the critical difference is that there are jobs to aspire to. For one classical Indian arts administrator, *BBC Young Dancer* may work to change the career path for a single dancer, but this is of little consolation to all the many excellent South Asian dancers who might aspire to work in dance, but for whom there is no obvious way to achieve this (fieldwork notes, 23 August 2017). In the words of the artistic director and producer of the arts company zeroculture, Hardial Rai, 'there is still no industry to support those artists... So we are relying on factors outside our sector for support' (Rai 2021). Within the context of *Young Dancer*, this means that in the competition finals, dancers in the South Asian category, who must make time for their dance training amid a range of priorities, are competing against dancers in other categories with sometimes two or even three years of full-time vocational training under their belts – of time spent absorbed in studying, training in and thinking about dance. This clearly presents a risk that South Asian dance forms could end up appearing less technically rigorous than other dance forms – simply due to the lack of time available for study. I put this to Kaushik, whose reply was characteristically feisty,

> That's not the risk – that's the reality. Ballet is supported by numerous institutes that enable intensive and dedicated training at all levels – we haven't anything parallel to this. However, it *is* worth the risk to take part. Yes, it is not a level playing field, but South Asian dancers have been remarkable in competing on a par with ballet and contemporary dancers despite this. We should not undermine what we have achieved given our circumstances. We are daring to be on a par with these well-nurtured sectors. This comes from the passion and determination of the community. (Kaushik 2017b, emphasis in original)

In announcing the category winner, choreographer Shobana Jeyasingh, 2017's General Judge, and hence member of all judging panels, spoke of the courage and commitment it takes to decide to be a dancer in a context where there is 'no professional training'. 'You need', she said, 'dedication. You need the support of your family. But above all, these forms require *time*.'[36] The winner, despite stiff competition, was a dancer (Shyam Dattani) who had made the decision to 'take up full-time training . . . under the support of his Guru' (*BBC Young Dancer* 2017, South Asian Category Finals, programme notes).

'Contemporary' Dance, Category Confusion and Cultural Inauthenticity

At the performance in Manchester, one piece presented by the prodigiously talented Jaina Modasia struck, for me, a jarring note. Her duet, as described above, was performed together with a contemporary dancer, and featured several lifts and other partner work completely alien to kathak technique or repertory. While experimentation is to be welcomed, and Erika Fischer-Lichte et al. (2014) remind us that cultural 'interweavings' are both inevitable and nothing new, the choice of choreography left me with several questions. Why would a dancer like Modasia, whose proficiency in kathak is stunning, choose choreography likely to be so much more difficult for her to perform? As a collaboration in another context, I could see the appeal – but as part of a competition on national television? When the whole point is to show yourself at your very best – to reveal your artistry in a context where, as choreographer Matthew Bourne put it, 'technique is a given' (*Young Dancer* press event, 2015)? Modasia is a confident and flexible performer and acquitted herself with impressive competence in a sequence well out of the range of classical kathak – but overall, I was left feeling cheated. I did not want to see Modasia working hard to perform a set of (by contemporary dance standards) indifferent lifts. I wanted to see her fly in a complex battle of rhythms, in a dazzle of *chakars*,[37] in a weaving in and out of floor patterns and changing proximities to her partner. The duet felt forced. Would any of the contemporary or ballet dancers, I wondered, attempt to make a battle of footwork central to their duets? I expressed my frustration to an audience member. 'Eh', he sighed, 'It is because they don't have confidence in their own form' (field notes, Lowry, 23 January 2017). Was that it? As I discuss later in the book, the South Asian dance sector certainly does show occasional signs of being beset by an internalized inferiority complex. As Shay (2008: 9) describes, this is not uncommon among formerly colonized communities, in which 'many of the colonized individuals accepted and continue to accept and even exaggerate the denigrating opinions of themselves and their forms of cultural expression held by representatives of colonial powers, long after the presence of the colonial administration'.

A similar point is made by the revolutionary Brazilian educationalist Paulo Freire when he writes,

> Cultural conquest leads to the cultural inauthenticity of those who are invaded; they begin to respond to the values, the standards, and the goals of the invaders . . . In cultural invasion it is essential that those who are invaded come to see their reality with the outlook of the invaders rather than their own; for the more they mimic the invaders, the more stable the position of the latter becomes. (Freire 2017: 126)

Was Modasia's duet the result of playful creativity and a transgressive exploration of artistic boundaries? Or was it a (perhaps unconscious) attempt to align the aesthetic of her piece with that of (dominant) Euro-American contemporary dance practice? An instance of what sociologist Anibal Quijano terms the 'colonization of the imagination of the dominated', whereby 'cultural Europeanization was transformed into an aspiration' and 'European culture became a universal cultural model' (Quijano 2007: 169)?

Researching this chapter, I reread the rubric for the competition. In the Repertoire section for South Asian dance, the rules stated,

> The second solo could show a more contemporary style and/or show movement vocabulary from another South Asian dance form.
>
> Your partner work *should* be a contemporary duet. (*BBC Young Dancer* competition guidelines, 2017, my emphasis)

I asked Hackett about this. 'Doesn't it say could?' she asked – but the guidelines read 'should': not choice, but obligation. The rationale, she explained,

Is because the forms are traditionally performed solo – duets do not form part of the tradition. It is a very interesting point. The duet is not part of the traditional form – it wouldn't be part of an existing catalogue of pieces. So, in this sense any duet choreographed will necessarily be contemporary in that it departs from tradition. We took advice from a lot of people in the sector – Shobana and Piali and others – and the consensus we received was that a duet with a musician would be part of the tradition, while a duet with another dancer probably wouldn't. (Hackett 2017)

So far, so good. 'But', I asked, 'What does the word "contemporary" mean in this context – Isn't it quite a loaded term?' Hackett's response was, 'I think of the term as "contemporary" with a small "c" – meaning "of this time" . . . As I remember for the 2015 round, we didn't have any contemporary entries – though Urja [Desai Thakore] choreographed a contemporary piece for Vidya [Patel]'s final' (ibid.).

While this may have been the intention, I am not convinced that this was the interpretation put on this condition by the participants. As argued above, the openness to a 'transgressive' interpretation of the forms lent the original form of the competition both depth and integrity; however, I found the coercive 'should' in this section of the competition's rubric uncomfortable. Where a duet is specified, and granted that this already takes South Asian dance forms out of their conventional format, is there any further need to assert what form that duet should take?

This raises a further question, which is what it is that should count as normative, and what as transgressive, and from whose perspective. Author, scholar and martial artist Janet O'Shea argues that 'lack of familiarity with choreographic codes often leads non-South Asian viewers to assume that bharatanatyam choreography, no matter how recent its composition, is "ancient" and "traditional"' (O'Shea 2007: 57).[38] This is an example of the kind of misperception identified by McFee (2005: 369) that I touch on above, whereby the artwork is incorrectly understood because it is read with 'inappropriate assumptions . . . [that are] imported'.

The responsibility lies here with the panel of specialist judges to pick up on such nuances and convey to the watching public that, for example in Prakash's first solo, the leaps in the air he performs with knees bent and soles of the feet pressed together show an inclusion of vocabulary from another dance style, kathakali. It is an indication of *Young Dancer*'s weight and seriousness that in the broadcast South Asian category final, the bharatanatyam specialist judge, artist and academic Chitra Sundaram, explained to viewers what made Modasia's interpretation of 'Krishna Nee Begane Baro' unusual (Sundaram on *BBC Young Dancer* 2017).

An additional problem in interpreting the term 'contemporary' as a South Asian dancer is that being historically used to an audience that might, for example, see nothing new in Seeta Patel's interpretation of the classical *margam* (*Something Then, Something Now*, 2014) – which made use of unconventional spatial arrangement (and included sections of dance performed with her back to the audience, something classical Indian dance traditionalists would regard as taboo) – and being used to funding guidelines that have been seen to privilege a specific interpretation of innovation, a lack of confidence in what will be *perceived* or *accepted* as contemporary may result in pushing boundaries in a manner more forced than organic. This is scarcely surprising given the commonly held equation of 'contemporary dance' with Euro-American contemporary dance practice. Arguably any performance by a contemporary performer is 'contemporary' in that it is rendered by a performer in the present moment, but if the rubric means by 'contemporary' something more than this (as it clearly does) – and yet does not mean to refer to 'Contemporary' dance – it is not clear what in fact it does mean. Unambiguous definition is even more important given the deeply entrenched 'rhetoric of modernity' (Mignolo 2007: 463) that has aligned, since the Enlightenment, the contemporary, the 'modern' and the 'new' with the values and cosmology of Western Europe (and later the USA) as opposed to the perceived 'traditionalism' of alternative cosmologies. That this is not mere theoretical nitpicking is borne out by the experience of the competition producers themselves. Independent arts manager Anita Srivastava (founding director of New Dimensions arts management) explains,

> In 2014, for the first time, [the] BBC advertised the young dancer competition – and because the brand name BBC was there – and because for the first time they were including ballet, hip-hop, contemporary and South Asian, they were expecting quite a few applications. But up to the first deadline, they did not receive a single one [for the South Asian dance category]. (Srivastava 2017)

She was then recruited by the BBC to help with 'reaching out and getting in touch with the South Asian dance sector' (ibid.).

Srivastava attributes the lack of applications (which was a continued problem with the second round of the competition in 2017) to a variety of reasons. One of these was the use of the troubled and vague term 'contemporary'. Srivastava recounts,

> In the application you had to write about . . . what you were going to present. And the classical work you were going to present as a second piece had to be slightly different from the first piece – it had to be more contemporary. So, at this point I picked up the phone to the BBC and

checked directly with them – what do you mean? Because none of these dancers are contemporary students and they have not had any contemporary dance training – so what are you expecting? So, then they explained that the second piece had to be different from the first piece. So, if the first piece was more technique-based, the second should be more *abhinaya*- or more fusion-based . . . the word that they used . . . that was definitely one of the stumbling blocks for many of the teachers thinking, 'I don't teach contemporary, so how can I present this?' (Srivastava 2017)

The suggestion that the second solo might 'contain elements of vocabulary from another South Asian dance style', is again, I feel, a 'category confusion' and a misapplication of what is appropriate for contemporary dance onto South Asian forms. Granted, 'contemporary dance' covers a multiplicity of techniques – from Martha Graham's to José Limón's, from Merce Cunningham's to contact improvisation. The crucial difference is that contemporary dancers expect to train in a variety of these techniques. Whether or not South Asian dancers should train in more than one technique is up for debate. The fact remains however that asking a bharatanatyam dancer to use vocabulary from kathak, for example, is more like asking a ballet dancer to use vocabulary from release technique than asking a contemporary dancer to play with a combination of Graham and Cunningham. The historical development of the forms means that dancers still struggle to accept or perform different *banis* or schools of their *own* style, let alone introducing vocabulary from another style altogether. Indeed, the *guru–shisya* (teacher–student) system[39] is based on exclusive training with one guru, such that even taking a class from another teacher within the same *bani* or substyle is seen as potentially confusing and corrupting, and has not, until very recently, been accepted. And even now, it is tolerated rather than encouraged. Prakash Yadagudde makes this point, highlighting how far he has come from '*bani*' orthodoxy: 'I don't stick to something rigidly. That is the reason that when we run the Summer School [at the Bhavan in London], we call different people . . . We don't want to say, "you have to do only your *bani*" . . . many people think like that – but that's not how I think' (Yadagudde 2017a).

In this context, to suggest that dancers use vocabulary from a whole other dance form represents not so much an encouragement to extend the canon as to step outside the canon entirely. It is the mistaken application of the norms of one aesthetic cosmology on another. Having said this, there are pervasive examples of exchange between classical Indian dance forms, where aspects from another classical dance form – or from a folk dance or a martial arts form – are quite naturally incorporated into the performance of a different style, as with Prakash's use of a kathakali jump in his bharatanatyam piece (referenced above). Such exchange can be typified as what the philosopher and literary critic Mikhail Bakhtin (1981) termed 'organic hybridization' (see also Meduri 2020). What

Young Dancer promotes or even compels by contrast, through the prescription of a hybridization that goes beyond such organic flows, is, I suggest, what Bakhtin (1981: 417) describes as a 'reaccentuation' – a hybridization that can result in a representation of the language hybridized that at best lacks 'nuance' (ibid.: 419) and at worst represents a 'crude violation' (ibid.: 420) of that language. This tendency is arguably exaggerated in the 2022 format, as I discuss below.

In both these ways, in the use of the term 'contemporary' and in the suggested use of vocabulary from other dance forms, the production of *Young Dancer* reveals how hard it is, despite the best of intentions, to escape a dominant framework of understanding, and thereby, as Mignolo (2007: 459) puts it, to change 'the terms in addition to the content of the conversation'. The attempt at 'equal representation' founders on the lack of a 'profound understanding of each [dance] language's socio-ideological meaning' (Bakhtin 1981: 417). In other words, it founders on a continued 'gross underestimation' of 'the whole significance of Europe's colonial domination of the world' (Mbembe 2010), and a continued enactment in this small section of the cultural sphere of that 'hidden and not so hidden violence at the core of what Western hegemony takes to be its "knowledge" of others, knowledge which most of the time takes the form of ignorance' (ibid.). It betrays a failure to recognize the full extent to which the Western ideological framework has been and continues to be accepted as universal – a recognition that must be the starting point for any meaningful engagement in decolonization.

'All Dances Are Ethnic, but Some Are More Ethnic Than Others'

Developing the point made above, I use the title of dance anthropologist Theresa Buckland's (1999) article[40] to draw attention to the final issue I want to raise in connection with *Young Dancer* before considering the wider context. Perhaps the most important while also the most worrying aspect of *Young Dancer* is how close it came to being something else entirely. Hackett explains, 'When I joined [the *Young Dancer* Advisory Panel], they were going to have three categories – ballet, contemporary dance and "Other". They seemed to think that everything else – from Irish dance to musical theatre, to South Asian dance forms, to hip-hop – would go into one category' (Hackett 2017).

In one sense such a categorization would do no more than reflect funding divisions within British dance. As an illustration, looking at the funding for National Portfolio Organizations (NPOs) for the years 2018–22,[41] the funding for the Birmingham Royal Ballet alone (leaving aside English National Ballet, the Royal Ballet at the Royal Opera House and other companies) was £7,891,000/annum – or 18.7 per cent of the total annual dance budget for this time period. The funding for the Contemporary Dance Trust in London alone (aside from funding for any other contemporary dance organization) was £1,793,985/annum – or 4.2 per cent of the budget. This is in contrast to the funding for all seven of the South Asian Dance Alliance organizations that are NPOs (Akademi, the Bharatiya Vidya Bhavan, Gem Arts, Kala Sangam, Milapfest, Sampad and South Asian Arts UK) put together, which came to £1,351,813/annum for 2018–22, with the important qualification that six of these seven organizations cater for all South Asian art forms, not only South Asian dance, and that this figure includes the funding for the South Asian Youth Orchestra co-ordinated by Milapfest.[42] The 2023–26 portfolio has brought significant changes, as I discuss in Chapter 5. Yet even here, the funding for all the South Asian NPOs within dance put together comes to £2,690,356/annum, and this is with the contentious inclusion of Akram Khan Company.[43] This is in comparison to the £2,164,253/annum allocated to Rambert Dance Company alone – and is 33 per cent of the annual funding allocated solely to Birmingham Royal Ballet.[44]

The BBC's initial thinking along these lines is clearly not anomalous. In his reflections on the programme, dance critic Bruce Marriott wrote, 'Ethnic dance came down to South Asian, but what of other ethnic dance? . . . I hope a wider view can be taken next time and perhaps a catch-all section introduced' (Marriott 2015). Similarly, Ismene Brown suggested as a possible improvement, 'Rethink the categories more broadly to admit jazz, tap and any ethnic dance – rather than only hip-hop and kathak' (Brown 2015).

Such commentary, as with the competition prescriptions detailed above, highlights the deep-rooted Eurocentricity that persists within the British cultural sector, which assigns to the primarily Euro-American, white-dominated forms of ballet and contemporary dance an ahistorical universalism, contrasted with the 'ethnic' particularity of other forms. As dance anthropologist Joann Keali'inohomoku (2001: 39) pointed out in 1969, almost half a century ago, 'By definition, every dance form must be an ethnic form. Although claims have been made for universal dance forms . . . it is doubtful that any such dance form can exist except in theory'. It is an illustration within the dance world of the way that 'a particular ethnicity' (that of Western Europe) has been 'taken as universal rationality', imposing 'a provincialism as a universalism' (Quijano 2007: 177). This perception immediately privileges two white, Euro-American dance styles that do not have, historically, a much greater claim to represent 'British' dance than South Asian dance or hip-hop (see Chapter 5).

Competitions, Meritocracy and South Asian Dance in Britain

The original format of *Young Dancer* was a considered, intelligent competition with a commitment to artistic integrity that avoided the 'fast art' and 'vision-bites' that characterize so many other televised dance competitions and talent shows. As a competition it treated with respect all the dance forms with which it engaged, and it sought to avoid stereotypes through a model of dialogical performance. The deliberate engagement with and invocation of the artistic narratives of different cultural forms, through the judgement and commentary of dancers and choreographers from these forms, at least in part fulfilled Mignolo's (2007) plea for the 'pluriversality' that he believes is key to the ongoing project of decolonization. At the same time, the competition has been 'a huge profile raiser and has created a lot of excitement, and an environment of ambition within students and parents – healthy competition' (Ray 2017b).

However, *Young Dancer*'s goals and purposes have remained to an extent thwarted and undone by the sheer weight of the cultural sphere that surrounds it, which is one that continues to hold 'the elite values of European art . . . as the pinnacle of human endeavour' (Buckland 1999: 8), with ballet symbolizing the 'apogee of the performing arts' (Keali'inohomoku 2001: 35). This framework is one that, despite its intentions, *Young Dancer* remains unable to fully recognize and therefore escape. This 'entrapment' is one it shares with the wider British cultural sector, where the continuance of 'West-' or 'white-centredness' is apparent, from the allocation of state funding to the unexamined and unrecognized aesthetic bias of arts funders, programmers, producers and managers. In 2017, a contemporary dancer won the *Young Dancer* Grand Final for the second time, and once again, the Wild Card space was awarded to a contemporary dancer.[45] For the Grand Final, which features judges from each category of dance, the judges must rely on their aesthetic rather than their artistic assessment (following McFee and Best's definition) for each of the performances not from their own discipline. Even if (as one would hope) they made the effort to inform themselves about the other dance styles before the competition, such cursory education cannot be expected to shift a lifetime of acquired aesthetic preferences. In the Grand Final 2017, three out of the six-member jury panel had a contemporary dance background, which, as *Dance Tabs* commentator Graham Watts observed, seemed 'a bit too contemporary-heavy' (Watts 2017). 'It seems that contemporary dancers have the advantage in this contest', he writes, something he attributes to 'the absence of rigid discipline' while 'the robust reliance on specific disciplined technique [for ballet and kathak] makes even the tiniest blemish more obvious, as well as diminishing the opportunity for self-expression and freedom of movement' (ibid.). While acknowledging the symptom, I would contest this diagnosis – in the 2017 competition, for example, I felt that Prakash expressed himself through the character of Hanuman with as much individuality and wit as could be found anywhere else in the series. The bias is, I believe, much more deep-seated, and relates to the 'enduring enchantment' (Mignolo 2002) of a culturally specific reading of newness and modernity that privileges 'individualism, the right to criticism, autonomy and action' (Mignolo 2007: 467), and which deliberately defines itself in contradistinction to 'tradition'.

The dominance of the Euro-American contemporary and classical dance traditions within the British dance world is pervasive, painful and frequently not recognized by contemporary dancers, who, coming from a context that is nonconformist and eclectic (as well as predominantly liberal and left-wing), are too often inclined to think themselves beyond prejudice. Bisakha Sarker, a creative Indian dancer in the Tagore style who has worked in Britain for over thirty years, reflects with some sadness on the contemporary dance world: 'They do not know us. They only know Shobana Jeyasingh . . . and Akram. But why? We know so many people's names and go to so many things. But why? Because it never came on to their radar. There is no need for it to' (Sarker 2017). For a senior arts administrator in the sector, *Young Dancer* is problematic in the attention it receives, which seems to diminish the importance and value of awards made within the sector itself. For him, it is almost as if the acknowledgement and appreciation of institutions and assessors from outside the sector is required for the sector to appreciate and value itself (fieldwork notes, 23 August 2017).

In this light, Freire's words become all too poignant,

> For cultural invasion to succeed, it is essential that those invaded become convinced of their intrinsic inferiority. Since everything has its opposite, if those who are invaded consider themselves inferior, they must necessarily recognize the superiority of the invaders. The values of the latter thereby become the pattern for the former. The more invasion is accentuated and those invaded are alienated from the spirit of their own culture and from themselves, the more the latter want to be like the invaders: to walk like them, dress like them, talk like them [and, we could add, dance like them]. (Freire 2017: 126)

The argument thus returns inexorably to the question of competition and meritocracy, and the myth both that hard work can get you anywhere and that a social structure that awards 'special privileges to special talent' can at the same time respect the fundamentally equal worth of every person. The failures of the competition are visible not only for South Asian dance. Again, to quote Watts (2017), 'It seems oddly counter-intuitive that 80% of the finalists in the first two iterations of this event have been young men, which is probably in inverse proportion to the gender balance amongst those seeking entry into the vocational schools'. Are we to understand from this that young male dancers are intrinsically more talented? Or should we ask rather what are the structures, ideological and institutional, that allow young male dancers to showcase their dance in a manner perceived as 'finalist material'? Ultimately, the attempt to present a competition of equals cannot overcome the structures and bias that continue to favour the white and the male.

Afterword – *BBC Young Dancer* 2022

In 2022, after the bulk of the research for this book was complete, the BBC aired *BBC Young Dancer* 2022. This iteration of the competition was immediately notable in two main ways. First, the BBC had brought in a new artistic director for the programme, Emma Gladstone, who revamped the competition framework substantially. Second, 2022 brought the first overall competition winner trained in South Asian dance – 17-year-old Adhya Shastry, an A level student trained in bharatanatyam, ballet and contemporary dance. These two factors demand some reflection.

The new competition format is much broader in scope – and enables the participation of dancers from any genre. This meant that for the first time, the competition featured tap dancers (one of whom, Kai Scanlan, reached the final ten) and also a clog dancer. In the new format, from the entry videos submitted, seventy-two dancers were shortlisted for face-to-face auditions, which were held over four days. As with the previous competitions, judges were recruited to represent different dance form expertise, and for the initial round included the bharatanatyam dance artist Geetha Sridhar, the ballet dance artist Begoña Cao, street and freestyle dance artist Gianni Gi and hip-hop dance artist Dickson Mbi, with Emma Gladstone as the Chair of Judges.

Each group of twenty-four dancers started their audition day by taking part in workshops 'designed to test their versatility and openness to explore new ground' (narrator Clara Amfo, BBC 2022a: 1:03), before performing their solos. The plan was for the group of seventy-two to be whittled down to twenty by day four, though the wealth of talent meant that the 2022 competition featured twenty-two dancers for this second callback. A further three judges joined the panel at this stage – bharatanatyam dance artist Seeta Patel, independent dance artist Annie Hanauer and multidisciplinary artist Ivan Blackstock. For the callback audition, 'As the judges have already seen the dancers in the solo auditions, this callback is all about how they respond in workshops . . . the dancers need to show they can improvise, work together and learn new dance moves from one another' (ibid.: 45:47).

The dancers took part in workshops led by contemporary dance artist Theo Clinkard and multidisciplinary artist Julia Cheng, improvising, interacting, creating dance phrases and learning them from each other. On the strength of these workshops, the judges selected the final ten competitors.

These ten dancers then took part in a week-long residential dance intensive termed the 'BBC Young Dancer Academy' at the Dartington School of Arts in Devon. During this intensive they were set a number of challenges including working in pairs to create a dance film, working on duets and trios choreographed by some of the judges of the initial auditions, working on an ensemble piece created by Ivan Blackstock and developing and polishing their solos. For the Grand Finale they performed their solos, duets and trios, and the ensemble piece at the Roundhouse theatre in London, where they were judged on their performance across these pieces by a fresh set of judges. Again, these judges were chosen to represent a range of dance form expertise and were the bharatanatyam dance artist and director of Akademi (2019 to the present) Subathra Subramaniam, ballet artist Ryoichi Hirano, contemporary dance artist Arthur Pita and hip-hop dance artist Kate Prince.

Abandoning the previous format, which, as I note above, Judith Mackrell felt had been thought through with 'unusual care', was a bold move. Its most striking advantage was the opportunity it provided to include a wider range of dance styles, meaning (among other things) that viewers were treated to sections of Kai Scanlan's sparky and virtuoso tap routines. The young dancers themselves spoke of how much they enjoyed the time at the residential 'academy', with the opportunity to work intensively alongside other young people with a passion for dance. The time spent in the academy working together and developing pieces also helped to some extent to shift the focus of the competition away from product to process. This reduced the reliance on the time-pressured performance that is often a concern in relation to competition dance, as discussed earlier in the chapter. Thus, Adhya Shastry's win in the Grand Finale was based on her performance for that evening, but it built on a week's worth of dancing in which she consistently demonstrated her strong technique, her versatility, her strength in collaboration and her leadership skills. In this way, the new competition format arguably better identifies what the Centre for Advanced Training in Birmingham terms an 'industry-ready' dancer than its previous incarnation (see Chapters 3 and 4).

Yet despite this apparent greater space for other dance forms, a space seemingly underlined by Shastry's win, a closer look raises questions about the space the new format purports to offer. From the initial auditions, this format lays emphasis on participation in workshops, on improvisation, creation of movement, engagement in tasks, collaboration with other dancers and thinking beyond the parameters of one's dance form. Such skills are required to a greater or lesser extent, and in a variety of ways, across dance forms. The framework in which they are sought for the competition, however, is the framework of contemporary dance. Bharatanatyam and kathak dancers, for example, are used to improvising in response to a specific lyrical phrase, or in dialogue with a musician. They are used to creating movement phrases to a particular rhythm and to learning such phrases from others. South Asian dancers without additional training in contemporary dance, however, are unlikely to have encountered the need to improvise to music from a genre utterly removed from their own, or to learn dance moves that fall entirely outside of their classical canon. After all, it is the perfecting of a set repertoire of movement that characterizes a classical form.

In the initial auditions, Emma Gladstone reassures the participants, saying, 'I'm fairly sure that for everybody there is going to be something that feels a little odd, or that you haven't done before' (BBC 2022a: 2:50). This may be true. Certainly, in Episode 3, we see the other nine dancers, with no bharatanatyam training, learning a bharatanatyam phrase for Blackstock's ensemble work. Similarly, we see all the dancers taking part in a hip-hop cypher. Yet this very framing, that so readily seeks to absorb the characteristics of another dance style, is that of contemporary dance. From the daily 'academy' classes, led (in what looks like contemporary dance) by movement director Ingrid Mackinnon, to the emphasis on going beyond the 'same sort of movements' and 'drawing from each other' (workshop leader Julia Cheng describing what she is looking for; BBC 2022a: 19:00), the overarching 'rules of the game' are those of Euro-American contemporary dance.

This framing has also been picked up by the ballet audience. One commentator observes, 'The entire thing seems to be structured in such a way as to disadvantage ballet dancers. Most classical dances are based around repertoire and known variations, whereas [with] other styles ... [dancers] are expected to devise their own work' ('taxi4ballet' 2022). Given this, it is perhaps unsurprising that of the twenty-two dancers called back before the 'final cut', two were street/hip-hop dancers, two were tap dancers, three were ballet-trained and three South Asian dance-trained, while the remaining twelve were contemporary. Of the final ten, five were contemporary-trained, two street/hip-hop, one tap and one each trained in ballet and bharatanatyam. With both ballet and bharatanatyam, the dancers selected for the final ten either had a neoclassical edge (as with Olivia Chang-Clarke) or substantial additional training in contemporary dance (Adhya Shastry has trained in contemporary dance as part of the Centre for Advanced Training at London Contemporary Dance School). The more classically focused Ai Suzuki (ballet) and Piya Varma (bharatanatyam), despite their technical brilliance, were left behind. Where the previous competition format both limited yet freed competitors through a focus on the specific parameters of particular dance techniques, the 2022 format reflects the realities of the professional dance world in demanding dancers with the 'hyperflexibility' (Kedhar 2020) to accommodate a variety of dance techniques and aesthetics (see Chapters 3 and 4).

A further comment on the BalletcoForum attracts some agreement: 'I quite liked the format which yielded winners in different categories before they were pitched against each other' ('Capybara' 2022). It is easy to understand why. The separate categories allowed, as Hackett had intended, an assessment of the dancers of each dance style within the specific conventions and narratives of their forms. This meant that in the competition's 2019 iteration, for example, bharatanatyam dancer Shree Savani won the South Asian dance category in large part on the strength of her compelling *abhinaya*. In the new format, by contrast, Gladstone mentions as factors contributing to how the dancers will be assessed 'the things you can mark like articulacy, musicality, how to partner, how they use a complex range of dynamics' (BBC 2022b: 3:14), immediately highlighting one area that traditionally plays little part in South Asian dance (how to partner), while omitting an aspect that is fundamental to its performance (*abhinaya*).

Any dance form depends not only on its physicality, but also on its accompanying mindset – the 'set of beliefs' that govern its performance, the specific narrative that gives it context. In the revised competition format, I suggest, while

Figure 1.2. Shree Savani, the winner of the 2019 BBC Young Dancer South Asian dance category final, performs Maa *(Shree Savani and Dimple Chauhan, 2019) with her dance partner Shreya Vadnerkar. 2019. © BBC Photo Archive.*

a wider range of physicalities are welcomed, this is on the basis that they are all positioned within the overarching ideological framework of contemporary dance. As is often the case with any ruling ideology, its contingency and the particular cultural conditioning that inform it are so entrenched as to be assumed to be universal, neutral, without cultural valence.

Furthermore, as if to emphasize how very far we have still to travel, despite the ostensible commitment to diverse representation, the narration of *BBC Young Dancer* 2022 includes comments that thoughtlessly but damagingly reinforce long-standing prejudices. In Episode 1, for example, the narrator Clara Amfo describes ballet as 'the most demanding dance form, requiring precise technique, line and strength' (BBC 2022a: 24:01) – as if the performance of other dance styles can somehow dispense with these attributes. In Episode 4, Shastry's dynamic performance of *Kali Khautvom* is described as 'Adhya providing us with a beautiful celebration of her culture' (BBC 2022b: 17:09), when if anything the programme has shown how complex and multifaceted the cultures of the various dancers featured are – and therefore how meaningless such a statement is. It appears that even in 2022, some dance styles are more ethnic than others.

An apparent win, then, for a greater range of dance styles and in particular South Asian dance on closer examination turns out to be a loss, whereby non-contemporary dance styles (including ballet) are stripped of the chance to be judged on their own terms, with respect to their own artistic narratives and aesthetic conventions. In many ways this no more than mirrors the reality of the dance world today, where dancers are increasingly valued for their versatility and their ability to meet the ever more eclectic demands of choreographers. Adhya, as a dancer able to transverse the boundaries of contemporary and classical Indian dance, represents a dancer especially likely to appeal to contemporary choreographers, while the space for the exploration of ballet or bharatanatyam on their own terms becomes increasingly anachronistic. Whether this reality is healthy either for dance or dancers is a question I discuss further in Chapter 4.

Deciding the best format for *Young Dancer* is undeniably a challenge. Ideally all dance forms performed across the UK would benefit from the kind of profile and legitimacy that the competition offers. One commentator questions 'why we can't have a separate competition for each genre – there are potentially large audiences for each if done properly' ('Emeralds' 2022). There are likely to be financial and logistical obstacles to this approach – apart from which a particular attraction of *BBC Young Dancer* is surely the way that it has brought together artists and audiences from different dance styles. One possibility might be a changing set of categories for each iteration determined by the largest numbers of entries. Whatever form it takes, it must not come at the cost of the stylistic integrity of the dance forms represented. The current version of *BBC Young Dancer* expands the range of dance forms presented, but paradoxically contracts Mignolo's 'space of experience' and 'horizon of expectations'. Dance forms have been brought from across the range of experience – but they have all been locked within one room.

Conclusion

An examination of the competition *BBC Young Dancer* brings into focus both how far South Asian dance forms have come in this country and how far they have yet to go (in terms of infrastructural support as well as wider appreciation and acknowledgement). The challenges faced by the young classical Indian dancers entering this competition, with its self-conscious and deliberate links to the world of professional British dance, reflect the wider challenges faced by classical Indian dancers aspiring to a career in dance in Britain. Like any artist attempting to make a living from their art forms, they face the same questions as the producers framing this competition – how to present dance that is accessible without being comfortable, that is legible without surrendering to a 'vision-bite' stereotype and that is commercially viable without being driven by commercial ends. How can one be a 'professional' in the sense of making one's living as a dancer or performer while continuing to be 'professional' in the sense of honouring a 'concern for the laws of form demanded by aesthetic autonomy' (Adorno 1975: 14)?

For classical Indian dancers in Britain, as for the young South Asian dance artists in this competition, together with these challenges, there are additional demands that can make the engagement with the wider world of British dance a particularly complex and enervating venture. There is the constant negotiation of a self-representation that avoids the pitfalls of either essentialism or assimilation (Kedhar 2020). The common conflation of the term 'contemporary dance' with 'Euro-American contemporary dance' places on other dance forms the burden of proving their contemporaneity (Kwan 2017), a problem exacerbated by the 'rhetoric of modernity' (Mignolo 2007), which positions 'tradition' as something in the past. There is the persistent labour of insisting on the need for their work and their dance forms to be assessed in the terms of their own artistic narratives. After all, in the words of artist and cultural theorist Brenda Dixon Gottschild, 'One of the easiest ways to disempower others is to measure them by a standard that ignores their chosen aesthetic frame of reference and its particular demands' (Gottschild 1997: 171). Yet, as *Young Dancer* shows, particularly in its most recent iteration, so entrenched is the assumed and unexamined universalism of Euro-American aesthetics and conventions that this is hard to ensure even where the need has been acknowledged. As in the *Young Dancer* competition, professional classical Indian dancers in Britain must 'compete', in this case for funding and for audiences. And as with *Young Dancer*, this competition takes place in a landscape in which multiple social structures mean that in many ways, the 'winners' are always already determined.

The illustration of this competition therefore encapsulates several of the themes and challenges that I discuss further in this book. Its focus on passionate and talented dancers at the start of their professional lives is a reminder of what is lost when these dancers turn to medicine, engineering or dentistry, and thereby lends a sense of urgency to the question of a developing classical Indian dance profession in Britain and what might obstruct its growth. Meanwhile the very format of a dance competition brings starkly into focus the continued need for the critique first brought to bear through critical race theory (CRT) in the context of interpreting law in the United States in the 1970s and 1980s. To truly challenge the inequities of race, racism and power necessitates not only challenging the most blatant examples of discrimination (such as grouping all non-Euro-American dance forms under a category of 'ethnic dance') but questioning 'the very foundations of the liberal order' (Delgado and Stefancic 2011: 3), which ultimately 'affirms the underlying ideology of just desserts' (Crenshaw et al. 1995: xv) without considering who has written the rules of the game.

In the next chapter, before I consider the structures and organizations supporting the professionalization of classical Indian dance forms in Britain, how they succeed and where they fail, I will first rewind a little and take some time to consider the controversial concept of 'professionalism'.

Acknowledgements

This chapter is derived in part from an article published in *South Asian Diaspora* 11:2, (163–78), 2019, copyright Taylor & Francis, available online: https://www.tandfonline.com/doi/full/10.1080/19438192.2019.1568537.

Notes

1. Figures provided by the BBC to Anita Srivastava, sent to me via personal communication, 3 May 2017.
2. I assume. The BBC was unable to provide me a figure – but merely from the circumstantial evidence of talking to friends and colleagues, I believe this to be a safe assumption.
3. Hip-hop, like 'South Asian dance', is also disadvantaged by comparison with ballet and Western contemporary dance, for example by not having a dedicated vocational school. There are interesting similarities and contrasts between the cases of hip-hop and South Asian dance – see Prickett (2013b) for an insight into hip-hop's journey to legitimacy in Britain.
4. Very sadly, Emma Gladstone died of cancer in February 2024 at the age of 63 – less than two years after *BBC Young Dancer* 2022 was broadcast.
5. Jane Hackett has a long and impressive history of involvement in dance in various capacities. Apart from working herself as a dance artist and choreographer, prior to her post at Sadler's Wells, she was director of two national conservatoires, Director of Learning for Birmingham Royal Ballet (BRB) and director of schemes for the Royal Opera House and BRB to increase diversity and access to training and careers in dance, as well as of professional development programmes for dance artists, choreographers and teachers. She also holds an MA in Dance Studies from the University of Roehampton. Perhaps it is not surprising in this context that *BBC Young Dancer* is, as I argue, though not without its problems, qualitatively different from and more nuanced than other televised dance competitions.
6. Sadler's Wells is a leading arts venue in London with a fascinating history. It started out as a music house, in which the owner, Richard Sadler, discovered a mineral spring in 1683. It remained a venue for the arts, becoming more focused on dance in 1925 under the leadership of Lilian Bayliss. It has a particular significance for dance in Britain, with both the Royal Ballet and the Birmingham Royal Ballet starting out there. It currently hosts the National Youth Dance Company and aims to be 'a global leader in presenting fresh and innovative dance' (Sadlers Wells. n.d.).
7. This is *unless* that contract ended before the competitor's sixteenth birthday. The age range is 16–25 for disabled dancers.
8. To ensure that competitors are not put off by the cost of hiring a videographer and editor, the regulations state: 'The video should be unedited within the performances and its quality should be good enough for us to assess your dancing. It does not have to be of a professional broadcast quality and you will not be penalised for poor quality of video or sound as long as an assessment of your performance is possible' (*Young Dancer*, entry brochure, 2017).
9. These judges for the video entries change each year, as they do for the other stages of the competition. See Appendix 2 for a list of judges and mentors engaged for the South Asian dance category finals.

10. In 2017 this was Sadler's Wells, London. In 2019, it was the Birmingham Hippodrome main stage. In 2022, it was the Roundhouse, London.
11. *Strictly Come Dancing* is a British televised dance competition broadcast on BBC 1, which pairs celebrities and other participants from all walks of life with professional dance artists in a ballroom and Latin dance competition. It is an updated and revised version of the show *Come Dancing*, which ran between 1950 and 1998.
12. *Strictly Dance Fever* was a similar competition solely for amateur dance artists also broadcast on BBC 1. *Got to Dance* was a British televised dance competition for amateur dance artists that was broadcast between 2009 and 2014 on Sky 1. *So You Think You Can Dance* is an American televised dance competition airing on Fox TV that premiered in 2005. It is the flagship show for the *So You Think You Can Dance* franchise, which has seen local variants in more than thirty countries. A British version premiered in 2010 on BBC 1.
13. *Move Like Michael Jackson* was a one-off after the singer's death in 2009; *Strictly Dance Fever* was axed in 2006 after two series and *Got to Dance* ended in 2014.
14. This was by transmission – no figure was available for iPlayer.
15. A highly prestigious international ballet competition for ballet students aged 15–18.
16. In a discussion of different philosophical approaches to determining what should constitute an artwork, Carroll (2001) resolves that 'historical narration is a reliable way for identifying art' (ibid.: 84) and that 'whether or not an object is to be regarded as an object or art depends on whether or not it can be placed in an evolving tradition of art in the right way' (ibid.: 63).
17. The same concern can be heard within bharatanatyam circles – for example, one artist commented of the famous bharatanatyam training school Kalakshetra, 'Kalakshetra teaches you to be a very good robot. No emotion, no understanding, no understanding of how your body works' (fieldwork notes, Yuva Gati, 12 April 2017).
18. Oliver Cromwell was a Puritan military commander of the anti-Royalist Roundheads, who served as Lord Protector of the Commonwealth of England, Scotland and Ireland between 1653 and 1658. In 1647 the Puritan parliament made the celebration of Christmas a punishable offence, and it remained such until the restoration of the monarchy in 1660. Thus, while it was not Cromwell alone who 'cancelled' Christmas, this period is associated with him, together with a particularly austere form of Puritanical religious observance.
19. The question of dance as paid labour and of the necessity for many dance artists to work multiple jobs is discussed more fully in Chapter 2.
20. 'Flaubert was smarter than us . . . He had the wit to come into the world with money, something which is indispensable for anyone who wants to get anywhere in art' (Theophile Gautier to Feydeau, quoted in Bourdieu 1983: 349).
21. Though, as several commentators have pointed out, *Young Dancer* does not actually give the competitors much, with the grand prize of £3,000 being sufficient to cover the tuition fees for only a third of one year of training, in contrast for example to the Prix de Lausanne, which offers a prize of a year's free tuition plus expenses. It does, however, provide competitors with tremendous exposure. The young kathak dance artist Vidya Patel, who won the South Asian Dance Category final in 2015, was catapulted to fame as a result, feted both within the South Asian and contemporary dance worlds, and has not had any shortage of work since.
22. In his lively monograph *Why Are Artists Poor?* (2002), Dutch artist and economist Hans Abbing explores the notion of the artist single-mindedly devoted to their art, heedless of

market pressures. He builds on Bourdieu's notion of the reversed economy to present the concept of the 'exceptional economy of the arts', whereby, paradoxically, art gains a greater market value the more it purports to ignore or go beyond the market.
23. Dodds uses the case studies of burlesque striptease; pogoing, headbanging and skanking at punk, metal and ska music gigs; and the dance culture of the British Caribbean weekend dance club 'Sunday Serenade'. Dancing at music gigs is a 'free activity' (in that one would pay for the gig whether one danced or not); the 'Sunday Serenade', charging £5 a ticket for a Sunday evening of dance, is clearly not aiming to do much more than cover costs; and burlesque striptease, while hoping to be marketable, clearly has many more complex interests and ideals as its overriding goal (unlike the Cabaret of Angels).
24. Soma is a drug that produces a feeling of well-being.
25. The pathological underpinnings of such competitions are arguably highlighted by the number of competitors (including 'winners') who go on to suffer serious mental health issues, some even committing suicide. See Adegoke (2020). Thanks to Ann R. David for highlighting this point.
26. Such use of the competition format is nothing new. Dodds notes how in the early twentieth century, in response to the 'sense of social unease' prompted by the 'bodily aesthetics of play . . . casualness, [and] inventiveness' (Robinson 2009, cited in Dodds 2011: 59) of ragtime dance, forms of ragtime were 'codified and set as a disciplined technique that could be taught as competition dancing' in a manner 'refined to suit North American tastes through exhibition dance' (Dodds 2011: 59).
27. *Young Musician* was conceived by BBC producers Humphrey Barton and Walter Todd to encourage more home-grown participation in classical music. (BBC n.d.)
28. The 2022 format gives more time to recording the process of the competition during the week-long Young Dancer Academy, together with the competitors' responses to this process.
29. The Place is a dance and performance centre in central London, home to London Contemporary Dance School.
30. This 'assumption of technique' is sadly undermined in the 2022 competition, which shifts the emphasis away from the performance of acquired technique, focusing instead on the flexibility and versatility of the 'hired body' (Foster 1997: 255; Kedhar 2020).
31. 'The reason we went for bharatanatyam and kathak was to ensure that there would be enough specialists for each style. Challenging as it is to find specialists for bharatanatyam and kathak, it would be even more so with other styles. Also, at present we have a bharatanatyam and a kathak specialist on the panel. To allow for a specialist judge for each style, we would have to recruit five or six judges to sit on the panel' (Hackett 2017).
32. The final decision as to which dance artist stays or goes rests with the 'layperson' audience vote. Hence the suggestion made that the audience is the 'fifth judge' for the competition.
33. Connor Scott was the overall winner of *BBC Young Dancer* 2015. He went on to train at the Rambert School of Contemporary Dance. As a result of the competition Connor and Vidya created a piece together to open Navadisha 2016. They were subsequently commissioned by Sampad to create and tour a new show, *About the Elephant* (2018).
34. After seeing Patel perform, the well-respected contemporary choreographer Richard Alston invited her to join his company as a guest artist for the creation and tour of his new work *An Italian in Madrid*. In fact, however, it was not at the *BBC Young Dancer*

competitions that Alston first saw Patel dance. It was at the U Dance Festival 2015, where Patel was dancing as a guest performer (Patel, personal communication, 2019).
35. I observed this at a performance of Prakash Yadagudde's (2017) *Kadiragama Kuravanji* by students and alumni of the Bharatiya Vidya Bhavan (field notes, 12 February 2017).
36. Jeyasingh made these comments while announcing the judges' decision for the *BBC Young Dancer* category final at the Lowry Theatre, Manchester (field notes, 23 January 2017).
37. Spinning movements within kathak dance.
38. Indeed, the concept of 'choreography' itself raises questions in relation to classical Indian dance forms, as I discuss in Chapter 5.
39. See fuller discussion in Chapter 3.
40. This itself riffs on Joann Keali'inohomoku's (2001) article, 'An Anthropologist Looks at Ballet as a Form of Ethnic Dance'.
41. The latest NPO round, 2023–26, shifted the balance of funding to include more investment in diverse-led dance. The new portfolio is discussed in greater detail in Chapter 5.
42. Source: National Portfolio Organizations spreadsheet, 2018–2022. (Arts Council n.d.).
43. Contentious because while Khan draws on the vocabulary of classical Indian dance forms (particularly kathak), he classes his work as contemporary dance and uses primarily contemporary-trained dance artists.
44. All figures from the NPO 2023–26 spreadsheet are available at Arts Council n.d.b..
45. In 2015, a further space was awarded a hip-hop dance artist – and I do feel that the competition could helpfully reserve a further Wild Card space for a hip-hop or South Asian artist.

Chapter 2

Professionalism: Of Work, Love and Money: Living to Dance – or Dancing to Live?

What It Means to Be a 'Professional' Classical Indian Dancer in Britain

> Understanding and acting on these economic trajectories is what makes the difference between dance as a noble hobby and dance as a professional career.
> —Shobana Jeyasingh, in Rachel Gibson, *Navadisha 2016*

> 'Professionalism' is about serving the art and your art form *solely*, as the centre point of your life. That for me is professionalism. It's not about money. It's not about how much money you make or how successful you are.
> —Akram Khan, interview, 2018 (emphasis original)

> Guruji has trained many students [in dance] who have gone on to be top professionals and work in top establishments.
> —Compere, Bharatiya Vidya Bhavan, field notes, February 2017

> The lack of distinction between amateur and professional is a major problem in our sector.
> —Dance artist, personal communication, field notes, May 2016

Introduction: Professionalization, a Preoccupation for South Asian Dance in Britain

I am at my old dance school, the Bharatiya Vidya Bhavan or Institute of Indian Culture, based in West Kensington in London. A former church, it is now a thriving centre for Indian arts and languages. I have returned to see another

Figure 2.1. Students of the Bharatiya Vidya Bhavan in a production of the Kadiragama Kuruvanji bharatanatyam dance drama. Bhavan, London. 2018 © Dinesh Mahathevan.

performance by Akshay Prakash, the dancer from *BBC Young Dancer* with whom the last chapter opened, this time in the context of a dance drama, as one performer among an ensemble. I enjoy the familiar feel of the Bhavan, finding my seat in the Mountbatten Hall where images of Earl Louis Mountbatten[1] and (the then) Prince Charles gaze down benignly at the assembled audience. Where in India anglicized names such as Madras and Calcutta have been replaced with the non-Anglo-inflected Chennai and Kolkata, in this London outpost of Indian culture, Louis and Charles remain comfortably settled. As anticipated, the performance starts somewhat late; equally as anticipated, I enjoy it very much when it eventually starts. The cast, all made up of volunteer or unpaid dancers, are committed and confident, with a couple of outstanding performers, including Akshay. Sometime before the performance finale there are speeches. Even as I stifle a sigh, there is a part of me that welcomes this interruption. For as long as I can remember speeches lauding the performers and the creative team have been an integral feature of performances at the Bhavan. Somehow not to have them would seem improper or incomplete. My mind wanders as the compere starts the customary round of thanks and congratulations. My attention is caught, however, by a proud reference to Guruji's (Prakash Yadagudde's) achievements, as someone who 'has trained many students [in dance] who have gone on to be top *professionals* and work in top establishments' (field notes, February 2017, my emphasis).

The term catches my attention, in part, inevitably, because of my focus for this book on what it means to 'professionalize' Indian classical dance forms in Britain, but also in part because it is unexpected. I am used at the Bhavan to hearing about the 'legal eaglets' or the well-organized medics who combine their careers with weekends and evenings spent at the Bhavan, often resulting in good quality performances, such as this evening's show. The two leads in this piece are both medics, Akshay studying at medical school, and the heroine of the dance drama already working as a medic in London. What does the compere mean, I wonder, by her invocation of 'professionals'? Does she mean top professional dancers, and in this case, which 'top establishments' is she referring to? I can certainly think of a number of my guru's students who are professional dancers, but they work in the main for their own companies. Or does she mean that they are top professional dancers, but also working as professionals in other fields, in top establishments outside of dance? Is she referring to the unpaid dancers of tonight's performance? Does 'professionalism' not have a monetary association in her understanding of it? Whatever her intention, her investment in the importance of 'professionalism' is clear.

As I discuss in the introduction, 'professionalism' has become an increasing preoccupation for the South Asian dance sector in Britain. For example, as seen in the previous chapter, for Akademi's Mira Kaushik, the recognition of South Asian dance forms as 'professional' rather than 'community' art forms[2] is partly what made the inclusion of a South Asian dance category in *BBC Young Dancer* so significant. Writing in a magazine belonging to an organization representing the wider British dance sector (One Dance UK), London-based kathak dancer Parbati Chaudhury reflects on a series of meetings that were run over two years by the South Asian Dance Alliance (SADAA). What interested her most in these meetings, she observes, were the discussions that focused on 'the professionalisation of practitioners' (2019: 28). In a very different part of the sector, at the Bharatiya Vidya Bhavan, which, unlike Akademi, is an institution less concerned with building links to the wider community of dance in Britain and more interested in 'stick[ing] to what we do best . . . concentrat[ing] on promoting our classical dance forms' (Nandakumara 2017, the awareness of the currency of the 'professional' is likewise present, as the compere's speech indicates.

So, why is this Anglo-American-derived sociological concept (Bourdieu and Wacquant 1992; Rueschemeyer 1983) of such significance for South Asian dance in Britain? While the status of the 'professional' is evidently desired, it is not clear what being a 'professional' entails. Indeed, as the opening epigraphs demonstrate, there are multiple and at times opposing understandings of what it means. Like 'beauty', it appears to be a good and desirable quality, but one that means different things to different people. And yet, unlike 'beauty', which has a contingency that is generally recognized, being 'professional' continues to be upheld as a quality that adheres to some objective standards. Unfortunately, it seems, there is not much agreement as to precisely what these are. For classical Indian dancers in Britain keen to demonstrate 'professionalism', therefore, this involves chasing a chimera – and it is anybody's guess when this status has been achieved. Unsurprisingly then, the anonymous dance artist cited in the last epigraph above finds that there is no clear distinction between what defines an amateur and a professional practitioner.

This chapter attempts to put a shape to this chimera that has such a hold on the South Asian dance sector in Britain. In doing so, I hope to impose some parameters on the concept's current, somewhat inchoate influence. Starting with an overview of sociological understandings of 'profession' and its cognates, I then look at the complications of defining 'professionalism' within the arts (particularly dance) and more specifically, South Asian dance. In order to do so I briefly trace the history of classical Indian dance forms, their suppression and their revival, showing how this history impacts on current 'professional' practice both in India and Britain, particularly by encouraging the pattern of the 'dual-career' dancer. I conclude by asking: given both its contingency and its ambiguity, is the concept of the 'professional' (and hence 'professionalism') in fact useful at all, or is it best abandoned? This was the preferred approach of Bourdieu, for whom '[p]rofession is a folk concept which has been uncritically smuggled into scientific language and which imports into it a whole social unconscious' (Bourdieu and Wacquant 1992: 242), a concept 'all the more dangerous because . . . it has all appearance of neutrality in its favour' (ibid.). His suggestion was that the concept be replaced altogether in favour of that of 'field'. I evaluate how far his suggestion of 'field' serves as a viable substitute for understanding 'professions' and 'professionalism' and suggest three key 'features of professionalism' that I argue hold across occupations and across cultures.

Profession, Professional, Professionalize – the Sociological Context

On one level the meaning of 'professional' is very straightforward. Sociologist Stephen Ackroyd acknowledges, 'In everyday speech to be professional requires only that a person is paid for their work and/or adopts a business-like approach to it' (Ackroyd 2016: 15). Or, in the words of a musician friend, 'it's when you get paid, innit?'[3] The *Oxford English Dictionary* defines 'professionalization' as 'The action of making or fact of becoming professionalized; the process of professionalizing',[4] with 'to professionalize' being 'To render or make professional; to give (a person, occupation, activity, or group) professional qualities or characteristics.'[5] 'Professional', in turn, is defined as 'A person who engages in a specified activity, especially a sport, as *a paid occupation*. Frequently opposed to *amateur*' (my emphasis).[6] Sequentially, the definition of 'profession' is listed as 'An occupation in which a professed knowledge of some subject, field, or science is applied; a vocation or career, especially one that involves prolonged training and a formal qualification.'[7] This is echoed in Jeyasingh's understanding of the term, quoted above: 'Understanding and acting on these economic trajectories is what makes the difference between dance as a noble hobby and dance as a professional career' (Jeyasingh, in Gibson 2016: 38).

Using this understanding, 'professionalization' would refer to the process of transitioning from an amateur (or unpaid) to a paid pursuit. This is not the whole story, however, as Akram Khan's perception of the term makes clear. For him, professionalism has nothing to do with 'economic trajectories'. On the contrary, '"professionalism" is about serving the art and your art form *solely*, as the centre point of your life . . . It's not about money' (Khan 2018 emphasis original). Rather than an economic alignment, Khan's understanding of 'professionalism' invokes commitment, integrity and surrender to one's work.

Part of the challenge of understanding what it means to be 'professional' is that the term has come to signify both an understanding of someone who is 'paid for their work' (with the implication that they merit such pay for their acquired expertise) at the same time as invoking someone who 'puts their work first' (with the implication that they will carry out their work to the best of their ability regardless of what they might be paid). In this way, in common parlance, while at one level, as Ackroyd observes, 'professional' equates to 'being paid', it is at the same time widely touted as signalling desirable qualities such as competence and commitment to work above and beyond 'being paid'. It suggests a level of engagement with one's occupation that takes it beyond simply being a 'job'. The same term is used, therefore, both to invoke monetization and to reject it.

This inherent tension in the understanding of what it means to be 'a professional' is reflected in the sociology of professions, where theories about 'professions' and 'professionalism' can be seen to fall into two main camps (Ackroyd 2016), labelled by Thomas Brante (1988) as the 'Naïve' and the 'Cynical'. What Brante terms the 'Naïve' understanding stems from 'functionalism', a theory that argues that institutions emerge and persist because of the use or the 'function' they serve to a society (Ackroyd 2016). This account of professions assumes that they 'serve the public good and are altruistic' (ibid.: 17) and is presented by Brante as 'Naïve' in that it rests on the ideal of a 'utopian professional focussed on the common good' (Brante 1988: 121). A more recent restatement of this position can be found in the work of scholars such as Eliot Freidson, who argues that an emphasis on 'professionalism' can uphold the ideal of an 'ideology of service' and 'devotion to a transcendent value' in the face of the growing pressures of the market (consumerism) and organizations (managerialism) (Freidson 2004: 116). This view, I suggest, corresponds to Khan's understanding of professionalism as involving a selfless devotion to one's craft.

A counter-view of professions, presented by Brante (1988) as 'Cynical', arose in part in reaction against the idealist functionalist view, and is possibly best summed up in the aphorism attributed to philosopher and dramatist George Bernard Shaw: 'All professions are conspiracies against the laity' (cited in ibid.: 119). Under this interpretation, professions attempt to impose what the pioneer sociologist Max Weber termed 'closure' (Weber 1979) on the occupations they regulate, where closure means the 'monopolization of opportunities by various social groups' (Brante 1988: 127). A key proponent of this position was Terence Johnson, who argued that professions are not types of occupations so much as 'a peculiar means of occupational control' (Johnson 1972: 27). Under this construction, 'professions', far from being altruistic, 'promote professional practitioners' own occupational self-interests in terms of salary, status and power' (Evetts 2014: 38). While it misrepresents Jeyasingh's view to align it too closely with this 'cynical' position, and I discuss below the problems with overly romantic notions of 'art as above money' below, there is nonetheless a correspondence here with the perception of professionalism as connected to 'understanding and acting on economic trajectories'.

There are elements of truth in each of these understandings of 'professionalism', both the 'Naïve' and the 'Cynical'. Part of the complexity pertaining to the concepts of 'profession' and 'professionalism' stems from the fact that they have come to represent both an ideal of commitment to excellence as well as a pragmatic acceptance of the need for income and the means of making a livelihood. Inherent in 'professionalism' is the tension that arises from the necessity to monetize one's craft, or one's practice, in particular within a capitalist economy. The 'Naïve' and 'Cynical' perspectives merely highlight different ends of the same conundrum.

The earliest understandings of 'the professional' sidestepped this conflict by making 'the professional' someone who, though he might make some financial gain from his practice (and at that point in time it was almost exclusively 'his'), did not depend on it for his living. American sociologist and early thinker on professions Everett Hughes points out that the very 'earliest meaning of the adjective "professed" was "one that has taken the vows of a religious order"' (Hughes 1963: 656). As the term was secularized, it took with it some of the qualities of involvement in a religious order, including entry into a closed group with its own specific code of practice, an appeal to a specialized body of knowledge, a set of expected relations between members of the order and finally a commitment to that which has been professed, entailing a commitment to a more universal entity and a wider good than the service of a particular client (or one's own livelihood). The earliest established 'professions' were those of 'divinity, law and medicine. Also, the military profession' (ibid.), practised by those for whom their profession was a supplement to independent means. Consequently, there developed, to follow sociologist of professions Julia Evetts, the early image of the professional, which was one of 'the doctor, lawyer and clergyman, who were independent gentlemen, and could be trusted as a result of their competence and experience to provide altruistic advice within a community of mutually dependent middle- and upper-class clients' (Evetts 2014: 42). These professionals being 'independent gentlemen', their need to make an income was not paramount – and thus they would not be corrupted by it. Their economic independence safeguarded their integrity.

This elite status and impression of trustworthiness and competence is in part what drove twentieth-century occupations not previously considered as such to seek the status of a profession, with its concomitant benefits of 'more independence, more recognition, a higher place, a cleaner distinction between those in the profession and those outside, and a larger measure in choosing colleagues and successors' (Hughes 1963: 661). Hence Hughes's conclusion in 1972 that 'The concept of profession is . . . one of *value and prestige*' (Hughes 1972: 339–40, cited in Joffe 1977: 19, my emphasis). This association with 'value and prestige' drove the anxiety within manifold occupations to lay a claim to the descriptor, leading American sociologist Harold Wilensky to write an article entitled 'The Professionalization of Everyone?' critiquing the tendency for everyone, including 'barbers, bellboys, bootblacks and taxi drivers', to claim to be 'professionalized' (1964: 138). Sixty years on, the association of 'professionalism' with status and worth remains as potent as ever – and South Asian dancers (in Britain) are no more inured to its allure than anybody else.

Clearly, a quality open to everyone loses its claims to distinction or privilege, and much early writing on the professions and professionalism focused on attempting to determine what kind of occupation could legitimately be called a 'profession' and in what context. Hence the approach sometimes termed 'trait theory'[8] developed, espoused by sociologists such as Wilensky (1964), Millerson (1964), Greenwood (1957) and others (see Ackroyd 2016),[9] whereby an attempt was made to establish what distinguished a profession in line with a number of identifiable 'traits' or characteristics. The problem with this theory was and is that there is 'only limited agreement as to what the traits of professions are' (Ackroyd 2016: 16). As a result, there is now a widespread recognition 'that definitional precision [of professionalism] is . . . a time-wasting diversion' (Evetts 2013: 780) and that 'it no longer seems important to draw a hard-definitional line between professions and other (expert) occupations' (Evetts 2014: 33). Nevertheless, there has been some agreement, and it is worth bearing in mind that most lists refer to 'expertise', 'a consistent body of knowledge' and 'certification of competency' (Ackroyd 2016: 16).

While the amount of time scholars have spent unravelling the finer points of 'professionalism' could, with some justification, provoke accusations of sophistry, it remains the case that the attribution of 'professional' and 'professionalism' does matter. It matters where the line is drawn between who is 'amateur' and who 'professional'. Just as doctors discuss 'frauds' or 'quacks' whom they regard as betraying the ideals of their profession (Wahlberg 2007), for dancers there are a range of 'wannabe' dancers, 'housewives' or 'amateurs'[10] who are thought to tarnish the way the field is perceived, and from whom they wish to be clearly distinguished. As sociologists Mark Neal and John Morgan (2000: 10) observe in their millennial reprise of Wilensky's article, 'The ethnographic approach to the professions . . . demonstrates that the issues of definition and social closure are not mere academic constructs but are everyday concerns for professionals as part of their work'. Hence the frustration of the dancer cited at the beginning of the chapter with 'the lack of distinction between amateur and professional' in the world of classical Indian dance. While the choice of the label 'profession' or 'expert occupation' for a particular area of work may be an academic exercise, the attempt to achieve 'occupational control of the work', to determine who is 'competent to work' or to establish who merits the legitimacy of the title 'professional' is not.

In the context of the arts, standards of practice and guidelines for what distinguish a 'professional' are important both in the 'idealist' (Naïve) sense, to ensure excellence in artistic practice for those the practitioners serve (the audience), and in the 'Cynical' sense, because, as social geographer Alison Bain points out, 'without a professional guarantee, it can be difficult to ensure that society and the marketplace compensate artists for their works' (Bain 2005: 34). While the 'Cynical' view of professionalization rightly alerts us to the dangers of the exploitation of a relatively disempowered public by a privileged professional class, in the context of work by artists (who have historically struggled to have their labour properly recognized), occupational control can be seen as essential to prevent their own exploitation. Contrary to the 'Cynical' view, in ensuring a certain level of artistic practice, occupational control can also work to safeguard both artist and audience, art (or dance) teacher and art (or dance) student. As Theresa Buckland shows in her article 'Crompton's Campaign', the Victorian dance master Robert Crompton's efforts to impose standards on the practice of dance teaching in Britain in the 1900s and to 'exercise collective control over the artistic standards of the profession' were motivated as much by a desire to root out charlatans, to prevent a situation whereby 'pupils are spoiled and Art suffers' (Crompton 1892, cited in Buckland 2007: 26), as to 'protect employment rights' (of bona fide teachers) (ibid.: 2).

A hundred years later, the young British South Asian dance sector finds itself facing a similar task. As the epigraphs at the start of the chapter suggest, at present there is no clear basis for 'occupational control' within the sector – rather, it is assessed on very different and sometimes opposing criteria. I explore some of the social and historical reasons behind these disagreements below.

Working to Live, or Living to Work – the 'Professional' Artist

> Go to the British funding authorities and say, 'We are professional dancers with a positive contribution to make to the British cultural scene . . . we must have *money*'. (Massey 1982: 11, my emphasis)

What makes a 'professional' artist? A 'professional' dancer'? Debates about what or who might constitute a 'professional' are additionally complicated in the field of the arts where the lack of necessity for formal qualification (see below) and yet the importance of training; the lack of a clear career progression, and yet the existence of understood status markers within the field; and the existence of a 'reversed economy' valuing 'symbolic' over 'economic capital' (Bourdieu 1983; Svensson 2015) all transgress commonly cited traits of 'professionalism', including 'certification of competency' or 'vocational qualifications', 'salaries' and a 'full-time occupation' (Weber 1979, cited in Ritzer 1975; Ackroyd 2016),[11] making 'occupational control' particularly challenging. As Bourdieu (1993: 43) observes, 'one of the most significant properties of the field of cultural production is its extreme permeability'. Thus, Bain (2005: 25) writes in her discussion of the construction of artistic identity, 'with no degrees, licenses, prerequisites or credentials, there is an inherent difficulty in separating . . . professionals from amateurs'. The lack of clear boundaries is far from being a problem unique to South Asian dance in Britain.

Even in areas such as European classical music, contemporary dance or ballet, where there are clear vocational programmes and an elaborate framework of certification, ultimately, as psychotherapist Jon Frederickson and sociologist James F. Rooney observe in their study of the 'music occupation', 'the fact remains that an individual can become a musician without attending a school or conservatory . . . the reason for this is simple: success in music is measured through readily available skill, not through certification of knowledge' (Frederickson and Rooney 1990: 198). Sociologist Roger Stebbins echoes this: 'Artists and entertainers are also validated as professionals when they are invited or hired to present their art in places renowned for displaying professional talent' (Stebbins 1992: 29) without completing any certified training.

Returning to the Oxford Dictionary, or the 'commonly understood' definition of a professional as someone 'paid for their work', again, working within the arts makes this complicated. As Stebbins (1992: 29) points out, 'It is well known that only a small minority of artists and entertainers can live solely by the income from their vocation . . . most professionals in these fields are forced to be part time practitioners to some degree'. This is all the more so within dance, considered by many to be the 'Cinderella' of the arts (Burns and Harrison 2009). An article on an American financial advice website, forbiddingly entitled 'Think You Can Dance for a Career? Think Again', starkly reinforces this point. John Munger, then director of research and information for Dance USA, is quoted as saying, 'The vast majority of dancers cannot make a living off dancing alone as a performer . . . I believe less than 3000 actually do in the entire nation' (Macdonald 2006).).[12] This finding is supported in the report *Dance Mapping*, produced by Susanne Burns and Sue Harrison for Arts Council England in 2009, who note, 'Many dance workers . . . operate what have been termed as "portfolio careers", defined as "no longer having one job, one employer, but multiple jobs and employers within one or more professions" . . . This idea of having a portfolio career is symptomatic of the working life of a dancer' (2009: 127).

What does the understanding of a 'professional' as one who is 'paid' mean in this context? If one is paid for a single performance, does this make one a professional? Does it matter how much the payment was for? For Kaushik, one is professional 'from the moment you sign a contract' (Kaushik 2017c). So, is one a professional for as long as one is contracted, no more, no less? Or does a single contract entitle one to admission to the 'professional artists club'? Does it matter if the contract does not involve any financial exchange?

The difficulties inherent in this equation between 'professional' and 'being paid' are highlighted in a random search of 'professional dancers' on Google. The website dance.net features as responses to the question 'What makes a person a "professional" dancer?' both 'By most competition rules, it's if 40% of your income is from dance', and 'where I train – it's when you earn the majority of your income from dance . . . about 80%' (Dance.net 2019). Even supposing a suitable percentage were agreed on, what should count as 'earning an income from dance'? Does teaching count? Or leading workshops as well as performance? How about dance management? In 2009, Dance UK suggested that thirty thousand people were employed in the dance sector, yet only 2,500 members of Equity (the British trade union for performers and creative practitioners) described themselves as dancers (Burns and Harrison 2009). Even allowing for performing dancers who may not have belonged to Equity, these figures show a striking discrepancy. In what capacity were the remaining 27,500 employed? What distinguished the 2,500 people who considered themselves to be 'dancers'?

The bar set by Equity does not seem prohibitive, asking that

> You have earned £750 or more from professional work in the entertainment and performing arts industry.
> OR
> You can provide proof of membership of an FIA-affiliated union.
> OR
> You have undertaken a job on an Equity contract. (Equity n.d.a)

Notably, an 'area of work covered by Equity' includes not only performance work, but also work as 'a teacher or voice coach engaged in the teaching of performing arts' (Equity 2022). The key determinant is evidence of (some) pay. Medical anthropologist Caroline Potter, in her discussion of the process of making a professional contemporary dancer, 'Learning to Dance', found that for contemporary dancers, completion of training was insufficient grounds to count oneself as professional, but so, apparently, was being paid in itself. Professionalism also had to do with the status or the legitimacy of the work undertaken:

> Recognition as a professional is largely linked to performance and/or choreographic experience, for instance through acceptance into an *estab-*

lished company, participation in *recognized* dance festivals (e.g. London's annual Dance Umbrella), or paid teaching at *recognizable* venues . . . Recent graduates of dance training programmes, while officially (according to School administrators) part of the professional community, often do not recognize themselves or their peers as successful professionals until they have secured a first performance or choreographic contract. (Potter 2007: 266, my emphasis)

Dance scholar Judith Alter cites dancer and psychologist Carol Ryser's study among dancers who likewise felt that 'professional' was not determined only by remuneration, but by 'consecration' (Bourdieu 1983: 320) or the 'act of dancing regularly with a *recognized* company' (Alter 1997: 73, my emphasis).

In the particular case of South Asian dance in Britain, the difficulties with 'professionalism' as defined in relation to both 'consecration' and remuneration are especially pronounced. As I discuss in Chapter 1, while employment for many dancers is precarious, the 'ready-made' employment option of work as a company dancer is, for South Asian dancers in Britain, almost non-existent and where opportunities do exist, they are less likely to receive mainstream legitimation or 'consecration'. Contemporary dance artist Georgia Redgrave reflects on her experience of working with bharatanatyam dancers: 'I thought that we had it hard as contemporary dancers, but it sounds like there are really very few opportunities for bharatanatyam dancers, so much so that dancers are just happy to get opportunities to dance, even if it's really low paid or unpaid' (cited in Agrawal 2019a). As a result, for South Asian dance, the 'professional' marker of securing a contract with a 'recognized company' is proportionally less likely. This is true to such an extent that former Yuva Gati director (2008–18) and bharatanatyam artist and teacher Anusha Subramanyam felt constrained to advise young South Asian dancers wishing to pursue a career in dance to apply to contemporary dance courses:

> I *have* actually been telling my dancers that they should apply to do a contemporary course. And I have been asked – why? And my thing is – why not? If you want to be a performer in this country – a full-time performer and a choreographer . . . if any one of us was to train at one of the contemporary dance schools, there are more opportunities. (Subramanyam 2017)

Against this backdrop, it is hardly surprising that an Akademi report commissioned in 1997 found that South Asian dancers felt that

> Professionalism should be redefined and not solely determined by taking as its criterion that of performing and teaching dance as the principal

source of income . . . *professionalism is to do with excellence of performing standards and should not be taken as commensurate with the earning potential of the performer.* They feel that this is a cultural issue of great consequence, an imposition of values tantamount to cultural imperialism . . . in a culturally diverse society one should be allowed to retain the freedom of performing without this being linked to earning money from dance, if one so wishes, without a perceived consequent lowering of one's performance standards. (Iyer 1997a: 57, my emphasis)

For these dancers, the notion of tying the concept of 'professionalism' to the economic reality of money and contracts is dangerously reductive. Dancer, choreographer and coach Mavin Khoo makes this case eloquently:

So just as an example, as a dancer I think one of the limitations of working within a professional setting in the West is of course that then dance becomes your job. And when it becomes your job, the boundary that this places in terms of, I guess things that for me are important, like truly living and surrendering to your craft . . . the more I work, the more experience I have working in a range of contexts and it's a very ambiguous line about how many professional dancers are actually invested in becoming artists, and how many are doing their jobs. (Khoo 2017)

For Khoo, the only meaningful and abiding contract for an artist is with their art form – and other contractual agreements must yield to the overriding demands of this most important commitment.

While Khoo distinguishes the 'limitations of working within a professional setting in the West', there is in fact a long-established rhetoric within the arts world in the West that underlines the importance of 'the theory of art for art's sake, which is to the field of cultural production what the axiom "business is business" . . . is to the economic field' (Bourdieu 1983: 343). The arts operate, Bourdieu (1993: 40) argues, within a 'reversed economy', or within a field that places a value on 'disinterestedness'. He draws a comparison with the case of prophecy, which 'demonstrates its authenticity by the fact that it brings in no income'. Consequently, Bain (2005: 29) remarks, there has been and still lingers 'A spirit of romanticism embodied in the stereotypical image of the starving artist in a garret' (see also Abbing 2008). The artist, this romantic image suggests, cares nothing for income so long as they can commit themselves to their art. As with understandings of who or what makes a 'professional', such mythical ideals within the arts world matter because they impact on how people live. An investigation into the career of the independent dancer by dance scientist Imogen Aujla and dancer and academic Rachel Farrer revealed that

> Some dancers and choreographers were reluctant to talk about money, firstly because it appeared to compromise their artistic integrity: 'no one likes talking about money, whether it's institutions or a funded company. You feel like you've got to maintain artistic integrity . . . I think there's this notion that it's about producing your art, so it's about your artistic identity and the fulfilment of the project. But then it's hard to earn anything [laughs]'. (Aujla and Farrer 2015)

Contrary to Massey's exhortation cited at the beginning of this section ('We are professional dancers . . . we must have money'), the understanding in this case is 'We are professional dancers . . . we don't talk about money (because our commitment goes beyond it).' Thus, the debate returns to the very first understandings of 'profess' and 'professionals' in which the understanding of 'professed', referring to one who 'has taken the vows of a religious order' (Hughes 1963: 656), was carried into succeeding understandings of 'professionals', in that the 'professor' was assumed to have avowed their commitment to a more universal entity and a wider good than the service of a particular client (or their own livelihood).

'Jobbing Professionals', 'Noble Hobbyists' – and a Historical Interlude

It would be interesting (though beyond the scope of this book) to trace when the widely understood meaning of 'professional' switched from having at its heart the idea of a 'nobler' or broader goal than payment, to the point at which the dictionary defines the concept in terms of 'being paid'.[13] A significant part of the kudos attached to the earlier understanding of 'professional', as I argue above, pertained to the professional's relative indifference (or at least apparent indifference) to monetary reward.

Given the sociological evolution of Indian classical dance forms (described below), it is worth observing that in the historical context of British sport, the term 'professional' referred to a player requiring payment (as opposed to the 'amateur' who played for love of the game alone). In this context, the 'amateur' typically held greater status than the 'professional' (Wagg 2000). This was essentially on the same basis that had afforded the professional (in other contexts) part of their original status – that of pursuing the chosen activity free of economic interest. Thus, sports sociologist Stephen Wagg shows how until as recently as the 1960s and 1970s, within English cricket, 'amateurs' were upper-class 'gentlemen' players who played with no fee, while the 'professionals' were 'usually hired by gentlemen to play for their teams' (ibid.: 32). Accordingly, team captains were almost always 'amateurs', with 'the inherent leadership qualities of the gentleman amateur often fiercely asserted', thanks to their 'educated minds' and 'logical power of reasoning' (ibid.).[14] The thinking behind this is made plain in the framework on amateur status drawn up by the International Amateur Athletics

Federation (IAAF) in 1948, which states in its first clause, 'An Amateur is one who practises and competes ONLY for the love of the sport' (cited in Polley 2000: 93, capitals in the original). This is by contrast with the (by implication) less noble paid professionals, pejoratively known as 'mere jobbers' or 'instrumentalists' (Allison 2001: 157). These same values found within British sport also applied to the practice of Indian classical dance forms in the early to mid-twentieth century. Given the impact this history has had on understandings of 'professionalism' in South Asian dance in Britain today, it is worth a slight digression to consider this in some detail.

As is well documented elsewhere (Srinivasan 1985; Gaston 1996; Allen 1997; O'Shea 1998; Meduri 2001, 2004; Soneji 2010), Indian classical dance forms have a long history of professional performance, albeit in the context of temples, courts and private salons rather than in the contemporary (Euro-American) context of ticketed stage performance. From at least the sixteenth century (and probably earlier), the various dance forms that were later reconstructed as 'Indian classical dance forms' were performed by dancers known by different names in different part of India, but now most commonly recognized as *devadasis*.[15]

As Amrit Srinivasan's now classic ethnographic work identified, at least within the south of India, these hereditary dancers had established an occupational 'devadasi "way of life" or a "professional ethic" (*vrtti, murai*)' (Srinivasan 1985: 1869). While 'the office of *devadasi* was hereditary', it 'did not confer the right to work *without adequate qualification*' (ibid., my emphasis). Rather, 'recruitment to the profession was restricted on the basis of criteria such as – sex, inheritance, initiation, training (the public demonstration of skill in one's art subsequent to a ritual and social apprenticeship . . . was the necessary preliminary to a professional career)' (ibid.: 1870).[16] The early nineteenth-century Telegu Brahmin, P. Ragaviah Charry, writing in 1806, gives us a further insight into the rigour involved in being a 'Dancing Girl'. He records,

> The young girls are sent to the dancing school at about 5 or 6 years of age, and at 8, begin learning music; either vocal or instrumental – some attain great proficiency in dancing, or others in singing; but the first art is limited to a certain period of life, for dancing in the Hindoo style requires great agility of constitution – thus no woman after the age of 25 is reckoned competent to the task. (Ragaviah Charry 1808: 546)

He goes on to explain the manner of professional qualification – 'when the Girl attains a certain degree of proficiency . . . the young student is introduced to the assembly and her merit is examined and assayed' (ibid.: 547). What emerges from these accounts is an impression of working dancers who performed their occupation in a manner demonstrating several of the traits Ackroyd (2016) notes as receiving some sociological consensus as attributes of professions, such as specialized training, professional duties, a distinctive way of life and a particular clientele.

Ragaviah Charry also refers to the dancers' means of income or 'Revenues'. Here, 'the first source of emolument', he states, 'proceeds from their destination as public women – When the young lady arrives at the age of puberty, she is consigned to the protection of a man, who generally pays a large premium, besides a suitable monthly allowance.' (Ragaviah Charry 1808: 547). As his observation makes clear, and is well attested elsewhere, the 'dancing girl' commonly combined her work as a dancer with work as a professional courtesan. This was part of her accepted function and, as Pillai (2020) points out, often relied on long-standing relationships between a woman and a particular client. It is this aspect of the lifestyle of hereditary dancers, viewed through a lens of British Victorian values that falsely equated it with prostitution, that led to it becoming the subject of much controversy in the early twentieth century, as well as the focus of a number of aligned but differently motivated campaigns for its prohibition.[17] These campaigns ultimately led to a series of regional bans on the hereditary dancers (including the influential State of Madras 'Madras Prevention of the Dedication of Devadasis Act' in 1947),[18] as a result of which, and combined with the diminished status of their customary patrons in the face of British imperialism, the hereditary dancers were effectively prevented from continuing their profession, including their traditions of dance and music, by the beginning of the twentieth century.

While condemning the hereditary dancers, abolitionists remained largely positive about the art forms – the music and dance – that these dancers had practised. Keen that the art forms should not disappear with the hereditary dancers, advocates for their preservation, like the lawyer and nationalist E. Krishna Iyer, who was involved in the Indian independence movement in the 1920s and 1930s, directed their efforts towards taking dance out of the 'hands of the exponents of the old professional class with all its possible and lurking dangers . . . and introducing it among cultured *family* women of respectable class' (Krishna Iyer 1949: 24, cited in Soneji 2010: xxiv, my emphasis). The reformist Muthulakshmi Reddy, herself from a hereditary dancer family, likewise held that 'the arts must be restored to their original purity and grandeur, so that respectable, good and virtuous women may come forward to learn and practice them' (Reddy in *The Hindu*, December 1932: 5, cited in Srinivasan 1983: 82). It took a while to overcome the stigma associated with practising dance, but slowly opinion shifted so that in 1943, the highly influential founder of Kalakshetra, Rukmini Devi Arundale, was able to write to a student and teacher in her school, S. Sarada, 'They used to think that, except the usual class of people, no one else would be able to dance. Now there are so many girls from *good* families who are excellent dancers' (in Sarada 1985: 50, cited in Allen 1997: 65, my emphasis).

These 'excellent dancers', coming as they did from 'good families', were, unlike the hereditary dancers, not dependent on dance for their livelihood. Thus, one of the keys to distinguishing this new class of dancers from their forebears was that they did not dance for money. The arts, in Rukmini Devi's vision (a vision that reflected the wider approach of the period), were to be followed with dedication, but without commercialism. For Devi, the success of the Indian nation, as well as the Indian arts, depended on restoring woman from her degraded position to that of 'a divine influence, rising above the material aspect of things' (Devi, cited in Weidman 2003: 208; see also Meduri 2005). The obvious candidate to acquire such non-monetarily oriented expertise was the financially supported housewife. To quote a 1930s advertisement for violin lessons, in a programme for the Madras Music Academy, 'A modern wife has tons of unemployed leisure and a wise husband must provide hobbies for her leisure being usefully employed' (cited in Weidman 2003: 210). In providing such a 'useful occupation', following the rhetoric of the times, the 'wise husband' would be upholding not only Indian culture but also the Indian nation and Indian moral integrity. Thus developed the ideal of practising dance as, in the words of Jeyasingh, a 'noble hobbyist', whereby 'My mother's generation had an ideal of dance as a noble pursuit untainted by the economics of earning a living' (Jeyasingh, in Gibson 2016: 37). Where for the hereditary dancer, her 'freedom from household responsibilities (*grhastha*)' (Coorlawala 2004: 50) meant that she could dedicate herself to her artistry, in the twentieth-century reconstitution of the dance forms, being a womanly representative of *grhastha* values was almost a precondition of being permitted to perform them.

Not quite everyone was convinced of the practicality of this. The great Sanskrit scholar and patron of the arts V. Raghavan voiced his reservations, arguing that 'family women are not capable of devoting the time and attention to develop to perfection this art of Bharata Natyam. Domestic circumstances of work and care are not promotive of the spirit of it' (V. Raghavan Bhava Raga Tala 1933, cited in Soneji 2010: 188). He was in the minority, however, and Srinivasan (1983: 82) suggests that by the time the 1947 Madras Act banning the dedication of hereditary dancers came into effect, it marked 'the birth of a new, elite class of "amateur" dancers' as much as it sealed 'the death of the old professional class of temple dancers'. Accordingly, mohiniattam and kathakali dancer and founder of Akademi Tara Rajkumar recalls, 'on my father's side there was this feeling that yes, I should perform and get a name, but never take a fee because it was beneath you to get money out of your artistic performance' (Rajkumar 2017).

This ideology of the 'noble hobbyist' was institutionalized in one of India's most significant training schools, Kalakshetra, in part due to Devi's idealism and wish to avoid commercialism. As a result, while standards of training were similarly rigorous, the question of making money from one's work and expertise was ignored almost on principle. Kalakshetra alumna Mira Balchandran-Gokul reflects,

> I never really planned my career – and nobody was there to help me plan it. Everyone who was there was very idealistic. My parents were

idealistic, and even in Kalakshetra, there was no focus on how do you develop dance into a career. I don't think that played a part *at all*. (Balchandran-Gokul 2017, emphasis original)

As another illustrative example of the institutionalization of this ideology, dance writer Ashish Khokar suggests that in the late 1980s,

Kalakshetra was so staunchly unprofessional where money matters were concerned that it returned unutilized a grant of Rs. 25 lakhs from the Ford Foundation on the grounds that 'never having been a wealthy institution, it was at a loss as to how to use these funds.'[19] (Khokar 2012 193)

The message was that 'Kalakshetra's creed was to do with art, not the business of art' (ibid.).

The reconstructed classical Indian dance forms have thus developed with an inbuilt aversion to performing art for money, going beyond that found within Euro-American artistic practice, due to the desire to maintain distance from a supposedly disreputable past. As dance scholar Judith Lynne Hanna shows, again due to associations with prostitution, 'the "ballet girl" had a pejorative connotation in the U.S. until the mid-twentieth century and in some places still does' (1988: 124). Likewise in the UK, 'dance' was denigrated as 'entertainment', not 'art', until well into the twentieth century owing to the connection with the supposed sleaze and immorality of the music halls, where dance in nineteenth-century Britain was most commonly performed (Siddall 1999).[20] Yet, I suggest, there did not develop a divide between the legitimated (unpaid) and proscribed (paid) practice of ballet. Rather ballet's 'rehabilitation' took place on the understanding of the dance artist being paid, while for classical Indian dance forms this 'rehabilitation' was on the basis of the artist being unpaid. To understand some of the complexities of the development and professionalization of South Asian dance forms in Britain, it is essential to recognize this context.

Dance, Art and Pay – the Indian Context

Of course, the problem with the practice of the arts as described above, as indeed with the economically buffered 'professions', is that it almost necessarily restricts the field concerned to those privileged or wealthy enough to be able to work without pay: in these cases, the upper-middle-class housewife, or the gentleman of independent means. Bourdieu makes this case in his essay on 'The Field of Cultural Production' (1983). Reflecting on the 'reversed economy' he makes the fairly obvious point that

The propensity to move towards the economically most risky positions, and above all the capacity to persist in them . . . even when they secure no short-term economic profit, seem to depend to a large extent on possession of substantial economic and social capital. This is firstly because economic capital provides the conditions for freedom from economic necessity, a private income (*la rente*) being one of the best substitutes for sales (*la vente*). (Bourdieu 1983: 349)

The ideology of arts as best practised shielded from financial imperative is one that only stacks up in the context of not having to earn one's living as an artist – it better suits the 'noble' (unpaid) 'amateur' rather than the (paid) professional artist. Certainly, though there are signs that this is now changing, it has been the case within India that the serious practice of bharatanatyam and other classical dance and music forms has largely relied on having a significant disposable income. Dancer and scholar Avanthi Meduri makes this point forcefully, observing that for student dancers,

> If they have the economic means, they buy the best instruction available. If they do not, but have the talent, then they struggle. The path to fame is not easy. The students with economic power shop around for the best teachers and test them out. It used to be the other way around . . . *At all times money is needed*. (Meduri 2001: 110, my emphasis)

The personal reality of this was brought home to me during a visit to Chennai in 1998. I spoke to a young girl in the audience of a dance show who was clearly keenly absorbed and interested in the programme. I asked if she was a dancer. 'No', she sighed. 'I was taking lessons – but then I couldn't afford the *arangetram*' (the debut stage performance for bharatanatyam dancers). The situation is exacerbated by the interaction with NRIs (non-resident Indians) who come to India to train and pick up dance materials. Dance anthropologist Ann R. David explains: 'NRIs (non-resident-Indians) from the UK, USA and elsewhere bringing in foreign money to pay teachers, promoters and musicians are 'in part responsible for creating inflated expectations' and 'inflated prices' (David 2005b: 41–42).

In addition, unlike careers like medicine or engineering where one can expect a salary to reimburse training costs, as a classical performer in India, one's costs do not end with training. With the exception of a select few, to perform in India frequently involves not only paying for one's own training, but also to a greater or lesser extent subsidizing one's own performances. Thus, theatre practitioner and anthropologist Shanti Pillai writes:

> In Chennai, almost all dance concerts are free. Patronage of the performing arts has all but disappeared and government support is minimal. This means that the individual dancer not only receives nothing for the performance, but also that she or he must frequently meet all of the production costs. (Pillai 2002: 17–18)

Award-winning Chennai-based bharatanatyam dancer Chris Gurusamy, whose calibre is well attested (among other achievements, he was chosen by *New York Times* dance critic Alistair Macaulay as one of his 'best dancers of 2017' and was also selected as Junior Fellowship Awardee 2017–18 by the Indian dance organization Kalavaahini), describes his experience of working as a dancer. He notes that while 'there is a possibility' of being paid for work in 'group choreography',

> If you want to be a soloist like I do, then you kind of have to learn to live meagrely . . . a dancer might get paid the same amount as a singer might get paid. Which is to say 5,000 rupees . . . But then we have to pay the five orchestra members, and each one of them might demand INR 4,000 *EACH* – so it's very rare to have a *kachheri* [concert] situation where you end up breaking even. Breaking even is like . . . when I break even in a *kachheri* – like I've had a couple where I've been able to break even because the sponsors have given a bit of money – those are like the *best kachheris* because you just feel like you know you are actually *earning* something – but most of the time you end up shelling out I'd say at least INR 6,000 on top of what they've given you *if* they give you anything. Some people still believe that it's OK to *not* pay artists, which happens quite regularly, and we have to fork out the entire payment for the orchestra.[21] (Gurusamy 2017)

As a result, as Janet O'Shea (2003: 178) comments, 'Dancers who strive to maintain professional lives in Chennai perform internationally in order to attain a level of financial reimbursement that offsets the generally low honoraria offered by Chennai venues'.

Furthermore, unlike in Britain, there is not significant state funding available in India for individual artists. Post-independence, the Indian government had founded a set of Indian Akademis for the arts, based, as dance historian Joan Erdman explains,

> on the Western concept of government patronage through academies, the most explicit model being the French Academy.[22] The new Government of India defined its responsibility for the arts as 'the rebuilding of [India's] cultural structure' and the continuation of support for arts previously patronized by the princes. (Erdman 1983: 253)

The three Akademis were the Sangeet Natak Akademi (for music and dance) established in 1953, the Sahitya Akademi (for literature) and the Lalit Kala Akademi (for visual and the plastic arts). Similarly to the Arts Council in England, these three institutions, along with the Indian Council for Cultural Relations

(ICCR), which aims to 'revive, establish and strengthen cultural relations between India and other countries' (ibid.), are supported by government grants, yet are supposed to be autonomous in terms of their broad programmes and decisions. However, as Erdman points out,

> Involvement of the government of India in the cultural sphere was not intended to pre-empt other support for the arts . . . At the time of their founding, the Akademis had as their objective the revival and promotion of India's artistic traditions. *They did not include programs to support individual artists.* (Erdman 1983: 253, my emphasis)

Moreover, such funding as there was available was relatively sparse. The dance scholar and Indian cultural policy adviser Kapila Vatsyayan wrote in 1972 that

> Culture, in spite of the basic approach, was now to receive comparatively low priority when pitted against the needs of a developing economy, backward industry, badly requiring colossal funds and state administration, not to mention the targets of free and compulsory education, adult literacy drives. (Vatsyayan 1972: 17)

Funding for the arts came from the Ministry of Education – and cultivating a literate population was a funding priority. As a result, 'cultural activity, both of a participative nature and of a professional nature, was sustained in pre-independent India mainly through private effort . . . This is still true' (ibid.: 23), and remains true nearly fifty years later.

The lack of state funding, the lack of clear progression routes, combined with the complicated relationship to money or to 'material concerns' that was woven around the classical art forms make the issue of 'making a living through dance' particularly difficult. Thus, ethnomusicologist Anna Morcom observes that in comparison with the commercial world of bollywood dance,

> In classical performing arts, there has not been such an easy or open relationship to earning raw money. Indeed, in South India, fees given to teachers by students or for performances are still not seen or termed as a salary or wage, but as *gurudaksinas*, fees similar to a priest receiving gifts from the patrons of the temple for assisting them with experiencing the divine, rather than as an assertion of their ownership of the performance through monetary compensation. (Morcom 2015: 293)

Dutch anthropologist Stine Puri (writing specifically about bharatanatyam, though the situations with other Indian classical dance forms are similar) makes a blunt assessment.

> Bharatanatyam is mostly respected as a kind of cultural education for young females, but not as a career path . . . For most bharatanatyam dance students today, the dance is therefore an expense rather than a source of income . . . Bharatanatyam dancers of today, as opposed to *devadasis*, thus have the luxury of not having to dance for an income. *Dancing shows that one has the money to dance rather than the need to dance for money.* (Puri 2014: 221, my emphasis)

If one does not have the good fortune to be independently wealthy, and cannot be adequately compensated for one's artistry, the only available option is to work at two jobs, something that continues to be taken for granted as a means of sustaining one's practice within India today. On a panel at 'World Dance Day' organized by Khokar in 2015, one of the panellists, Ananda Shankar Jayant, advised the young dancers in the audience,

> You will all be facing this journey of having a successful career and a successful dance career. They are two different things. The trick is to find something that will cross subsidize your dance . . . I have been very successful that I am a rail manager . . . so don't let anyone tell you that you can't do two things. (Shankar, in Kanakarathnam 2015)

Chapter 3 draws attention to the methods of training in dance – and it is important to recognize that dance teaching in India has proved an effective economic vehicle for many dancers, particularly women, providing a respectable semi-professional designation and a means to mediate between amateur and professional status. Yet the continued unease around dance and money highlighted in Morcom's quotation above increases the precarity around teaching as a means of income. A successful teacher is likely to have started from the basis of strong social, symbolic and economic capital – which might offer them, for example, the luxury of space to teach a class in their own homes, or a subsidy to support them in the initial stages of establishing a class. This means that even where dance teaching becomes a significant source of household income, it is often married women who take the step to establish an independent dance school, aiming at a career that enables flexibility around household tasks and childcare while the husband provides the secure income offered by conventional employment. One remains more likely to encounter a male teacher in India within the comparative security of institutional employment, for example as a teacher for Kalakshetra.

Dance, Art and Pay – from India to Britain

This model of dance practice in India cannot be ignored in Britain because, as Kaushik puts it, 'the dance sector relies on what is happening back home' (cited in Gorringe et al. 2018: 61). Several of the prominent figures in the South Asian dance world in Britain today (including the directors of the influential organizations Sampad and Kadam, as well as until recently Akademi) only came to Britain as adults, meaning that their formative understandings of dance and its practice (or their primary *habitus*[23] and *doxa* – or axioms[24]) were developed in India. In addition, as Gorringe et al. (ibid.: 59) observe, 'There is a constant exchange between India and the UK, and artists and teachers from India are regularly brought to the UK to perform and to run summer schools, intensive training sessions and masterclasses'.[25]

Given the significance of India and the constant exchange between India and Britain, the transfer of ways at looking at the arts, and in particular dance, is almost inevitable. The acceptance and respectability of teaching as a means of earning within India, for example, as discussed above, has subsequently enabled the proliferation of sites of community practice that inform the South Asian dance infrastructure in the UK. Yet there has also remained a deep-seated perception among some practitioners, teachers and (importantly) parents of young dance students that dance either should or could not be performed for money and that therefore the pursuit of dance must be undertaken alongside another career – or by the independently wealthy. Nina Rajarani recalls her mother's initial reaction to her decision to pursue a career in dance,

> She said that all these dancers in India come from very rich backgrounds – they have inherited wealth – they don't need to earn a living and we are a typical middle-class family and have to work really hard – and unless you think you are going to marry someone rich who will support you when you are dancing, I really don't see how this will work. . . (Rajarani 2018)

This perception is exacerbated by a situation whereby, as I discuss elsewhere, while employment for many dancers is precarious, the option of work as a company dancer is, for South Asian dancers in Britain, yet more limited.

In this way, a combination of factors – the historic suspicion of dance as a means of livelihood; the precarity of migrant communities, which in the absence of securely recognized cultural or social capital seek occupations that offer secure economic capital;[26] and the lack of available jobs for classical Indian dancers – has meant that the 'dual-career dancer' continues to feature prominently in the world of classical Indian dance practice in Britain. Thus, it remains commonplace for a serious classical Indian dancer practising in Britain to also be working as a doctor, a dentist or a lawyer, something reflected in the aspirations of young dancers. Gorringe et al. found in their study among young South Asian dancers that 51 per cent of their respondents aimed for a 'dual career' (compared to 7 per cent aiming to commit to dance full-time), with almost 40 per cent of these hoping to combine dance with medicine (Gorringe et al. 2018: 17). Grau's 2001 report draws attention to 'a copy of the law society gazette. . .which featured a picture of a "professional Bharata Natyam dancer" while announcing her new full-time job as a solicitor for Landau Zeffert Dresden' (Grau 2001: 64). Almost twenty years later, a performance at the New Art Exchange in Nottingham in 2018 featured a professional bharatanatyam dancer who was also a 'practising dentist' (New Art Exchange 2019).

The Dual-Career Dancer

This pattern of the 'dual-career dancer' and the perception that it is not only possible but desirable to maintain professional practice in a career such as medicine or law without compromising the professionalism of one's artistic practice is a contentious subject among classical Indian dance practitioners in Britain. Its acceptance or rejection as a model has significant implications for the shape of the developing field of professional classical Indian dance and for the understanding of 'professionalism'. It is therefore important to unpick and examine some of the key issues in this debate.

In some ways, the 'dual-career' route can be seen merely as an extension of the pattern adopted by many artists of working at a secondary occupation in order to fund a primary artistic occupation (Abbing 2008; Sommerlade 2018). The very limited availability of jobs with long-term contracts means that the reality for most dance practitioners in the UK is one of a 'portfolio career' defined as 'multiple jobs and employers within one or more professions' (Burns and Harrison 2009: 127). Indeed, the very condition of portfolio working, and of working at a variety of often menial, non-career-oriented jobs during gaps between employment, to make ends meet and to allow flexibility to continue in one's vocation as a dancer, can be a further source of occupational identity for those independent dance artists who constitute the majority of the sector. Dancers exchange stories of the times they have worked waitressing or stuffing envelopes to make ends meet – like bharatanatyam and contemporary dancer Archana Ballal, who had 'a whole host of part-time jobs – non-dance jobs – doing like promotions or as a telephone fundraiser . . . because there's always the gaps in between' (Ballal 2017).

Combining work as a dancer, however, with a dance-related activity (such as yoga teaching or physiotherapy), or with work requiring minimal expertise or long-term commitment (such as working as a waiter or waitress or as a temporary administrative assistant), is qualitatively different from combining such work with another profession requiring intense levels of training (six years in the case of medicine), expertise, focus and time commitment. Dance sociologist Kristine Sommerlade's research among contemporary dance theatre artists highlights both the precarity of dance work and the scarce availability of long-term contracts and the fact that 'dance artists undertake secondary jobs mainly to fund working in their primary artistic occupations as performers, performer/creators or choreographers' (Sommerlade 2018: 174). Nevertheless, many of her interviewees 'rank their artistic practice as more important than paid employment, leisure time and consumption', and for one respondent 'as soon as one of her employers refused to accommodate her intermittent absences due to her artistic commitments, she resigned from the post' (ibid.). In the case of dance, which like sport, depends upon a level of physical fitness and of consistent training (see Chapter 4), it is especially hard to move in and out of artistic practice – arguably more so than in other creative arts such as writing or painting. Thus, while a 'portfolio career' may be standard among dance artists, the pursuit of professional work as a dancer alongside work as a doctor, dentist, accountant or solicitor is a pattern peculiar to the South Asian dance sector in Britain. Obviously, many doctors, dentists and accountants pursue other forms of dance in their spare time – but in this case, it is uncommon for their professionalism as dancers to be in question; dance is a leisure pursuit. When I worked with a contemporary dance choreographer on a dance project in 2016, his reaction to hearing that classical Indian dancers commonly work as dancers alongside other careers or occupations, not as yoga teachers or bartenders but as doctors and accountants, was one of disbelief (field notes, November 2016). I encountered a similar reaction among the contemporary dance category finalists at a *BBC Young Dancer* event in 2017 when I explained that two of the competitors they were watching were medics: 'You would never get a professional contemporary dancer who was also a doctor' (field notes, January 2017).

In part, this pattern merely represents a pragmatic response to finding a viable way to pursue one's chosen art form in the face of severely restricted employment opportunities. Akram Khan suggested at Navadisha 2016 that this is not a problem confined to Britain. He spoke of conversations with leading Indian bharatanatyam and kathak artists who voice the same challenges:

> I am often in dialogue with classical artists, like Malavika Sarukkai, Priyadarshini Govind, and Kumudini Lakhia . . . [about] the concerns they have about the lack of support, and the lack of opportunity. They feel that the younger artists slowly become disheartened to pursue a career in that field. And then some of those younger artists reluctantly move into the contemporary dance world. Simply because there isn't enough opportunity to develop or sustain themselves as a classical artist. (Khan, in Gibson 2016: 26)

Kathak dancer, choreographer and teacher Sonia Sabri agrees: 'We train dancers to study bharatanatyam, kathak, whatever the classical form is – we make them study *so* hard – but actually they then divorce themselves from that and they end up doing contemporary dance . . . getting work in classical technique – it's a real struggle' (Sabri 2018).

A dual-career route therefore seems a logical means to find a way to do the work to which one is truly committed, rather than being forced into doing the (more contemporary) work that is more readily available. Yadagudde (2017a) explains his reasoning for encouraging his students to take this approach: 'One is a psychologist, everyone is working. I told them, "Earn money. Keep some money, do a performance every two years – it will fund you."' The reliability of the income of their day job ironically improves their consistency as performers of work they believe in. The remarkable energy, passion and determination shown by dancers who follow this dual path can, in many ways, only be applauded, especially as it is arguable that this has been an important way in which the Indian classical dance forms have been kept alive in Britain thus far.

The pattern of a dual career, however, also raises problems. It requires those practitioners who follow this route to work double-time, meaning that the practitioner, although no longer economically stressed, continues to be stretched physically, emotionally and intellectually. While there has not hitherto been research conducted specifically on the 'dual-career dancer', the case of nineteenth-century British sport is once again instructive, in which Wagg (2000) clearly describes how the commitment to amateurism started to unravel. Relying exclusively on a practitioner's love and respect for their art form to maintain standards of performance did not ultimately work out too well for the field, putting the Amateur Athletics Association (AAA) in the bizarre position of legislating against excellence. Thus, rules were put in place that no individual might 'gain advantage' through a job that might allow them to train at more than an amateur level (ibid.). After all – to practise would be cheating! Asked about the subsequent professionalization of the sport, the rugby player Stuart Lancaster reflected:

> I suppose improved fitness is the main thing . . . a sense of having fulfilled one's potential. You don't have to train in the evening when you are already tired, but you can concentrate on it. So, I'm glad to have played rugby as well as I could have done. I think it's probably only a 5 percent difference to being a serious amateur, but it is different. (Lancaster, in Allison 2001: 116)

Stebbins's research into amateurs and professionals raises a similar point. He observes, 'The fact that many amateur activities are scheduled during late weekday afternoons or early evenings presents another problem – fatigue . . . a large majority of amateurs talked about fatigue as an obstacle to doing one's best' (Stebbins 1992: 51). Yadagudde describes how he feels inspired to continue teaching because

> In the Bhavan, everyone is very dedicated. They come with seriousness – they don't come to play around. Some are doctors, some are accountants, some are financial experts – they work – every one of them – in a profession, and yet they still come. Some work 'til 2 a.m. Some girls work as nurses – they work all night and come at 8 o'clock in the morning for

a class – and then go home and sleep. What I mean is the passion – the interest they show – that makes me feel that . . . I am doing nothing. (Yadagudde 2017a)

While on the one hand, such commitment is both admirable and, as Yadagudde finds it, inspiring, how far is this level of training after a full day's (or night's) work sustainable, or even desirable? One immediate risk factor is clearly that of injury due to fatigue, or (potentially) insufficient time spent on warm-ups and cool-downs. One South Asian and contemporary dancer spoke both of her admiration and yet her scepticism for the dual-career route:

I think it's really difficult. When do you get the time to train, to keep in shape? . . . To be honest I'm amazed that all these South Asian dancers have these careers – and that is what makes me question the commitment – I don't know . . . I automatically question the commitment to the dance aspect of both careers – to how well you are keeping your practice – to how much time and thought you manage to give to your practice, to someone else's work . . . to your own work. (Anonymous interviewee, 2017)

Essentially, the problem with having another job for money is that one ends up with less time. This is a problem because, as Jeyasingh puts it, 'above all, these forms require *time*'.[27]

Time is required not only to maintain one's fitness and develop one's craft, but also to contribute to the development of the sector more generally. Returning to Chaudhury (quoted at the beginning of the chapter), her reflection on professionalism within classical Indian dance in Britain continues,

It is essential to formalize professionalization further, which would hopefully result in more considered programming. Practitioners who want to be programmed by arts venues and theatres of any scale should be dedicating the majority of their time to dance or dance-related work, with an open approach so that they are not only developing their practice, but also taking time to understand the sector better. (Chaudhury 2019: 28)

The restriction on the time of dual professionals, in Chaudhury's view, means that they are unable to really inhabit their sector.

Additionally, the experience of artistic practice is qualitatively different for dual professionals as compared to dance artists who 'dedicate the majority of their time to dance' because they are not subject to the same economic pressures. Aujla and Farrer (2015) rightly emphasize the hardships of the life of a dancer – the demands of intense physical training, the ever-present risk of injury, 'hardships . . .

exacerbated by working in the independent dance sector, with its undefined roles, constantly changing working schedules, and lack of financial security'. This is a precarity from which dual-career dancers are cushioned. It is understandable in this light that dancers dependent on dance work for their income might feel a sense of proprietorship over the scarce paid work that is available.

A further concern is that dance practitioners who are not dependent on their art practice for an income can afford to undercut other practitioners who are. Rajarani (2018) makes this point clearly:

> If you have a full-time job doing something else as your main sources of income . . . you can afford to do things at a lower rate – so you can afford to undercut or do things entirely for free. Or you can afford to do things on a more casual basis. For example, if someone is running a school, and they are combining this with a full-time career – they are not going to be too worried about whether they receive fees or not, if the student pays on time, etc. – whereas if this is your only job, you need to put systems in place to make sure that you are not losing money, or paying to run the classes. So, someone running classes on a casual basis makes it harder for someone who is running classes as their only source of income.

Ultimately, both in terms of economic necessity and personal identity, dual-career dancers are not subject to the same imperative to seek work within the field. For Stebbins this imperative marks a key difference between professionals and amateurs: 'Professionals know they must stick to their pursuit when the going gets tough . . . Amateurs can be choosy, professionals cannot' (Stebbins 1992: 51). Gurusamy makes a similar point, adding that this imperative is not necessarily always a negative:

> Having a career to back yourself up with is always a good thing – but if you really want to make it, I don't know how good it is. Because a fall-back plan is always great – but how far are you going to push yourself if you have something to fall back on? I feel like I work as hard as I do because I don't have that luxury of a fall-back plan . . . you know – I *have* to make it . . . *I have no other option*. (Gurusamy 2017, my emphasis)

For London-based arts and dance producer Hardial Rai, this imperative is critical as it impacts upon the very nature of the work produced. For him the 'struggle' of being an artist summons a calibre of work that comes from a place of necessity. Where this is not the case, 'The artist is not challenged'. In this light he has made a decision not to programme artists for whom their artistic practice is not their primary career: 'I say – I am not going to programme you just because you are very good at it. We know what struggle is in terms of being involved in the arts. The struggle is what makes the work' (Rai 2021).

This view is echoed by another dancer, who spoke at the World Dance Day mentioned above. For her it is precisely the preparedness to embrace precarity because of an overriding commitment to one's art form that marks the boundary between (she implicitly suggests) 'real' dancers and others. Questioning Jayant's assumption of a dual career cited above, she observes,

> A lot of us spoke about the problems we have pursuing dance as a career, as something you want to do full-time and not with a parallel job. But then I tend to think, isn't this what filters us to want to be dancers? There is no fixed salary, there is no proper status . . . so you know to some extent, I believe, that being a dancer comes from having to make this very difficult choice. (Kumudu C., in Kanakarathnam 2015)

In this way the dual-career route, while allowing dance artists to perform on their own terms rather than those of others, and while attesting to the remarkable commitment of many to continuing their dance practice, can also be seen to present a challenge to the professionalization of classical Indian dance forms in Britain, both from the idealist perspective, whereby time constraints can compromise standards of practice, and from the cynical perspective, whereby the lack of an economic imperative on the part of the dual-career practitioner can undermine the demand among the wider sector for proper pay.

Unpaid Work = Amateur (Professional = Paid?)

The tensions engendered between those whose artistic work is their primary source of livelihood and those for whom it is not, as well as by the inherent ambivalences in the understanding of 'professionalism', are not confined to the South Asian dance sector. The following example, drawn from a set of heated email exchanges posted on the Standing Conference of University Drama Departments (SCUDD) mailing list in March 2017, is useful in positioning this debate in a wider context.

The thread was prompted by an email from actor and theatre producer Justine Malone posting a 'Call out to musicians of Oxford' for a theatre production, offering them the opportunity to 'ply their trade in a professional setting' in return for 'beer/wine, free nights out, fun, new friends, a credit in the programme and exposure of your talent', but no fee (Malone 2017). Responding to this call-out, Caroline Radcliffe, a lecturer in theatre, asked that the SCUDD list 'veto giving advertising space to companies not prepared to pay musicians and actors . . . [an] appalling practice [which] just perpetuates the idea that musicians and actors should be prepared to tolerate unprofessional conditions "because they love it"' (Radcliffe 2017). In the course of a series of responses, Malone defended her use of the term 'professional' because 'The company I'm working with have professional practices and create incredible work . . . the only thing that makes us am-dram is that everyone involved has a "day job", but those who choose to be involved are too talented and dedicated to not create new work'. In a subsequent email she adds, 'Cash and quality do not always go hand in hand'. The response from another member of the list is unequivocal: 'Unpaid work (of a polished and professional standard) = AMATEUR' (emphasis in the original). Radcliffe is likewise unimpressed, echoing Bourdieu: 'some people are very privileged and happy to be able to commit time to projects without being paid, but as with the dreadful system of internships, it is only people who have another source of income who can do this.'

As an indication of how widespread this problem is, Equity states, as part of its 2019 'Professionally Made Professionally Paid' campaign, that

> Low and no pay is a major issue for many Equity members. Too often performers and creatives are expected to give their time and energy for free, exchanging hard work for 'exposure' or 'CV points'.
>
> This particularly affects members at the start of their careers, and those without savings or economic support also find themselves priced out of the industry. (Equity 2021)

The dual-career route can be seen to contribute to this problem. While it can offer artists financial flexibility and protection, this very flexibility and protection can undercut the demands of the wider sector, and a more fundamental pursuit of a proper valuation of and respect for the arts. After all, in the words of a further panellist at Khokar's World Dance Day, 'If we could give dancers better salaries, why would they need to do ten other jobs?' (Mayuri Upadhya, in Kanakarathnam 2015).

Profession, Field and *Virutti*

To summarize my argument so far, while 'professionalism' is a coveted attribute (not least among classical Indian dancers in Britain), what it actually means to be 'professional' remains subject to dispute. The inherent tension within the concept between holding an overriding commitment to the occupation professed (or working for the 'love' of one's work)[28] and safeguarding the right to be properly remunerated for one's laboriously acquired skill (working for money) is exacerbated within the 'reversed economy' of the arts, which places a value on 'disinterestedness'. It is further exacerbated within the field of classical Indian dance (in Britain and beyond), which remains influenced by the historic stigma attached to dancing for an income, and (in part as a consequence) a dual-career pathway is a popular choice. Attempts to enumerate the required characteristics of a professional are futile because, returning to Bourdieu's contention, highlighted at the very beginning of this chapter, despite the term's 'appearance of neutrality' (Bourdieu and Wacquant 1992: 242), understandings of 'professional' and 'professionalism' are contingent and subjective. There is apparent agreement, returning to the Oxford Dictionary definition, that a professional is one who is paid for their work, but even this seemingly unexceptional condition is questioned in the light of whether one is being paid for 'recognized' work with a 'recognized' organization. The layers of interpretation attached to the term mean that there are some practitioners, as shown above, who feel that 'professionalism should be redefined' to make not income, but more ambivalent attributes such as 'excellence' and 'commitment' its primary determinant.

An additional complication arises in the form of what sociologists have dubbed 'organizational professionalism' (Evetts 2013: 787). The appeal to 'professionalism' here becomes a disciplinary mechanism, both a 'technology of the self' and a 'technology of power/domination' (Foucault 1980) to 'convince, cajole and persuade employees, practitioners and other workers to perform and behave in ways which the organisation or institution deem appropriate, effective and efficient' (Evetts 2013: 790). These 'appropriate' and 'efficient' ways of behaving are inevitably assessed by a particular criterion, one that has largely been determined from an Anglo-American or 'white' perspective. Scholars and activists have therefore increasingly critiqued the concept of 'professionalism' for ushering in a set of culturally subjective values (normalizing and institutionalizing 'whiteness') under the guise of an 'objective' good (Gray 2019; Urgo 2019; Balarajan 2020). Thus, when it is invoked in the context of dance, Khoo (2017) asks pointedly, 'When we talk about professionalism, what are we really talking about? We are talking about the West and how the West has defined what professionalism is, and unfortunately even in India they are looking to the West to define what that model is.'

As an example, the performance at the Bhavan described at the beginning of this chapter started late, something that constitutes a serious breach of established (Anglo-American) notions of 'professionalism'. However, as Jeyasingh explains, with characteristic clarity,

> The definition of 'professionalism' will depend on me and the kind of people I want to perform to. If they don't mind if I arrive a little bit late or that there is no signed contract – that might be okay if the contract between the audience and the performer is very clear. On the other hand, if I want to perform at Sadler's Wells, then I would have to understand that that's a different contract between audience and performer – and this would mean that I have to have an administrator, that I make sure I am on time, I would have to make sure my copy is good, my marketing is done and I that pack up and leave when I say I will. So, it has to do with the contract between the performer and the audience. One kind of

'professionalism' is different from another kind – depending on what the expectations are. (Jeyasingh 2018)

How has 'professionalism = good timekeeping' come to be an axiom?

In this way 'organizational professionalism' becomes a fresh manifestation of colonialism, a fresh means by which to pursue mastery and subjugation (Singh 2018), and to perpetuate the delusion that one particular group of people has more command and understanding of what it is to be human and how humans 'should' behave than another.

For Bourdieu, a way of sidestepping the definitional morass and the value-laden entanglements of the concept of 'profession' in order to focus more clearly on the underlying concerns that make it important is to dispense with the concept entirely, replacing it 'with the concept of field' (Bourdieu and Wacquant 1992: 242). For him, the most important struggles are those around defining the 'boundary of the field' (ibid.) – who is legitimately classed as belonging to a 'field' and who is not – or in other words, the question of occupational control.

Bourdieu's concept of 'field' is, as discussed in the introduction, and like many of his concepts, (deliberately) hard to pin down. It is a 'network, or a configuration, of objective relations between positions' (Bourdieu and Wacquant 1992: 97). It can be compared (with caution) to 'a game (jeu)', following 'rules, or better regularities that are not explicit and codified' (ibid.: 98), but that are nonetheless recognized and followed by all the 'players' in the game, or agents in the field. In other words, it is a social space populated by agents who recognize the same values, the same weighting as regards different forms of capital and the same 'logic, transcending individual agents' (Bourdieu 1990: 58) as to how the 'game' (or the 'field') functions. Using this shared logic, the agents within the field negotiate their position in relation to others.

Following Bourdieu and adopting the concept of 'field' rather than 'profession' as the tool of analysis (relegating 'profession' and its cognates to their 'proper' position as 'objects'),[29] an investigation into the 'professionalization' of classical Indian dance is a study of the sector's pursuit of its own 'autonomy', or self-definition. It is a question of determining what constitutes the sector's own 'rules' and 'logic' (*doxa*), what it acknowledges as valued knowledge or skills and thereby who is recognized as a legitimate or 'bona fide' member of the field – of determining, in other words, what constitutes 'professionalism' for the specific field of classical Indian dance in Britain.

In this light, a significant source of the tensions and frustrations for classical Indian dance practitioners in Britain can be understood as arising from a situation in which they are uneasily caught between two existing fields, or between two sets of rules and expectations: the field of classical Indian dance on the Indian subcontinent, and the field of (Euro-American) professional dance in Britain.

They are trying to construct a field of British classical Indian dance, which is not yet sure or secure in its own identity. Caught between two worlds, it is hardly surprising that Khoo's perception of the world of classical Indian dance in Britain is that it is 'very confused'. To move forward, he suggests,

> People have to be clear about what they want. Do they want dancers to come out like Kalakshetra dancers? Or do they want dancers who will have the physicality and versatility to be adequate to serve some of the South Asian choreographers in terms of form, but are able to have the versatility of some of the contemporary dancers, etc.? What do you want out of it? (Khoo 2018)[30]

In part, however, the excitement and the frustration endemic in the world of South Asian dance in Britain arise because it does not want to choose. The task of professionalization of classical Indian dance forms in Britain, I suggest, is the task of finding a sustainable and legitimized way of being both, within the same field.

At present, as I discuss throughout the book, and as highlighted by other scholars (Thobani 2017; Kedhar 2020; Meduri 2020), the pursuit of classical dance in the manner that Khoo characterizes as producing 'Kalakshetra' dancers is largely carried out within the South Asian diasporic community, often in the context of long-distance cultural nationalism (see the next chapter), largely unpaid and with little reference to the broader British dance context, which dictates the dominant view of what is valued knowledge and what is legitimate (sharing this view with other fields within an overarching 'field of power'). Arriving from the newly constructed field of (amateur, but expert) classical dance in India, as discussed above, dancers made an uneasy space for themselves within the field of British professional dance by aligning themselves with the (also newly emerging) independent dance field, or field of freelance dance practitioners, a field governed primarily by the standards, values and aesthetics of Euro-American contemporary dance. This positioning is easily understood given both the privilege and relative exclusivity of the world of ballet (another field that classical Indian dance could have attached to), and the catholic ability of contemporary dance to absorb many forms into itself.[31] It was also, as Anusha Kedhar (2020) cogently argues, a positioning that was actively encouraged by Arts Council funding policy from the late 1980s, which encouraged 'innovation' and placed artists seen as innovative 'in not just a different funding category, but also one with more resources' (ibid.: 38). 'Innovation' was defined from a very particular perspective and essentially meant, in the words of dance scholar Alessandra Lopez y Royo (2004: np), 'being expected to engage with a western dance aesthetics – constantly pushing boundaries in terms of presentation, stagecraft, music, the unfolding and development of the theme, and doing so in a fashion recognisably informed by western performance standards'.

Through this adoption, classical Indian dance forms have arguably undergone 'a form of symbolic violence that leads them to recognize the legitimacy of a symbolic order that is unfavourable to them' (Hilgers and Mangez 2014: 11). South Asian dance in Britain, then, in its process of professionalization, remains in the process of determining the specific *doxa* that define it, as well as establishing a 'legitimate recognition' (ibid.: 6) of such *doxa*.

Thus, in the case of the professionalization of classical Indian dance in Britain, layered on to the question of how an occupation monitors itself, attains status and ensures standards is the more specific question of how an immigrant art form from a former colony negotiates its place and identity within the mainstream framework of a formerly colonizing power. A particular harm of the colonizer was that of operating 'as if there were no law, reason, or civilization other than his own' (Mbembe 2021: 227). As touched on in Chapter 1, a corresponding focus in the attempt to decolonize is the bid to rid the imagination of this sense of univocity – both in the minds of the former colonizers and the formerly colonized. Looking at the case of classical Indian dance in Britain, how does it retain its voice, its distinctiveness and its specificity without surrendering to the still potent, almost gravitational pull of an assumption that there is 'one right way to be'? Returning to my seat in the Bhavan's auditorium, with the house lights up, the smiles on the faces of the portraits on the wall seem less benign. Certainly, the dancers are performing bharatanatyam, but let us not forget that they are doing so within the Mountbatten Hall.

Bourdieu provides a necessary caution against the unthinking embrace of the notion of profession without a recognition of the cultural baggage that it imports. The concept of field highlights how occupations develop an internal set of rules, standards and thereby conditions for legitimacy specific to themselves. Considering fields in the light of their relative proximity to an overarching 'field of power' helps explain the relative levels of influence of different fields, and why classical Indian dancers might be keen to be part of the field of contemporary dance, despite the confusions and contradictions this entails.

The notion of field, however, useful as it is, does not ultimately equate to the concept of 'profession'. One could have a 'field' of amateur philatelists – but not a 'profession' of amateur philatelists or indeed of amateurs of any sort. The term 'profession' serves a specific purpose in its invocation of both working for 'love' and working for 'livelihood'; it thereby has an association with economics that 'field' lacks. This is a condition also signified, I believe (from a very different cultural context), by the Tamil word *virutti* (விருத்தி). *Virutti* is a word used to describe a way of life (including the way of life of the hereditary dancers). It also means 'conduct' or 'behaviour', 'nature' (as in one's nature), 'employment', 'business', 'devoted service', 'means of livelihood' and even 'slavery' (Agarathi n.d.). The overlap of meaning with the English word 'profession' is notable, particularly in terms of its dual focus on devoted service at the same time as a means of livelihood. The means of livelihood does not necessarily equate to pay, but it does equate to a means to sustain oneself granted in return for the performance of one's occupation. Returning to the original sense of the word in English, a professional is determined by what they profess – and their life is primarily shaped and patterned by their commitment to the professed occupation. In part, the expertise and legitimacy associated with the professional stems from the expertise they acquire precisely through such focused commitment and allocation of time. As discussed above, unless one is independently wealthy, such focus and commitment necessarily mean that one's profession, as well as shaping one's lifestyle, must also be a primary or significant source of one's livelihood. I suggest that one way to retain the particular meaning of 'profession', while discarding the disciplinarian force (rooted in Euro-American values) that it has acquired, might be to employ instead the term *virutti*.[32]

Of Love, Money and Merit

In this light, counter to the views of several of the dance artists cited in this chapter, I argue, following the lead of Equity, that it is essential that any understanding of profession, professional or professionalization must be understood to be as much about livelihood (which in today's world usually equates to money) as it is about service, commitment and selflessly developed skill (time and love). This is not so as to call into question the expertise of someone who is not properly paid for their skill, but to underline our obligation as a society to pay for and value such expertise. Such a recognition would restore the practice of Indian classical dance forms to their performance outside the realm of the *grhastha* (lit. 'householder') and outside the exclusive realm of the wealthy (and typically high-caste). In this way, while accepting the justice of Bourdieu's critique of the term, resulting in his conclusion that each field (or profession) must set its own terms of legitimacy, I submit that nonetheless, certain attributes can be seen as common across and distinctive to professions. These, I suggest, are expertise, livelihood and legitimacy.

Professionalization, therefore, is about both acquiring expertise and achieving a means of livelihood through that expertise. Where Bourdieu's concept of separate fields is helpful is in understanding that each separate profession (and subfield within that profession) will have certain types of skills that it denotes as indicating 'expertise'. Each profession will also determine how this expertise should be assessed (what is deserving of merit), and thereby at which point to ascribe legitimacy to the 'professional'. The ability to achieve a livelihood will, of course, then depend to some extent on the level of value that the wider society (in particular the 'field of power') places on one's expertise – or to what extent one's expertise is then more widely 'consecrated' or legitimized.

Conclusion

In this chapter I have taken a detailed look at the contested subject of 'professionalism'. A moot topic in any context, it is a status that is especially difficult to determine within the arts, and even more so in relation to Indian classical dance forms, where historic stigma associated with earning money through dance leads to a common perception of 'professionalism' as separate from economics. This has led, both in India and the diaspora, to the phenomenon of the 'dual-career' dancer, distinguished from other dancers and artists with portfolio careers by the demands, both in terms of training and ongoing commitment, that these 'non-dance careers' require. Bourdieu presents an important critique of the concept of 'profession' as importing a specific (Anglo-European) set of cultural conceptions under the guise of neutrality. In response to this, I examine the concept together with the Tamil concept of *virutti* and argue that despite the justice of Bourdieu's reservations, there nevertheless remains a space for the concept of 'profession' as one that connotes an occupation marked by 'expertise', means of 'livelihood' and 'legitimacy'. Where I agree with Bourdieu is that 'the rules of the game', or the principles governing the field, such as what constitutes both the nature and the measure of the expertise that is valued, must be determined by individual professions. One possible way to invoke this concept without its historic Euro-American baggage (though with some wariness as to its possible Indo-Tamil associations) might be to replace the term 'profession' with that of *virutti*.

A notable advantage of *virutti* is its radical incompatibility with precarity. As touched on both in this and the last chapter, precarity increasingly characterises the nature of working lives, particularly the working life of the freelance artist, subject to employment on a succession of time-limited projects – and thereby caught, as Bojana Kunst (2015: 153) puts it, within 'projective temporality'. This is a condition that comes accompanied by a constant sense of 'temporality and alertness' (Van Assche et al. 2019: 139); a permanent sense of being on 'standby'. In contrast to this, *virutti* foregrounds the durational nature of work – and the necessity of such duration for the development of skill. The need for duration to develop expertise is indeed already a condition demanded by a profession, as explored above and in Chapter 4. It is an irony that the increasing clamour around behaving 'professionally' comes at the same time as the increase in short-term and fractured working conditions makes the scope for developing such 'professionalism' less likely. As Kunst (2015: 156–57) argues, 'under the dictatorship of the accelerated time conditions of contemporary production, constant flexibility and nomadism', it can be said that 'everything the artist does is amateurism'. It is understandable that in response, 'the notion of artistic practice has gained so much currency over the last years ... [revolving around a] durational activity that is more sustainable than a project' (Van Assche et al. 2019: 139). Artistic practice becomes a way to maintain expertise *despite* rather than within the demands of work. *Virutti*, in its emphasis on a way of being and a continued way of life, insists on constancy rather than precarity. In this way it confronts this short-termism, together with some of the demands of 'hyperflexibility' that Kedhar (2014, 2020) highlights as part and parcel of the working life of a South Asian dancer in Britain. Against the demand for endless bodily flexibility, *virutti* invokes commitment to an established set of skills; against the non-stop and crisis-based demands of project work, *virutti* demands regularity.

Dance theorist Randy Martin evocatively characterizes precarity as teetering 'between prayer (precor) and debt (precarius), between a wish tendered on a promise, and a claim to inhabit a space or *tenancy held at the pleasure of others*' (2012: 62, my emphasis). As discussed above, despite its apparent opposition to precarity, the meaning of *virutti* likewise overlaps with the idea of 'slavery', bondage and 'devoted service'. In the pursuit of professionalism, aiming to serve both 'love' and 'money', to combine commitment and devotion to one's art form with the need to earn a living, I suggest that 'precarity' comes from the bondage to 'making a living' (within which precarity space must be made to develop skill), while *virutti* comes from bondage to one's profession or skill (which also serves as one's means of making a living). In this sense, *virutti* can also be seen as positioned against 'mastery', the pursuit of which, both in colonial and post-colonial discourse, the English and gender studies scholar Julietta Singh (2018: 3) argues, 'informs and underlies the major crises of our times'. *Virutti*, in its emphasis on service and duration, signals, without ostentation, the necessary incompleteness and the necessary repetition of endeavour, not as cause for despair, but as an act of love. In this way, the promise of 'flexibility', both in terms of the dance idioms and 'flexible hours' of precarious work, turns out only to enslave, while the 'enslavement' of a *virutti*, through its very parameters, turns out to offer a form of freedom. Of course, such freedom only arises when facilitated by the recognition of the need (and therefore financing) of that *virutti* by wider society (its legitimacy) – and I consider the significance of this at the end of the book.

In studying the professionalization of classical Indian dance forms in Britain I will examine the ways in which the field identifies and ensures expertise, its struggles to secure the practice of these dance forms as a means to livelihood and its battle for legitimacy. Although these areas inevitably overlap, each of the next three chapters will focus on one these three areas in turn: Learning (training and expertise); the demand for a specific kind of dancer (and thereby access to markets and the means of livelihood); and the pursuit of legitimacy.

Notes

1. Earl Louis Mountbatten was a British statesman, naval officer and colonial administrator. In February 1947, Mountbatten was appointed Viceroy and Governor-General of India and oversaw the Partition of India into India and Pakistan. After Indian Independence, he served as the first Governor-General of the Union of India until June 1948.
2. Within the British context, there has been an important community dance movement since the 1970s, which emphasizes the importance of dance for all, regardless of age or ability. Community dance can involve people dancing together as a means of expressing cultural identity or as a means to explore a particular dance style. Community dance groups can be led by a dance specialist, but the majority of group participants will practise dance as a hobby rather than as a profession.

3. Mark Broadhead, cellist, personal communication, 20 June 2017.
4. *Oxford English Dictionary*, s.v., 'professionalization (n.)', July 2023, https://doi.org/10.1093/OED/8850904365 (retrieved 16 May 2024).
5. *Oxford English Dictionary*, s.v., 'professionalize (v.), sense 1', September 2023, https://doi.org/10.1093/OED/1106584645 (retrieved 16 May 2024).
6. *Oxford English Dictionary*, s.v., 'professional (n.), sense 1.a', December 2023, https://doi.org/10.1093/OED/9491132837 (retrieved 16 May 2024).
7. *Oxford English Dictionary*, s.v., 'profession (n.), sense II.7.a', March 2024, https://doi.org/10.1093/OED/1119222773 (retrieved 16 May 2024).
8. This is not related to the 'trait theory' found in other areas such as psychology or criminology, other than in referring to specific characteristics.
9. Much of this summary draws on Ackroyd's (2016) clear and helpful summary of the development of sociological theories of professionalism.
10. These are all pejorative terms used by dance artists within the field to describe other dance artists they wish to distinguish themselves from.
11. Bourdieu (1983: 320) writes: 'Thus at least in the most perfectly autonomous sector of the field for cultural production, where the only audience aimed at is other producers (e.g. Symbolist poetry), the economy of practices is based, as in a generalized game of "loser wins", on a systematic inversion of the fundamental principles of all ordinary economies, that of business (it excludes the pursuit of profit and does not guarantee any sort of correspondence between investments and monetary gains), that of power (it condemns honours and temporal greatness), and even that of institutionalized cultural authority (the absence of any academic training or consecration may be considered a virtue).'
12. The link to this page is unfortunately no longer extant. Munger is quoted making a very similar point in a 2012 Huffington Post article (Darst 2012: np).
13. Jeyasingh used this term to describe the middle-class performers of the reconstructed Indian classical dance forms in her keynote speech at Navadisha, May 2016, MAC Birmingham.
14. Wagg relates the tale of Jack Hobbs, a professional player for Surrey in 1904, who was superlatively talented and came to be regarded as the best batsman in the world. Due to his talent, he was claimed as an 'honorary amateur' by the game's elite, with Pelham Warner, the Middlesex captain, affording him the high praise of being a 'professional who played just like an amateur' (Wagg 2000: 33).
15. Literally 'female servant of God'. The term *devadasi*, however, as Nrithya Pillai highlights, is in fact a term 'that comes out of Sanskrit materials that were the focus of European Orientalist scholarship about India. It is not a term used frequently in the historical record (texts, inscriptions, literature, etc.), and more importantly, within these communities that held exclusive rights to performative traditions that were part of their intangible culture' (Pillai 2020: 13). Pillai, who is herself from the Isai Vellalur caste that many hereditary dance artists came from, argues that 'the continued use of the term [*devadasi*] . . . inflicts violence and dissuades women from engaging in both their hereditary dance form and its critical history' (ibid.: 14). Out of respect for her argument and position, I substitute the term 'hereditary dance artist' for *devadasi* in my subsequent argument, except in citations.

See Soneji's (2010, 2012) rigorous work on this area. He agrees that there are references to professional dancing women before this time period, but notes, 'it is only in the Nayaka period [early sixteenth to mid-eighteenth centuries] . . . that the identity of the

devadasi as we understand her . . . with simultaneous links to temple, court and public cultures, complex dance and music practices . . . emerges' (2010: xiii).
16. This performance, called the *arangetram* within bharatanatyam, remains an important social performance today, though ironically rather than announcing the start of a career, it now more often heralds the dance artist's retreat from regular training in dance in favour of pursuing a more lucrative profession (see Gorringe 2005).
17. These included campaigns led by both British and Indian reformers concerned about child marriage and prostitution; members of the Hindu reformist Brahmosamaj and Aryasamaj movements concerned with returning to the 'original' truths of the Hindu scriptures and with 'rescuing' old traditions from a condition of present degeneracy; and one led by men from the community of hereditary dance artists who hoped to challenge the rights of only daughters to inherit property (Sreenivas 2011).
18. As Marglin (1985: 8) comments, 'Even though the new law applies only to the province of Madras, it influenced enormously the consciousness of most English educated Indians regarding the *devadasis*'.
19. Currency converters and inflation calculators suggest that INR 25 lakhs was equivalent to around £30,000 in the 1980s – which is equivalent to about £85,000 in 2024.
20. This may be why the Arts Council was initially slow to create a separate Dance department. It is also why London Contemporary Dance Theatre started out as the Contemporary Ballet Trust, 'the word "ballet" being more respectable than "dance"' (Siddall 1999: 14).
21. Clearly here it is not all artists' pay that is overlooked. The dance artists are still required to pay the musicians.
22. The French name was deliberately misspelt for the Indian context, 'possibly with the transliteration of Nagri [*sic*] script in mind' (Erdman 1983: 253).
23. This can be understood as an embodied lens. See Chapter 4 for a fuller exploration of this concept.
24. By *doxa* Bourdieu means unquestioned beliefs or axioms – 'the world of tradition experienced as a "natural world" and taken for granted' (1977: 164).
25. The importance of India in the hearts and minds of dance artists training and working in Britain comes across clearly in their study, in which 74 per cent of respondents felt that incorporating a link with India in a suggested training programme was either important or extremely important (Gorringe et al. 2018: 79).
26. As the stand-up comic Nish Kumar remarked to Akram Khan during a conversation as part of Dance Umbrella 2020's 'Continental Breakfast', in the context of understanding their parents' reservations about careers in the arts, 'if you immigrate somewhere, you have to try to push your children to do something that the society you are living in deems necessary, so that they don't just kick you out' (Kumar, 2020).
27. She made this point in a speech while serving as General Judge for *BBC Young Dancer* 2017 (field notes, January 2017).
28. Somewhat ironically, this understanding of the professional carries substantial overlaps with the definition of the amateur – or one who pursues a practice or study with no view to financial gain, but only for the love of it ('amateur' deriving from the past participle *amatus* of the Latin *amare*, to love).
29. I follow the lead of, for example, Sahin-Dikmen (2013) and Schinkel and Noordegraaf (2011).

30. By 'Kalakshetra dancers', Khoo means dancers whose training has centred on thorough knowledge of the bharatanatyam vocabulary and *margam*, together with associated skills such as Carnatic vocal performance, *nattuvangam* (the use of cymbals and rhythmic recitation to accompany a bharatanatyam performance) and accompanying theory from texts such as the *Natyashastra* and the *Abhinayadarpana*.
31. For Chitra Sundaram, the more obvious field for classical Indian dance forms to align with was indeed that of classical ballet. Its inclusion instead within the less evidently compatible field of contemporary dance has left the forms with further challenges, not least the emphasis within the world of contemporary dance on innovation and the new (Kedhar 2020). Thus, Sundaram asks, 'How do we work *within* [the contemporary sector in which we have been positioned] and not lose the classical?' (SADAA meeting, field notes, 27 June 2017). While in some ways classical Indian dance is more aligned with ballet, particularly in the valuing of an established canon, an adoption into the field of classical ballet would not have protected classical Indian dance forms from a similar acceptance and espousal of the norms and aesthetic values of Western dance.
32. This would have the added advantage of leaving scope for an emphasis on the aspect of devotion or surrender contained within both *virutti* and 'profession' but eclipsed by a latter-day association of professionalism with 'mastery'. On the contrary, I argue that *virutti*/professionalism is premised on the *impossibility* of mastery.

Chapter 3

Learning
Migration, Identity, and Making Professional Dancers

Introduction

In a warm, brightly lit studio in what looks like a converted house in the suburbs of north-west London, a group of children aged between 7 and 10 are learning the first elements of bharatanatyam. They wear a *kurti* (or long shirt) with trousers, and a scarf wrapped around their waists. They recite a nursery rhyme in Tamil and perform movements along with the rhyme. They leap, knees pushed out to the side in a sort of mid-air *muzhamandi* (a position where the knees are bent out to the side with the heels together, the bottom almost resting on the heels) – heels touching their bottoms, arms sketching a circle in the air, with both hands held in *shikara* (or a thumbs-up position). They practise the seventh *nattadavu*, one of the extensive series of *adavus* or units of movement that every bharatanatyam dancer must learn in order to perform the art form. 'Make sure your back knee isn't bent', the teacher urges. They finish with some *abhinaya*. The teacher asks them to make up stories, and to illustrate their stories with facial expressions and with the *mudras* or hand gestures they have learned. One girl catches a fish and 'puts it in the oven' for her tea. There are no mirrors. The children's mothers sit at one end of the room and quietly observe. Later on, many of these mothers themselves swap places with their children and participate in their own class, their children watching or getting on with their homework. The older women wear 'dance saris' – saris tied to come to just below the knee, to allow ease of movement.

In a leafy part of Birmingham better known for its chocolate factory, two teenagers attend a bharatanatyam class. They are in the teacher's house. Both they and the teacher are dressed in T-shirts and leggings. They perform the *tattikumbattu* or prayer danced at the beginning and end of classes, and after a short warm-up start with *tattadavu* (the first set of *adavus* that a bharatanatyam dance artist learns). The dining table has been pushed back to create space, but it re-

Figure 3.1. A bharatanatyam class taking place in the Dance Xchange studios, Birmingham. 2018 © Magdalen Gorringe.

mains cramped. As the dance sequences become more complex and cover more space, the dancers cannot entirely stretch out their arms to perform some of the movements, and their jumps are necessarily constrained to avoid banging into the ceiling light.

In a large, converted church in West London, smells of the Indian snacks served by the canteen and sounds of the vocal and instrumental Indian music taught in other parts of the building provide the backdrop to classes in a range of classical Indian dance styles. The hall is colourfully painted with images of Hindu gods and goddesses. Here, a group of primarily young girls, clad in uniform white dance saris with a red border, are put through their *adavus*. In another room, dancers dressed in *salwar kameez* (an outfit made up of a long shirt over loose-fitting trousers) and wearing kathak *ghunghrus* (stringed bells wrapped round the ankles) recite the *bols* (or spoken rhythm patterns) for their next movement sequence, their hands keeping time with the sophisticated combinations of finger and palm claps that form the basis for keeping *tal* or *talam* – rhythm – within Indian classical dance and music styles.

In central Birmingham, sharing space with the Birmingham Hippodrome, which houses the main theatre space and the rehearsal studios for the Birming-

Figure 3.2. Prakash Yadagudde teaches a bharatanatyam class in the Hathi Hall of the Bharatiya Vidya Bhavan, West Kensington, London. 2023. © Magdalen Gorringe.

ham Royal Ballet (BRB), are the studios of the Birmingham dance agency Dance Xchange. From one studio issues the slightly unexpected music of the *Natesha Khautvom*.[1] The studios are beautiful, spacious and warm, with sprung floors and mirrors, and built-in sound systems. In one, about twenty young people dressed in tracksuit bottoms and T-shirts learn to embody the different iconography of Lord Shiva. Next door, another group similarly attired is engaged in a contemporary dance class. In yet another, a group of kathak dancers are at work.

Back in London, in a university PE hall, a group of young adult ballet and contemporary dancers are given a short experience of bharatanatyam dance – some basic *adavus*, and a modified version of a dance piece dedicated to Lord Ganesha. 'This movement', says the teacher, showing her arms crossed in front of her body, the fingers of each hand held in a *kartarimukah* or 'scissor' gesture, as if to clasp each ear, 'is an adapted version of a movement performed by non-dancers when worshipping Lord Ganesha. It is an adaptation of a movement from everyday life.'

The settings and demographic of these five 'snapshot' classes reflect a broader reality. Taking a closer look at the pupil make-up of the classes, of all students observed, only two are boys. As with many other styles of dance in Britain, this gender ratio is representative of the broader practice of classical Indian dance. Unlike other dance styles, however, in the first four classes described, the children and young people in attendance are without exception of South Asian heritage, or mixed race (predominantly mixed South Asian and white). Again, this reflects the broader reality of Indian dance training. Despite differences in practice space and attire, four of the five classes are uniform in catering predominantly to children of school age. This is also representative, in part because there is as yet no school offering vocational training for classical Indian dance forms in Britain, as I discuss below.

Looking more widely at the spaces holding the classes, two of the five classes described are taught under the auspices of cultural centres, which serve as gathering points for the South Asian diaspora: a Tamil school and a centre for Indian culture. As I consider later, this is typical of the context of classical Indian dance tuition in Britain, as is the fact that only one of the five classes described is being taught in a purpose-built studio with a sprung floor and mirrors. The fifth class, in a university setting, forms part of a broader dance degree (focused primarily on Euro-American contemporary dance techniques), and aims to give contemporary dancers a brief taste of, and introduction to, bharatanatyam (as one of several dance techniques from the global majority to be 'sampled'). Like the other classes, the students are predominantly female. In this case, however, while a range of ethnicities are represented, the participants are largely white. Again, this single snapshot reflects a wider pattern: where classical Indian dance forms are taught at universities and further education colleges in Britain, they are normally taught as part of a broader dance course aiming to extend the knowledge and range of contemporary dancers, and the majority of these dancers are female and, while from a range of backgrounds, predominantly white. This chapter unravels what some of the different demographics and contexts seen in these snapshots mean for professional training in classical Indian dance forms in Britain.

The performance of almost any dance style requires some degree of training – whether this be a brief rehearsal at a country dance where the 'caller' walks participants through the moves in the following dance; a single dance class, as salsa dancer and scholar Sydney Hutchinson describes her formal salsa training;[2] or the prolonged and intensive training of a ballet dancer in a conservatoire. The nature and duration of the training depends on the demands of the dance form and the context in which it will be performed – the training provided needs to be fit for purpose. In this way training overlaps with livelihood, as where there is employment for dancers trained in a particular style, there is clearly more of an incentive to train intensively in that form. Conversely, where there is limited employment available for dancers trained in specific dance forms there is clearly not the same imperative for training that is considered to meet a 'professional' standard.

The next two chapters look at how a classical Indian dancer is trained in Britain today. More specifically, they look at how training and livelihood are intertwined by asking: how is a *professional* classical Indian dancer trained in Britain today? What marks the distinction between amateur and professional training? What measures are in place to ensure high-quality training – and how is a dancer's competence to practise determined? How does the role that classical dance forms play in nurturing a sense of Indian subcontinental identity within the diaspora impact on the training and development (and recruitment) of professional dancers? What is the impact on a dancer of training in a form outside the context where that form originated? In a context where there is a demand for the ever more versatile dancer, what does this mean for training in classical Indian dance forms?

Though they are interrelated, the range of these questions means that addressing them in a single chapter would be unwieldy. I have therefore divided my examination of the training that is so critical to the creation of a professional dancer into two. While both chapters necessarily deal with both topics, this chapter focuses more on 'training and learning' and the following chapter more on 'livelihood'.

In this chapter I look at the 'how' of training in terms of the broader infrastructure that supports it. What are the institutions available for teaching classical Indian dance forms in Britain, and how do they monitor standards of practice? What are the pressures that these institutions have to navigate? I consider how training in classical Indian dance forms in Britain is pursued for its broader role in providing an education in cultural heritage and the implications of this for the development of a professional dance practice. I also reflect on the increasing professional demand for the versatile dancer, the dancer able to slip seamlessly across dance forms, with a competence in multiple physical vocabularies. Against this reality, how should institutions tasked with creating professional dancers combine the provision of a thorough grounding in classical Indian dance forms with the moulding of an 'industry-ready' dancer? Finally, the chapter looks at the 'who' in this equation. Who trains in classical Indian dance forms in Britain, and who trains in them professionally? Who are the teachers and who regulates them? This chapter combines a sociological and a historical approach, providing a context to training both in India and Britain that will serve as a background to both chapters, before turning to current provision.

The Context: Training Routes in India, Past and Present

To understand the current provision of training in Britain, it is necessary first to situate contemporary practice in its historical context. In the professional practice of the precursors of kathak, bharatanatyam and other dance styles now considered 'Indian classical dance forms', the trajectory of training and the consequent transition from training or apprenticeship to 'professional practice' were relatively straightforward. Looking for example at the model of *dasi attam* (a dance form that was a precursor to bharatanatyam),[3] Ragaviah Charry, the commentator encountered in the previous chapter, writes that a girl who intended to become a dancer would take her place within the teacher's household at an early age (between 5 and 6) (1808: 546) and train under the *guru–shishya parampara*[4] model of teaching – a system of teaching whereby skills and knowledge are passed down through a lineage of teachers.

The *guru–shishya* teaching mode was and remains employed in India across a range of disciplines, from martial arts, dance and music to philosophy and theology, and is in many ways similar to the European model of an apprentice living with the master craftsman to learn their trade. In common with other systems of apprenticeship, this manner of training was immersive, and relied both on 'imitation and intuition' (Chatterjea 1996: 75) – a combination of unquestioning repetition and an understanding of professional practice acquired through osmosis. The *guru*, or teacher, modelled the route to correct practice not only on a professional but also on a personal level (Vatsyayan 1982; Chatterjea 1996; Prickett 2007).

In the case of *dasi attam*, when the correct level of proficiency had been obtained in the eyes of the *nattuvanar* or teacher, the dancer was ceremonially presented to 'an assembly' made up of a knowledgeable audience, including potential patrons. Ragaviah Charry explains: 'when the Girl attains a certain degree of proficiency, the friends and relatives of the Old Mother are invited . . . and the young student's merit examined and assayed' (1808: 546–47).[5] This performance was called the *arangetram* (meaning 'the ascent of the stage', from the Tamil 'arangam', 'stage', and 'erru', 'to climb'). An equivalent ceremony, the *rangmanchpravesh*, was used for kathak, and it appears that with regional variations, training in other dance forms such as modern day odissi followed a similar pattern. Ragaviah Charry continues, 'After this ceremony, and not until then, the set gain admittance to the favours of the public and are asked to attend marriages and other feasts' (ibid.: 547). In this way the 'debut performance' can be seen to have functioned similarly to a large public audition and led presumably to a flourishing or a mediocre career depending on standard of performance.

As discussed in the previous chapter, the erosion of *dasi attam* or *sadir* as a professional way of life led to a shift in the rationale underlying why the dance forms were performed. Instead of being practised as a form of livelihood, they were pursued primarily as a 'serious hobby' or 'recreation', which served at the same time to reinforce a particular understanding of Indian nationhood. Different regional dance forms, deliberately reconstituted and redefined as 'classical', with the reconstructed bharatanatyam serving as a model (Shah 2002), were used in the service of 'cultural nationalism' (Meduri 2001, 2005, 2008b; Weidman 2003; Soneji 2010; Putcha 2013; Purkayastha 2017b), whereby art forms are used to 'regenerate the distinctive . . . character of the nation, mainly through literature and art' (Fleming 2004: 230). In a nationalist 'sacralizing [of] the past' (Guha, cited in Purkayastha 2017b: 125), bharatanatyam in particular was given a pan-Indian status, used symbolically to gloss over local distinctions and differences in an endeavour that 'disassociated the dance from its social roots in highly localised non-Brahmin communities', and enabled a 'nationalised "pan-Indian" reading' of its 'aesthetic history' (Soneji 2010: xxv). Or, as dance studies scholar Prarthana Purkayastha words it, 'Indian dances became major symbols of an embodied national heritage that was consciously constructed to counteract the violence of colonialism in the early twentieth century' (2017b: 127). Applying the lens provided by Bourdieu's (1986) identification of different forms of capital, this meant that while the reconstruction of the dance forms resulted to a large extent in a loss of their role in providing 'economic capital',[6] this loss was made up for by the enhanced status accorded them in terms of 'cultural' and 'symbolic' capital, in serving as the 'poster art forms' for the newly formed Indian nation. Far from the separation from dance as a means to earn a living leading to a relaxation in standards, therefore, it was almost a point of honour for the performers of the new 'bharatanatyam' that the practice of the dance forms maintained the same levels of expertise. Thus, while the significance of dance practice shifted substantially from being a means of earning a living (at the same time as representing 'cultural capital') to being a means to demonstrate individual and collective commitment and investment in the rich art forms of the new nation of India (predominantly representing 'cultural capital'), the value of dance practice remained the same.[7] The emphasis on rigorous training, therefore, remained.

While several prominent dancers from the early period of bharatanatyam's history (the 1930s and 1940s), including Ram Gopal, U.S. Krishna Rao, Chandrabhaga Devi, Mrinalini Sarabhai and Rukmini Devi, received their tuition within a version of the *guru–shishya* tradition, the ban on the hereditary dancers who had supported and been supported by this method of teaching for dance and music meant that this was necessarily in a different form from the teaching tradition as it had existed for the hereditary dancers themselves. Thus, as with the dancers named above, the change in the provenance of students from being dancers of the same caste and possibly even the same family as the teacher to being wealthy individuals from a higher caste (not dependent on the arts for a living), together with the change in the intention behind learning the dance forms, inevitably altered the nature of the *guru–shishya* relationship. It gave it (and its succeeding form, when the middle-class dancers themselves became gurus in their turn) a necessarily different quality and emphasis to that which had characterized the training ground for the hereditary dancers. While the student was still the guru's apprentice in terms of continuing the lineage of the guru's particular style of dance, their chances of employment and livelihood were no longer so closely tied to their relationship with that guru.

During the same pre-independence period, again fuelled by a nationalist commitment to preserving and propagating the Indian arts, a number of institutions were established, offering another model of instruction that incorporated elements from the *guru–shishya* mode of instruction, and yet fundamentally altered it. One of the earliest of these was the Kerala Kalamandalam, established in

1930 by a remarkable man, Vallathol Narayana Menon, who (long before the use of the National Lottery by Arts Council England) conducted an all-India lottery to establish the school (Daugherty 2000).[8] The Kalamandalam specialized (and continues to specialize) in the art forms of Kerala, kathakali, kudiyattam and mohiniattam. Shortly afterwards, Rukmini Devi, with the initial support of the Theosophical Society,[9] established Kalakshetra in 1936, focusing in particular on training in bharatanatyam and associated arts such as Carnatic music and *nattuvangam* (the art of reciting the correct rhythmic syllables and keeping time for the dance with the cymbals).[10]

Post-independence, under the auspices of the government-founded Sangeet Natak Akademi (see previous chapter), two training schools were established, one for kathak (Kathak Kendra in 1964) and one for manipuri (the Jawaharlal Nehru Manipuri Dance Academy in 1954). The first four officially recognized Indian 'classical' dance forms in 1958 were bharatanatyam, kathakali, manipuri and kathak. With Kalakshetra and Kalamandalam already in existence, this meant that there was now a training school for each of these now nationally recognized styles. Since that time a plethora of dance training schools and courses has emerged, offering training at varying levels of intensity. Universities offer degree courses in different Indian dance styles across India, and further dance schools offering training of an intensity similar to that of Kalakshetra or Kathak Kendra have been established – most notably the dance village Nrityagram, established by Protima Gauri Bedi in 1990, which offers training in odissi.

As a result, the current training routes in India include, as dancer, choreographer and scholar Ananya Chatterjea delineates in her dated yet still relevant article: training under the modern-day variant of the *guru–shishya* model; studying at a college or university for 'a BA, MA or even a PhD in Dance' (Chatterjea 1996: 81); training at independently run 'dance schools'; and finally, training at one of the dance institutions mentioned above. Of these, the dance institutions clearly offer the greatest intensity of training. Training with the 'neo-guru',[11] where rather than living with the guru full-time, the student 'lives periodically with him/her . . . or a teacher might hold two-week or two-month intensives', offers 'intensity in bursts', while with independent dance schools, students 'attend class 2/3 times a week and are expected to practice at home' (ibid.: 80–84). Of this method of training, Chatterjea observes, 'training in dance schools can be discounted as a serious system of training for those who wish to become professionals. It is more of a response to the growing middle-class demand for easily accessible visibility, even glamour' (ibid.: 87).

Training Models in Britain – First Steps

Given Chatterjea's sceptical assessment of independent dance schools, it is interesting to note how much of the training within Britain is achieved through this model. There is now an array of dance schools teaching predominantly bharatanatyam and kathak, but also odissi, kuchipudi and mohiniattam, located across Britain. Classes in these schools are offered mainly during the evenings or at weekends, with students usually attending once or twice a week. There are students who train more frequently and there are also instances where students experience a more intensive *guru–shishya*-style relationship in the 'neo-guru' model, staying with the teacher for days and weeks at a time during school holidays. Such intensive one-to-one training is generally arranged privately between student and teacher without institutional support – and the training customarily takes place out of 'standard' working hours: at evenings, weekends, during holidays and (frequently) during a student's 'gap year'. The usual pattern is that the student will receive the bulk of their training with their chosen guru, though it is increasingly accepted for students to attend masterclasses or workshops with other teachers, with the knowledge and consent of their primary guru.[12] In line with this, the regular summer schools run by organizations such as Milapfest, or by the Bhavan, provide important periods of intensity that supplement students' regular training, and many students make a point to keep the dates for these intensives clear to ensure that they can attend (Dutta 2017; Agrawal 2019).

Yet it remains the case that there are no vocational dance schools such as Kalakshetra offering immersive and intensive training, and there are no degree courses available for classical Indian dance. There have been several universities (see Appendix 3) that have offered some training in classical Indian dance as part of an overall degree in dance – most notably the University of Surrey in Guildford, which for many years (until its closure in 2019) offered a Dance BA that provided students with training in four types of dance – ballet, contemporary, African people's and 'Asian' (most recently bharatanatyam, though for several years prior to this the style offered was kathak). As with the example at the beginning of the chapter, however, the training provided in these instances has been aimed not at producing professional classical Indian dancers but more at extending the physical and mental versatility and understanding of contemporary dancers for work within the world of Euro-American contemporary dance.[13]

Some of the earliest classes for classical Indian dance training established in Britain, by contrast, were based on a model different to any of those described above and had a very specific professional agenda – the training of dancers for a company. Ram Gopal first set up classes in Kensington, London in the early 1960s, and attempted to attract recruits through a series of advertisements (including in *The Times* and the *Dancing Times*) in 1962 and 1963 (David 2001). He offered daily classes in four different classical dance styles – Kathak, Kathakali, Kandyan and 'Tanjore' (*sic*) taught by Gopal himself, together with 'other qualified instructors from India'. To attend the classes, one had to apply (by letter only), and attend an audition and an interview.[14] A young Naseem Khan responded to an advertisement in *The Times* and started training at the school, where dancers were expected to train in all four styles. However, only a 'handful of students' (Khan 2017) ever attended and in the end the school 'sort of disintegrated . . . I turned up one day and they said I'm sorry the school is finished and Ram's gone' (ibid.).

A few years later, the Asian Music Circle set up the first 'organised and lasting series of Indian dance classes in Britain' (Khan 1997: 26), employing first Gopal and then the dancer couple U.S. Krishna Rao and Chandrabhaga Devi for a period of two years. In the absence of Gopal, Khan joined these classes. She recalls, 'We had classes in the staff canteen of the Indian consulate on South Audley Street. We did them after hours . . . so the whole place smelt slightly of curry. And that was four times a week – it was very intensive actually. It was Tuesday, Thursday, Saturday and Sunday . . . Many more people came than had come for Ram's classes' (Khan 2017). In terms of the class participants, 'They were a great mixture – a terrific, really good mixture of people who had come through yoga, people who were of Indian origin, some were Indian students who were studying here and then there were English people who were fascinated by it' (ibid.). The students learned repertoire and attained a sufficient level of competence to perform in dance dramas choreographed by their teachers, which toured the UK, Ireland and Belgium. They did not get paid for these performances, but from Khan's perspective, 'we were learning, you know – we didn't expect to get paid anyway – it was part of the training' (ibid.).

At the same time as the Raos were teaching, other teachers were establishing independent classes, among them Sunita Golvala, whose school, Navakala, founded in 1968, is the longest-standing Indian dance school in Britain; the Indian film star Suryakumari, who started teaching in London in 1965 and later founded the (now defunct) Centre for Indian Performing Arts (Harpe 2005); and Balasundari, a Kalakshetra graduate.[15] For these teachers, while there was not a clear agenda to create professional dancers (unlike for Gopal), the emphasis remained on the study of distinctive movement styles. Any knowledge of culture that came with these styles was secondary. Students were often adults, and with these early classes, tended to be more of non-Indian than Indian origin.[16]

Training in Contemporary Britain: Dance as the Tuition of Heritage

> Most of the new recruits [students] are from families keen for their children to remain connected with their culture. Bharatanatyam is not just a dance, but a whole package of Indian culture and identity.
> — Chitralekha Bolar, panel discussion, Navadisha 2016

As this quotation from Birmingham-based dancer and teacher Chitralekha Bolar suggests, the context of Indian classical dance training today has changed significantly from these early models, with their explicit performance and professional focus, and their even mix of Asian and non-Asian participants. Independent arts producer Anita Srivastava[17] believes that there are in all approximately 350 teachers of classical Indian dance forms working across the country, either independently or attached to an institution, with student numbers ranging from a handful to over a hundred (see Gorringe et al. 2018).[18] The largest number of schools is in London, where the director of the Bhavan, M.N. Nandakumara, estimates there to be between sixty and eighty schools teaching Indian classical music and dance (Nandakumara 2017). True to the samples cited at the beginning of the chapter, the students at these schools are most commonly British Asians with parents or grandparents from the Indian subcontinent. As an illustration, of the students taking the exams in classical Indian dance forms offered by the Imperial Society of Teachers of Dancing (ISTD), kathak artist, teacher and choreographer Sujata Banerjee, who is Chair of the Classical Indian Dance Faculty (CIDF),[19] reports that they are 'predominantly Asian – with a very small scattering of non-Asian students' (Banerjee 2017). They are also predominantly of school age (between 5 and 17), though there is a significant minority of young adults in their twenties, and a few older students.[20] Students are largely female – the 2017/18 Yuva Gati[21] intake had fifty students (forty-five bharatanatyam and five kathak), of which two were boys. This ratio is fairly typical and reflects the pattern of gender distribution found within most dance classes in India as much as it does that of ballet and other dance styles practised within Britain. As mentioned above, students usually attend classes with their teachers at evenings and weekends once or twice a week.

Some of these schools are run by South Asian arts agencies and institutions: the Bharatiya Vidya Bhavan (or the Bhavan) in London, Milapfest in Liverpool, South Asian Arts (SAA-UK) in Leeds and Kala Sangam in Bradford[22] all host weekly classes in bharatanatyam, kathak or both, with the Bhavan also offering classes in kuchipudi and odissi. However, most dance classes are organized privately by independent dance artists and teachers, and their schools are primarily run as businesses with the school fees covering the costs of the overheads for teaching, space hire and administration. Over fifty years after classical Indian dance took root with classes as well as performances in Britain, class teachers remain predominantly first-generation immigrants from the Indian subcontinent. Yuva Gati, for example, employs as 'home tutors' twenty-three bharatanatyam and kathak tutors across Britain, the majority of whom are first-generation immigrants from India (Subramanyam 2017). This reflects the wider pattern of classical Indian dance training in Britain. There is, however, a growing number of teachers who were born and trained in Britain, some of whom, including bharatanatyam artists, teachers and choreographers Nina Rajarani of the Srishti dance company in Harrow and Kiran Ratna of India Dance Wales, run very well-attended dance schools.

In common with many other dance forms in Britain, including ballet, jazz and contemporary dance, the first classes in Indian classical dance forms are often given to very young children as an enrichment activity (physically, culturally or socially), with the majority of these classes introducing children to dance with no expectation that they will necessarily go on to take dance as a career. A key difference, however, between the emphasis of the tuition of contemporary dance or ballet and that of classical Indian dance forms, as the opening quotation highlights, is that classes in the latter are for both children and adults, and are often seen primarily as a way of 'keeping in touch with cultural heritage' or roots. Though dancers may go on to start exploring the dance form for its own sake, the original impulse to learn frequently stems from a parental desire that the child is enabled to cultivate links to a cultural heritage outside that of the cultural mainstream (David 2012). Bharatanatyam dancer Saijal Patel reflects, for example, '[It was] mainly culture [that] made me start dancing, because I knew it was related to my god, my religion' (FABRIC 2012). Or as another young second-generation Asian dancer put it, 'In my generation there are many people who don't know anything about their culture. Dance is the only way of getting to know about it.'[23] Similarly, during a discussion group at a training day for Yuva Gati tutors, teachers cited 'preserving heritage and cultural education and awareness' as being a significant role for dance.[24] In their research on the feasibility of instituting a vocational training course for classical Indian dance forms in Britain, Gorringe et al. (2018: 47) found that for 40 per cent of pre-university respondents, 'keeping in touch with my cultural heritage' was the most important reason for studying dance. Writing about the practice of Indian classical dance forms in Britain for the Indian newspaper *The Hindu*, bharatanatyam artist, teacher and choreographer Divya Kasturi sums up this attitude: 'With Indians sprinkled all over this island, the first intent that has come to stay in the minds of every aspiring Indian parent is – "I want my children to learn classical dance, just so they are in connect [*sic*] with our culture"' (Kasturi 2019).

In this way, much of the training in classical Indian dance forms in Britain is delivered in the context of providing a 'tool for cultural retention for a diaspora community' (Nova Bhattacharya, Navadisha 2016, in Gibson 2016: 43). This approach is encapsulated on the website for West London Tamil School, which presents the reasoning behind the introduction of examinations for the (curiously named) Oriental Fine Arts Academy of London (OFAAL) that operates under its auspices, explaining: 'The trustees also realised the value of providing the examination to the children who are living outside the homeland ... OFAAL examination promotes the cultures and values to the younger generation' (West London Tamil School 2018). Clearly, as Priya Srinivasan puts it, 'maintaining links to Indian [or Tamil] culture has become a vital pedagogical tool in immigrant communities' (Srinivasan 2012: 40). Hence, as the title of this section notes, dance as the 'tuition of heritage'.

'Cultural Long-Distance Nationalism', Cultural Policy and the Professionalization of Classical Indian Dance Forms

One catalyst for the marked change in demographic and intention between the classes discussed above and the earliest British classes was, of course, an increase in immigration. As discussed in the introduction, immigration rose initially in response to the call from the British government to Commonwealth citizens to fill the gaps in the British labour market after the Second World War, followed in the 1960s and 1970s by the arrival of the East African Asians and, from the late 1950s on, by the arrival of Sri Lankan Tamils, initially primarily for university education, and increasingly through the 1980s, fleeing the Sri Lankan civil war or the 'troubles' (see David 2005b). Naseem Khan recalls of the arrival of the East African Asians, 'Here – almost overnight – was the support for the Bharatiya Vidya Bhavan, leapfrogging between 1972 and 1977 from a small office to a vast West London cultural centre. Here were the participants for . . . Navakala . . . the Gujarati theatre scene . . . [the dancers] for Navaratri' (Khan 1997: 26).

Unsurprisingly, the new migrants gravitated to cultural centres where they could combat some of the isolation and threat of a frequently racist new home. In 1968 parliamentarian Enoch Powell had made his now infamous 'rivers of blood' speech in which he set the 'ordinary, decent Englishman' against the 'immigrant and immigrant-descended population'.[25] Powell was stripped of his position in the shadow cabinet as a result, but his view was far from anomalous, as evidenced by the many letters in his support and demonstrations in his favour that his sacking elicited. The racial climate of the nation was probably better gauged by these responses (of ten thousand letters and seven hundred telegraphs Powell received, only eight hundred took issue with his views)[26] than by his demotion. Against the background of such animosity, cultural associations provided important focal points through which to provide support networks, reinforce a sense of identity and combat isolation.

There is clearly both a need and a place for the role that art can play as a means for migrants to assert identity in an often hostile and bewildering environment. Artist and activist Rasheed Araeen makes the case eloquently:

> When people are confronted with a hostile or an un-inviting host population, their own cultures can provide comfort. Culture in this instance can provide shelter against what is unpleasant and also compensate for what one is not able to achieve in the new country. It is the right of all people to maintain themselves within their own cultures, wherever they are, and it is also their right to protect their cultures, their creative forms and values. (Araeen 2011: 50)

From the perspective of the professionalization of these dance forms, however, the commitment to dance as primarily a means for a specific regional cultural connection or identity, or, to use the phrase coined by diaspora studies scholar Sau-Ling Wong (2010), for 'cultural long-distance nationalism',[27] means that for many of those attending classes, their sense of identity as a class member is framed first in terms of keeping in touch with Indian or Tamil roots, and only then in terms of being a kathak or a bharatanatyam dancer. In other words, ancestral, geographic or familial connections are privileged above artistic allegiance.

The impact of this prioritization of learning on the development of a professional classical Indian dance sector is such that it is worth considering in greater detail. To do so I draw on Wong's concept of 'cultural long-distance nationalism', which she derives from Benedict Anderson's (1992) concept of 'long-distance nationalism', a term that 'succinctly conveys . . . suggestions of genocentric orientation, the subject's physical removal from the homeland, and his/her lack of embeddedness in the nation-state of origin' (Wong 2010: 10). Where 'long-distance nationalism' is primarily concerned with political intervention in the former homeland (Glick Schiller 2005), Wong's (2010: 9) focus is the 'cultural dimension' of this relationship, whereby 'practices of culture in the diaspora . . . as much as possible given altered circumstances, derive their sense of legitimacy, their standard of authenticity, and often their content from the perceived source of culture – the nation-state from which the practitioners are now physically removed' (ibid.: 10).

This role for dance is by no means unique to Indian classical dance forms. To cite just a few examples, Wong coins the term in relation to the practice of Chinese dance forms in America; ethnographer Barbara O'Connor (2013) makes a similar point related to the diasporic role of Irish dancing; and dance scholar Alexandra Kolb (2013) draws attention to the intriguing role that the Bavarian folk dance *Schuhplattler* played in this regard among anti-Nazi German exiles during the Second World War, as well as to its present-day role in the US. In these contexts, as well as a form of 'cultural long-distance nationalism', dance serves also as a mode of what cultural anthropologist Arjun Appadurai (1996) terms 'cultural reproduction', which Janet O'Shea (2007: 52) helpfully summarizes as representing the way in which 'immigrants seek out emblems of cultural identity because their diasporic position requires the transmission of culture to be explicit rather than tacit'. Periods of significant sociopolitical upheaval or change (such as India's coming to terms with the legacies of colonialism) provoke a similar pattern of explicit cultural transmission, as the precarity of the social context means that cultural reproduction cannot be taken for granted. Thus, as anthropologist Kalpana Ram puts it, 'Predicaments of breakdown, loss and corresponding anxieties about one's culture do not begin with migration for people who have experienced colonisation. Indeed, for Indians, the immigrant situation recreates and gives life to the predicament of colonisation faced by earlier generations of Indians' (Ram 2000: 263).

In this way the function of the classical Indian dance forms in the diaspora continues and builds on the role they had already assumed within the newly developing Indian nation, meaning that they are turned to as a means to allay migrant cultural anxieties because they are 'already understood . . . as a transmitter of what is most representative and prestigious about Indian civilization' (Ram 2000: 264). Thus, just as classical Indian dance forms (particularly bharatanatyam) became a rallying point for a pan-Indian sense of national identity both pre- and post-Indian independence, in the diaspora, they serve to provide a single focal point of common inheritance for 'immigrants [who] left home with [a variety of] local or regional identities' (Glick Schiller 2005: 571).[28]

This role for immigrant art forms was bolstered by British government policy initiatives in the 1970s and 1980s, which promoted a strong sense of identity among 'ethnic minority communities' as a way to mitigate social problems. The rationale for this followed that of the Organization for Security and Co-operation in Europe (OSCE)'s 1975 Helsinki declaration (to which Britain was a signatory), which recognized the importance of 'migrant workers' and sought to ensure the well-being of these workers by encouraging both 'free instruction in the language of the host country', as well as 'supplementary education in their own language, national culture, history and geography'(OSCE n.d.).The belief was that a 'minority' community secure in its own identity would be less likely to cause social unrest – an argument reiterated by Lord Scarman in 1981, in a report commissioned in response to the racially instigated Brixton riots that had taken place earlier that year, when he recommended special funding for the promotion of 'ethnic minority communities' as a solution to socio-economic problems (Araeen 2011).[29] As a result, 'money was channelled by the central and local state into ethnic minority community centres and arts in an attempt to combat widespread alienation that had its roots in racism and material discrimination' (Weedon 2004: 65). At the time, Shobana Jeyasingh recalls, 'there was a huge political agenda around multicultural arts, and it was interpreted as respecting separate identities and allowing space for those separate identities to develop' (Jeyasingh 2018).

While much of this funding stream may have been well intentioned, its effect was double-edged. The result for arts, such as Indian classical dance forms, was that much of the opportunity for engagement with these arts was offered as a vehicle to keep in touch with the 'home culture'. Subsidy for 'ethnic arts' within 'ethnic' community centres immediately distinguished these art forms from art forms such as ballet or European classical music, with their presumed universal appeal. Such framing underscored the idea of these art forms being needed 'to fulfil a specific need of a specific people', rather than taking their place within society as a 'common asset' (Araeen 1987: 19). In this way the 'entertainment and endorsement of cultural diversity' came with a 'corresponding containment' (Bhabha 1990: 208). This move in Britain, though purportedly instigated by the Brixton riots, was paralleled in America. Srinivasan (2012: 39) notes, 'Beginning in the 1980s, the US supported a multicultural policy aimed at a celebration of cultural diversity. In this scenario Asian Americans are valued and encouraged for the exotic, traditional and ancient practices they bring to American culture, but are relegated to the margins and are thought of as aliens, not American citizens.' Srinivasan relates this to theatre studies scholar Karen Shimakawa's theorization of such positioning as creating Asian American bodies that are 'abject bodies' – 'always at the margins, repudiated by the centre' (ibid.).

In this way, it was not only the role of dance within the newly formed India that, as Ram (2000) shows, was replicated in the diaspora, but also the more invidious hierarchies of colonialism itself: the differences, 'politically . . . between rulers and the ruled; ethnically, between a white *Herrenvolk* [race, nation or group believed to be superior to other races] and blacks; materially, between a prosperous Western power and its poor Asian subjects; culturally, between higher and lower levels of civilization' (Guha, cited in Purkayastha 2017b: 127).

The critique of these early efforts at multiculturalism and their effective (if unintended) replication of the dynamics of colonialism is now well rehearsed (Appiah 1994; Bhabha 1994 Taylor 1994; Rattansi 2011; Cantle 2014; Mbembe 2021). While the term 'cultural diversity' was meant to be a fresh concept that addressed some of these issues, for many, it has failed. Its failure is clearly articulated by writer and editor Richard Appignanesi, who states bluntly, 'cultural diversity is a meaningless tautological expression' (Appignanesi 2011: 5). His point is that all cultures are inherently diverse. As literary theorist Edward Said puts it, 'Partly because of empire, all cultures are involved in another; none is single and pure, all are hybrid, heterogenous, extraordinarily differentiated and unmonolithic' (Said 1994: xxix). Or, in the words of historian and philosopher Tzvetan Todorov, 'There are no "pure" or "mixed" cultures, but only cultures that acknowledge and value the fact that they are mixed, and others that deny or repress this knowledge' (Todorov 2010: 420). Used to replace the tautologous 'ethnic arts', 'cultural diversity' merely substitutes a different tautology. Playing on Theresa Buckland's article cited in Chapter 1, 'All Dances Are Ethnic, but Some Are More Ethnic Than Others' (Buckland 1999), the implication of 'cultural diversity' is effectively 'all cultures are diverse, but some are more diverse than others'. The problem with this is that while there have been concerted (and to an extent successful) efforts to improve representation of 'diverse' cultures, the very label conjures something apart. Diversity connotes variety and distinctiveness, but it also connotes difference, unlikeness, 'Otherness'. The effect of this is to immediately question for whom these 'diverse' art forms are relevant or pertinent. Said (1994: xxviii) notes that 'CLR James used to say that Beethoven belongs as much to West Indians as he does to Germans since his music is part of the human heritage'. The early funding of art forms such as classical Indian dance as a means of consolidating 'Indian' identity acted to call into question the universality of a *tarana* or a *varnam*. Cultural studies scholars Chris Weedon and Glenn Jordan argue that in this way the concept of 'ethnic art' conflated 'phenotype . . . and culture' and hence served as a 'form of policing as much as . . . a space for enjoyment' (Jordan and Weedon 1995: 487). Lest 'policing' seem too harsh a word in this context, they remind us that in Britain it was 'often the case that funds granted by central government to "Ethnic Arts" and "Multiculturalism"' came 'not from budgets for arts and culture, but from the Home Office' (ibid.). Rather than the creative and cultural life of the country, the key concern of the Home Office within the

UK is 'to keep citizens safe and the country secure' (Home office n.d.). 'Cultural diversity' was an attempt to shift and improve on this model, but, as Appignanesi shows, while the words may have changed, the underlying import really did not.

In her insightful article 'Decolonising Dance History', Purkayastha (2017b) highlights two forms of 'invisible violence' that she sees as 'constructing Indian dance heritage', which she identifies as Orientalism and Indian cultural nationalism. This latter 'invisible violence', in itself a reaction to the violence of colonialism, has resulted, she argues, in the 'erasure' from the national memory of 'certain dancers and their work' (ibid.: 127), replicating the colonial 'tendency to grant cultural legitimacy to certain bodies, while denying it to others' (ibid.: 129). These same invisible violences, while erasing the bodies of some, have worked to constrict and distort even those bodies they have legitimized. Their legitimization of 'Indian classical dance forms' has at the same time encouraged the status of these forms as (to draw on a distinction made by dance and theatre studies scholar Royona Mitra) 'danced' heritage, as opposed to 'dancing' heritage (Mitra 2017: 41). They emphasize dance forms as 'cultural artefacts' (Agrawal 2019b) as opposed to 'knowledge that is inhabited, relived and transformed' (Akram Khan, in Mitra 2017: 34). They have worked to evoke, in the words of bharatanatyam practitioner Navtej Singh Johar, a 'cultural chauvinism [that] is fed into dance pedagogy', representing 'the antithesis of where I want to go with my dance' (Johar 2021). They have worked to mean that, as Jeyasingh expresses it in the case of bharatanatyam, '[B]haratanatyam came to be valued chiefly as an example of culture and religion and Bharatanatyam dancers to be valued as race relation officers, cultural ambassadors, experts in multiculturalism, anthropological exhibits – everything save as dance technicians' (Jeyasingh 2010: 182).

Lest violence seem too strong a label to use with reference to the development of classical Indian dance forms in Britain as a professional pursuit, I suggest three ways in which it has had a substantive and material impact. These are, of course, interlinked, but I have attempted to analyse them by reference to 'framing', 'standards' and 'constituents'.

Framing

First, 'framing'. As I discuss above, the combination of the natural instinct of new migrants to congregate with others who will relate to their experience of dislocation and anxiety (Ram 2000), combined with Home Office policies aimed at supporting community centres and an immediate Arts Council response to place the burgeoning new art forms 'within the remit of the new community arts panels rather than the artform departments' (Khan 2006: 21), reinforced a perception that 'ethnic minority arts' were 'the province of the communities from which they had sprung and not of any wider relevance' (ibid.). These factors conspired to mean that most classes in Indian classical dance have been and continue to be taught within a context in which the focus is less on the art forms in themselves (with a resulting incidental knowledge of cultural mores) and more on cultural heritage studied through the means of dance classes. This emphasis has simultaneously picked up the reconstructionist casting of dance as a 'noble hobby' – and the two framings combined have served to divert attention away from the possibility of dance as a career, building on and reinforcing the reconstructionist emphasis on dance as a means of cultural rather than economic capital: as a serious 'hobby', rather than a *virutti* (or way of life). Thus, kathak artist Kajal Sharma, in an interview for the ISTD magazine, *DANCE*, laments 'the status that dance still holds as a hobby for South Asians' (Agrawal 2017: 45). Another dance teacher explained to me, 'Parents think of the dance as a cultural thing. They do not consider it a profession' (field notes, Yuva Gati residential, Dance Xchange, 12 April 2017).

Standards

Second, 'standards'. While for the reconstructionists, keen to prove themselves worthy performers of their adopted dance forms, standards of performance were critical, it is not clear that the same emphasis on standards of performance has entered diaspora practice – certainly not uniformly. Where the overriding aim of training in the arts is about 'keeping in touch with one's roots', it stands to reason that the success of this training should be assessed on how far it has achieved this goal, not necessarily on the quality of the training provided. Once this primary aim is achieved, any extra provision in terms of a high standard of training is a bonus. Bharatanatyam artist, teacher and choreographer Stella Subbiah observes of her own classes, held under the auspices of London Tamil School,

> When the mothers come with their children, they come with the idea that they are Tamil. 'You have to learn bharatanatyam'. *Iyal, Isai, Natakam*.[30] So they come with the idea – to learn that. Whereas . . . I still think you need to offer the rigour. Because if you offer something without that rigour, it doesn't stay – there is no residue of it. (Subbiah 2018)

In a bid to open parents' eyes to the possibilities and the impact of standards within dance, Subbiah started a class for mothers.

> As parents, I feel, give them the experience and exposure of coming to a dance school . . . with my ladies I give them the chance to perform in the universities. They used the studios at Roehampton to rehearse. They are going to perform in [the University of] Surrey. So, imagine the impact of this – of rehearsing in studios like that. And this is the first time they have done this. So, in my mind, these are the mothers, these are the parents . . . I'm not saying that they will say no to their kids becoming doctors or engineers, but side by side maybe some doors have opened

for them – I don't know. At least some of their assumptions have been challenged. (ibid.)

In this way, Subbiah hopes to take parents beyond a 'modality of anxiety' about keeping 'the culture alive' (Ram 2000: 262), to take a level of interest in the standards at which the culture is being 'kept alive'.

Lest I be misunderstood, there is a great deal of excellent training taking place in Britain, in some cases as good as or better than training available in parts of India. It is equally the case that people have every right to practise these dance forms as a leisure pursuit for a variety of reasons, in the same way as contemporary dance or ballet, with no particular regard for standards. The way classical Indian dance forms have developed in Britain, however, in large part because of the ambivalent approach to dance as a career, means that as opposed to other dance forms, even where high standards are desired, there is no clear reference point to set a bar for standards of practice. Standards are often compared (frequently unfavourably) to standards of practice in India, though as Shivaangee Agrawal (2019c) argues compellingly, the very different contexts of performance mean that this is not really a comparison of like with like. In the meantime, much training, without the benefit of a clear professional benchmark or motivation, is conducted, in the view of Mira Kaushik, 'like a cottage industry with individual teachers running their own schools'. In her view, 'a lot of the teachers in Britain did not train professionally in India[31] – they trained as a hobby – but they come here and set up schools' (Kaushik, in Gibson 2017: 2). As they lack professional training, she feels that South Asian dance artists entering the professional dance world are like 'school leavers' competing with the 'Oxbridge graduates'[32] who have received professional contemporary or ballet training (ibid.). Continuing with this analogy, the problem for classical Indian dance forms in Britain is not so much that training might start out in a community centre or a draughty town hall, but rather that there is no 'Oxbridge' equivalent of training to either set a standard or to aspire to. Monique Deletant Bell, the former chief executive of Dance Hub Birmingham (and administrative director of Akademi, 2009–15), observes, 'a lot of what you are saying about South Asian dance is paralleled by ballet – I remember going to a church hall . . . but I think the difference is that [with ballet] there are ways, routes . . . to push you up through . . . South Asian dance doesn't have those routes. So, if you are a teacher who recognizes that your student had talent, what do you do with them?' (Deletant Bell 2019).

The reality of 'dance as heritage' and its impact on standards of dance training and on creating an environment likely to nurture a 'dance profession' was recognized by Jeyasingh as far back as 1993. Speaking at a conference coordinated by Dance UK (now One Dance UK) entitled *Tomorrow's Dancers*, she commented, 'the culture of Indian dance training here does not encourage people to look at dance as a full-time profession . . . not to belittle the very good work that exists . . .

but a dance form that relies on weekend, evening and summer school provision is just not going to produce large numbers of professional Indian dancers' (Jeyasingh 1993: 56).

Constituents

Third, constituents. This is, I believe, the most insidious and far-reaching result of the positioning of art forms like classical Indian dance within, as Naseem Khan puts it, 'the province of the communities from which they had sprung' (2006: 21), in that this framing has worked to restrict a broader engagement with the dance forms by presenting them as particularly representative of a specific 'diverse' culture. This has had an impact on who practises and performs the forms, on who is perceived and targeted as a suitable audience and thereby, inevitably, on how successful the dance forms have been in the professional arena. In other words, it has had an impact on the 'constituency' of these dance forms. While it is true that there remain practitioners from a heartening range of backgrounds who work in Britain as professional dancers (in Akademi's 2007 kathak ensemble production *Bells*, for example, three out of the ten dancers involved were of non-South Asian heritage), for a country that has had consistent training in Indian classical dance available for over fifty years, and is purportedly committed to the project of cultural diversity, as discussed above, the number of non-South Asian heritage students of classical Indian dance forms is shockingly small.

An interesting case study pointing to how different policies and initiatives could had led to a very different present is that of odissi dancer Katherine (Katie) Ryan. Ryan, whose family had previously had no connection to India or Indian art forms, started taking odissi classes at her primary school in Bedford, where the odissi dancer (now director of Kadam Dance and editor of *Pulse*) Sanjeevini Dutta was employed as a dance animateur.[33] Importantly, Dutta was employed not (primarily) to increase cultural understanding through a one-off workshop (as is usually the case with classical Indian dance work in schools), nor to explore another aspect of the curriculum through classical Indian dance, but actually to teach odissi as an after-school activity every week. Ryan 'just got interested . . . and as I progressed through primary and into secondary school, with some of my classmates, we started to learn classical repertoire . . . it was an extra-curricular activity and quite a social activity for myself and my friends' (Ryan 2017). Ryan subsequently chose to commit to dance more seriously and is now a professional odissi dancer. What is telling about Ryan's case is that it is exceptional. Where she was offered odissi classes as part of a regular after-school club – and thereby as a routine part of a British cultural inheritance – the more common experience of classical Indian dance forms for non-South Asian heritage children in Britain is of a one-off educational workshop, most often provided as part of a study topic related to 'India' or 'Hinduism'. Where a regular class emphasizes a world 'cultural tradition . . . alive in our countries . . . available to each one of us' (Jordan

Figure 3.3. Odissi dancer Katie Ryan in an abhinaya-*based dance piece.* © *Simon Richardson.*

and Weedon 1995: 482), the more common 'sample' workshop may point to the existence of these dance forms in Britain, but in a context that underlines their Otherness. Hardly surprisingly, the participation of non-South Asian heritage students in classical Indian dance classes in Britain today is something of an aberration, sufficiently unusual to occasion comment.[34] Compared to the fairly even numbers of white and South Asian heritage students reported in the earlier dance classes, it seems hard to dispute Jordan and Weedon's claim that while art forms such as classical Indian dance have been supported, they have simultaneously been 'ghettoized'.

Beyond the recruitment of dancers, the 'different but equal' or 'separate identities' approach that characterizes the discourse underlying the policy both of 'ethnic arts' and 'cultural diversity' has had a significant impact on developing audiences. Obviously classical Indian dance forms have been immediately deprived of all those school children such as Ryan whose more 'normalized' exposure to the dance styles could have led to a wider audience. At the same time, the approach has led to, in the words of theatre producer Tony Graves, the view that more 'traditional' work 'will be of interest to people of South Asian origin . . . whilst also assuming that it appeals to them alone' (2006: 154). Thus, Rajarani speaks of her frustration in attempting to perform classical work 'because the minute you speak to a programmer about it, they will insist that it won't sell'. As a consequence, 'you can't offer a product that no programmer wants to buy, so you have to create something else' (Rajarani 2018). This 'something' has usually meant a contemporized version of South Asian dance judged to hold a wider audience appeal. As a result, as dancer and scholar Sitara Thobani notes, there has developed a situation whereby the division between classical and contemporary performances parallels the division between community and professional, with the 'professional designation . . . most often reserved for performances of *contemporary* South Asian dance – more likely to take place in venues in the affluent city centre and draw more mixed or predominantly white audiences' (Thobani 2017: 108, my emphasis). The diminished audience for professional classical work restricts the need for such work, which restricts the need for classically trained dancers at a professional level. This was reinforced, as discussed in the last chapter, by an Arts Council policy focused on 'innovation', which meant that 'Indian classical dancers, whose work was seen as a re-presentation of a received cultural form, were largely excluded from the Arts Council's funding portfolios' (Kedhar 2020: 38). The resulting lack of employment opportunities then leads inevitably to questions about how worthwhile it is to invest time and finances in training to this level, leading to kathak artist, teacher and choreographer Sonia Sabri's sense of futility about the long years of training in classical Indian dance forms, as seen in the last chapter: 'we train dancers to study bharatanatyam, kathak, whatever the classical form is . . . but actually they then divorce themselves from that and they end up doing contemporary dance' (Sabri 2018). A critical issue relating to the professional training of classical Indian dance forms in Britain, in other words, is the question voiced in the 2010 report into progression routes for classical Indian dancers, 'what are we training for?' (Ramphal and Alake 2010: 9), and one could add 'who will we be performing to?' In this way, while the practice and pursuit of these classical Indian dance forms has been encouraged, their legitimacy has been confined to a very particular sphere – they are practised not as 'British dance', but as the dance of South Asian communities within Britain.

Each of these factors – framing, standards and constituents – can be seen to have a specific impact on three different institutions (or attempts at institutions) involved in training classical Indian dance forms in Britain. While each factor applies to a greater or lesser extent to each institution, it is helpful to look at each case from the perspective of one key factor. The chapter turns now therefore to framing and the failure of the attempt to establish vocational courses; standards and the significance of the ISTD; and constituents and questions for Yuva Gati.

Framing – and the Failure of the Vocational Courses

The interest in a school able to offer intensive, vocational training for classical Indian dance forms has long been present, as I highlight in the introduction, 'for years' before Naseem Khan wrote her landmark report in 1976.[35] Almost twenty years after Khan's report, at the *Traditions on the Move* conference (1993) mentioned in an earlier chapter, observations from the plenary discussion record: 'There was an acceptance that there is no full-time training here, [and] dancers from the subcontinent are better trained; there is a great need for full-time training courses for dancers with accreditation and that the dance training here must prepare students for the performance structure of Britain' (Tucker 1993: 4). A further twenty years after this conference, at a meeting of the South Asian Dance Alliance in 2017, the question of a conservatoire was still moot, and it was noted that Akademi 'has done a lot of ground-work talking to key partners about progressing a conservatoire' as 'currently there is no level playing field in training between South Asian Dance and contemporary dance and ballet' (Gibson 2017: 6). Asked what one thing she would change if she had a magic wand to improve her position as a young person aspiring to be a professional classical Indian dancer in Britain, kathak dancer Tulani Kayani-Skeef answered: 'a vocational school for kathak in the UK' (Kayani-Skeef, quoted in Gorringe et al. 2018: 14). Firmly established in his career, kathak artist and choreographer Akram Khan voiced the same desire: 'my dream is that there is this high-level conservatoire for Indian classical dance, like the stories I heard of Kalakshetra – I wish there was something equivalent to that here' (Khan 2018).

Reflecting this level of consistent interest, there have been a number of attempts to provide such training (see Appendix 2). In 1992, De Montfort University attempted to set up 'the first degree in Britain to offer South Asian dance as a major subject of study in its own right' (David 2003: 6). However, 'due to difficulties experienced in recruiting and retaining staff' (ibid.), and low student demand, the course was disbanded within a year. A little over a decade later, Akademi worked together with London Contemporary Dance School (LCDS) to offer a BA in Contemporary Dance with a South Asian dance strand (either bharatanatyam or kathak). The course opened in September 2004 and closed, after only three cohorts, in 2009. Again, according to Veronica Lewis, then director of LCDS,

> The course didn't work because we didn't have the groundswell of people who wanted to do it . . . We couldn't sustain it. A conservatoire model is a very costly model. We had to have different tutors for bharatanatyam and kathak, as well as for ballet – and we couldn't continue to pay for it . . . The course would never have closed had we been able to attract more students to make it viable. (Lewis 2018)

An attempt by Trinity Laban to set up a BA in Indian Music in partnership followed the same seemingly inevitable trajectory. The Bhavan's director, M.N. Nandakumara, explains,

The first year we had five students. Five was the lowest number that we were allowed to have. So, we were able to run . . . But to get even those five we really struggled. Maybe there are about sixty to eighty schools in the whole of London teaching Indian music and dance. Imagine if each one of those sent one of their students, or even if ten each sent a student, we would have been able to fill a cohort. But when it comes to taking it as a full-time course there remains doubt in the minds of people. For them, taking a medicine degree or an IT degree or an engineering degree is the one that helps them to run their families – and this is a side activity. Very few want to take this as their profession. (Nandakumara 2017

For this reason, the idea of establishing full-time dance training forms no part of the Bhavan's present ambitions – 'We don't have that kind of facility here – and you only to look at what happened to our music degree course!' (ibid.).[36]

As indicated above, this lack of participants for vocational courses is very far from reflecting a wider lack of engagement in classical Indian dance and music, as the number of dance teachers running schools across the country highlights – and some of these schools have students attending in their hundreds. In 2016, for example, bharatanatyam artist and teacher Chitralekha Bolar's school had more than 250 pupils enrolled (Gibson 2016: 38). In 2017 the Bhavan had 140 dance students enrolled, ninety for bharatanatyam and forty for kathak (Nandakumara 2017). Nina Rajarani's school had about 'a hundred' students enrolled in 2017 – and she could have more if she wished; she deliberately restricts the numbers she teaches and has a waiting list (Rajarani 2018). In 2016, the CIDF of the ISTD conducted 1,643 exams for classical Indian dance students in Britain, 911 for bharatanatyam, 497 for kathak and 235 'primary' exams (Brown 2018). This number accounts only for those teachers who choose to admit their students for ISTD exams (according to the CIDF chair Sujata Banerjee, this was about seventy at that time; Banerjee 2017) and does not include students from, for example, the Bhavan and the many Tamil schools that conduct their own examinations. If Srivastava's estimate cited above of 350 dance teachers is correct, there are about another 280 teachers across the country who have chosen not to send their students for ISTD exams.

With such a groundswell of uptake at the level of pre-vocational training, what accounts for the lack of uptake for vocational training? The framing of the pursuit of classical Indian music and dance as primarily a means to maintain links with cultural heritage – as 'noble hobbies', or as Nandakumara puts it, 'side activities' – diminishes the attention paid to these art forms as potential careers. Equally, the restricted constituents, or the perception of restricted audiences, for classical Indian dance forms means that there are then limited employment opportunities for classical Indian dance artists who might opt to be vocationally trained. In this way, the 'framing' and the 'constituents' of pre-vocational training, together with the wider 'framing' and therefore 'constitutive audience' for classical Indian dance in Britain, combine to impact upon 'standards' by effectively restricting the numbers of those likely to pursue a vocational course – making the running of such courses unsustainable.

As I discuss throughout, while the difficulties of finding work as a contemporary or ballet dancer are well known (Burns and Harrison 2009; Sommerlade 2018), there are nonetheless over a hundred established contemporary dance companies based in Britain and Europe alone.[37] These companies offer auditions and employment to contemporary dancers, meaning that a young student can embark on their training with the aspiration to work for companies such as those of Rambert, Jasmin Vardimon or Hofesh Shechter. The strength of this dream encourages the risk to devote everything to dance on the chance of making it. There is little such incentive for a classically trained Indian dancer – even as an aspiration. For many years, Jeyasingh's company and subsequently Angika (1998–2008)[38] provided the 'aspiration push' at least for bharatanatyam dancers. As described in the introduction, however, Jeyasingh's company now more often primarily comprises Euro-American-trained contemporary dancers. If a classical Indian dancer wishes to take dance as a career, therefore, the dream must involve being prepared to choreograph, coordinate, market and fundraise themselves (as well as dancing in their own work). This is a tremendous ask from a young school leaver. Indeed, for Agrawal, expecting young dancers to make this choice without clearer career pathways in place borders on the unethical: 'I don't think there are any 16/17-year-olds who would commit to doing this full-time – and that it is not realistic or even fair to ask them to do this when there are no career prospects available. I don't think that it is right to ask them to finance such a course with no career prospects' (Agrawal 2018).

While the lack of employment, or the necessity to form and run their own company, may turn out to be the reality for many (even most) young graduate contemporary dancers, they are at least able to embark on their training with the goal of working as a dancer in one of many existing companies. The addition of the classically focused Seeta Patel Dance (bharatanatyam), Amina Khayyam Dance, Pagrav Dance (both kathak) and Jaivant Patel Dance (kathak, but with an interest in showcasing other classical forms) as 2023–26 NPOs promises to make a significant difference here – at least as long as they remain in the portfolio. However, while there is no repertory company equivalent to Rambert for contemporary dance or a national ballet company, the demand for the classically trained dancer will always depend on the interests of the company's artistic director.

The framing of classical Indian dance forms as particularly relevant to their own communities has thereby impacted both on the likelihood of students to perceive these forms as a potential career, and, through restricting potential audiences, on the possibility of providing those interested with a viable career should they want one. This has led to the lack of a critical mass of students for vocational courses, meaning that despite the perceived need for more intensive training and despite the committed attempts to make this provision, as yet there is none. In terms of professional dance training this means that there is no obvious progression route for committed and talented dancers beyond school age; there is still not the central institute to set standards that Naseem Khan hoped for in 1976; and finally, the best provision for classical Indian dancers in Britain – whether aiming to be amateur or professional – is through weekend and evening classes, with supplementary intensives with their gurus or at summer schools. For Jeyasingh (1993: 56) such training 'attracts a different kind of person – either enlightened amateurs or a few very determined mavericks who will make it despite all obstacles. It is certainly not conducive to producing dancers, a profession of dancers, saying "this is what we want to do for a living."'

Jeyasingh wrote this over twenty-five years ago, but her words remain relevant to the practice of Indian classical dance in Britain today. Under this model, as is borne out by the trajectories into dance of many of the professional dancers currently working in South Asian dance in Britain, dancers emerge into the professional world more by accident than design. They continue to be 'the determined mavericks' who make a decision to give a career in dance 'a go', often after they have made their first steps towards a different career.[39]

Standards and the Classical Indian Dance Faculty of the ISTD, or 'Kaushik's Campaign'

Given this lack of options for more serious study, the standards of teaching in these weekend and evening dance classes assume a proportionately greater significance in laying the groundwork for the British professional classical Indian dancers of the future. It was in part the recognition of this, together with frustration with unqualified teachers, tutor isolation, a lack of structured learning and uneven standards of dance training, that led Mira Kaushik in 1999 to initiate one of the significant attempts to professionalize the teaching of classical Indian dance in Britain, leading ultimately to the creation of a South Asian Dance Faculty within the ISTD (now the Classical Indian Dance Faculty).

In this attempt, Kaushik was treading a familiar path – in fact her concerns echoed those of the founder of the ISTD, no less, the Victorian dance educator and reformer Robert Crompton, briefly mentioned in the previous chapter. At the end of the twentieth century, the position of dance teachers in England was marked by many of the same issues that beset South Asian dance in Britain today: insularity, the lack of means for professional representation and a lack of clarity around standards for dance practice, meaning that a number of dance classes were taught by 'so-called professors . . . who . . . certainly had no qualifications to teach that which they themselves but imperfectly performed' (contemporary periodical *The Novice*, cited in Buckland 2007: 10). A key figure in addressing these challenges was Robert Crompton, and he conducted a 'systematic campaign for the realisation of a British professionalised society of dance teachers' (Buckland 2007: 22) as part of his efforts to unite and regulate dance teaching in Britain. This resulted in the foundation of the ISTD (or the ISDT – as it was originally the Imperial Society of Dance Teachers)[40] in 1904, of which he was the first president. I title this section 'Kaushik's Campaign' (echoing Buckland's 'Crompton's Campaign') in recognition of the common motivation behind both these attempts at reform.

The ISTD has grown over the years to encompass eleven faculties, offering syllabi and examinations for a range of dance styles including Classical Ballet, Latin American Dance and Disco/Freestyle/Rock 'n' Roll, with the CIDF being one of the younger faculties. The ISTD's focus is on ensuring and monitoring excellence of teaching standards, as well as ensuring that teachers cover an agreed syllabus or structure of content through their teaching. The completion of ISTD examinations does not in itself equate to vocational training for a performing artist, and the majority of those taking them focus on dance as a recreational pursuit (Brown 2018). However, just as with music grades in European classical music, the examinations provide a clear structure for students who may then proceed to more intensive vocational training, and the ISTD does now offer a selection of examinations geared more towards those wishing to take dance as a profession (the Advanced 1 and Advanced 2 levels). Despite many dancers pursuing the examinations as a leisure activity, as the ISTD's Artistic Director Ginnie Brown points out, 'there is a healthy through flow of dancers [taking ISTD] exams who go into the profession', so 'there is a strong connection between the recreational and vocational side of things' (ibid.). The ISTD also offers a Diploma in Dance Pedagogy, with a route from this to obtaining the QTLS (Qualified Teacher Learning and Skills) status that is equivalent to a PGCE (Postgraduate Certificate in Education), allowing for salaried employment within a school.

Prior to the creation of this faculty, there had been no central body within Britain to monitor the teaching of Indian classical dance forms within independent dance schools and to provide a sense of quality assurance to parents and students. A number of schools connected to larger institutions, including the Bhavan, the Centre for Indian Classical Dance in Leicester (CICD) and certain of the Tamil schools (including West London Tamil School), devised their own syllabi and examination systems, or adopted syllabi and examinations from India to both motivate students and provide some means of assessing standards. While these measures were sufficient for many, for Kaushik, this meant the adoption of 'many South Asian qualifications and imported systems [that] suffered from outdated syllabi irrelevant to the British education system and incoherent assessment infrastructures' (Kaushik, cited in Sundaram 2014: 3). She was further informed by her own experience as director of Akademi, overseeing the classes that the then Academy of Indian Dance itself ran in different locations across London in its early days. She recalls taking over as director in 1988 and realizing that 'Akademi had teachers who were teaching classes in different locations . . . Surbiton, Holland Park, etc. [different suburban areas of Greater London] – and there was no way of managing these classes. They were the personal territories of the individual dancers who were being paid by Akademi but doing whatever they wanted. A lot of the classes, I was told, were being used as rehearsal spaces' (Kaushik 2017a).

A desire to raise standards, together with a sense that Akademi should avoid replicating work being done by other organizations, such as the Bhavan, motivated Kaushik to rethink the role she wanted her organization to play, with the result that Akademi hired 'someone to look at the strategic development of Indian dance and a project that would impact the whole country and the world. And that was the beginning of [the Classical Indian Dance Faculty] of the ISTD' (Kaushik 2017a).

The formation of a faculty required the submission of syllabi for kathak and bharatanatyam, and Akademi's research for acceptable syllabi was lengthy and inclusive. It took the form of a three-year research project, notably funded by Arts Council England, led by kathak dancer Sushmita Ghosh, and 'involved consulting over a hundred teachers of classical Indian dance in Britain and abroad and sampling their existing curricula' (Sundaram 2014: 2). Recognizing the variations among the different schools or styles of bharatanatyam and kathak taught in Britain (*banis* for bharatanatyam, *gharanas* for kathak), the syllabi have been deliberately designed to be sufficiently flexible to accommodate the manifold variations in style. The bharatanatyam syllabus, for example, specifically acknowledges that *adavus* 'vary from school to school' (ISTD South Asian Dance Faculty 2000: 19). The agreed syllabi are delivered to match the examination structure that applies across all faculties in the ISTD (a Primary Class exam, a general grade 1 to 6, followed by four 'vocational' training qualifications), examinations that 'operate in the Regulated Qualifications Framework by the Office of the Qualifications and Examinations Regulator (Ofqual)'. Further, 'the Customer Services and Quality Assurance Department monitors the activities of the organization and working of the examinations processes to ensure that the ISTD meets the criteria of the Regulators in every respect' (ISTD n.d.a). The ISTD 'achieved Government recognition in November 2000 and was further recognised to operate in the Qualifications and Credit Framework in 2010 (now the Regulated Qualifications Framework) by the Office of the Qualifications and Examinations Regulator (Ofqual) in England' (ibid.). It is dependent for its knowledge of the different dance styles it examines as well as for its 'development of a particular technique through courses and syllabi updates', on its individual Faculty Committees, each made up of genre representatives elected by a ballot of their 'full-teaching and life members' every three years (ISTD n.d.b).

In several ways, the creation of the CIDF within the ISTD has been a remarkable success story. The faculty is growing every day (Banerjee 2017) – and even the Bhavan (which has long been content with its own examination structure) has made clear its preparedness to offer ISTD exams to those who would like them (Nandakumara 2017).[41] In September 2013, the ISTD faculty newssheet reported that 'the number of ISTD's classical Indian dance examinations has increased by about 300% over the past year!' (ISTD 2013). As mentioned above, in 2016, the CIDF conducted 1,643 examinations for students in Britain.[42] In 2017, at Navadal, a national youth dance competition for young dancers organized by Akademi, the winners for both solo and group performances for bharatanatyam and kathak were ISTD students, as were the *BBC Young Dancer* South Asian category winners for the three original versions of the competition – Vidya Patel (2015), Shyam Dattani (2017) and Shree Savani (2019).[43] Several of the younger generation of successful professional or semi-professional Indian classical dancers who have trained in Britain are ISTD students, including Aakash Odedra, Jaina Modasia and Vidya Patel. Teachers who have adopted it are warm in its praise. Pushkala Gopal, one of the most respected and sought-after of the bharatanatyam teachers in Britain,[44] feels that it is 'one of the most brilliant things' to have happened for the teaching of classical Indian dance forms in Britain, arguing that 'the ISTD movement has awakened the community' (field notes, 27 March 2018). Admittedly, as an ISTD examiner and long-term faculty committee member (as well as being prominently involved in the consultation process for the syllabus), Gopal's perception of the ISTD's role is likely to be positive. The very number of teachers who have adopted it, however, testifies to its value, and to its success in offering a syllabus with a sufficiently coherent structure to be useful to teachers, while remaining sufficiently flexible to embrace variations in technique without teachers feeling forced into a single mould. The emphasis placed from the beginning on inclusivity has led to an acceptance of and respect for stylistic variations that is built into the syllabus and helps it to resist any tendency towards homogenization or the flattening of distinctions in style that a single syllabus might otherwise encourage.

The CIDF has achieved much in terms of professionalizing the teaching of Indian classical dance forms, and thereby in helping to develop potential professional dancers. It provides a clear framework of achievement for students; it encourages collegiality and combats isolation among teachers by providing an umbrella body that can offer support, opportunities for networking and continued professional development, together with a route to qualified teacher status for work within schools. It also encourages a baseline of good practice in terms of urging teachers to be DBS-checked,[45] insured and committed to continued professional development. The health and safety of students is integral to its thinking – and the syllabi emphasize the importance of warm-ups and cool-downs, as well as offering suggestions for style-specific body exercises. It offers two qualifications specifically geared to the vocational practice of dance. Moreover, the inclusion of the faculty has helped to establish classical Indian dance forms more firmly on the map of dance practice within Britain. There are a number of events run by the ISTD including some student showcases and teacher-training residencies that are open to members from across the different faculties, and this provides an occasion for a growing awareness of classical Indian dance styles, and conversely, a growing awareness among classical Indian dance practitioners of the culture and practice of other genres. In 2017 Shyam Dattani featured on the cover of the July–September edition (issue 480) of *DANCE* (the ISTD membership magazine), and the magazine regularly features news and images from the CIDF. Such exposure is critical in normalizing the presence of classical Indian dance forms in Britain and underlining their presence in the 'mainstream'.

In the face of this glamorous appearance of commercial, international and artistic success, however, there are those who raise concerns. Part of the work of SAA-UK in Leeds is to provide classes in bharatanatyam and kathak. The director, Keranjeet Kaur, was keen to take on the ISTD model. She trained in ballet as a child, and for her the 'ISTD offers the framework that we need to take a young person on a complete journey where they develop all the techniques that you need, on par as I did with ballet'. However, she soon found herself facing a situation in which 'parents got into the habit of wanting [their children] to jump through hoops and just get grades' (Kaur 2017). In an attempt to counteract such speed grade taking, she has made it a rule that at SAA-UK, pupils only take grades every two years. After all, as she points out, 'Given that they [the students] are only meeting once a week and probably only for an hour – you have to do your file work, theory, technique, dance piece, music – on a once-a-week basis thirty weeks a year is just unrealistic to achieve a grading – if you want to do it with excellence and quality' (ibid.).

This echoes a concern that dancer, teacher, animateur and former director of Yuva Gati Anusha Subramanyam (2009–2018) raised with dance scholar Stacey Prickett while Prickett was writing about the ISTD exams in 2004. Subramanyam had been involved in the consultation process for the syllabus and explained that it offered an idealized vision of a training programme – what would be accomplished without time constraints. When her own students took the exam, however, she realized how difficult it was to really cover the material suggested in the space of a year (Prickett 2004). Kathak artist and teacher Nilima Devi makes a similar point. Talking about the process of devising the syllabus, she comments, 'I sent my syllabus to Sushmita [Ghosh] and said – I've developed a course based on once a week for one hour. Then Sushmita developed a course based on thrice a week for three hours plus one-hour everyday training at home. And I objected, saying that my experience shows that people will not do it. It is unrealistic' (Devi 2017).

The concern is that if students are studying for an hour a week what they should be studying for three hours (with five hours of independent practice), how far can they genuinely grasp and embody what they are taught? And if students are passing exams without such genuinely embodied knowledge, what does this say about the exams and their standards? Yadagudde (2017a) commented on his experience of pupils joining his classes from other teachers: 'many people come here [and] they say they have done the fifth grade or fourth grade, but I don't know what they have learned . . . The syllabus is very strong – I'm not questioning that . . . but some of them, they come with a certificate, but they still have to start from the beginning.'

This inevitably raises questions about the quality of the examinations and the examiners themselves. Kaur (2017) explains that a number of teachers she encounters are resistant to the ISTD because 'they are not sure about how skilled the adjudicators are. So, there are questions about how they adjudicate, whether they have got a bias about certain things. How neutral, or how objective are these adjudicators – and what training do they go through in order to be an adjudicator?'

From the perspective of professional dancers, when these standards are in doubt, the value of passing the vocational exams is then immediately spurious, as one dancer found to her cost: 'We already have a series of robust qualifications for the sector in the shape of the ISTD exams, and people don't care about that. It wouldn't [sic] matter. I have aced all my ISTD exams, and it makes no difference' (cited in Gorringe et al. 2018: 44). Indeed, for Yadagudde (2017a) the very focus on examinations is bewildering: 'When I was learning there was no exam for anything . . . It's my ability to dance that got me a job here [the Bhavan]. My qualifications . . . nobody bothered about it . . . Only in the Western culture you have to have such things.' Akram Khan voices a similar scepticism.

> My exam was on stage – that's the real exam. An exam in an academic environment – an exam in a school kind of way – to tick off something, to get a percentage – that was not my training. My training was on stage – in the class and the stage. I enjoyed the study for the exams but they are not what made me – absolutely not. (Khan 2018)[46]

The most forthright criticism of the ISTD exams comes from the visionary behind them, Kaushik herself.

> When I dreamt of [the] ISTD, it was an opportunity for contemporization and updating and for bringing classical Indian dance teaching practices into [the] twenty-first-century UK . . . It's a great achievement for the sector to have reached where they are. But the problem is that they think that [the] ISTD is the beginning, middle and end of everything. They think that an ISTD grade 6 certificate is going to make the future of dance in this country . . . but they don't see that aged 18 a student

who has done part-time training and graded exams is now barely ready to go for an audition to get into a dance school. They are not professional dancers . . . So, this is where we need to really open up, we need to see, we need to become brave, we need to look beyond that and say what is it we really mean by a professional dancer? (Kaushik 2017b)

Once again, as Jeyasingh raised in her role as judge on *BBC Young Dancer* (see Chapters 1 and 2), the question of standards collides with the question of time. The body is a stubborn instrument, and takes time to embody movement patterns, as I discuss at greater length in the following chapter. Where such time is not allocated, what does this say about standards of practice?

Chitra Sundaram, echoing Khan and Yadagudde above, argues that for a performing artist, exams are an irrelevance, and standards are best assessed in the context of performance to an informed audience: 'If you are focusing on performance – this is where we return to the market economy – you give dancers the chance to perform. Then the audience will decide – or the critic – those learned among them will decide' (Sundaram 2018). This viewpoint suggests a return to a modern-day equivalent of the *arangetram* or *rangmanchpravesh* described at the beginning of the chapter, and resonates with the findings of Potter and Alter, mentioned in the previous chapter, that success as a professional is associated with the 'act of dancing regularly with a recognized company' (Alter 1997: 73). This confronts us again with the inescapable interweavings of cause and effect as we are returned to the familiar question of performance of what and for whom, which leads naturally to the next section – on 'constituents' and Yuva Gati.

Constituents and Questions for Yuva Gati

As discussed, a lack of clear employment opportunities for classically trained Indian dancers, partly due to the actual or perceived lack of audiences for classical Indian dance, has contributed to the non-viability of a school for vocational training in these styles. While the opportunities and demand for classical dancers wane, however, there is increasing demand for the bilingual dancer, fluent in classical Indian as well as Euro-American contemporary dance. One choreographer told me, 'There aren't enough dual-trained [Euro-American contemporary and classical Indian] dancers' (personal communication, post-show event, South Bank, 24 May 2017). This demand was a key motivator in setting up the short-lived BA in Contemporary Dance (South Asian Dance Strand) at LCDS, a school established in 1969, initially to train dancers in Graham and Cunningham contemporary dance techniques to equip them for work with London Contemporary Dance Theatre (see also Chapter 5). Veronica Lewis explains that the course was instituted to meet 'the perceived need for adequately trained dancers who could traverse the boundaries of contemporary and bharatanatyam/kathak, to serve the needs of working choreographers . . . We were hoping to create dancers fluent in both South Asian and contemporary dance – versatile in both' (Lewis 2018).

This emphasis on versatility reflects a global trend that impacts across dance styles. Dancer, choreographer and scholar Melanie Bales describes the process within contemporary dance practice whereby 'Training has become eclectic . . . dancers engage in a wider range of styles and classes in order to be technically and stylistically viable to more choreographers' (Bales 2008: 16). As Susan Leigh Foster argues, this trend is fuelled by economic need – dancers train to increase their employability. The result is what she calls the 'hired body', whereby the dancer's body 'does not display its skills as a collage of discrete styles, but rather homogenizes all styles beneath a sleek, impenetrable surface. Uncommitted to any specific aesthetic vision, it is a body for hire – it trains in order to make a living at dancing' (Foster 1997: 255). The demand for the versatile dancer had an impact not just on this course at LCDS. Its influence can also be seen on the third training initiative for classical Indian dance forms in Britain that I wish to discuss – Yuva Gati.

Yuva Gati is the South Asian dance strand of the Centres for Advanced Training (or CATs) and is the only way by which government funding is directly channelled to support training in classical Indian dance forms in Britain.[47] The CATs were initially established as the result of research commissioned by the Advisory Panel for the Music and Dance Scheme (MDS) (now part of the Department for Education), in 2003. The research recognized a need to ensure that all young people are able to access music and dance training regardless of their background, and the MDS started to establish CATs across the country to address this need.[48] CATs are about nurturing talent for the dance profession, their aims explicitly including 'raising the profile of dance as a career option', 'providing opportunities for students involved in the programme to engage with professionals working in the world of dance and providers of vocational training' and 'to nurture the next generation of dance students – and ultimately dance artists'.[49] Aimed at 11–18-year-olds, they provide a 'pre-vocational' training, aiming to give young students a sufficiently solid technical foundation, together with the motivation, inspiration and information to encourage them to pursue dance as a career.

While they initially focused on contemporary dance or ballet, a South Asian dance CAT (named Yuva Gati in 2013) was piloted between January and August 2009, with the first full academic year starting in September of the same year. It is based at and administered by the Birmingham-based national dance agency Dance Xchange,[50] working in partnership with South Asian arts agency Sampad, also in Birmingham. Unlike the CATs for other dance genres, which operate for a whole day on the weekend every week during termtime, and which cater for students from the region, the South Asian CAT in Birmingham serves students across the country. It therefore operates on an intensive project basis, running residential courses during school half-terms and holidays. Training during the week is supported by 'home tutors', or the students' regular teachers.

Given their professional orientation, the test of success for other CAT schemes lies in part in how many of their graduates progress to vocational training courses. As discussed, no such courses exist for classical Indian dance forms, to the frustration of Subramanyam: 'This year we have three people graduating, who want to be professional dancers – we can't send them anywhere. Last year we had two dancers who wanted to take up dance professionally – we couldn't send them anywhere' (Subramanyam 2017).

In the absence of such a measure, programme administrators suggest as a marker of success for the programme the production of 'industry-ready dancers' (Henwood and Lewis 2018). This inevitably begs the questions for which industry, and in what capacity? As 'classical Indian dancers' in classical Indian dance choreography? Or as 'South Asian' dancers with the versatility to perform within contemporary dance work? As discussed, the latter is the work where there is a demand, the most likely to provide a dancer with an income and the work most commonly designated professional (Kedhar 2014, 2020; Thobani 2017; Meduri 2020). Given this reality, how should these potential professional dancers be trained?

Life coach and dance manager Jane Ralls, part of the team who initially helped set up Yuva Gati (then simply the South Asian dance CAT), recalls the complexities involved in drawing up a suitable programme: 'there was a lot of discussion around how far it should be contemporary/fusion and how far it should be classical, so the content of the curriculum took a while to be shaped' (Ralls 2018). For Subramanyam, an element of contemporary dance training is a critical part of Yuva Gati training because 'our young dancers – they are training here in the UK . . . whether or not they take it as a career, they *live* here. I would like to see them have a dialogue with the wider dance sector, their peer groups' (Subramanyam 2017, emphasis original).[51] For Dance Xchange's Head of Learning and Participation, Alexandra Henwood, the overriding aim of Yuva Gati training is in 'the more classical form – the repertoire and the set vocabulary' (Henwood and Lewis 2018). However, the character of the professional dance world, as discussed, means that this aim then conflicts with Yuva Gati's other aim to 'nurture and develop confident, highly skilled, creative and adaptable dance artists, with exceptional dance technique, who are well prepared for the rigours of professional dance training and future careers in dance' (CAT Associate Artistic Director call-out, email, 30 August 2018). Thus, 'over the years we have introduced yoga and contemporary dance alongside the bharatanatyam and kathak training to enhance the classical training, and also to add another element to their learning to *keep it in the contemporary context and in the professional world* as well' (Henwood and Lewis 2018, my emphasis). Ultimately it is this pragmatism that leads the way:

> Some of our students are very classical and traditional and that's fine, we support that journey, but we also want to equip them with the skills to

operate in the dance world in any form, so what we try and do is make them versatile enough to ensure that they can have a self-sustaining dance career, whether that is in the wider dance sector or whether they stay true to their own traditional dance roots . . . and obviously contemporary has a much wider spread. South Asian dance is definitely present, but it's a smaller strand in some senses – so we try to give them everything we can in terms of skills so that they can be in whatever area they decide to be in. (ibid.)

Thus, as Subramanyam (2017) puts it, the students are offered 'training to enable our young pupils to become a versatile dancer. So, we are training them in bharatanatyam, in kathak – they also get training in contemporary dance, yoga, Pilates, so they have an understanding of their own body – safe dance practice, efficient dancer, dancing body.'

In 2018, as part of a ten-year programme review, Dance Xchange and Sampad made changes to the management structure and training approach of Yuva Gati to 'ensure the programme remains current, in order to prepare our students for the ever-changing demands of the dance industry' (email to all CAT parents and home tutors, 30 August 2018). In part there was a need to address the tension between nurturing exceptional technique (in classical Indian dance forms) and preparing dancers for 'future careers in dance'. This tension remains (CAT tutor, personal communication, 2019), which is unsurprising, as to fulfil both objectives the South Asian dance CAT relies either on the development of a wider audience (and hence more demand for work) for professional Indian classical dance, or the CAT's ability to produce dancers trained 'both in contemporary and South Asian' styles to meet the current market demands. Audience development is beyond the CAT's remit, and attempting to create a versatile dancer with 'exceptional technique' in at least two dance forms within the 132 hours (or approximately sixteen working days) a year that the artistic team spends with the students[52] is of course an impossible ask. Dance Xchange's then executive director Claire Lewis cites their then CEO Debbie Jardine as believing that while '"contemporary dance" at the moment is something that can be quite set, she sees it in the future being something much more open . . . where there is a fluidity and a flexibility and a fusion that allows people with South Asian dance skills as well [as] contemporary dance skills to all work together . . . and adapt and absorb, without watering down styles' (Henwood and Lewis 2018). While this is an interesting vision of the future, this is certainly not the present case (see Chapter 4).

In attempting to create a classical Indian professional dancer, then, Yuva Gati is caught between two constituencies: the constituency of their student recruits – largely children of South Asian heritage learning dance to keep in touch with their culture, coming from a context where geographic takes priority over artistic identity – and the constituency of the professional dance world, where the place of classical Indian dance forms remains peripheral. This professional dance world, as I discuss further in the next chapter, remains largely defined by 'the world of contemporary or independent dance in which South Asian dance forms have found themselves uneasy guests' (Gorringe et al. 2018: 47).

Thus, the choice faced by classical Indian dancers remains, as discussed in Chapter 1, the tediously familiar binary of exoticism or assimilation, sameness or difference. This is a binary that was reinforced (if unintentionally) by an early Arts Council decision to position art forms such as classical Indian dance 'within the remit of the new community arts panels rather than the artform departments' (Khan 2006: 21). This was succeeded by a policy privileging 'innovation' in a way that encouraged a level of conformity with the *doxa* of Euro-American contemporary dance. A revealing exchange at an event at Sadler's Wells in 2018, at the classical Indian dance and music festival Darbar (In Conversation with Akram Khan: Contemporary to Classical), shows just how long 'innovation' served as a guiding criterion for funding. The exchange was between the director of Kadam, Sanjeevini Dutta (who was in the audience), and Alistair Spalding, who was chairing the conversation. Dutta welcomed the way that Darbar 'was making classical dance "fashionable" again' after the years in which 'the Arts Council . . . put out the message that unless you can contemporize your forms, your classical work is not going to have a place in the UK.' Spalding reassured Dutta that 'as one of those people who sat in those rooms with Arts Council deciding things, that's now over . . . if you apply as a classical artist, you are as likely to get money as any other.' Dutta queried, 'But that was only something like five years ago?', to which Spalding replied, 'Yes' (fieldwork notes, 23 November 2018).[53] The implication is that between the late 1980s and the early 2010s, or for about twenty-five years, funding was allocated in a way that 'created a false distinction between professional dance artists and community-based dance practitioners' (Kedhar 2020: 40) and actively encouraged classical Indian dance to present itself as something other than it is. Small wonder then that dancers have felt, as seen in the introduction, that classical Indian dance is 'not what is wanted in the UK'.

Conclusion

This chapter has considered the institutions involved in training classical Indian dancers in Britain – the weekend and evening dance schools, the CIDF, Yuva Gati and the failed attempts to create a vocational school. It demonstrates how the natural instinct of immigrant communities towards 'cultural reproduction' (Appadurai 1996) was reinforced by British Home Office and Arts Council policy in the 1970s and 1980s to create an environment of 'contained' diversity (Bhabha 1990), replicating the divisions and hierarchies of colonialism within the frame of 'multiculturalism'. This has impacted on the teaching of Indian classical dance forms in Britain, such that their framing has prioritized identity with an ancestral 'homeland' over artistic identity. It has impacted on the dance forms' constituency (or the range of their practitioners and audience) by emphasizing their importance as symbols of a specific geographically tethered cultural identity rather than recognizing their universal appeal. This restriction of constituents has had a knock-on effect on standards of practice by preventing the development of a critical mass of practitioners who might have made a school for intensive vocational training in these dance styles a viable project. As a result, there is no clear training route for dancers wishing to train in these forms professionally beyond the evening and weekend classes, the private one-to-ones with teachers or gurus and the summer school intensives that equally characterize the training routes for those pursuing these dance forms as amateurs. A more intensive and immersive training as a dancer can be achieved only by following a training course in contemporary dance or by training in India (see next chapter). While the CIDF of the ISTD has been largely welcomed as a way of developing professional attitudes and of enabling long-term and consistent engagement with training, some raise questions about the standards that the ISTD, with predominantly non-professional examinations, is able to ensure. Such critics suggest that the true test of a dancer's quality lies not in exams, but in success as a performer – or to use the measure employed by Yuva Gati, their preparedness as 'industry-ready dancers'. However, the restriction of 'constituents' that has circumscribed the pool of practitioners has equally also stymied the development of a wider audience. This has led to limited demand for performances of these dance forms and hence for dance artists with this specific training. This situation has been exacerbated if not necessarily constructed by an Arts Council policy that discouraged what was seen as the replication of a 'received cultural form' (Kedhar 2020). The cumulative result has been that classical Indian dancers in Britain cannot be 'industry-ready' because there is no 'industry' ready to receive them. In this light, as Gorringe et al.'s feasibility study concluded (2018), even were there to be a vocational course, it would merely create rather than solve a problem in training dancers then left with nowhere to go.[54]

It is no accident that when the Academy of Choreographic Art (subsequently the Royal Ballet School) opened in 1926 and the London Contemporary Dance School in 1969, it was in close conjunction with partner repertory companies. For obvious reasons, the demands for training and for employment go hand in hand. In the current professional market, however, dancers are typically valued for their versatility. Thus institutions such as Yuva Gati, or individual dancers serious about their careers, find themselves pushed to cross-train in Euro-American contemporary dance as a means to enhance employability.

More widely, then, this chapter draws attention through the case study of the teaching of classical Indian dance forms in Britain to the limits of a multiculturalism that is predicated on the benevolent finding of space for different 'cultures' while clearly positioning these cultures as beyond the 'norm'. As with *BBC Young Dancer*, space is made for different manifestations of the world, so long, as cultural theorist Homi Bhabha (1990: 208) puts it, as we are 'able to locate them on our own grid'. The result is a world where bharatanatyam and kathak can be taught either as part of the 'tuition of culture', as a cultural artefact or as a way to expand a dominant dance vocabulary, as a cultural accessary. The 'dancing' heritage of these forms (Mitra 2017), whereby there is a recognition of 'everyone's universal right to inherit the world in its entirety' (Mbembe 2021: 75), is swamped by the claims of essentialism and commodity.

I turn in Chapter 5 to consider what it might mean for 'everyone to inherit the world in its entirety'. This would provide the necessary context for a widening of taste and an audience generation that might make employment for classical Indian dancers a reality, not as an artefact or an accessory, but as part of a universal 'dancing' heritage. Before this I take a more detailed look at the push towards versatility, where it comes from and what it means for the professional practice of classical Indian dance forms in Britain.

Notes

1. A short bharatanatyam dance about Lord Shiva in his form as Nataraja, Lord of Dance.
2. 'My formal training consisted of a single dance lesson in a nightclub, which was soon shut down' (Hutchinson 2015: 1).
3. *Dasi attam, china melam* or *sadir* was the professional dance form practised by the hereditary dance artists of southern India, one of the key dance traditions used as the basis upon which the bharatanatyam of the present day was constructed. However, as scholars have argued (notably Soneji 2012), in the process, the dance form was so modified as to end up presenting a very different aesthetic to that of *sadir*. Bharatanatyam's relationship to *dasi attam* therefore is not that of straightforward successor. Thus, while it is undeniable that *sadir/dasi attam/china melam* is where bharatanatyam starts, the reclamation of the dance form represented less of a revival than a reconstitution.
4. The phrase in Sanskrit literally means 'teacher–student', 'from one to another'.
5. There is evidence to suggest that the tradition of the *arangetram* as a marker of entrance to professional practice goes back as far as the ninth century. The 'Old Mother' referred to is the matriarch heading the hereditary dance artist household with whom the dance artist lived and trained. See Gorringe (2005) for a fuller discussion of the *arangetram*, its history and its contemporary manifestations.
6. It should be noted, however, that there were several dance artists who had successful paid performance careers despite the widely held mistrust of the 'professional' dance artist, for example Uday Shankar, Ram Gopal, U.S. Krishna Rao and his wife Chandrabhaga Devi, Kumudini Lakhia and Kamala Laxman ('Baby' Kamala).
7. Albeit for a very different socio-economic class of people.
8. The great Bengali poet Rabindranath Tagore had established Shantiniketan in 1901, a school that 'attempted to replicate to a large degree the ashram or forest school of ancient India where gurus and their pupils lived in a residential hermitage or gurukulum' (Lal 1984: 34), and where students were educated in arts and crafts in parallel with academic instruction. At its inception it was primarily a school for younger children. In 1921, Tagore added what he called a 'world university' to this school, Viswa Bharati (Gupta

2002), where dance became 'an integral part of university education' (Purkayastha 2017a: 70). The dance taught at Shantiniketan drew on many different classical and folk-dance forms, developing its own 'modern dance aesthetic' (ibid.). It therefore offered a different approach to the schools aiming to instil proficiency in specific inherited techniques.
9. They later withdrew their support, forcing Devi to move the school to its current location in Thiruvanmiyur, Chennai in 1948.
10. In 1938, the dance artist and choreographer Uday Shankar established the 'Uday Shankar India Cultural Centre' near Almora in northern India, which offered tuition in bharatanatyam and manipuri among other subjects. However, the school struggled for funds and closed not many years after.
11. Dance scholar Stacey Prickett, inspired by O'Shea, uses this term to describe the contemporary variant of the guru (Prickett 2007: 30).
12. It is now fairly common practice for gurus to send their students to other teachers in India for a month or two of intense training prior to their *arangetram*.
13. The course was set up in 1995 with kathak classes taught by Nahid Siddiqui. Despite not providing professional training, it nonetheless provided vital experiential knowledge of a classical Indian dance style for hundreds of students over the years. The kathak and contemporary dance artist Jane Chan started her kathak training on this course before opting to train seriously under her guru Amina Khayyam. The closure of the course therefore represents a great loss to South Asian dance in Britain in particular, as well as to dance in Britain more widely.
14. An advertisement in the *Dancing Times* can be seen at https://www.vads.ac.uk/digital/collection/SADAA/id/370/rec/21 (retrieved 18 August 2024).
15. Golvala's services to South Asian dance were acknowledged in the Queen's Honours in 2016 when she was awarded an OBE.
16. Information on Balasundari's classes comes from Shakuntala (Sheila Cove), who trained with her in London in the late 1960s and early 1970s. In Sheila's class with Balasundari in 1970, of fourteen students, only two were Asian.
17. Srivastava has worked variously with Kadam, Milapfest, Yuva Gati, *BBC Young Dancer*, the South Asian Dance Alliance (SADAA) and as producer for several independent South Asian dance artists. Her perception of the field is thus well grounded.
18. Akademi market research in 2010 reckoned that there were '120 teachers of bharatanatyam and kathak teachers in the UK' (cited in Ramphal and Alake 2010: 14). There are many more teachers offering classes in Indian cinematic or bollywood dance.
19. The CIDF was originally launched in 1999 as the South Asian Dance Faculty.
20. The first 'snapshot', for example, describes Stella Uppal Subbiah's classes taught under the auspices of London Tamil school, where she has made a deliberate effort to teach the mothers of the children attending class. I discuss this example at greater length later in the chapter.
21. Yuva Gati (Sanskrit for the 'youth path' or 'youth movement') is the South Asian strand of the government-funded 'Centres for Advanced Training', or CATs, administered by Sampad in partnership with the Birmingham-based NDA Dance Xchange (now FABRIC).
22. See Appendix 3 for further information about each of these organizations.
23. Participant at Yuva Gati Teachers' Continuous Professional Development (CPD) day, Dance Xchange, Birmingham (fieldwork notes, 29 March 2018).

24. Yuva Gati Teachers' CPD day, Dance Xchange, Birmingham (fieldwork notes, 29 March 2018).
25. The full text of this speech can be found at Press Association (2007).
26. See Brooke (2007) for an illuminating discussion of Powell's speech and the public response.
27. Thanks to Alexandra Kolb for drawing my attention to this article and highlighting the concept of 'cultural long-distance nationalism'.
28. I refer particularly to 'India' because while classical Indian dance forms are commonly referred to in the UK as 'South Asian' dance forms, recognizing their provenance and practice in a range of other countries outside of modern-day India (e.g. Pakistan, Bangladesh, Sri Lanka – see Introduction), in effect the majority of classical Indian dance practitioners in the UK have familial links with India and Sri Lanka. This is in part due to the ambivalence of Islam (the dominant religion of Pakistan and Bangladesh) towards the practice of dance, and in part due to differences in class (migrants from Pakistan and Bangladesh have tended to be from poorer, working-class backgrounds, whereas those from India have been predominantly middle-class). There are prominent classical Indian dance practitioners with roots elsewhere, most notably kathak dance artist and choreographer Nahid Siddiqui, who was born and trained in Pakistan, and Akram Khan and Amina Khayyam, who both have Bangladeshi heritage. However, they are in the minority. The context of migration from Sri Lanka is quite different from that of India, driven as it has been in large part by the painful conflict between the minority Tamils and majority Sinhalese. This conflict has led to waves of Sri Lankan Tamil refugees to Europe, the United States and Canada since 1956 (David 2012; Jones 2014) and has meant that the practice of dance (bharatanatyam) by these immigrant Sri Lankan Tamils has had more overtly political overtones and a closer affinity with straightforward 'long-distance nationalism' than the less explicitly political long-distance *cultural* nationalism of the Indian diaspora (David 2007, 2012; Satkunaratnam 2013).
29. A series of violent clashes between predominantly black communities in Brixton and the police. There had been earlier riots in different parts of the UK protesting police racism – but these riots were sufficiently intense to force an institutional response in the form of the Scarman report.
30. *Iyal* (Literature), *Isai* (Music) and *Natakam* (Drama) are considered to be the three 'pillars' of Tamil culture (*Mutamizh*). Bharatanatyam combines all three.
31. By professional training she means the kind of intensive training given by a full-time degree, or a course such as at Kalakshetra, rather than weekly 'hobby' classes.
32. 'Oxbridge' is a contraction of Oxford and Cambridge, which are internationally renowned and highly regarded and sought-after universities in Britian.
33. As an aside, along with Sanjeevini Dutta, others mentioned in this chapter, Sujata Banerjee and Veronica Lewis, also worked as dance animateurs, Lewis being one of the first to take up an animateur post in the UK (see Stevens 2016/17).
34. When the ISTD South Asian dance course first started, Prickett's respondents felt that 'the ISTD's inclusion of the forms enhances their accessibility for those without a South Asian heritage' (Prickett 2004: 17), a belief that would, on face value, appear well founded, as the ISTD provides classical Indian dance forms with a platform in the 'mainstream'. However, more than a decade on, those without South Asian heritage taking the exams

are conspicuous by their absence, forming less than 1 per cent of those who take the exams (Banerjee 2017).

35. In many ways the London branch of the Bharatiya Vidya Bhavan (an Indian cultural institute offering classes in music and dance, among other subjects, established in 1972, though classes started some years later), could be argued to fulfill this role. Certainly, the Bhavan has provided a focal point for Indian music and dance, a place where visiting artists are able to perform and conduct workshops. The centre has endorsement in the form of frequent visits to perform and teach from a range of established professionals, mainly from India, including, for music, the world-renowned sitarist Ravi Shankar, and for dance, bharatanatyam icons such as Padma Subrahmanyam and Chitra Visweswaran and the kathak maestro Birju Maharaj. Since 1984, the Bhavan has followed a prepared syllabus and conducted its own examinations to assure standards, with the examiner usually being a visiting artist from India, and many of its graduates have gone on to set up their own schools in Britain. For all the Bhavan provides, however, it does not provide a full-time vocational course.

36. Other, not specifically vocational courses have also been pioneered – and followed the same seemingly inexorable trajectory. University College, Bretton Hall launched a Certificate for South Asian Dance Artists working within schools in 1995, working in partnership with the South Asian dance umbrella organization, ADiTi, and Middlesex University. This course closed in 2000 with the folding of ADiTi (Ramphal and Alake 2010). It was replaced by a module in South Asian dance as part of a BA; this subsequently became a wider Diversity in Dance module. The University of Roehampton established an MA in South Asian Dance in 2005, which closed in 2016. Courses boldly envisioned and brought into being with energy and drive, for one reason or another, proved to lack staying power, most commonly due to a straightforward lack of demand. See Appendix 2.

37. This is apparent from a quick glance at the list compiled here: https://www.danceonline.co.uk/list-of-dance-companies.html (accessed 19 July 2024).

38. A bharatanatyam company established by Subathra Subramaniam and Mayuri Boonham. It achieved RFO status (regularly funded organization – now termed NPO) in 2008 but closed the same year. See Kedhar (2020) for a detailed analysis of Angika's work and trajectory. Kedhar argues that RFO status, while it 'can make companies less precarious financially, can also put added pressure on them to produce and perform at a higher, and often untenable, rate' (ibid.: 67).

39. See, for example, Seeta Patel, who had started her training as a medic before turning to dance, or Shivaangee Agrawal, who had secured a job as a systems analyst.

40. The incongruity of the CIDF's positioning within the *Imperial* Society has not escaped attention. In 2004 Prickett wrote a detailed article looking at the opening of the CIDF, including some wry observations on the ironies of the inclusion of this faculty within a body with such advertised imperial roots.

41. This is largely due to the convertibility of ISTD exams to UCAS (University and College Admissions Service) points. Both the Bhavan and Subbiah have been urged by parents to offer ISTD exams in classical Indian dance forms not for the sake of assessing quality in the dance styles themselves, but because ISTD qualifications count towards UCAS points (Nandakumara 2017; Subbiah 2018), allowing for a stronger application to study a subject affording work in a more stable and lucrative sector. When I contacted the Bhavan in March 2023, no student had taken up the option to pursue an ISTD exam, though the

Bhavan was prepared to offer the option if desired (Nandakumara, personal communication, phone call, March 2023).
42. Interestingly, in 2012, the faculty presented its examination curricula and criteria to dance teachers in Mumbai and Delhi – the first initiative in India for the ISTD (Sundaram 2014) – and in 2017 there was one ISTD CIDF registered teacher in India, and there had been enquiries from two or three others (Banerjee 2017).
43. Shree studied to Grade 5 and then stopped. She is, however, interested in taking the exams up again and is particularly interested in the vocational exams (Savani, personal communication, 23 July 2019).
44. As an indication, Pushkala was awarded Milapfest's Acharya Ratna (literally 'Jewel of Teachers') in 2015, in 2016 was honoured at Navadisha (the South Asian dance conference referred to in the introduction) for her teaching legacy in Britain, and in 2020 was awarded an MBE for 'outstanding and exemplary achievement in service to the community'.
45. DBS stands for Disclosure and Barring Service. This is a safeguarding service designed to protect vulnerable groups, including children and young people, by preventing the employment of individuals in sectors from which they may be barred.
46. Khan's exams were run by the Indian classical music institute Prayag Sangeet Samiti (see https://prayagsangeetsamiti.in/, retrieved 18 August 2024).
47. As some dance schools are run by South Asian arts agencies, such as the Bhavan, Milapfest, South Asian Arts (SAA-UK) in Leeds and Kala Sangam, which receive Arts Council Funding, the running of these classes, at least in terms of overheads, is to some extent state-subsidized. However, most dance classes are run privately by independent dance artists and teachers. These dance artists may receive project-based funding for discrete initiatives, but their schools are primarily run as businesses.
48. The National Dance CAT website states, 'CATs exist to help identify, and assist, children with exceptional potential, regardless of their personal circumstances, to benefit from world-class specialist training as part of a broad and balanced education. This will enable them, if they choose to proceed towards self-sustaining careers in music and dance.' CATS/National Centres for Advanced Training (n.d.).
49. These quotations and much of the information in this paragraph is taken from DanceXchange (2009), obtained with thanks from Dance Xchange and Anita Srivastava.
50. Now amalgamated with the Nottingham-based dance agency Dance4 to form FABRIC.
51. Subramanyam also believes that contemporary dance CAT students should receive some exposure to and training in classical Indian dance forms.
52. This is independent of the time spent with home tutors, which follows the weekend and evening class pattern already discussed.
53. This was about the time that the Arts Council launched the Creative Case for Diversity in 2014 (see Chapter 5).
54. See Chapter 5 for further discussion on the audience generation that makes employment a realistic prospect.

Chapter 4

Livelihood, Learning, Embodiment
'Technical Habitus', Classical Indian Dance Forms and the Limits of the 'Versatile Dancer'

> When we started South Asian classical dance was still of interest to the West. It's not any more. It has slowly been driven out. It's all about how you take the form and 'fuse' it. 'Fusion' is the big thing. And there are so many wonderful, professional dancers who are being forced to make contemporary work – and some of it is bad and some of it is good. But the point is that they are having to do it because they need to survive. And that infuriates me – that they are put in that situation. It makes me sad.
> —Akram Khan, interview, 2018

> And I realized that you need a lifetime, more than a lifetime to train in one art form. Where there is a question of two and three art forms, you can get a feel for other art forms, but you can really, really immerse yourself completely only in one.
> —Shaalini Shivashankar on Manch UK, 9 May 2020

> I also say very proudly that there are people who live in India who speak brilliant English. Similarly, there are those who live in England who perform excellent kathak. You don't need to live in England to speak the best English. You don't need to be in India to perform the best kathak.
> —Sujata Banerjee, interview, 2017

> The cultural context in which people in India live definitely does enhance their dance. You just don't get the right body language out of students who are born here – it just doesn't fit in.
> —Nina Rajarani, interview, 2018

> Someone did once say to me – unless you have trained in India, you are a kind of half-cooked artist.
> —Sonia Sabri, interview, 2018

Introduction

I am in the Hathi Hall in the Bhavan in London. On the walls are brightly coloured images of Hindu gods and goddesses, including a striking image of Saraswathi, goddess of arts and learning. Standing about a head above most other students in the class, with my dirty blonde hair and pale skin, I don't exactly blend in with the shades of brown skin and the black hair of most of my peers. I feel slightly awkward – a *muzhungakai* (the Tamil word for the 'drumstick' vegetable, also used pejoratively to refer to someone especially tall and lanky) with large feet and jutting elbows. Guruji (Prakash Yadagudde) comes into the class, and standing in our rows, we perform the *tattikumbattu* (the danced prayer performed before and after dancing). Guruji recites: *Talangu takadhiku taka tading gina tom*, and our bodies respond to this signal to prepare to dance. Suddenly my Otherness drops away. My deep *aramandi* (a position with both knees bent out to the side in a diamond shape, somewhat akin to a demi-plié in ballet, but deeper), hard-won over years of training, makes my height less conspicuous. *Tahatajamtari ta*. As my hands form the familiar *mudras*, as my feet beat out the well-known rhythm, as my body reaches in the movement that it has performed so many times, and amended through so many corrections, my awkwardness slowly falls away. I know this. My body breathes. I am dancing.

Another time, another place. I am in a studio in East London. I have come for an audition to work with a company that takes dance performances to schools and community groups. I wonder if my training in *abhinaya* and storytelling, or the highly developed skills in foot percussion given me by my bharatanatyam training, might work for the company. I don't look out of place among the other dancers gathered for the audition, now warming up in the studio, who have a range of heights and skin colours. With my long legs and neck and straight-backed posture, people have often mistaken me for a ballet dancer. As the audition starts this illusion is soon corrected. Coming from training in which legs are often bent and rarely lifted above waist height, I feel distinctly uncomfortable waving my legs around, not to mention that I don't have the muscle control to do so gracefully. I manage to roll to the floor when required, assisted by the supplementary training I have taken in contemporary dance, but my body still holds a resistance, not helped by the voice in my head of one of my bharatanatyam dancer friends, who once innocently asked of me what contemporary dance meant by all this 'rolling about on the floor'. I feel awkward and flustered and only just manage to limp through the sequence of movements. Unsurprisingly, I don't get through the audition. As I sit on the tube back home, I only wish there had been a chance to demonstrate what I could do rather than showcase what I couldn't.

In the previous chapter I looked at some of the 'hows', the 'whos' and the 'whats' of training in classical Indian dance in Britain, looking at the institutions available to provide training to young dancers, and at the demographics to which these young dancers and their teachers largely tend to belong. I looked at the constraints and restraints on the development of the professional classical Indian dancer in Britain occasioned by the role that these dance forms play as a means to sustain links to Indian and South Asian cultural heritage. I also touched upon the dilemma facing schools in terms of deciding what and how to teach their dancers, particularly Yuva Gati, the only institution in the country with a remit for providing young dancers with professional training in classical Indian dance forms. How best should they balance providing a robust grounding in the technique of a classical Indian dance style with ensuring that students are sufficiently multiskilled to work within a sector where the professional demand is increasingly for the versatile dancer? I therefore looked particularly at the tensions and the choices faced by institutions.

The epigraphs and the short personal anecdote cited above reflect the focus of this chapter, which is about how these tensions manifest in the embodied reality of individual dancers, and in the choices they make in order to take dance as a profession or make it their livelihood. The chapter is divided into two sections, the first looking at the context from which the professional dancer emerges, the second turning to the context within which that dancer must then find work. In the first part of the chapter, I consider the impact of training within Britain in dance forms that originated and developed in India. As I discuss, for some teachers there is a cultural 'dissonance' between the body language and disposition that comes with being, for example, a twenty-first-century Londoner and the body language and disposition demanded of a bharatanatyam dancer. Rajarani's experience, grounded in over thirty years of teaching, is that 'You just don't get the right body language out of students who are born here – it just doesn't fit in. It doesn't come to them naturally' (Rajarani 2018). From a different perspective, kathak dancer, choreographer and teacher Sujata Banerjee observes, 'You don't need to be in India to perform the best kathak' (Banerjee 2017). The implications of this debate on the practicalities of training and working in classical Indian dance in Britain are such that it demands attention.

In the second part of the chapter, I turn to the question highlighted by the first two epigrams above – the impact of the professional demand for the versatile dancer, and how the classical Indian dancer must adapt their embodiment of these classical forms in order to better access the dance labour market. Once a dancer has gone through the arduous and time-consuming process of shaping their body in line with classical Indian dance training and acquiring the physical and cultural capital of that particular form, what does it mean for that dancer and that dancer's body to then be required to fulfil the demands of the professional dance world for versatility – and thereby, to get work? What does it mean when, as Akram Khan puts it, a classically trained Indian dancer is 'forced to make contemporary work to survive'? If it is true that 'it takes more than a lifetime to train in one art form', what is the impact of the demand for versatility on the way that the body of a professional dancer (in this case, particularly a professional classical Indian dancer) is shaped?

Rehabilitating the 'Habitus'

In considering these questions, I draw on Pierre Bourdieu's concepts of *cultural capital* and *habitus*, together with the notion of *physical capital*, coined by sociologist of the body Chris Shilling (1991). Bourdieu (1984) pointed to the idea of physical capital in identifying *embodied capital* as one of three manifestations of cultural capital (the others being objectified and institutionalized). Shilling argues, rightly in my view, that 'the "physical" is too important to be seen merely as a component of cultural capital' (1991: 654) and therefore introduces the notion of *physical capital* to describe the physical assets pertaining to an individual, automatically through genetic inheritance, or acquired through training. I use this concept together with that of *habitus*, a concept that forms a key part of Bourdieu's sociological analysis. It is also, as the Bourdieusian sociologist Diane Reay remarks, 'probably Bourdieu's most contested concept' (Reay 2004: 432). I will therefore take some time to explain my understanding of habitus and to highlight why I have decided to use it before returning to the main questions of the chapter.

As a starting point, Bourdieu explains habitus in his essay *Outline of a Theory of Practice* as 'a system of lasting, transposable dispositions which, integrating past experience, functions at every moment as a matrix of perceptions, appreciations and actions' (1977: 82–83). It is the 'immanent law, *lex insita*, laid down in each agent by his [sic] earliest upbringing' (ibid.: 81). Further, it is 'close to what is suggested by the idea of habit, while differing in one important respect. The habitus, as the word implies, is that which one has acquired, but which has become durably incorporated into the body in the form of permanent dispositions' (Bourdieu 1993: 86). Bringing these ideas together, habitus can be described as an embodied disposition or inclination, serving, as sociologist Lindsay Garratt vividly and helpfully suggests, as a kind of 'somatised lens' (Garratt 2016: 80), both shaped by and in turn shaping a person's knowledge and experience.

Bourdieu's intention in 'reviving', as he puts it, the term from its earlier use by sociologist Marcel Mauss, and even Aristotle (Bourdieu 1993: 86), was to describe 'the embodiment of social structures and history in individuals' (Power 1999: 48), in such a way as to tread a middle ground between determinism and subjectivism (Power 1999; Morris 2001; Edgerton and Roberts 2014), or to acknowledge the influence of an individual's environment and cultural context while leaving space for their agency and choice as an individual.

The range of contexts in which the concept is used, not least by Bourdieu himself, together with its different inflections of meaning,[1] has led to it being critiqued as vague and 'overburdened' (Shilling 2012: 160). It has also been read as overly deterministic and ahistorical, which is somewhat ironic given Bourdieu's intention in its use (Jenkins 2002). In the specific context of dance anthropology, a notable critique has been presented by anthropologist Brenda Farnell, for whom Bourdieu's attempt to 'avoid objectivist, behaviourist accounts of human activity . . . without returning to their subjectivist opposite' founders in its failure to sufficiently account for human agency, with the use of habitus locating agency 'somewhere ambiguously behind or beneath the agency of persons' (Farnell 2000: 402–3). Furthermore, Farnell sees in Bourdieu's understanding of habitus as something that functions 'below the level of consciousness and language, beyond the reach of introspective scrutiny and control by the will' (Bourdieu 1984: 466) an unhelpful perpetuation of 'a misconception in dualist thought, that thinking is what goes on in the head or brain quite distinct from the actions of the body', based on an assumption that a lack of 'discursive facility entails a lack of consciousness' (Farnell 2000: 409).

There are certainly occasions on which Bourdieu can be seen to perpetuate dualist thinking. While discussing the term '*l'esprit de corps*', for example, in 'Program for a Sociology of Sport', he argues that 'if most organizations . . . put such a great emphasis on bodily disciplines, it is because obedience consists in large part in belief and belief is what the body (*corps*) concedes, even when the mind (*l'esprit*) says no', and that bodily disciplines serve as 'a way of obtaining from the body a form of consent that the mind could refuse' (Bourdieu 1988: 161). The body appears here as supplying an obedience that the mind withholds. There is clearly a strong image here of a mind–body divide. The overall impact of Bourdieu's work on habitus, however, has been a renewed focus on embodiment – and the lack of a 'hard separation between bodily conduct and intelligent conduct' that he extended from the thinking of Merleau-Ponty (Moya 2014). Sociologist Nick Crossley argues that it has 'put embodiment centre stage, facilitating a strong sociological grasp on it' (Crossley 2001: 88).

Farnell makes a convincing case for the need to talk 'from the body' rather than, as she believes Bourdieu does, 'about the body', and proposes a 'semasiology of action' as an alternative to habitus. To illustrate her point she uses a case study centred around seeking route directions from a young Nakota woman (Nakota is the endonym for the First Nations people also known as Assiniboine) in northern Montana in the US. The woman provided directions using 'pointing gestures' orientated to the cardinal directions 'even though she had no visible landmarks to guide them'. Farnell's extensive fieldwork among the Nakota suggests that this response was typical, as for the Nakota, 'North, south, east and west, plus "earth" [and] "sky" constitute an indexical form intrinsic to many social situations and events' (Farnell 2000: 410). For Farnell, Bourdieu's understanding of habitus diminishes the personal agency of her conversant in using these gestures. She proposes that by contrast with habitus, which makes Nakota people 'unconsciously disposed to use the symbolic form of the four directions . . . when they give route directions', according to a 'semasiology of action', when Nakota people give route directions, 'they are causally empowered dynamically embodied persons utilizing resources provided by the systems of signifying acts into which they have been socialized' (ibid.). In other words, if I understand her correctly, when viewed from the perspective of 'habitus', a person has no choice as to whether or not to use the systems of signification into which they have been socialized, but do so habitually – or on 'autopilot'. By contrast, according to a 'semasiology of action', 'semiotic modalities of vocal and action signs' provide Farnell's consultant with 'culturally shaped means of conceptualizing (using) her corporeal space' (ibid.: 412), which she then *chooses* to employ.

Farnell makes an important point. As she argues, there is certainly a tendency within social theory to attribute agency to 'internal mechanisms' and 'macro-social' forces, whereby it is not clear how these entities then effect causality, as it were, on the ground. My understanding of Bourdieu, however, is that what Farnell means by 'semiotic modalities of vocal and action signs providing a culturally shaped means of conceptualizing space' is very much what Bourdieu means by 'habitus', though he would include a greater range of physical (and mental) 'modalities'. Furthermore, as Crossley (2001), Reay (2004) and Wainwright et al. (2006) among others maintain, arguing that habitus exerts an influence not consciously registered by the agent is not to say that the agent is robbed of all scope to act as a 'causally empowered dynamically embodied person'. It is to acknowledge the rather unremarkable point that our bodies are predisposed to follow and respond to familiar patterns of movement and behaviour, unless we make the effort to act otherwise. To use an example picked up later in the chapter, I might signify assent either by nodding my head, or by tilting it from side to side, an action I would most likely unconsciously choose depending on the social context I am in. This unthinking and habitual gesture does not imply a lack of autonomy in other areas, however, just that my body holds a predisposition to a certain pattern of response that would normally remain unconscious and unexamined. Moreover, contrary to a Cartesianism whereby thought is privileged as a space with greater autonomy than action (as indeed is suggested in Bourdieu's comments on the *esprit de corps* cited above), such lack of reflection is not confined to actions. Elsewhere, Bourdieu is clear about the 'unthought categories of thought which . . . predetermine thought' (Bourdieu and Wacquant 1992: 40). Rather than being restricted to action, for Bourdieu, 'unconscious bias' is the logical extension of an engrained habitus.

Foster (2009: 7–8), like Farnell, finds habitus an overly deterministic concept, reading it as possessing a 'conservative, retentive function', resting on an understanding of culture as 'relatively stable, cohesive and distinct'. It is true that Bourdieu does insist on the pull of 'inertia', and the gravitational pull of the 'status quo', arguing that 'Cumulative exposure to certain social conditions' can mean that the individual 'internalizes the necessities [and constraints] of the extant social environment' (Bourdieu and Wacquant 1992: 13).[2] He also describes habitus, as seen above, as a pattern incorporated into the body as a 'permanent' disposition. So far, so determinist. He moderates his view elsewhere, however, to argue that though an 'enduring disposition', habitus is not in fact 'permanent'. Rather, 'habitus change [*sic*] constantly in response to new experiences' (Bourdieu 2000: 161). Notably, habitus can be changed through 'awareness and . . . pedagogic effort' (Bourdieu 2005: 45). Dispositions are 'long lasting; they tend to perpetuate, to reproduce themselves, but they are not eternal' (ibid.). Rather, they are 'subject to a kind of permanent revision' (Bourdieu 2000: 161).

A key to the modification or 'revision' of habitus is 'awareness', or a recognition of the force of the structures and conditions that constrain us. This awareness is what allows for the toppling of convention and offers the escape from the 'conservative' and 'retentive' force not only of the habitus, but of other social forces. In Bourdieu's (1990: 141) words, 'The specific efficacy of subversive action consists in the power to bring to consciousness, and so modify, the categories of thought which help to orient individual and collective practices'. To change, he is saying, one must recognize and acknowledge both one's physical and mental 'unconscious bias'.

As I argue in the introduction, Bourdieu's theoretical tools (including habitus) are best understood in the context both of his own personal circumstances and of his vehement opposition to 'rational action theory', which understands the functioning of society on the basis of individual behaviour as directed by a series of individually calculated decisions or choices. For Bourdieu this 'founding myth of the uncreated creator . . . is to the notion of habitus as the myth of genesis is to the theory of evolution' (Bourdieu and Wacquant 1992: 132–33). Thus, while he does not deny 'strategic choice and conscious deliberation as a modality of action' (ibid.: 131), he does want to emphasize the extent to which 'the individual is always trapped, save to the extent that he [*sic*] becomes aware of it . . . within the limits of the system of categories he owes to his upbringing and training' (ibid.: 130). His contention is, he points out, 'in a sense very banal . . . that social beings are at least partly the product of social conditioning' (ibid.: 132). He asks, with some impatience at his critics, 'What is it about this that is so shocking?' (ibid.).

It is in this light that I find habitus a useful tool through which to look at dance, dance fields and how they are shaped, particularly when researching how non-dominant dance styles struggle to stake their space within a field governed by dance forms that characteristically evince and favour a different aesthetic, a different *doxa*, a different habitus. The term provides a shorthand through which to recognize the way that a person's actions, stance, gestures and gait are all socially and environmentally inflected – 'how any individual moves, speaks or symbolizes emerges from the intricate process of living in society' (Cohen Bull 1997: 270) – something that it seems unhelpful to discard.

Habitus and Dance – Building on Wainwright, Turner and Williams's Tripartite Distinction of Habitus

Part of the reason for the level of disagreement about what Bourdieu intended by his various concepts (especially that of habitus) is that he conceived of them as being open to modification in the light of empirical work – he 'sees his concepts as in a continual process of being reworked' (Reay 2004: 439). He explicitly requested that scholars and researchers employ a method of 'comprehension through use' (Bourdieu, cited in Wainwright et al. 2006: 553) in approaching his work. In this light, a number of Bourdieusian scholars (Reay 2004; Wainwright et al. 2006; Thatcher et al. 2016) see the extension and development of his concepts, or their 're-appropriation . . . in creative ways' that 'he himself did not use' (Thatcher et al. 2016: 1), as part of a necessary and legitimate updating of his work that he himself would have sanctioned. In this spirit, sociologists Steven Wainwright and Bryan Turner and social scientist Clare Williams (2006, 2007) build on his work to identify three variants of habitus they perceive as operating in the field of ballet, which they label 'individual', 'institutional' and 'choreographic'. I have found this tripartite extension of the concept a helpful frame through which to consider some of the struggles faced by classical Indian dancers in Britain. While some Bourdieusian purists may balk at this use of Bourdieu, I hold that it is an extension that remains true to the intention of his work, not least in adapting his concepts through a 'twenty-first century exegesis' that allows 'the relevance' of his work 'to endure and expand' (Wallace 2016: 52). For the remainder of this chapter, therefore, I adopt the tripartite schema of habitus that Wainwright, Turner and Williams propose. To this schema, I add a fourth variant of habitus, which I term 'technical habitus'. This fourth variant is necessitated by the extent to which training in classical Indian dance forms is provided within Britain (and to a lesser extent within India) outside of a formal institutional structure.

Within Wainwright et al.'s schema, 'individual habitus' refers to the habitus the person acquires due to the environment in which they are born. This habitus develops in relation to a person's 'physical capital' in the sense of their physical (and genetically acquired) attributes such as height, a long Achilles tendon or hypermobile feet. It also includes the physical (and mental) predispositions they acquire through living in a particular social environment – such as sitting more naturally on the floor than on a chair (or vice versa) or learning to eat with one's hands or a knife and fork. A dancer's individual habitus means that one dancer might favour, for example, movements in *chowka talam* (a very slow tempo) rather than a higher speed because *chowka talam* suits their particular physicality and temperament better. 'Institutional habitus' refers to the habitus dancers acquire through 'schooling' or training within a particular institution and adopting the habits, skills and mannerisms of the 'field in which they are located' (Wainwright and Turner 2006: 551). Wainwright et al. use the example of the 'fast footwork' of the Royal Ballet, or the emphasis on flexibility and extensions in dancers of the Paris Opera, to illustrate how different institutions inflect the habitus of their dancers. Within classical Indian dance, 'institutional habitus' manifests in the different stylistic traits of different *banis* or *gharanas*. Bharatanatyam dancers following the Kalakshetra style for example characteristically pride themselves on their clear lines and precision, while dancers of the Vazhavur style are marked by more rounded movements and a softer energy. 'Choreographic habitus' refers to the habits, skills and mannerisms acquired through 'rehearsing and performing in a certain style' (Wainwright et al. 2006: 545). Choreographic habitus extends physical capital in a dancer's ability to perform fluently the signature movements of a particular choreographer and again predisposes them to a particular sequence or emphasis of movement. Where choreographic habitus builds physical capital in one context, it can compromise physical capital in a different context. Even a short spell as an apprentice dancer in one dance company, for example, left my body with a wish to push any still position into an imbalance and transform a stillness into a suspension, an inclination I needed to consciously moderate in performing classical work.

I suggest 'technical habitus' as a fourth variant to describe the moulding of habitus acquired through training and 'pedagogic effort', yet not necessarily acquired within the formalized context of an institution. It also serves as a way of referring to the habitus imbued by training with a broader scope than that offered by institutional habitus. Training in a particular dance form can unite the practitioners through a 'technical habitus' while their specific institutional habitus may differ. Technical habitus extends and inflects a dancer's physical capital through building strength and developing skill in ways dictated by a particular dance idiom. In a bharatanatyam context, this might mean the capacity to sustain a deep *aramandi* over long periods, or to hold the arms in the specific position of the *natyarambhe* (a position in which the arms are held stretched out to the side with the elbows raised). It also imbues a dancer with a particular physical bias or expectation. A bharatanatyam dancer, for example, may experience a sense of unease if they do not perform a short, danced prayer (*tattikumbattul namaskaram*) before and after dancing, or a sense of incompleteness if a movement pattern performed to the right is not then repeated to the left.

'Technical habitus' allows for the recognition that the formalized actions, stances and techniques of particular dance forms, independent of the physicality of the specific dancers who embody them, and independent of the institutions in which they may be taught, likewise bear the imprint and carry the history of the context in which they originated. As Keali'inohomoku famously argued in 1969 (see Chapter 1), ballet continues to carry the cultural codes of its courtly European origins despite its contemporary status as a globally recognized art form,[3] and the expectations (physical and mental) of ballet dancers are modified accordingly. A ballet dancer's habitus is modified therefore to expect that taking the right leg behind the left and bending the knees while tilting the body slightly forward is a way to express a respectful greeting. Classical Indian dance forms likewise retain, and to a certain extent embody the cultural imprint of their place of origin – which is of course what makes them so attractive as a form of 'cultural education' for certain groups of young British Asians (as well as elsewhere in the Asian diaspora – see Srinivasan 2012). The dances drawing on the Hindu texts and traditions, the languages of the songs to which the dances are performed, the flora and fauna referred to within them (lotuses, creepers, deer, elephants, crocodiles), the aesthetic values placed on (for women) a bare midriff, large eyes and covered legs, all speak as eloquently of the specific customs, 'morals, ethics and values' of their specific cultural origins as ballet does of its Western European provenance.[4] A dancer's habitus is modified through the performance of bharatanatyam, for example, to expect that arms stretched out in a straight downward diagonal, with open hands, palms facing down, should move from right to left before being bent to allow the palms to touch the eyelids, as a means to express respect and devotion.

'. . . If You Have Never Drawn a *Kolam* before in Your Life, How Are You Going to Show That on Stage?'

Dance Forms, Changing Space and Individual Habitus

> Not one of them could hold the *veena* [a long-necked stringed instrument played horizontally across the lap] properly and I assume it's because half of them haven't seen a *veena* and even less have actually held a *veena* and [they] don't understand it. But if you grew up in Chennai – you know what [a] *veena* looks like – you have 90 per cent touched one . . . if you have never drawn a *kolam* [a pattern sketched with rice flour][5] before in your life, how are you going to show that on stage? (Bharatanatyam dancer observing a class of British-born bharatanatyam dancers, fieldwork notes, 12 April 2017)

In this quotation the bharatanatyam dancer quoted voices a question that preoccupies – one could even say troubles – a number of the practitioners teaching classical Indian dance forms in Britain, returning us to the first of the two questions that form the focus of this chapter. If we accept that an individual's habitus reflects their social and environmental context, and if we likewise accept that a dance technique bears the imprint of its place of origin, given that any dance technique necessarily builds upon a dancer's individual habitus, what happens when the cultural contexts of these different forms of embodiment are mismatched or non-aligned? How does this culturally inflected social conditioning of an individual's body interact with the body's more formal conditioning through training in a (culturally inflected) dance form? As the epigraphs opening this chapter reveal, different practitioners take different views on this.

The view of the dancer quoted, restated in Bourdieusian terms, suggests that the individual habitus acquired through the absorption of the cultural context of living in India is a prerequisite for full, convincing or authentic embodiment of the institutional habitus of classical Indian dance forms: it is easier to create the image of someone playing a *veena* if you have held, and possibly played, a *veena* yourself. The same dancer explains,

> I think it's really important [to spend time in India] because there are so many things . . . If you haven't woken up because a rooster has woken you up instead of a clock, how are you going to understand that? . . . I believe that you should go and see the temples that you are dancing about . . .the Thanjavur temple. You can see it in a book a thousand times, but it's not until you stand *in* the courtyard and you look *up* – that you understand what all those *varnams* are about. That's what I'm saying – that you need to have that certain amount of rootedness in the country. (Fieldwork notes, 12 April 2017)

This is not a lone voice. As I continued my training in London as a teenager, after our family had returned from India, my dance teacher expressed a similar sentiment, remarking on the ease with which I embodied the bharatanatyam movements compared to my peers (who, though of South Asian heritage, had been born and brought up here) because I had 'more of India in me'. Sonia Sabri refers to the view she has encountered that 'unless you have trained in India, you are a kind of half-cooked artist'. Rajarani, quoted at the beginning of the chapter, likewise experiences problems with a cultural mismatch between the everyday environment of her students and that of bharatanatyam. For her,

> The cultural context in which people in India live definitely does enhance their dance. You just don't get the right body language out of students who are born here – it just doesn't fit in. It doesn't come to them naturally . . . I think sometimes that if you do it with them when they are young, they are not inhibited. If you try to teach them when they get older – pre-teens – there are so many inhibitions and they are so self-conscious. So, I try and do *abhinaya* really early on – as early as possible to get over all of that. For example, I'll ask them to move their head like this [moves head side to side] – it's a cultural thing – they just won't do it – even when I say that it is simply *parivahitam*.[6] They just

refuse to do it. Even doing their eyebrows in *alarippu*[7] – they just don't like that. (Rajarani 2018)

In a frequently cited image, Bourdieu describes a habitus that 'encounters a social world of which it is the product' (or a familiar 'field') as like 'a fish in water', taking 'the world about itself for granted' (Bourdieu and Wacquant 1992: 127). What Rajarani and the dancer quoted above describe here is how trying to construct a classical Indian habitus within Britain is the reverse – it is 'a fish out of water'. The impact is less categorical, as one can still train in classical Indian dance forms in Britain (it is not quite a dead fish) – it is just a harder or a less natural proposition. Yadagudde articulates this perspective clearly:

It's not necessary for them to go to India and learn . . . but if you go for some time and see . . . that is much better because dance is a mirror of culture. And culture you can see only in the people – by going to the market, going to the temple . . . going to the festivals. There are many festivals in India – here there are very few. This is the reason that we do festivals in the Bhavan . . . it's to help the girls who come . . . because the girls are never usually exposed to this. (Yadagudde 2017a)

Dancers for whom a clenched fist with an outstretched thumb (the *shikara* hand gesture) represents questioning within their everyday context (inflecting their individual habitus) will find it easier to assimilate a technical habitus that seeks to embed the same movement for a similar meaning. Dancers who customarily signal assent by swaying their heads from side to side (*parivahitam*) in their social context will find it easier to reproduce that particular movement pattern in an artistic context.

While this is to some extent undeniable, this apparently unexceptional position demands some interrogation, particularly in relation to the way in which some of the quotations above could be interpreted as seeing the development of the individual habitus most suited to classical Indian dance forms as somehow geographically tethered. I consider this question firstly in the light of what social geographer Doreen Massey (1994, 2005) describes as a 'relational' understanding of space, and secondly in relation to the significance of both 'technical' and 'institutional' habitus.

I turn first to Massey's understanding of space. Under this construction, space (and within this wider dimension, the specific location of 'place')[8] is not static but is 'always being made' (Massey 2005: 90);[9] it is 'continually built and rebuilt by relations' (Sergot and Saives 2016). This dynamic, creative understanding of space questions the modernist organizing of space, which 'refuses to acknowledge its multiplicities, its fractures and its dynamism' (Massey 2005: 139).

It is an understanding of space that displaces an India evoked as a repository of cultural forms with a fluid India under permanent recreation (as are all places) by 'histories which are ongoing in the present' (ibid.: 245). Spaces and places change, and the impact of the processes of globalization means that these changes are ever more rapid and unpredictable. Rajarani voices concerns about the ability of her pupils to embody certain movements. Similar reservations, however, about students' ability to truly understand what they are representing are found increasingly within India. Shanti Pillai notes,

> The narratives that abhinaya seeks to express have also simplified. This is in part because many dancers do not have thorough knowledge of the languages in which songs are sung. Young middle-class residents of Chennai do not even have a firm command of Tamil, the language of many dance compositions. Furthermore, many lack an overall knowledge of the mythology and literature that would permit them to explore poetry with greater sophistication or to improvise for longer periods of time upon any single line. (Pillai 2002: 21)

Considering the disjuncture between the world of classical Indian dance students in Britain and the dance world they seek to represent, the dancer quoted at the beginning of this discussion asks, how many of the Britain-based students 'have ever been awoken by a rooster'? But it can equally be asked, how many dancers in Delhi have had this experience, or in Mumbai? How many students of classical Indian dance forms today, in India, Britain or anywhere else, have experienced churning milk into butter with a stick (a commonly depicted motif), or hunting with a bow and arrow, or herding cows? The dancer speaks of the importance of visiting the temples one is dancing about, but how far does a visit to Thanjavur today provide anything like the experience of Thanjavur two hundred years ago when the *varnams* were written? In this time period, the Thanjavur temple has ceased to function as a temple for daily worship, instead forming part of a world heritage site, and bharatanatyam has become a global phenomenon, or in the words of Janet O'Shea, 'a dynamic global practice characterized by local variation' (2007: 166). The danger of too great an emphasis on place lies in too small an appreciation of the effects of time.

It is true that a child in India is more likely to find themselves frequently in environments where, for example, a *shikara* is understood to mean a question and *parivahitam* is understood to mean assent. As Rajarani recognizes, one response to any such lack of experience (both in Britain and in India) would be to try and work with dance students 'as early as possible', so that the teacher's own classical Indian dance habitus (including their bodily *hexis*[10] or that part of habitus which particularly concerns physicality or motor function) can be absorbed by their students. Bourdieu spells out the reality we all encounter, that children learn by imitation:

> The child imitates not 'models' but other people's actions. Body *hexis* speaks directly to the motor function . . . in all societies, children are particularly attentive to the gestures and postures which, in their eyes, express everything that goes to make an accomplished adult – a way of walking, a tilt of the head, facial expressions, ways of sitting and of using implements, always associated with a tone of voice, a style of speech, and (how could it be otherwise?) a certain subjective experience. (Bourdieu 1977: 87)

A child does not limit themselves to a single model, however. A model embodying the habitus of an Indian classical dance style can have a profound influence especially if the child encounters that person consistently from a young age. Katie Ryan, whom I mention in the previous chapter as having had early and consistent lessons with odissi dancer Sanjeevini Dutta, describes her own experience of absorbing the *hexis* and the technical habitus of odissi:

> I think that's all quite subtle and I think I learnt it – I just absorbed it – and I had the advantage of having started at a young age, so I observed my teacher on a weekly basis and picked up mannerisms that way. And I was still at the age that I was developing mannerisms outside dance. I think children do pick up the way they talk, the way they move, the way they act from the people around them. And because I had a lot of contact with the dance teacher during those years, I think it was quite a natural way of learning it. (Ryan 2017)

Such learning through example, however, is not tied to a specific location. Ryan's description relates to her experience in the historic market town of Bedford in the east of England. Her experience of Bedford the place is dictated by the specific confluence of social relations she has encountered in that location – which for her included exposure to the *hexis* of odissi dance through her relationship with Dutta. The same place of Bedford will mean something very different to someone else who experiences a different set of social interweavings that this location has to offer. Habitus responds to the influences of the environment – but the reality of globalization, migration and social movement; the pervasive reach of cable TV and the internet; and the increasing ability of the global rich to insulate themselves from the demands of the physical environment mean that the greater divide today is arguably not the geographical divide between middle-class children in an affluent suburb of London and middle-class children in an affluent suburb of Chennai, but the more substantive economic and socio-relational divide between both these groups and those children for whom poverty makes dance classes impossible.

'An Ear for Rhythm Most Europeans Lack'?

A Brief Note on Race

A further danger of the identification of classical Indian dance forms with a particular place is that this can too easily elide into their identification with a particular race. At Navadisha 2000, a conference on South Asian dance in Britain, the then director of Birmingham Royal Ballet, David Bintley, argued against the practice of South Asian dance forms by non-South Asian dancers, his concern being the 'purity of dance' and the 'need to preserve the origins of each traditional dance form'.[11] I discuss below some of the difficulties involved in ensuring that the vocabularies that make each dance language distinctive are practised and maintained. This may well have been Bintley's overriding concern. However, a response that conflates culture with race highlights just how easy it is to slide from concern about particularity into the chimera of essentialism. When I was working as a dancer with a colleague in the Devonshire town of Totnes (in southwest England) in the early 2000s, a (white) audience member remarked on how 'the stamping of the feet' of my (brown) colleague was so much more distinct than that of mine and asked why this was the case. My colleague responded by saying that she hadn't noticed this and asked the audience member to explain why she felt this, something the lady found impossible to identify except as a 'feeling'. While footwork can be more or less distinct as a result of better or worse technique, a lack of a clearly articulated 'stamp' has not been highlighted by my (expert) teachers over the years as one of my more obvious flaws. In this case it seemed likely that the lady in question was responding less to my footwork than to my (white) race. While her comment was intended as a compliment to my colleague, it was a double-edged compliment along the lines of Agnes De Mille's 1963 assertion highlighted by Keali'inohomoku that 'barefoot savages have an ear for rhythms most Europeans lack' (De Mille, cited in Keali'inohomoku 2001: 39). Like Bintley, she exhibited, as Grau reflects on Bintley's comments, a 'romantic ethnocentrism' (Grau 2001: 38) or exoticism. And, as the politician David Lammy puts it, in the preoccupation with the 'exotic', with 'marketable objects of wonder . . . the underlying force is still racism, even if it has a smiley face' (Lammy 2019). Keali'inohomoku (2001: 38–39) reflects on Walter Sorell's 1967 ascription of differences between dance forms 'to "race" to "racial memory", and to "innate" differences which are "in the blood"', commenting that 'these ideas are so outdated in current anthropology, that I might believe his book was written at the end of the nineteenth century rather than in 1967'. Such beliefs, however, have so pernicious a hold that thirty years later a senior figure in the dance world felt unembarrassed to proclaim them. A further twenty years after this, a quick search on the American question and answer website Quora brings up 'Why are black people so good with music?' and 'Why do Africans have so much energy to dance vigorously all the time?' (Quora 2020). As we know too well, racial stereotypes die hard.

In her witty exploration of sexism, *How to Be a Woman*, journalist Caitlin Moran observes,

> I have a rule of thumb that allows me to judge, when time is pressing and one needs to make a snap judgment, whether or not some sexist bullshit is afoot. Obviously, it's not 100% infallible but by and large it definitely points you in the right direction and it's asking this question; are the men doing it? Are the men worrying about this as well? (Moran 2011: 86)

Combining Moran's approach with that of Keali'inohomoko (2001), I have adopted a similar rule of thumb for classical Indian dance forms, which is asking the question: would the same observation apply to ballet? Are ballet dancers worrying about this as well? So, in terms of spending time in India being a precondition to properly embody Indian classical dance forms, I ask, must a ballet dancer who wishes to embody Giselle first spend some time having a picnic on the banks of the Rhine? Is the ballet danced by ballet dancers in China less balletic because the dancers have not been to Paris? Individual habitus is shaped by place, environment and culture – however, place, environment and culture are not static, but subject to constant change. 'Habitus' is both structured and structuring in a constant exchange with its environment, which results in the incremental change of both.

While aligning one race as particularly suited to the practice of a certain type of dance (ideally) in a certain location, this same view excludes that race from the practice of a different type of dance in another location, the logical conclusion being the separation of cultures and races into different spheres, different places, different nations. India posited as the standard of authenticity for classical Indian dance forms at the same time calls into question the ability of these forms to represent Britishness. Under this construction, classical Indian dance forms in Britain are only ever given a provisional leave to remain.

Labour, Physical Capital and 'Technical Habitus'

This is not to suggest that the geographic or architectural particularities of a place are entirely irrelevant or unimportant. Returning to the reference to the Thanjavur temple, the significance for a bharatanatyam dancer of visiting, for example, the temples at Chidambaram or Thanjavur is something that many dancers and teachers subscribe to – I would certainly encourage my own students to visit these places if they went on a trip to India. As a keen dance student, I visited these temples myself, and it is undeniable that the majesty of the Thanjavur temple fires the imagination. It did so in part, however, because of the layers of interpretation I imposed on it through my reading about it and its role, and because of my sense of familiarity with and affection for it, which I had already acquired as a student learning dances that referred to it. Art historian Simon Schama argues that 'Before it can ever be a repose for the senses, landscape is a work of the mind. Its scenery is built up as much from strata of memory as from layers of rock' (1995: 7). The same applies to the architectural landscape. Returning to the discussion of aesthetic and artistry raised in Chapter 1, to achieve more than an immediate or sensual grasp of the significance of the Thanjavur temple relies on a proper grasp of the narrative in which this temple is a part. This in turn relies on the labour spent on acquiring this understanding, rather than some sort of transfer of meaning by osmosis through contact with the earth on which the temple is built.

In Bourdieu's terms, such an understanding of the significance of the Thanjavur temple relies on a particular cultural capital. Like all forms of capital, cultural capital represents 'accumulated labour' (Bourdieu 1986: 241). 'Embodied cultural capital' in particular 'cannot be transmitted instantaneously . . . by gift or bequest, purchase or exchange' but necessitates 'a process of embodiment . . . through a labour of inculcation and assimilation . . . invested personally by the investor' (ibid.: 244). It requires an investment 'above all of time' but also of '*libido sciendi*' (or a desire or thirst to know) 'with all the privation, renunciation and sacrifice that may entail' (ibid.). Culture, he argues elsewhere, is achieved through 'ascesis' (from the Greek *askesis*, or training) or discipline (Bourdieu and Wacquant 1992). Such discipline inflects and remoulds a person's individual habitus with one that is consciously and deliberately acquired (though it then becomes unconscious or 'second-nature'), through 'pedagogic devices' or 'awareness and pedagogic effort' (Bourdieu 2005: 45). In the dance context, this labour endows the individual with specific physical and cultural capital embodied within what I have called a 'technical habitus'. 'Technical habitus' relates to its social context but is also to an extent insulated from it in that is governed by the framework of its own 'field' and its own discipline.

Thus while 'technical habitus' builds on and can accentuate aspects of a person's 'individual habitus', there is obviously a difference, as dance ethnologist Deirdre Sklar (2008) points out, between everyday gesture and gesture as used in art, even when those gestures may appear 'the same'. 'Technical habitus' is not 'natural' but acquired and rests on the deliberate labour or exertion put into acquiring it. Very simply, a person living in India who does not study and practise kathak will not (despite all the advantages of a sympathetic social context) be as good a kathak dancer as a person who spends hours each day doing their *riyaaz* (practice) and perfecting their *chakars* (spins), though they might live in an environment less obviously aligned to their dance form. It is the distinction between what is absorbed (through one's environment) and what is acquired (through one's effort) that allows Banerjee to argue in the epigraph at the start of the chapter, 'there are people who live in India who speak brilliant English. Similarly, there are those who live in England who perform excellent kathak. You don't need to live in England to speak the best English. You don't need to be in India to perform the best kathak' (Banerjee 2017).

This is also why the technique of a dancer in the National Ballet of China may be inflected by individual and institutional habitus, but the technical habitus remains recognizably that of ballet. In this way, any dance technique necessarily builds upon a dancer's individual habitus, but beyond this relies on training to instil in the dancer the distinctive habitus of their distinctive dance style.

Ascesis, Sadhana, Technical Habitus and the Limits of Location

> For hours and hours, we would just do *'nadhindhin da, nadhindhin da'* . . . for one or one and a half hours . . . And I think that that precision of the *'nadhindhin da'* is so embedded within me that now I don't need to do four or five hours of *riyaaz* – one or two hours of good *riyaaz* helps me to go on stage. (Ashwini Kalsekar, in Manch UK 2020b)

The concept of a cultural form or a 'technical habitus' requiring patient cultivation and 'ascesis' is one that resonates for many bodily disciplines (see for example sociologist Loic Wacquant (1995) on the culture of boxing), and classical Indian dance forms are no exception. As Foster (1997) points out, such training tends to be repetitive, and is most effective when pursued every day because daily routines best create 'bodily habits'. She explains, 'Drilling is necessary because the aim is nothing less than creating the body. With repetition the images used to describe the body and its actions become the body' (ibid.: 239). As with Wacquant's boxers, the training that many dancers (including classical Indian dancers) undergo is such that it 'practically reorganizes their entire corporeal field . . . bringing to prominence certain organs and abilities and making others recede, transforming not only . . . physique, but also . . . body-sense' (Wacquant 1995: 73). It is a process that requires a level of discipline and self-denying commitment to the art form identified by classical Indian dancers as *sadhana*: a Sanskrit term meaning 'methodical discipline or exercise towards a desired knowledge or goal', which has a clear correspondence with the term 'ascesis', including in its religious connotations. The value of *sadhana* is high within the field of classical Indian dance. In 2018, for example, Akram Khan described his choice of a couple of bharatanatyam artists for the classical Indian dance and music festival Darbar, explaining, 'I was impressed not only by their virtuosity, but as you say, their way of thinking – their commitment to their dance – their *sadhana* – their devotion to their dance – it comes across in their work' (field notes, 23 November 2018).

Sadhana in the dance context (it is a concept found across several fields) takes the form of committed and rigorous practice of one's art form – the *riyaaz* that kathak artist Ashwini Kalsekar describes in the quotation above.[12]

Practice, or *riyaaz*, as any dancer knows, can be relentless and exhausting. Any structure, therefore, that can support the pursuit of this practice will make for a more conducive learning environment. In this sense, not in the sense of a determinist geographical tethering, but in terms of a recognition of the type of institutional support available, it absolutely remains the case that training within classical Indian dance forms in India is an easier proposition because, at present at least, the environment offers more opportunity for immersion within the field of classical Indian dance. Dancers in Britain, as discussed in the last chapter, train and acquire a technical habitus through a mixture of weekend, evening and holiday classes, not infrequently conducted in front rooms or converted garages (see also Srinivasan 2012). The acquisition of any specific institutional habitus within this is obviously hampered by the lack of institutions.

As discussed, there is currently no full-time training available in classical Indian dance forms within a British institution. This is a lack keenly felt by dancers within the sector. Gorringe et al.'s (2018) report cites one dancer saying, for example,

> I feel that if I had full-time training at some point, I would be better equipped as technique, stamina and understanding would be developed considerably compared to hav[ing] a once-a-week class and practising in my own time. Classes and practice in one's own time cannot be compared to full-time training in terms of rigour and intensity. (Cited in Gorringe et al. 2018: 35)

Another observes, 'I think I would be much more equipped to work as a dancer in the UK if I had more rigorous and constant training' (ibid.).

Additionally, the lack of a vocational school means that it is harder for dancers to find the motivation and energy that comes from training in a group. Pushkala Gopal explains:

> If you get to a good class in India, you find enough people of your standard in a particular group. Here you could be getting a little stagnant because you are the best among five or six others in your class – and . . . there isn't anyone else . . . whom you could pick up tricks from. And then also the pace of the class has to go at a mean level for the others to match the standard – and therefore you are more likely to find classes with more challenging material in India. (Gopal 2018)

This is a sentiment echoed by Rajarani,

> If I wanted to go to a morning class here, where would I go? There isn't one. A group class where there are ten people of the standard I am dancing to? I would have to dance on my own and pay a huge fee to somebody. And it's not the same thing. I found it so motivating to dance in a group of people in a similar situation to me – who just wanted to dance. (Rajarani 2018)

Without such support, dancers find that they need to be 'really self-motivating' (Patel 2017), with one dancer describing her training journey as 'years of solitary training and work being done in the background . . . to work as a dancer has been a slow and independent journey' (cited in Gorringe et al. 2018: 35).

Against this context, India remains, unsurprisingly, a favoured destination for dancers wanting to train intensively. Thus, Sabri:

> One of the advantages of training in India is that there is access to that full-time training. You are not only working with your peers – but you have the opportunity to work with musicians, poets, vocalists, yoga – all the constituent elements that make up the study of your art – you have full access to that in India. So, in an institute like a Kendra, in the morning you do your yoga. Then you do your tabla practice. Then your training – six hours – then back to theory – then body conditioning. That's a full day immersed in the art form. Here that's a huge void . . . To be embedded in the fraternity of your art, of kathak, or music – that positive energy, that constant thinking and questioning and talking – to be immersed in that is hugely, hugely important in your training – and that is non-existent here. (Sabri 2018)

Or again, Ryan: 'over there [India] I was able to train every day and I have not really been able to do that here . . . Summer schools did give me that kind of opportunity, but that's always for ten days at a time, and that's quite a short period' (Ryan 2017).

Does this present reality, however, mean a geographical tethering of Indian classical dance forms to the geographical location of India? While at present, on a number of levels, including institutional infrastructure, India offers an environment more conducive to the practice of Indian classical dance forms, does this necessarily mean that this will always be the case?

Choreographic Habitus and Training in Classical Indian Dance Forms in Britain

There is a further factor that limits the training of classical Indian dancers in Britain, in this case particularly with respect to the training of professional dancers, and this is the lack of (professional) demand for the 'technical habitus' that training in classical Indian dance forms affords. This brings me to the second key focus of this chapter and relates to the question raised in the previous chapter – 'what are we training for?' This is where Wainwright et al.'s third category – that of 'choreographic habitus' – becomes relevant. The term 'choreographic habitus' begs a question in the context of classical Indian dance forms, where the dance styles (as mentioned in earlier chapters) have characteristically been performed as part of a solo dance tradition. Whether the arrangement of movement for a solo dancer is rightly called choreography, and how far this term from the Euro-American dance context can appropriately be applied to classical Indian dance forms, are important questions but are not key to my point here. Rather, I use the term to signal the habitus that dance work in Britain demands, the kind of habitus that choreographers are looking for and thereby the kind of habitus that will be reinforced by 'rehearsing and performing in a certain style' (Wainwright et al. 2006: 545). In the cases where there is some limited institutional support for classical Indian dance training in Britain, such as through Yuva Gati, or through the short-lived BA at LCDS (see Chapter 3), these institutions, as illustrated, then face difficult choices about what they choose to teach and how they decide to train young dancers so that the 'technical habitus' they are imbued with can find a place within the 'choreographic habitus' of the professional world.

As touched on in earlier chapters, classical Indian dancers in Britain characteristically find themselves answering to two very different performance or choreographic demands – the demands of the diasporic community, or of others aiming to highlight and celebrate aspects of the culture of this community, and the demands of the professional dance world (O'Shea 2007; Kedhar 2014, 2020; Meduri 2020). As seen in the last chapter, until recently Arts Council funding criteria encouraged a situation whereby, as Sitara Thobani observes, 'dancers in London often contrast "professional" performances and venues with their "community" counterparts . . . the latter encapsulate classical performances presented to mostly South Asian audiences . . . in contrast, the professional designation is most often reserved for performances of Contemporary South Asian dance' (Thobani 2017 114).

The 'contemporary South Asian dance' referred to often requires a level of fluency with Euro-American contemporary dance styles. The audition call-out for Akademi's touring work *Paradiso* (Jose Agudo, 2016), for example, which aimed to 'illustrate how British Indian dance is integral to the UK dance scene,'[13] sought for the performance of 'British Indian dance' 'highly skilled and experienced contemporary dancers', with 'South Asian Dance experience desirable, though not essential',[14] and as discussed previously, contemporary dance experience is a frequent requirement of several of the more established companies that also draw on classical Indian dance styles, including Shobana Jeyasingh and Akram Khan companies. Gorringe et al. (2018: 36) cite classical Indian dancers describing how 'most dance company/project auditions value non-stylistic movement quality in the UK, which was obviously limited in my classical training';

how 'I have also found that I need to have some training in ballet/contemporary dance if I want to stand a good chance at a company audition'; and most damningly how 'I feel that my training has equipped me very well in classical Indian dance – but that this is not what is wanted in the UK'.

There are clearly some parts of Britain in which classical Indian dance forms are 'wanted'. As Banerjee observes, 'In some ways, ironically, South Asian dancers probably get more platforms to perform – in that they could be invited to perform for Diwali and on other such occasions' (Banerjee 2017). However, these are on the whole 'more community performances. There aren't many professional companies' (ibid.). Importantly for dancers, it is often the 'professional work' that is reasonably competitively paid, while dancers might be expected to give a community performance for free or for an honorarium. In Bourdieu's terms, within the field of British dance, the position of classical Indian dance forms, as non-dominant forms with limited legitimacy and establishment support, impacts upon a dancer's ability to transform the cultural and physical capital that they have acquired into financial capital. While classical Indian dance forms may retain high cultural and symbolic (if not financial) value within South Asian communities, within the field of British dance this value is yet to be established.

As seen in the last chapter, rather than the dancer trained intensively and in depth in a classical Indian dance form alone, it is the dancer who can 'traverse the boundaries of contemporary and bharatanatyam/kathak' who is in demand 'to serve the needs of working choreographers' (Lewis 2018). In this way, in order to succeed in the professional dance world, many dancers find themselves having to significantly alter or abandon the 'habitus' of their primary dance training, and training institutions such as Yuva Gati feel the pressure to try to make their students 'versatile enough to ensure that they can have a self-sustaining dance career whether that is in the wider dance sector or whether they stay true to their own traditional dance roots . . . and obviously contemporary has a much wider spread' (Henwood and Lewis 2018). In order for the cultural and physical capital painstakingly acquired by classical Indian dancers to be harnessed in the professional field of British dance, it has commonly needed to find a way of combining with, or in some other way integrating within, the values of Euro-American contemporary dance, with dancers often repeatedly facing the kind of discomfort and embarrassment I describe as my own experience at the beginning of the chapter.[15] Rather than do this, there are those who have simply chosen to opt out. Gorringe et al. (2018: 57) cite one dancer who admits, 'One of the reasons that I left dance was that I felt pushed into doing contemporary work', while others, 'rather than compromise what they see as the integrity of their art forms simply choose to avoid the professional context in Britain and find other ways to fulfil their dreams and ambitions as dancers' (ibid.).

Perhaps it is unrealistic to expect a career today for anything other than a versatile dancer. An article in the newspaper *The Stage*, which focuses on the world of Britain's performing arts, is unambivalent: 'Today's perfect dancer is versatile: "They have not one foundation technique, but two, with competency in a third style or more", says Rachel Rist, head of dance at Tring Park School for the Performing Arts' (Hanly 2016). Dancers across the board, as the previous chapter highlights, boost their employability with an ever greater range of skills, including circus skills such as juggling and gymnastics. The demand for the 'versatile dancer', then, can be perceived as a leveller. If all dancers are required to be ever more multitalented, what does it really matter what one's 'foundation' form is? All dancers will be required to have multiple competencies after all. The apparent logic of this position, however, founders in two main ways. First, because 'versatility' in dance, as I discuss below, characteristically comes at a cost, a cost more likely to be paid by non-dominant dance forms, or at the expense of the non-dominant technical habitus. Second, because 'versatility' is not a neutral entity, and the perception of one's 'versatility' largely depends on how that versatility is defined and on who decides what it looks like. Accordingly, I now take a closer look at 'versatility' in the context of British dance and what the demand for it means for the professional practice of classical Indian dance forms in Britain.

The Limits of Versatility

In a fascinating article reflecting on how different training styles differently shape the bodies of ballet dancers, Geraldine Morris (2003) draws on the work of the former orthopaedic surgeon for the Royal Ballet, Justin Howse, to illuminate her argument. He explains how 'Constant, exact repetition or practice will produce an engram – a condition where individual muscles or movement are not consciously considered' (Howse 2000: 19). In Bourdieu's terms, Howse describes here the mechanics behind the physical aspect of habitus, the *hexis*. This condition of an unconscious facility or instinct for movement is one dancers recognize, without necessarily appreciating the physiology behind it. Thus, in the quotation from kathak dancer Ashwini Kalsekar earlier on in this chapter, she describes the fluency of movement she gained through hours of repetition of a single movement. Pushkala Gopal makes a similar point in an interview: '"I trust in rote learning", she says. "Someone who learns their times tables processes maths much more easily." Can the same apply to the arts? "Absolutely. Repeat something 200 times and you know it completely – and in performance you can pull out things you didn't know were there"' (Gopal, in Chakrabortty 2009).

A reliance on engrams or being able to rely on one's body to 'pull out things you didn't know were there' is arguably vital for the professional dancer in that they 'allow a complicated movement to be performed far more rapidly than would be possible if conscious thought of each pattern were required' at the same time as producing 'inhibition of unwanted movements' (Howse 2000: 19). Dancer and choreographer Joshua Monten explains the benefits of 'engrams' in practice: 'considering the number of muscles, joints, dynamics, rhythms and outside events that dancers need to co-ordinate – it is often a blessing to be able to bypass deliberation and rely on one's instincts' (Monten 2008: 61).

What happens to the 'instincts', or more widely, the *hexes* pertaining to each distinct dance form when a dancer is required to train in a plurality of dance styles? For Monten, whose own experience of training was in a range of dance forms, 'To the extent that training is about making choices, developing versatility is a boon. But to the extent that it is about instilling instincts, having too many training techniques can be problematic' (2008: 61). As an illustration, he cites dancer and choreographer Twyla Tharp, whose eclectic training meant that she felt that her movements derived from 'rational decisions' where for her fellow dancers in the company they 'seemed like instincts' (Tharp, cited in ibid.: 62). She had to work to perform what to her colleagues came naturally. Ultimately, she felt, 'I was suffering from my eclectic training . . . I had been given too many options' (ibid.). In the course of Monten's own training in several different movement styles he found that he was forced to 'learn to negotiate physical imperatives that often seem mutually exclusive'. He describes vividly how his efforts to master the low crouch and groundedness of his capoeira training conflicted with the demands for lightness and extension in his ballet class. 'Although the cumulative effect of these varied subjects was a general, slowly increasing physical proficiency', he reflects, 'interferences and confusion did occur along the way' (ibid.: 60).

For Tharp, ultimately, while she never attained 'the level of seamless integrated classical training that she was aiming for', she found that she was able to combine the differing demands of her diverse training to find a 'new language capable of saying new things' (Tharp, in Monten 2008: 62). Monten cites the choreographer and critic Elizabeth Dempster, who likewise holds a positive view that eclectic training offers 'a body available to the play of many discourses. Post-modern dance directs attention away from any specific image of the body and towards the process of constructing all bodies' (Dempster, in ibid.). Yet, as Foster (1997) and Monten (2008) argue, such versatility comes at a cost. This is because, to quote Foster, 'Each dance technique constructs a specialized and specific body – one that represents a given choreographer's or tradition's aesthetic vision of dance' (1997: 241). Versatile bodies can apparently 'do anything' – but they cannot always embody the particular qualities of bodily bearing and dynamics that characterize a specific form.

The reality of this was memorably brought home to me in 2003 while watching *Polar Sequences*, a set of pieces choreographed for Wayne McGregor's Random company dancers by three different choreographers, including one piece by Shobana Jeyasingh. Random dancers have a justified reputation for brilliance and this occasion was no exception – their skill, strength and flexibility were such that it seemed they should be able to do anything. Partway into the dance Jeyasingh had choreographed a *tat tei ta ha* sequence – a commonly used bharatanatyam *adavu* set that requires the dancer to sit in *aramandi*, stamping alternate feet and jumping (while maintaining *aramandi*) onto the toes or balls of the feet, while the arms stretch out to the sides and across the body with the hands held in *tripataka* (a *mudra* where the fourth finger is bent forward). Suddenly the fluidity and poise that had marked the dancers to that point was replaced by uncertainty and discomfort. Their hands strained awkwardly to hold the unfamiliar position; their *aramandi* lacked groundedness as they jumped on to their toes. These dancers for all their brilliance simply did not possess the bharatanatyam habitus.

Clearly it is possible for certain dancers to possess a fluency in multiple dance languages to the extent that they are able to embody multiple *hexes* and switch between these as the occasion demands. One example of such a dancer would be the ballet, contemporary and bharatanatyam dancer Mavin Khoo. He has achieved this, however, not by replacing the hours spent on bharatanatyam with hours spent on ballet, but by increasing the overall time he has spent working. The same is true of Akram Khan, who in order to work as a contemporary dancer (after his initial training in kathak, Khan went on to train in contemporary dance at Northern School of Contemporary Dance and then at De Montfort University) without compromising his kathak, starts his day with 'three hours of classical Indian dance from 6 to 9 in the morning before my rehearsals begin'.[16] Just as with the dual-career dancers discussed in Chapter 2, however, this requirement to work overtime to continue one's practice of a classical dance style is highly demanding, both mentally and physically. How realistic is it to expect such commitment not from the exceptional, but from every dancer?

Without such labour-intensive and time-consuming efforts to counterbalance it, a danger with eclectic training (and with the 'versatile dancer') will be that the dancer's primary aesthetics and instincts default to those of the hegemonic dance discourse. Dempster enthuses about the eclectically trained body as 'a body available to the play of many discourses' – conjuring an image of a fluid to and fro between several discourses. In reality, however, just as in the wider conversations in a multicultural society, the minority viewpoint must fight to hold its own. In the Euro-American context the dominant discourse embraces a Euro-American aesthetic, and the body 'available to the play of many discourses' will reflect this dominance accordingly. In a reflective article on global trends in the representation of Asian dance forms, Ananya Chatterjea cautions that 'sharing space requires an interrogation of historic inequities and hostilities, and we need to be vigilant that these old violences are not perpetuated under the guise of the "new" global ventures' (Chatterjea 2013: 14). In other words, in the 'play of discourses', we must not forget which of those discourses is holding a microphone.

To continue with this image, this 'microphone' can take several forms, including, as touched on above, a better resourced infrastructure. Thus, a dancer attempting to train in contemporary dance as well as classical Indian dance in the UK will encounter a gravitational nudge towards contemporary dance at every step of their training – simply because this is the direction in which they are channelled by the available infrastructure. Without a clear route to vocational training, classical Indian dancers in Britain lack a further means that Bourdieu identifies to establish the value of cultural capital – 'sanction by legally guaranteed qualifications' (1986: 248). An aspiring professional dancer looking for full-time intensive dance training must therefore make their own arrangements without institutional backing in a manner, as Bourdieu points out, 'that can be called into question at any time' (ibid.). If they seek institutional support and affirmation, the options are to choose between training in India[17] or opting to study contemporary dance. Alex Croft, director of Bradford-based arts organization Kala Sangam, reflects,

> We have to find a way of picking up those young people who have that burning passion to be a kathak dancer, to be a bharatanatyam dancer, and what there is missing at the moment – is – if we found that gem of a person here at Kala Sangam, where would we push that person to? At the moment where I would push them to is into contemporary dance because you can go through high-quality contemporary dance training, here, in the North. At the moment there isn't anywhere else to send them. (Croft 2017)

In October 2019, Yuva Gati graduate Aishani Ghosh started a degree in Contemporary Dance at LCDS. However, her mother remarked that 'as a parent I feel that actually she is a South Asian dancer. Her body is a bharatanatyam body. Doing other things are an extra. If she could do a degree in South Asian dance and do other styles (e.g., contemporary) on the side, she could be true to herself' (cited in Gorringe et al. 2018: 53).

Once dancers have graduated, the infrastructural bias continues. Asked about her chief challenges as a bharatanatyam dancer working in Britain Shivaangee Agrawal replied,

> The biggest challenge is training. I don't have a regular and affordable way of training – it's really frustrating. Private classes with Guruji are great – but I can only afford them once a week. I want to be able to train like contemporary dancers train – to go to morning class as a thing I do every morning before I start my day. So that's probably the biggest challenge – funding this incredibly expensive training. Not that Guruji is incredibly expensive – his fee is reasonable relative to other options – but it just seems crazy to me that I have to spend that much money to maintain my skills when contemporary dancers are paying £4 a class. (Agrawal 2019b)

Archana Ballal, a graduate of the short-lived LCDS BA in Contemporary Dance (South Asian Dance Strand), makes the same point.

> Then I go to contemporary class. I'm not doing bharatanatyam class at the moment, but I practise. I have a friend who teaches yoga in Hackney – so sometimes I can use that space to do my *adavu* practice – or in my own home – in my kitchen . . . Contemporary classes are easier to fit in because they're central . . . and they are also a lot cheaper – like £4 or £5 – that helps doesn't it? (Ballal 2017)[18]

Cost and practicality make it substantially easier for a dancer to continue regular training in contemporary rather than classical Indian dance. The microphone stays with contemporary dance.

Whose Versatility?

This amplification continues through the types of technical habitus and the type of versatility that are then sought by choreographers. Who decides what constitutes versatility? It is not uncommon, for example, for classical Indian dancers in Britain to have a knowledge of two classical Indian dance styles (for example bharatanatyam and odissi, or bharatanatyam and mohiniattam), and many dancers extend their versatility through, for example, training in the martial arts form kalarippaiyattu. Such versatility, however, judging by the experience of the dancers in this study, is not usually sufficient to land regular work as a performing artist in Britain. The British dance field, it appears, seeks a different kind of versatility, one that takes as its starting point the aesthetics and the technical habitus of Euro-American contemporary dance forms.

Returning to the example of Jose Agudo's *Paradiso*, produced by Akademi, Archita Kumar, the only dancer in the piece without contemporary dance training, is not in the ensemble work, and for much of the piece remains on the outside of the drawn circle, looking at the dancers within. This is justified within *Paradiso*'s overarching narrative in that Kumar represents Beatrice, whose role is in itself somewhat apart from the other 'characters'. Equally, however, the lunges, leaps and floorwork of the ensemble choreography do not play to the strengths of a kathak dancer. Had the ensemble work featured fast staccato footwork, or the nuance of the distinctive relationship between text and movement found in *abhinaya*, the roles would have been reversed – and those dancers without a depth of training in classical Indian dance forms may have remained 'outside' the circle. Kumar's positioning within *Paradiso* offers, on a small scale, an illustration of the wider pattern of representation of dance in Britain, in which classical Indian dance forms remain on the outside of the drawn circle, looking in. It is telling that in *Paradiso*'s audition call-out, training in South Asian dance was 'desirable but not essential'. In the eventual piece, two of the six dancers had the

Figure 4.1. Dancers in Akademi's Paradiso *on the rooftop of the Royal Festival Hall, London. 2017*
© *Simon Richardson.*

'technical habitus' of a classical Indian dance form – Kumar and the contemporary and bharatanatyam dancer Kamala Devam.[19] The other four dancers had the 'technical habitus' of contemporary dance – perhaps unsurprisingly as choreographer Agudo, while trained in kathak, also has a primary habitus of contemporary dance.[20] Thus, when the other four dancers performed the vocabulary of classical Indian dance, their movements bore the unmistakable accent of their contemporary dance training.

Embodying a dance form is not simply about making shapes. As Foster puts it, when learning another dance technique, 'imitating movements and shapes is just the first step. It must be accompanied by studying and internalising elaborate anatomical, functional and expressive metaphorical systems that give colour and meaning to movement' (1997: 64). Or, in Bourdieu's terms, habitus relies not only on a physical disposition (*hexis*), but also on a particular mindset; being 'endowed with habitus implies knowledge and recognition of the immanent laws of the game', and includes not only a set of physical dispositions, but also a 'set of beliefs' (Bourdieu 1993: 72).

Whatever the physical dispositions demanded of a 'versatile dancer' in Britain, the 'set of beliefs' belong to that 'wonderfully unifying and legitimising aesthetic category of "contemporary dance" (really meaning Euro-American modern/contemporary dance)' (Chatterjea 2013: 10). Against this dominant set of beliefs, the technical habitus of the classical Indian dancer in Britain is positioned as always already a deficit, in a perspective that frames a group's qualities (or capital) 'based on what they lack' (Wallace 2016: 38). One tutor describes the insidious impact of this framing on students: 'they come to the course with a fairly open mind, but as things progress, they get to the idea that if they have not done ballet or contemporary dance, that they can't be professional. . . . This sense that they need to train in contemporary dance and ballet – is like the smoke in the air' (anon., interviewed by Gorringe for the Dance Hub Feasibility report, 2018).

Bourdiesian scholar Sam Friedman points out that such internalizing of a 'deficit perspective' should not be underestimated, but serves as 'an active constituent of the notion of barriers to success' (Friedman 2016b: 117). In this light, the 'play of discourses' is not even about who is holding the microphone. It is about who owns the stage.

'British Dance is Defined by Its Diversity'?

Serving on the panel of judges for the *BBC Young Dancer* competition in 2019, contemporary dancer and choreographer Wayne McGregor observed that 'British dance is defined by its diversity' (BBC 2019). On the same programme, hip-hop dancer and choreographer Jonzi D commented of the four dance styles featured that it was 'going to be difficult in future to isolate these styles as they are continually influencing each other' (BBC 2019). If Jonzi D is right, what shape will this intertwining of forms take? Given the dominance of Euro-American contemporary dance discussed, it is difficult to see how this 'intertwining of forms' will reflect any other than this dominant habitus, with elements from other dance styles, including the '*hugely* skilled practice' of classical Indian dance forms, being scattered within this habitus 'like putting sprinkles on ice cream' (Sabri 2018). Chatterjea's range of experience in her various capacities supports this view. Her perception is of a 'slow and steady erasure of difference in the name of globalization' (2013: 12):

> While the idea of the 'global' seems to offer the promise of a range of aesthetics and a range of bodies from different contexts marking widely different understandings of beauty and power, the reality of what materializes on stage seems to suggest that there are some unspoken conditions for participation on the global stage that ensure some kinds of conformity. (ibid.)

In this scenario, what happens to the 'diversity' that McGregor feels 'defines' British dance?

In raising this question, I share Chatterjea's discomfort about seeming to 'end up as some kind of champion for encrusted categories of tradition' who would deny choreographers their 'aesthetic choice' (Chatterjea 2013: 12). At the same time, it seems evident that, in the words of former Greater London Council dance officer Lynn Maree, 'These things are always organic, but *if you only teach to the developed and never go back to the roots, you lose something*' (Maree 2017, my emphasis). So how do we ensure, to repeat Akram Khan's question cited in Chapter 1, that 'on the one hand . . . South Asian dance [is] still protected in a sense of its form', while on the other, artists are allowed to 'find a way to . . . take aspects of South Asian dance to a more contemporary place'?

In 1999, cultural theorist Stuart Hall addressed a conference looking at the 'impact of cultural diversity on Britain's Living Heritage'. In his keynote speech, he cautioned that 'unless the younger generation [have access to] their repertoires, idioms and languages of representation . . . and can understand them and practise them to some extent at least, from the inside, they will lack the resources – the cultural capital – of their own "heritage", as a base from which to engage with other traditions' (Hall 1999: 22). What Hall, Maree and Khan advocate is a cultivation of 'repertoires, idioms and languages of representation' on their own terms, running parallel with the way that such repertoires are then transformed and entwined in the inevitable exchange of cultural flows.

An obvious question is whether the existing institutions and teaching schools, such as the Bharatiya Vidya Bhavan, the 'sixty to eighty' schools within London and the '350' teachers across Britain (see Chapter 3), are not sufficient to this end. Applying the previously cited 'Moran test' once again, would institutions offering part-time classes primarily at evenings and weekends be considered to provide a sufficient grounding in the 'repertoires and idioms' of ballet or contemporary dance forms? Possibly, for those taking dance as a hobby, but what about those taking it as a profession? What is the cultural, symbolic and economic impact on classical Indian dance forms of the continued lack of a full-time vocational course in Britain? What does this mean for these dance forms attempting to hold their own in the 'play of discourses' of the professional dance arena?

Almost thirty years ago, Jeyasingh argued that 'South Asian, African and Caribbean dance styles are major elements of British national dance culture, and should have their own schools and training institutions for the development of professional dancers and these styles in Britain' (Jeyasingh, in Brinson 1993: 56). To work with dancers trained in India was, she felt, like 'having the nursery in India and the orchard in England'. Rather, she argued for the establishment within Britain of 'an institution where somebody could undertake serious full-time training in Indian dance. Then the message would be given that this degree of specialisation can't be left to the domain of part time and evening classes' (ibid.: 57).

Gorringe et al. (2018) reflect likewise that for South Asian dance forms to maintain the distinctive aesthetic sensibility and rigour that characterize them, 'and yet equally reflect the distinctive quality and preoccupations of the UK that speak to our present moment', 'We need to decide whether these forms are central to our national culture, or whether they remain exotic imports that occasionally enliven our customary diet of ballet, Western theatre and contemporary dance. If the answer is the former we will need to invest – and crucially we will need to invest in training' (ibid.: 61).

Yet to invest in training, as this chapter and the previous chapter have argued, is of little use unless there are also jobs suited to the training that these dancers have received. To create such jobs also relies on building an audience for the type of work these dancers can perform. To put it another way, it involves shifting the onus of 'versatility' away from the dancer and onto the audience, away from the watched and onto the 'watcher'. The more versatile the audience, the broader their 'horizon of expectations' (Mignolo 2007: 494), the less the dancer must work overtime, distort their preferred dance form or otherwise contort themselves to conform to the narrowness of desire.

Conclusion

This chapter raises the challenges of training (or of acquiring a technical habitus) in a dance form that originated in one cultural context for a dancer whose individual habitus has been inflected and shaped by a very different cultural context. A dynamic view of both 'culture' and 'space' (Massey 2005) urges against a geographical tethering in which a culture and a territory are seen to have an unnegotiated link, while allowing for a wider sociopolitical framework that might enable one location to provide an artist with better infrastructural and institutional support than another (thus making the India of 2020 an easier place in which to immerse oneself in training in a classical Indian dance form than the Britain of 2020). The rise (in Britain and beyond) of the demand for the 'versatile' dancer loads the die against the development of a classical Indian dancer in Britain due to the weight of a dominant Euro-American dance discourse, amplified by greater resources and infrastructural support. A commitment to a Britain in which dance is 'defined by its diversity' rests on being able to provide dancers with facilities to acquire not only the *hexis*, but the *habitus* of classical Indian dance styles within Britain. Such provision is only viable where there is the development of a corresponding professional demand for the dancer with this particular 'technical' habitus. This is a demand that necessitates the development of versatility not of the dancer, but of the audience. Having thus far considered the creation of performers, therefore, the next chapter looks at the other, crucial factor in the equation of professionalization – the creation of demand, or in the case of dance, of audiences.

Notes

1. Wacquant observes that there seems to be 'a drift over time' in Bourdieu's thoughts on habitus from a more mentalist to a more corporeal emphasis (Bourdieu and Wacquant 1992: 120).
2. As a simple example, at a large gathering of academics in London participants might instinctively seek to shake hands by way of greeting, whereas in Chennai they might join their palms together in front of their chest.
3. 'Think how culturally revealing it is', she reminds us, 'to see the stylised Western customs enacted on the stage, such as the mannerisms from the age of chivalry, courting, weddings, christenings, burial, and mourning customs . . . Our aesthetic values are shown in the long line of lifted, extended bodies, in the total revealing of legs . . . in the lifts and carryings of the female . . . there are societies whose members would be shocked at the public display of the male touching the female's thighs' (Keali'inohomoku 2001: 40).
4. This also means, as dance scholar Anurima Banerji argues, that aspects of what I term the 'technical habitus' of Indian classical dance forms enshrine an 'identitarian politics of difference on the grounds of gender and caste' (Banerji 2021a: 133), which perpetuates damaging gender and caste stereotypes. Banerji's suggestion (which, no doubt, Bourdieu would have applauded) is that we treat the 'Laws of Movement' prescribed in the *Natyashastra* and subsequently embodied in the idiom of classical Indian dance forms with a 'critical consciousness' so as to employ 'radical and transformative interpretations' of textual and bodily languages and instead 'perform egalitarian social relationships' (ibid.: 149). Banerji raises here a very important point about ensuring that damaging power structures are not imported with a specific 'technical habitus' and the need for critical engagement with a prescribed idiom to transform and redeploy it.
5. A *kolam* is an intricate pattern of dots and weaving lines, characteristically made out of white and coloured rice flour, usually drawn outside houses in South India to repel the evil eye. Drawing a *kolam* is a common activity depicted within bharatanatyam dance pieces.
6. One of the nine *shirobhedas* or head movements for dance and drama set out in the *Natyashastra* involving tilting the head from side to side.
7. Usually, the first dance taught to students of bharatanatyam and the opening dance in the *margam* or repertoire, often performed together with a *Pushpanjali* (a short dance representing a greeting through an offering of flowers).
8. Massey describes place as not 'bounded', but as 'open and porous networks of social relations' (1991: 121).
9. This is a concept she links to Appadurai's understanding of 'areas' in motion, or 'process geography' (Appadurai 2000).
10. Habitus can be seen as *hexis* plus a certain socially conditioned way of being in the world. Thus, my bodily *hexis* means that I find the gesture of *anjali*, with both palms joined together at the chest, a natural one to assume, while my habitus means that it is the more automatic form of greeting I assume than a 'handshake'. Covid-19 temporarily shifted the habitus of many in this regard.
11. I was present at Navadisha 2000, and still recall the shock and disappointment I felt when Bintley raised this question. For this account, however, I draw on dance artist and cultural activist Anita Ratnam's record of events (Ratnam 2000).

12. See Srinivasan (2012: 29–38) for a beautiful and detailed description of the highly specialized labour that goes into the formation of a bharatanatyam dance artist's body.
13. Akademi Programme notes for *Paradiso*.
14. Akademi audition call-out by email for auditions on 15 March 2017 (sent 2 March 2017).
15. It is true that there are occasions when a contemporary choreography will seek out the distinctive cultural and physical capital of classical Indian forms for work in a piece, as for example with Richard Alston's use of Vidya Patel's kathak in *An Italian in Madrid* (2016) or Rosie Kay's use of Shivaangee Agrawal's bharatanatyam in *Modern Warrior* (2017) (Agrawal performed in the 2018 version). Such instances, however, remain, for the time being at least, very much the exception rather than the rule.
16. Akram Khan, in conversation with Mavin Khoo, Sadler's Wells, 23 November 2018 (field notes, November 2018).
17. Thus, the Scottish bharatanatyam dance artist Kirsten Newell decided to pursue a four-year degree in bharatanatyam at Kalakshetra (2009–13).
18. In September 2018 Greenwich Dance Agency professional classes were £5.50 a class. In spring 2020 (before Covid-19 forced cancellations), the Place offered professional classes at £5 a class or five classes for the price of four (in one week). In 2024/25, the Place's online professional classes were £8 a class. See https://theplace.org.uk/classes-courses/c-c-pro-class (retrieved 23 August 2024).
19. Devam is another dance artist who, like Khoo and Khan, has invested sufficient time training in both bharatanatyam and Western contemporary dance forms to allow her to switch between the *hexes* of both.
20. As Meduri (2020) documents, *Paradiso* was one of two pieces commissioned by Akademi that caused controversy in being choreographed by 'male, white male choreographers' (ibid.: 113) rather than South Asian choreographers. An additional concern was that the choreographers selected both had as their primary 'technical habitus' contemporary dance. This is likely to have influenced their choice of dance artists, thereby further limiting employment options for South Asian dance artists already struggling for work. Of course, most dance artists struggle for work, but for South Asian dance artists, work is, if possible, even more scarce than for other dance artists. As Meduri puts it, 'If dance in the UK is the Cinderella of the arts in terms of funding, South Asian dance gets less than two per cent of the overall dance allocation' – with a knock-on impact on available work.

Chapter 5

Legitimacy
Professionalizing Classical Indian Dance in Britain and Entering the 'National Cultural Canon'

Introduction

On 28 January 2021, Sadler's Wells Theatre in London teamed up with BBC Arts to present a three-part series called *Dancing Nation*. The ongoing Covid-19 pandemic meant that theatres were closed. In part in order to give dancers a chance to perform ('because they need to'; Alistair Spalding, BBC 2021: 46:26),[1] Sadler's aimed to bring 'world-class dance featuring UK companies' (ibid.: 00:42) to audiences watching on their screens at home. In curating the programme, Sadler's Wells chief executive Alistair Spalding expressed his wish 'to celebrate all the dance that is happening across our nation at the moment and make the centre of it Sadler's Wells' (ibid.: 46:12). Presenter Brenda Emmanus exclaimed, 'never has your programme, I guess, been so eclectic' (ibid.: 47:37). Spalding agreed: 'This was the idea – the idea was to represent not just the big companies but everything that is going on in dance . . . the whole range' (ibid.: 47:40). As a result, Emmanus continued, 'Dance in all its forms is on show in this festival, a testament to the really extraordinary range and diversity of work being produced across the UK' (ibid.: 49:13).

Given such a bold and inclusive aim for the series, it was particularly disappointing for classical Indian dancers watching it that classical Indian dance forms were conspicuous by their absence. Work was featured (now with a degree of predictability) by Shobana Jeyasingh and Akram Khan. Jeyasingh's featured piece, *Contagion* (2018), was a (movingly harrowing) contemporary work, employing exclusively Euro-American contemporary-trained dancers. In Khan's duet with Royal Ballet principal Natalia Osipova, *Mud of Sorrow: Touch* (2021), his 'technical habitus' as a kathak (as well as contemporary) dancer imbued the quality of all his movements, and the duet is a distinctive and beautiful work. Its dominant aesthetic conventions, however, remain the weight-shifting partner work of ballet or (Euro-American) contemporary dance – and the piece is unlikely to be recognized as representing kathak by the hundreds of students attending kathak classes each weekend (see Chapter 3). As a result, the series, for all its claims to diversity, offers no space in which classical Indian dance artists, including all those children and young people learning bharatanatyam, odissi or kathak in Britain, can see themselves and their art forms represented. It would seem that classical Indian styles do not form part of the 'dancing nation'.

This chapter discusses the role played in the professionalization of dance forms by their 'consecration' (Bourdieu 1991: 58) or their acquisition of 'legitimacy' – in particular by their inclusion into what Hage (2000) dubs the repertoires of 'national cultural capital', or the national cultural canon. The professionalization of classical Indian dance forms in Britain, as I have argued throughout this book, is only a viable proposition if there is sufficient audience demand for it. Moreover, the dance forms require enough symbolic capital to be able to secure the economic capital (through the patronage of either audience or state) to enable their practice. As sociologist of art Janet Wolff (1993) makes clear in her classic work on the subject, the field of art is also shaped not only by its production, but by its distribution and its reception. Inclusion within the 'national cultural canon' impacts upon the reception and distribution of art forms, thereby influencing the infrastructure supporting, and the circumstances surrounding, their production.

What constitutes a 'national dance canon' is contentious – there is no official list of dance works that comprise it; no set process by which a work achieves 'canonical' status. Moreover, the ephemeral nature of dance means that it is less amenable to the process of canonization than, for example, literature (the context in which the term is more commonly used). Nevertheless, there are some dance works that can be considered 'canonical' by virtue of their restaging, year after year, season after season; by their inclusion as set works of study within school and university syllabi;[2] by the attention paid to these pieces (and their reworkings) by the press and academia. Additionally, considered less from the specific perspective of canon and more in broader terms of what constitutes 'national cultural capital', this term can refer more generally to the kinds of literature, the type of art works and the forms of dance that are curated by institutions of national significance and standing (such as BBC Arts and Sadler's Wells). This is why, returning to the topic of the first chapter, the inclusion of 'South Asian dance' as a category in *BBC Young Dancer* was of such importance to the sector, and why, conversely, the lack of representation in *Dancing Nation* was felt so keenly.[3]

One measure of an art form's position in the 'national cultural canon' can be derived from the level of funding that it is assigned – by companies, by organizations and (where such funding exists) by government. The allocation of Arts Council dance funds to South Asian dance forms is 'basically . . . about 5 per cent' (fieldwork notes, November 2019), which contrasts with the about '55%' of the dance budget (Burns and Harrison 2009: 63) that Burns and Harrison noted that ballet still received in 2009.[4] This comparison may not seem notable until one considers that ballet is in fact not so very much longer-established as a 'British' dance form than classical Indian dance forms. It is therefore illuminating here to contrast the way in which other dance forms have been integrated into British dance practice to assume a centrality within the 'national cultural capital' that is now unquestioned.

Other Tales of Arrival – the Comparison with Ballet and Euro-American Contemporary Dance

On 10 February 1920, the Musical Association in London gathered to discuss the topic 'Why not British Ballet?' The discussion was launched by a paper delivered by the dance writer Mark E. Perugini, who argued strongly in favour of establishing British ballet, suggesting that all that was needed to achieve this were 'regular opportunities' for the English dancer to 'display . . . her art' (Perugini 1919: 53). Until the early twentieth century, as Perugini's plea makes clear, while ballet was performed in Britain, any attention and glamour attached to its performance were primarily focused around visiting artists (with home-grown dancers unceremoniously tucked away in the ballet *corps*).[5] This was the case to such an extent that another dance writer, P.J.S. Richardson, 'satirised this situation in his divertissement with [the] words, "No English Need Apply", which he published in *The Dancing Times* in 1923' (Genné 1995: 442), and British artists famously felt the need to change their names to succeed.[6] Unjust as it is to the many dancers who formed the *corps de ballets* at theatres such as the Empire and the Alhambra in the preceding decades (Guest 1992; Carter 1995), it is only within the last hundred or so years, therefore, that ballet has cultivated a status as a 'British' form.

It has done so remarkably successfully. Despite reforms within the Arts Council, and even though the 55 per cent of the dance budget it received in 2009 represents a significant reduction on the 77 per cent it had received ten years earlier (Burns and Harrison 2009: 63), ballet continues to receive the largest proportion of dance funding.[7] For the 2018–22 and 2023–26 portfolios, the three dance organizations allocated the largest Arts Council subsidies were all ballet companies (the Birmingham Royal Ballet, the English National Ballet and Northern Ballet Limited; see Tables 5.1 and 5.2 below).

In 1956, the queen's granting of the title 'Royal' to Ninette de Valois's[9] school and company, to form the Royal Ballet School and the Royal Ballet, secured ballet's status as an establishment art form, both legitimized by and helping to legitimize a particular version of 'Britishness', while the Ballet Rambert nurtured a new generation of choreographers, including Frederick Ashton, Anthony Tudor and Walter Gore, who brought a distinctively British sensibility to the established vocabulary.[10]

'Contemporary' dance – initially imported from America and Europe – has made a similarly successful transition to accepted 'Britishness', as dance scholar

196 ■ Towards a British Natyam

Table 5.1. Top ten funded dance NPOs (2018–22), including dance companies and agencies.
© *Magdalen Gorringe.*

	Company	Region	Art form	Annual NPO funding 2018–22
1	Birmingham Royal Ballet	Midlands	Dance	£7,891,000
2	English National Ballet	London	Dance	£6,214,000
3	Northern Ballet Limited	North	Dance	£3,112,000
4	Sadler's Wells	London	Dance	£2,456,000
5	Rambert	London	Dance	£2,237,000
6	Contemporary Dance Trust	London	Dance	£1,793,985
7	Re:Bourne	South East	Dance	£1,294,000
8	Dance East	South East	Dance	£810,153
9	Dance Xchange	Midlands	Dance	£760,126
10	One Dance UK	Midlands	Dance	£750,000

* Figures taken from Arts Council document on NPO funding 2018–22, compiled by M. Gorringe.[8]

Table 5.2. Top ten funded dance NPOs (2023–26), including dance companies and agencies.
© *Magdalen Gorringe.*

	Company	Region	Art form	Annual NPO funding 2023–26
1	Birmingham Royal Ballet	Midlands	Dance	£8,036,194
2	English National Ballet	London	Dance	£6,011,921
3	Northern Ballet Limited	North	Dance	£3,289,261
4	Sadler's Wells	London	Dance	£2,376,279
5	Rambert	London	Dance	£2,164,253
6	Contemporary Dance Trust	London	Dance	£1,826,994
7	FABRIC	Midlands	Dance	£1,376,001
8	New Adventures Charity (formerly Re:Bourne)	South East	Dance	£1,317,810
9	Dance East	South East	Dance	£825,060
10	One Dance UK	Midlands	Dance	£763,800

* Figures taken from Arts Council document on NPO funding 2023–26, compiled by M. Gorringe.
** (The top ten funded companies remain the same – however, FABRIC, which represents an amalgamation of the former Dance4 and Dance Xchange, now comes in at seventh place. New Adventures Charity was previously Re:Bourne).

Stephanie Jordan recounts in *Striding Out* (1992) – despite the initial wariness of 'British dance goers who . . . seemed to regard it as something best left to the Americans (and before the war, the Germans)' (Anderson 1993: 283). The establishment of the Contemporary Dance Trust (initially Contemporary Ballet Trust) by Robin Howard in 1966[11] and the transformation of Ballet Rambert from a classical to a contemporary dance company, Jordan (1992: 1) notes, rapidly brought a 'professionalism in contemporary dance that stood comparison with that of ballet, with wide public and critical recognition of a new genre of dance'. This led in the 1970s to a gradual development of a 'British contemporary dance with its own identity, independent of the American tradition' (ibid.). British contemporary dance schools such as the London Contemporary Dance School, Trinity Laban Conservatoire of Music and Dance and the Northern School of Contemporary Dance now attract students from across the world, and British contemporary dancers and choreographers such as the Cunningham-influenced Richard Alston and Siobhan Davies, who rose to prominence in the 1970s, the Limon-influenced Wayne McGregor, who founded his company in 1992, and, indeed, Akram Khan have received international recognition and acclaim. Despite their immigrant status, therefore, both ballet and Euro-American contemporary dance relatively swiftly acquired an unquestioned status and legitimacy as 'British' forms.

British 'Classical Indian' Dance?

There is some basis for arguing that classical Indian dance forms have been similarly accepted within Britain. Akram Khan's company, for example, with its blend of contemporary dance and kathak, had a starring role in the Opening Ceremony for the 2012 Olympics in London (Mitra 2015; Kolb 2018; Kedhar 2020; Meduri 2020). The Arts Council Corporate Plan for 2018–20 made specific mention of 'South Asian' dance forms, committing to 'work across artforms to investigate how dance can maximise available support networks and develop progression routes, with a focus on South Asian Dance, urban genres and new technologies' (Arts Council England 2018: 27). Chapter 3 draws attention to the 'Classical Indian Dance Faculty' within the (British) Imperial Society of Teachers of Dancing (ISTD). In Chapter 1, I discussed the inclusion of 'South Asian' dance in the *BBC Young Dancer* competition for British dancers. There has even been a bharatanatyam (or kuchipudi – it is not quite clear) dancer representing Britain as one of the images in the British passport (see Figure 5.1).[12]

Despite these symbolically significant examples, however, as the preceding chapters illustrate, the position of classical Indian dance forms in Britain remains precarious. A little over fifty years after the success of the first 'all British ballet', *Job* (Ninette de Valois, 1931), the Arts Council supported 'a full length Indian classical ballet for the first time' (Arts Council 1985: 7) in the form of Aka-

Figure 5.1. A bharatanatyam (or kuchipudi?) dancer on page 28 of the British passport (designed in 2015).
© Magdalen Gorringe.

demi's (then Academy of Indian dance) *The Adventures of Mowgli* (V.P. Dhananjayan, Pratap Pawar and Priya Pawar, 1984). Whereas twenty-five years after *Job*, however, ballet's place in Britain was endorsed by royal charter and patronage, with several established schools and companies, forty years after *The Adventures of Mowgli*, as previously discussed, there is still no training school for classical Indian dance forms in Britain; there is no repertory company with a primary aim to explore and sustain the dance styles rather than communicate the creative vision of a particular choreographer; and classical Indian dancers report feeling 'not wanted in Britain'. Where classical Indian dance forms have been accepted into the professional sphere, this has been largely on the basis of their 'hybridization with Western choreographic and movement aesthetics' (Kedhar 2020: 33; Thobani 2017; Meduri 2020).

Royona Mitra argues persuasively that choreography such as that by Akram Khan dances us along a path of 'new interculturalism', Khan's work destabilizing 'white mainstream culture from within' (Mitra 2015: 26). This was also the logic behind Akademi's work *Paradiso* (discussed in the previous chapter): 'Just as Dante composed *The Divine Comedy* in Italian (the common language, rather than Latin) so it could be enjoyed by the masses, we will take this show on a tour of London, performing on the streets reaching as diverse an audience as possible, on their ground' (Akademi programme notes for *Paradiso*). Such work can be read as occasions on which, as cultural theorist Robert Young explains Homi Bhabha's theory, 'the direction of the translation is reversed . . . the migrant . . . translates his or her own culture into that of the new host community', thereby intervening 'in the hegemonic culture that he or she finds him or herself confronted with' (Young 2010: 160).

This argument for the artist infiltrating the mainstream from within and thereby moderating and transforming settled aesthetic perceptions is a powerful one. The kathak featured in Khan's pieces, such as *Mud of Sorrow*, may shift the aesthetic range of a ballet fan without them even noticing it, while his unforgettable reinterpretation of *Giselle* (2016) for the English National Ballet both discomfited and recalibrated the understanding of ballet for audiences in packed theatres across the country.[13] Despite their success as touring pieces, Akademi's classically based *Bells* (Kumudhini Lakhia, 2007)[14] and *Sufi:Zen* (Gauri Sharma Tripathi, 2008) received a fraction of the press coverage afforded to the contemporary-based *Paradiso* and *The Troth* (Gary Clarke, 2017). In terms of reach and profile, and of introducing a wider audience to at least some of the elements of classical Indian dance forms, the advantages of this approach are evident. Akram Khan's company is the only company that can be seen to explore and represent classical Indian dance forms at any level that makes the list of the ten dance companies (excluding dance houses and agencies) in receipt of the highest Arts Council subsidies in the 2018–22 national portfolio (see Table 5.3 below; Aakash Odedra's and Shobana Jeyasingh's companies make the top twenty). The 2023–26 portfolio (though almost doubling the overall investment in South Asian dance forms, as I discuss below) does not feature a company exploring Indian classical dance forms in the top ten, though both Akram Khan's and Aakash Odedra's companies remain in the top twenty (see Table 5.4).[15]

Yet the successes of Khan's work, or Jeyasingh's, or of the two Akademi productions *Paradiso* and *The Troth*, which find their poetry in Bhabha's 'in-between' spaces, leave little space for employment for the classical Indian dancer.[16] While I agree with Mitra's assessment of the imaginative complexity of Khan's work, which 'interrupts banal representations of otherness' (Mitra 2015: 26), as yet his success has not had the effect of increasing the demand for, and employability of, dancers trained in classical Indian dance. Khan's own company uses primarily contemporary-trained dancers. Thus, while these translations may disrupt and unsettle the sensibilities of the mainstream audience, this disruption is certainly not more than that encountered by classical Indian dancers, who have largely been 'translated' out of the picture.

Table 5.3. Top ten funded dance company NPOs (2018–22). © Magdalen Gorringe.

	Company	Region	Art form	Annual NPO funding 2018–22
1	Birmingham Royal Ballet	Midlands	Dance	£7,891,000
2	English National Ballet	London	Dance	£6,214,000
3	Northern Ballet Limited	North	Dance	£3,112,000
4	Rambert	London	Dance	£2,237,000
5	Re:Bourne	South East	Dance	£1,294,000
6	Siobhan Davies	London	Dance	£582,018
7	Studio Wayne McGregor	London	Dance	£515,212
8	Akram Khan Company	London	Dance	£500,610
9	Motionhouse	Midlands	Dance	£468,806
10	CanDoCo	London	Dance	£447,889

* Figures taken from Arts Council document on NPO funding 2018–22, compiled by M. Gorringe.

Turning to classical practice, the shine attached to the classical Indian dancer placed 'in the picture' on the British passport is rather clouded by the accompanying commentary to the design, which makes clear that the dancer is used to represent a 'mela' and notes, 'melas reflect the diverse South Asian communities in the UK. They are usually large-scale, outdoor festivals, featuring dance, music, cuisine and many other aspects of South Asian culture' (HMPO 2015). While the intention is inclusive, this positioning marks the dancer's place within Britain as still contingent. Hers is not a British, but a 'South Asian' form and its inclusion serves thereby as a marker of Britain's diversity and multicultural credentials as much as a celebration of the art form itself.[17] It is telling that both South Asian and Caribbean aspects of British culture are featured on the passport on the same page in the context of 'mela' and 'carnival'. In the multicultural society, Hage argues, 'carnival' is often used to represent the spectacle and enrichment provided by the 'migrant' cultures to the host culture, a latter-day 'great exhibition' – presenting not so much what Britain 'is', but what it 'has' (Hage 2000: 140). Multicultural and cultural diversity policies, he argues, in presenting majority world (or non-white) cultures as cultural traditions that the white nation *has* (rather than *is*), thereby present them as within the 'sphere of influence' (ibid.: 89) of the white nation. In this way, 'Their belonging to the national environment in which they come to exist is always a precarious one, for they never exist, they are *allowed* to exist. That is, the tolerated are never just present, they are positioned' (ibid.: 90, my emphasis). Following this line of thought, the 'South Asian' dance that has developed what Anusha Kedhar calls 'the signature aesthetics of a dis-

Table 5.4. Top ten funded dance company NPOs (2023–26). © Magdalen Gorringe.

	Company	Region	Art form	Annual NPO funding 2023–26
1	Birmingham Royal Ballet	Midlands	Dance	£8,036,194
2	English National Ballet	London	Dance	£6,011,921
3	Northern Ballet Limited	North	Dance	£3,289,261
4	Rambert	London	Dance	£2,164,253
5	New Adventures (formerly Re:Bourne)	South East	Dance	£1,317,810
6	ACE Dance and Music	Midlands	Dance	£655,319
7	Siobhan Davies	London	Dance	£592,727
8	Phoenix Dance	North	Dance	£551,395
9	Ballet Lorent	North	Dance	£537,327
10	Studio Wayne MacGregor	London	Dance	£524,692

* Figures taken from Arts Council document on NPO funding 2023–26, compiled by M. Gorringe.

tinctly *British* contemporary dance genre' (Kedhar 2020: 118, emphasis original) is what Britain *is*, while the classical Indian dance forms unmediated by such (Euro-American) contemporizing influence are what it *has*.

As the exchange between Sanjeevini Dutta and Alistair Spalding signalled in Chapter 3, Arts Council policy is no longer one that encourages a particular interpretation of innovation. The changes to the Arts Council portfolio in 2023–26 testify to this, as does the experience of arts manager and promoter Anita Srivastava:

> None of the applications I have made have been for contemporary work. The claims that [the] Arts Council doesn't fund classical work or doesn't fund work from outside of London both are not a reality . . . For example, I wrote an application for Nina Rajarani's work *Jham* [2013], which was a purely classical work – there was no contemporariness in it. That was funded. Chitra Sundaram's *Sthreedom* [2013] . . ., Sujata Banerjee's *Draupadi* [2017], Swati Raut's various projects starting from *Basant Bells* [2013], *Half of Me* [2017] . . . *it's all classical work*. (Srivastava 2017 emphasis original)

This welcome shift of attitude within the Arts Council, however, cannot shift the reality that when artists and organizations promoting or practising classical Indian dance forms make the decision to engage with the wider world of professional British dance, they necessarily step into a field governed by a very different set of values, aesthetics and axiomatic principles (*doxa*), which are placed in a very different narrative (see Chapter 1) to that of the field of Indian classical dance forms. Thus a field that privileges nuanced and complex foot percussion; an integral relation to the visual arts (particularly sculpture); the ability of one performer to assume multiple roles; the reimagination of the archive as a fount of creativity; and the intimacy rather than the spectacle of performance must make its way in a field that values by contrast the interplay between two or more performers; the ability to make an impact on a proscenium stage; and creativity as the construction of the new.

Classical Indian Dance Forms and the 'National Cultural Canon'

What is it that prevents classical Indian dance forms from securing a more certain role in the 'national' cultural canon, and a larger stake in the national 'cultural capital'? In particular, what prevents the celebration of the classical forms as an expression of intrinsic British identity, rather than of 'South Asianness'? The Royal Ballet, for example, is not held up as 'reflecting the diverse Italian and French communities' within Britain. Why, as I ask in the introduction, is the 'South Asian' dance sector in Britain still in a similar state of infrastructural precarity to that noted by Naseem Khan in 1976?

I have argued throughout the book that the reasons for this are multiple (though interrelated). Chapter 2 highlights the deliberate distancing of classical Indian dance forms from the (professional) business of earning a living. Chapter 3 shows how this divorce between arts practice and livelihood is perpetuated in a diasporic situation whereby training in classical Indian dance forms takes place within the context of dance as providing a link with 'cultural heritage' and long-distance cultural nationalism. The identification of arts with 'heritage' is in turn consolidated by government policies of multiculturalism – 'a form of interpretation in which race and ethnicity are elevated and reified as absolutes and in which difference gets contained within symmetrical or at least similarly-configured social and cultural units' (Gilroy 2008: 671). This leads to a situation in which the training in Indian dance forms in Britain takes place (for participants who are overwhelmingly British South Asian and brown-skinned) in a space identified by the British passport designers as the 'mela' – the (brown) space of the 'South Asian community in Britain', the space of 'culturally diverse Britain' in which classical Indian dance artists are wheeled into primary schools at Diwali to 'enrich' students through exposure to 'other cultures'. In a pattern encouraged, if unintentionally, by the Arts Council, these same dancers attain wider marketability and acclaim, as I discuss in Chapter 4, only once they have left this world and entered the (white) space of contemporary dance (Thobani 2017; Kedhar 2020; Meduri 2020), with all the limitations and restrictions that this entails.

The failure of South Asian dance in Britain to make more headway than it has yet done is often also ascribed (by observers from both in and outside the sector) to insufficient vision, collegiality and 'joined-up thinking' among South Asian dance agencies and dancers. As noted in Chapter 1, Hackett's observation of the sector is that 'it is not as unified as it could be and there are a lot of people working on their own in their own little islands' (Hackett 2017). A representative of the Arts Council likewise expressed the view that there was not enough 'finding common ground' (interview, 2019), while a dancer and teacher from within the sector suggested that 'if these organizations *really* had a vision and a commitment to dancers and dance – rather than to themselves as organizations – I think South Asian dance would be in a better place' (interview, 2018).

The Arts Council *South Asian Dance and Music Mapping Study* (2020), which drew for its findings on conversations with eighty-four members of the sector and survey responses from 219, refers to the 'tribal nature of the sector' (Courtney Consulting 2020: 59) and states

> A core theme that ran through every conversation was the unhelpful politics and power paradigms of the sector. This has undermined collaborative and partnership working to date, resulting in a lack of joined up thinking and weak sector advocacy. Combined, these factors have impeded the sector's ability to be truly integrated and influential in the wider dance, music and cultural sector ecology in the UK and internationally. (ibid.: 95)

As Shivaangee Agrawal, Sanjeevini Dutta and Magdalen Gorringe comment in their response, it is disappointing to see the term 'tribal' repeated in the main body of the report, even though it is a term used by one of the report's respondents. The term serves to reinforce, they argue, 'a perception that the South Asian dance and music sector are somehow something Other, operating on their own terms and according to their own rules (Agrawal, Dutta and Gorringe 2021). Furthermore,

> although the attention afforded to the issue of the NPO leadership is undeniably important, it cannot be at the expense of acknowledging the structural racism that these NPOs have been navigating. By failing to acknowledge the deeper causes of NPO behaviours, we risk putting the next generation of South Asian NPO leaders under the same inequitable pressure, with the added expectation that they will carry through huge changes for South Asian arts. (ibid.)

As with any sector, there are certainly ways in which agencies and companies could work to develop better relationships, a wider sector vision and a more coherent national strategy. Yet caught between demands for (a culturally specific version of) 'innovation' and the frequently equally parochial concerns of the community organizations, the NPOs have faced an invidious task. The sector (and its leaders) faces cultural and political challenges posed by the context in which it is situated – which lie outside its own control or jurisdiction. Indeed, the very precarity of its positioning within this wider context in part predisposes the sector to greater factionalism – as Hackett concedes, 'To some extent this happens whenever a sector is poorly resourced and supported, so that people are competing for the same small pool of resources' (Hackett 2017).

Additionally, Agrawal et al. point out, a dissatisfaction with leadership is not unique to South Asian dance but is endemic within the charity sector. They cite charity sector commentator Andrew Purkis, who recognizes this dissatisfaction and acknowledges that there are undoubtedly occasions on which organization and leadership could do better, but points out that fundamentally, 'Some political and ideological roadblocks can be just too big to shift . . . Blame the umbrella bodies [NPOs]? You might as well blame the sea for "failing" to break down granite cliffs' (Purkis, in Agrawal, Dutta and Gorringe 2021).

Underlying the policies of multiculturalism and the greater marketability of the (Euro-American contemporary dance-oriented) versatile dancer, the disputes between different parts of the sector and the apparent failure to have made more significant progress are political and ideological roadblocks that overshadow the sector just as implacably as granite cliffs. Among the most striking and pervasive of these is clearly that classical Indian dance forms in Britain must stake their place in a context in which they transgress the 'somatic norm' (Puwar 2003); they must take their place within a framework of 'institutionalized whiteness' (Ahmed 2007: 157), in the context of the 'White nation' (Hage 2000). In this light, the Arts Council report's focus on failures in sector leadership seems naïve. After all, it is not only the 'South Asian' dance sector that appears to be in stasis. Programmer, researcher and writer Jemma Desai makes the point that this is a more widespread reality in the arts, and asks the more pressing question: 'Why, despite 30 years of sustained professional development programmes, recruitment drives and "mentoring" programmes resulting in a highly qualified, well networked and credible set of individuals from a range of ethnic backgrounds, [is] the industry in its static nature . . . still focussed on the individuals who are excluded rather than those who do the excluding?' (Desai 2020: np).

The Habit of 'Whiteness'

In one way the role of race in preventing the more wholesale incorporation of classical Indian dance forms into the 'national cultural canon' is very obvious. After all, probably the most immediate distinction between the dancers who brought ballet and contemporary dance to Britain and those who brought classical Indian dance forms is the colour of their skin.

The differential treatment of immigrants on the basis of race is woven into Britain's institutional and legal codes. The expansive inclusivity of the British Nationality Act 1948, which ruled that, as Arthur Marwick observes, all citizens of countries within the British Commonwealth were also 'all full British subjects and entitled, without let or hindrance, to settle in Britain itself' (Marwick 2003: 132), very swiftly unravelled. The minutes of a 1955 government working party record that 'it cannot be held that the same difficulties arise in the case of Irish as in coloured people . . . The outstanding difference is that the Irish are not . . . a different race from the ordinary inhabitants of Great Britain' (cited in Winder 2005: 342). This is a bureaucrat's rephrasing of the football hooligan chant 'There ain't no black in the Union Jack'.[18] As historian Robert Winder puts it, 'those of a different skin colour, it went without saying, presented difficulties' (ibid.).

A few years later, Harold Macmillan's Conservative government passed the Commonwealth Immigrants Act in 1962, condemned by then Labour leader Hugh Gaitskill as a piece of 'cruel and brutal anti-colour legislation' (cited in Younge 2020). This did not prevent the succeeding Labour government under Harold Wilson from introducing and passing a second Commonwealth Immigrants Act in 1968 reinforcing the earlier act, which, Winder observes, 'ninety-nine times out a hundred. . . would favour whites' (2005: 378). Though Britain has always been 'multicultural' in that, as Tzvetan Todorov argues (see Chapter 3), there are no 'pure' cultures, it is only when these cultures come linked to a particular skin colour that the term arises and sticks – as if prior to the migrations from the Commonwealth, Britain had been a culturally homogeneous unit. In this way the term 'multicultural', together with its successor, 'cultural diversity', ultimately serve as euphemistic expressions for 'racially mixed' (Winder 2005); or in Gilroy's words, 'multiculturalism is also often a coded way of speaking about race and about the dangerous processes through which race becomes a matter of culture' (Gilroy 2008: 670).

The insidious impact of this racialization of culture has been, as I argue in Chapter 3, to 'Other' South Asian dance forms, making them specific arts for a specific people. The hold of this perception is enduring and corrosive. Thus, while it is true that the Arts Council Corporate Plan for 2018–20 makes specific mention of its aim to develop South Asian dance forms (suggesting an inclusion in the 'national cultural canon'), at the same time, in a 2019 conversation with a representative of the Arts Council, a connection was drawn between the numbers of Asian people living in Britain and the allocation of funding for South Asian dance (suggesting a containment of their relevance):

> Basically, it's about 5 per cent – project grants are divided into under 15K and over 15K, and then also, national activities [NPOs], and then you have DYCP (Developing Your Creative Practice) – so I have looked at all four of those. So, it's kind of small. But if you think about Asian

people living in Britain, you could say – well actually it's representative. Because if I am not wrong, I think it's about 5 per cent. (Fieldwork notes, 25 November 2019)

The (perhaps unintended) implication is that the proportion of funding is appropriate because it reflects the proportion of those who may be interested in the dance form – *because they are Asian*. Such a perception anchors the place of South Asian dance as always already 'minority' arts.

Race impacts the choreography of the everyday – by potentially making it harder to fill in a form ('English is my second language, so ACE applications are very hard and complicated'), or by making it harder to approach an institution ('People are quite intimidated by the Arts Council; I am as well'; respondents in Arts Council report, Courtney Consulting 2020: 100). Rajkumar relates her initial struggles in her attempts to establish Akademi in the 1970s:

There was a lot of racism . . . If you walked around wearing a sari at that time, there was a presumption that you were not educated – that you couldn't speak English . . . but I am one of those rebels with a cause – so I used to wear a sari and a big *potthu* [bindi] deliberately. And I'm quite good with accents. So, I used to really put on an Oxford accent as far as possible – and people were shocked when they saw a woman in a sari speaking like this. (Rajkumar 2017)

Ram Gopal relates similar experiences of his time in London in the 1950s and 1960s:

Quite often in London I would be approached at parties and in galleries and someone would come up to me and say, 'Can you speak English?' I'd say, 'Yes, I can, can you?' And they'd say, 'What a lovely tan you've got.' I'd say, 'I'm sorry, I can't say the same for you. You look such a horrid, pallid white . . .'. I have a very quick, triggered reaction to these comments.[19]

In a reminder of how little things have changed, writing in 2019, Prarthana Purkayastha records facing a similar litany of questions (Purkayastha 2019: 139).

Race also impacts the choreography of the creation of dance works. As feminist and post-colonial theorist Sara Ahmed argues, race is not simply about prejudiced responses to different levels of melanin, but about a certain orientation towards being in the world encompassing 'styles, capacities, aspirations, techniques, habits' (2007: 154); it is about a particular (unquestioned) *doxa*; a specific (unconscious) understanding of what constitutes the norm. Hence, in Ahmed's words, the 'habit' of whiteness (ibid.). When art forms do not conform to this 'habit' and are not established as part of the 'national cultural canon', their practitioners are confronted with the need to communicate with an audience who do not recognize the narrative of their art forms, and do not understand their artistic conventions.

Performing for the White Gaze

> South Asian dance agencies (and dance companies) have had to choose whether they will play the 'heritage-in-multicultural Britain' game or the 'contemporary Britain' game. (Sundaram 2018)

> No, you're not listening to me. No, I can't perform Nritta. No, I can't because if I perform that part I'm not being who I am . . . I'm being who YOU want ME TO BE!!! (Excerpt from script of Shane Shambhu's *Confessions of a Cockney Temple Dancer*, reproduced by kind permission of the author)

In his classic work on how taste is formed, *Distinction*, Bourdieu observes, 'A work of art has meaning and interest only for someone who possesses the cultural competence – that is the code – into which it is encoded . . . A beholder who lacks the specific code feels lost in a chaos of sounds and rhythms, colours and lines, without rhyme or reason' (Bourdieu 1984: 2). This is true of any art form – an audience member who understands, for example, the mime code of ballet or the specific technique employed in a painting is likely to be able to place the artwork in its narrative context, to understand it more deeply and arguably to gain more from it. Returning to the distinction between the 'artistic' and the 'aesthetic' discussed in Chapter 1,[20] while a familiarity with the 'narrative' of an art form is essential for its artistic understanding, when the artwork originates from a cultural context different to that of its audience there can be barriers even to its 'aesthetic' appreciation. Beyond the understanding of any specific artistic code, sociologist Howard Becker argues, 'Only because artist and audience share knowledge of and experience with the conventions invoked does the artwork produce an emotional effect' (Becker 2003: 90). Small wonder then that the reporter for the *Brighton Herald* in 1838 (quoted in the introduction) felt that the performance of the hereditary dancers was 'not entirely consistent with our English tastes and feelings' and that '9 out of 10' audience members 'can't tell what to make of it'.

The conventions Becker refers to include not only the conventions particular to an art form, but wider cultural conventions, for example of dress, the meaning of a specific colour or the expected mode of relationship between young people and their elders. Where such a shared set of conventions does not exist, an art form is more likely to remain for the spectator, as Bourdieu puts it, 'a chaos of sounds and rhythms . . .without reason', or to be something that the audience 'can't tell what to make of'. To the extent that it is admired, this interest or admiration is likely to rely as much on its compelling and curious Otherness as on its offering a pathway to any sense of connection or understanding. The result of this for classical Indian dance forms in Britain, as Sundaram summarizes in the quotation above, has been either fetishized display or an attempt to fit the dance forms into the dominant aesthetic (and artistic) conventions.

While the route to 'Britishness' in the case both of ballet and contemporary dance certainly took some work,[21] with ballet adapting the themes, sets and costumes of its performance to align itself more securely to a representation of 'Britishness', and while it is also true that British ballet has a particular inflection that distinguishes it from French, Danish or American ballet, both ballet and contemporary dance have ultimately developed their own fields in Britain, with their own autonomy and aesthetic standards. As discussed in Chapter 2, classical Indian dancers, by contrast, in order to achieve a space for themselves as recognized professionals, have had to compromise their autonomy and adapt their aesthetics to make a space within the field of Euro-American contemporary dance practice.

Entering this space has meant performing the demanding and delicate dance mentioned in Chapter 1 between exoticism and assimilation, finding a way, in Kedhar's words, 'to perform both South Asianness and Britishness, to be simultaneously exotic and legible, particular and universal, different and accessible, other and not other' (2020: 3). It has meant a hyper-vigilance about costume to avoid 'succumbing to the exploitation of the exotica such as make-up, costume, flowers [and] jewellery' that make it seem 'more important for dancers to look "pretty" on stage than to focus on the dance itself' (Khayyam, personal communication, 21 May 2021). At the same time, it has meant being wary of criticism (from within the field of classical Indian dance) that says, 'you can't do this because you're misrepresenting bharatanatyam, that's not what bharatanatyam is about' (Agrawal, Manch UK, 2020d). It has meant the exhausting task of attempting to avoid commodification as a 'marketable object of wonder' (Lammy 2019), or as a spectacularized representation of the Other in Britain, while on the other hand playing catch-up in a world determined by the mores of contemporary dance. Unsurprisingly, the experience of black and African dance practitioners is very similar. Dancer and scholar 'Funmi Adewole notes that black and African people's dance is positioned 'on the one hand as traditional forms of dance as representative of lands of origin *for the migrant group* and on the other as fusions between traditional and social dance forms and Western dance technique as an expression of integration into Britain' (Adewole 2016: 145, my emphasis).

A 2019 interview with a member of the Arts Council with a record of being very supportive of South Asian dance forms reveals the unequal context in which practitioners of South Asian dance (and dances of the African diaspora) are required to work:

And I say this to the hip-hop people as well and they say, 'we don't want to do contemporary dance'. Well, no, but if you work within theatrical conventions that have been going on for X amount of years and where people have experimented – then it's a duty for you to know about those things and the things that have gone before and either accept things or reject them, but not be almost as if it hasn't existed. (Interview with the author, London, 2019)

Returning to the theorization of narratives of art, how much additional labour does this place on the South Asian (or hip-hop) dancer? A South Asian dancer must on this basis not only be familiar with the history and development of classical Indian dance forms and the significant developments in this field, but also be conversant with the conventions and developments in the field of Euro-American contemporary dance. Huge as this expectation is, it might not seem so unreasonable if it were matched by a corresponding desire for contemporary dancers to be conversant with the field of South Asian dance. This is not, however, the case. In the meantime, South Asian dancers are once again placed in a position of being valued according to a deficit-based reading of 'cultural capital' (see Chapter 4), disempowered by measurement to 'a standard which ignores their chosen aesthetic frame of reference and its particular demands' (Gottschild 1997: 171).

Kathak artist and choreographer Amina Khayyam relates a similar deficit-based reading of approaches to choreography found in South Asian dance:

I think choreography is a very hazy, cloudy area of dance – for example in contemporary or Western choreography, you would think that the choreographer would generate the vocabulary to give to the dancers, which is what happens with South Asian classical forms. The teachers or the choreographers give us the movement – and we just copy that – we copy – but we also make it our own. But here it's the opposite. The dancers generate the movement and then the choreographer takes that and shapes that to what they want. So, all this is totally topsy-turvy in a way from where I come from. And there is that hierarchy that we don't have choreographic knowledge – and it's true – we don't have choreographic knowledge in Western terms. But we do have choreographic knowledge in the way that we work – which is a very different approach to the contemporary or the Western approach. And I think this is something that has not been addressed, sufficiently analysed or looked at, except that I always hear the superiority when it comes to choreography of the Western concept, and the inferiority of the Eastern concept. (Khayyam 2018)

From a different perspective, the Ghanaian dancer and choreographer Nii Yartey makes the same point: 'The word choreography is alien to us as Africans. This does not mean that we as Africans did not do choreography, otherwise there would not be all these beautiful dances' (Yartey, cited in Ramdhanie 2017 80).

In the meantime, South Asian dancers are encouraged to make up for the 'deficit' in their practice by seeking the guidance and mentorship of contemporary dance choreographers in making their work. In fact, Khayyam relates that a significant London-based dance theatre

> wouldn't programme my work unless I went through a mentoring process with someone they chose. They might let me select – but they wanted a contemporary influence in it . . . I have to go through *their* mentorship in order for me to put my work out there . . . But how can a contemporary dancer give me guidance on my form when he or she doesn't have a clue about my form? (Khayyam 2018, emphasis original)

The invocation of 'choreography' licenses the non-South Asian curator or critic 'to assess and evaluate South Asian work' (Rai 2021), and the non-South Asian artist's deficit (in terms of knowledge of South Asian arts) is turned into the South Asian artist's deficit in terms of their adherence to a particular interpretation of 'choreography'.

In thinking about presenting their work, classical Indian dancers at every stage must consider how to adapt, hybridize, truncate or translate their work to make it legible and palatable for Euro-American audiences and (perhaps more importantly) Euro-American programmers. This means that on top of the extra labour of learning the conventions of the contemporary dance world is layered the further labour of working out how one's own form might fit within it. Given all this, it should not really be a surprise that South Asian dancers are often well into their twenties before they feel ready to present work,

> whereas contemporary dancers who are younger than me – they have created a piece and off they go – festivals, tours, building their repertoire of work that they are making . . . there is none of that kind of sand in your brain about what is the relevance or legitimacy of what I'm doing?! What am I doing – who's going to be interested in this . . . they just don't think about it. It's not an issue – it doesn't enter their brain. (Agrawal 2019b)

On the other hand, they may decide that the massaging and manipulation to which they will probably need to subject a loved dance form is simply not worth it. Reflecting on why she chose not to pursue dance professionally, the beautiful (and award-winning) bharatanatyam dancer Uma Venkataraman observes, 'Also – I really enjoy dancing, but *I really enjoy dancing what I want to dance* and I just thought that if it was my career I may not have the flexibility to do what I wanted in dance' (Venkataraman 2018 my emphasis). Counter to the intense frustration expressed by Shambhu in *Confessions of a Cockney Temple Dancer* cited at the beginning of this section, Venkataraman wants to dance what she wants to dance – and be who she wants to be.

In Chapter 3, I refer to the attempt made to set up a BA in Contemporary Dance (with a South Asian dance strand) established at London Contemporary Dance School (LCDS). At the time, there was some surprise and disappointment at the low level of applications received from the many South Asian dancers in Britain. However, as Gorringe et al. (2018: 52) point out, in being primarily a contemporary dance course, it 'immediately distanced itself from those whose primary goal and dream is to excel in classical Indian dance'. Dancers did not apply because the course did not offer them a way to be true to themselves. Similarly, when the way to reach 'a general public who doesn't understand the code that [a] dance is written in' (respondent in Courtney Consulting 2020: 88) is to 'come up with random ways that compromise their practice' (ibid.: 85) and to submit to the 'symbolic violence' (Bourdieu 1991) or the 'cultural invasion' of responding to the 'values, standards and goals' (Freire 2017: 126) of others, refusing to professionalize can be seen as an act of resistance.

At the beginning of the book, I ask the question 'why professionalize' in the context of a performance at the Bhavan that may not have met the criteria of 'professionalism' of some, but was entirely successful on its own terms. Across London, there are other organizations like the Bhavan that organize performances for predominantly Asian audiences whom they know will appreciate the performers they curate.[22] They have no interest in being part of the mainstream circuit of professional British dance because, as Sundaram points out, 'they are worried about what else will come with it' (Sundaram 2018). Where to professionalize means changing one's identity, it is unsurprising that the answer of many is simply to opt out.

'Visibility is a Trap'?

Feminist theorist Peggy Phelan (1993) articulates how visibility and representation (such as might come with further professionalization) are often grasped as a means to empowerment. She cautions, however, 'There is real power in being unmarked and there are serious limitations to visual representation as a political goal . . . Visibility is a trap. It summons surveillance and the law; it provokes voyeurism, fetishism, the colonialist/imperial desire for possession' (ibid.: 6). Are the many (potential) professional classical Indian dancers who have chosen a different route opting for the power of the 'unmarked'? Returning to the organizations that choose to remain 'off the circuit' mentioned above, Sundaram suggests that the desire for visibility would be greater if it was clear what the returns for this might be – 'If they were going to get more press reviews and financial help . . . that would be different' (Sundaram 2018).

Certainly, financial assistance has proved of significant help to some organizations, enabling them to achieve more ambitious programmes and secure a more robust infrastructure. For M.N. Nandakumara, director of the Bhavan in London, funding from the Arts Council has made a noticeable difference,

> It has helped us to streamline our activities, to ensure that we continue to provide all the services we offer. It has helped us to focus on improving a variety of activities offered. Then it has helped us to improve our facilities, our programmes – we can plan them well in advance, maintain our building. And it's a big, big recognition as well . . . We can complement our teaching by inviting external teachers to summer schools. We can concentrate on diversifying – for example until recently we didn't have kuchipudi or odissi classes. Now we know that we can use our marketing and other strategies to attract more people. All of this is thanks to the blessings of the Arts Council. (Nandakumara 2017)

At the same time, the limitations of visibility are evident when we consider a couple of British reviews of works featuring classical Indian dance forms. One review, which featured in a prominent national newspaper, of the major Indian dance and musical festival Darbar, held at Sadler's Wells, opened with a declaration that 'The eight Indian classical dance forms have been around for a couple of thousand years', going on to observe that 'for the uninitiated, classical art forms can feel impenetrable' (Winship 2018). The damaging Orientalist tropes of stasis and obscurity are thereby invoked within the review's first 150 words. In another, in this case a review written for the Place, the reviewer's level of understanding of classical Indian dance forms was so negligible that they were unable to make the fundamental distinction between the (markedly distinct) dance forms of bharatanatyam and kathak.[23] While reviews from prominent and internationally esteemed institutions continue to broadcast ignorance and Othering (and in the case of the Place, there was not even a recognition of the problems with their approach), the returns for visibility seem only to be, as Phelan warns, misrepresentation and myth.

South Asian Dance for South Asian People?

> I think it [classical Indian dance] cannot develop in another country being relevant only to a small group of immigrants from that country. For it to flourish it has to get its life source from the society and give out to everyone. (Sarker 2017)

One way to avoid the kind of misrepresentation described is to accept that classical Indian dance forms will necessarily have a restricted audience. For production company zeroculture's Hardial Rai, the attempt to adapt classical Indian dance forms to be read by a wider audience only results in compromised integrity – in work that tries to be 'all things to all people. And what's the point in that?' Rather we need to 'accept that certain art forms are only going to be patronized by and relevant to certain sections of the community' (Rai 2021). Instead of adapting work to meet the culturally specific vision of programmers with little understanding of the codes governing classical Indian dance forms, his answer is to seek out opportunities and spaces that will enable the commissioning and the framing of work to come from a place of understanding and knowledge. This will enable dance that is 'everywhere, every weekend – in community centres, theatres, theatres hired by community groups, local organisations' to take its space in the 'established theatres'. In this way, without attempting to moderate or adapt the codes and conventions that make it distinctive, 'the little story . . . told honestly, truthfully and in a heartfelt manner . . . can become the universal story' (ibid.).

Rai makes an important point about refusing to surrender the integrity of art forms in favour of accessibility. It should not be necessary to broaden the appeal of classical Indian dance forms by taking them into the (Euro-American) contemporary dance sphere, or by introducing mainstream audiences to other aesthetic conventions without their necessarily being aware of it – almost as if the (Euro-American) contemporary dance gives a 'sweet' coating to the 'bitter' pill of the (Indian) classical dance. This view echoes the call of American writer, teacher and activist Kelsey Blackwell for places in which black people can 'gather free from the stereotypes and marginalization that permeate every other societal space we occupy' (Blackwell 2018: 1).

While respecting the need for such safe spaces, the long-term vision must surely be that such spaces are made redundant by the 'making safe' of the wider environment. This is important because, as Sarker observes in the quotation that opens this section, classical Indian dance forms in Britain will continue to struggle to attain the symbolic and economic capitals necessary for them to thrive while they continue to be viewed 'as relevant only to a small group of immigrants' from another country. Or, in the words of Jeyasingh, 'if bharatanatyam is seen as having relevance only to a small group of people mostly of one ethnicity then it diminishes its influence and reach' (Jeyasingh 2018). To really develop a professional classical Indian dance sector in Britain, to genuinely make such space for the 'little story' in 'established theatres' demands, I suggest, an unseating of the (largely unspoken and often unrecognized) idea, and signature of colonialism, that one 'little story' is more 'universal' than another. It demands an acceptance that any 'universal story' is only ever accessed through multiple and various 'little stories'. This in turn demands a radical evaluation of both what constitutes Britain's 'national cultural canon' and of what is regarded as 'professional'. And the labour to achieve this, to echo Desai, must rest not upon those 'who are excluded' but on those 'who do the excluding'.

Un-Suturing, De-Linking:
Breaking the 'Habit' of Whiteness and Transforming the Canon

Establishing Indian classical dance forms as part of the 'national cultural canon' first necessitates acknowledging these art forms as part of Britain's collective heritage (in Hage's terms, making them what we 'are', not what we 'have'). Rather than accepting the parameters of a limited audience as Rai suggests, and equally, rather than inclusion within the cultural canon depending on these art forms abandoning their artistic codes and conventions to fit more into the dominant (Euro-American) culture, the task must be to familiarize a wider audience with those codes and conventions that will allow them to appreciate classical Indian dance forms on their own terms. It depends, in other words, as former director of Milapfest (1990–2019) Prashant Nayak urges, on 'making relevance'. Asked whom he felt might prove an appropriate audience for classical Indian dance forms, Nayak's response was that relevance is relative:

> It will depend on . . . how much these communities are exposed to it [classical Indian dance]. The more the communities are exposed to it, the more relevant it will become for them . . . I think it is up to us in the arts community to make it relevant. Relevance cannot be prescribed and it's not God-given – it's something that can be brought into existence by us. (Nayak 2017)

Returning to the examples of ballet and Euro-American contemporary dance, neither genre started off with an established British audience, but both worked to create one. At the same meeting with which this chapter opened, the music critic F. Gilbert Webb, who was chairing the meeting, observed in a post-talk discussion, 'I do not see that there is anything to prevent the establishment of British ballet on the same lines as Russian, except want of faith which would discourage financiers from supporting the concern. Of course, it must be several years before it would acquire sufficient public attraction to make it pay' (Perugini 1919: 55). Within a decade of this meeting, such 'public attraction' had been developed and British ballet was well on its way. Similarly, the place of contemporary dance in Britain was supported and secured in part through the efforts of the early British contemporary dance company Strider, which made a point of touring to 'colleges of education, small theatres, arts centres and art galleries' (Jordan 1992: 40), thereby introducing new kinds of dance content to audiences around the country (ibid.: 57). Later, Dance Umbrella, a London-based annual contemporary dance festival originally established as an Arts Council initiative in 1978, worked on 'building audiences beyond a narrow group of dance aficionados' (ibid.: 96).

Such 'bringing into existence of relevance', however, is not something that can be achieved by the South Asian dance companies and organizations alone. Piali

Ray, director of Birmingham's South Asian arts agency Sampad, argued in a focus group meeting, 'South Asian dance and music should not be only our responsibility. We cannot do it on our own' (field notes, 26 February 2020). This recognition was central to the Arts Council's launch of their fresh approach to equality and diversity, the Creative Case for Diversity, in 2014. In establishing the Creative Case, the Arts Council acknowledged, in the words of the then chair Sir Peter Bazalgette, that 'despite many valuable, well-intentioned policies over the past decade, when it comes to diversity, we have not achieved what we intended ... we didn't nurture diversity in all our work, across all our funded organisations and their audiences'; it accepted that 'we need to think about programming, the workforce, leadership and audiences, and how all these are interrelated' (Bazalgette 2014). In 1989, Graham Devlin, theatre director, cultural strategist and then Acting Chief Executive of Arts Council England (1996–99), wrote the report *Stepping Forward*, acknowledging the need for a more developed dance infrastructure and also recommending that some of the national dance agencies (NDAs) 'specialise in non-Western dance forms' (Devlin 1989: 39).[24] His report led, in the early 1990s, to the creation of a network of NDAs, including, for a brief period, the South Asian national dance agency ADiTi (1989–2001), which started out based in Bradford and moved to London in 1996 (see Appendix 3). Since its closure, other organizations, including Akademi and Kadam, have assumed many of the functions it served, and Akademi has a national reach.[25] It is significant however that Akademi has not been officially considered to be a national dance agency, as this is likely to have influenced its levels of funding (see Tables 5.5 and 5.6 below). This is particularly significant when one considers that while most of the NDAs are increasingly recognizing their responsibility across dance forms (as, for example, with FABRIC, formerly Dance Xchange, discussed in Chapter 3), this is not yet understood as a given. Rather, certain NDAs see South Asian-specific arts agencies as relieving them entirely of their responsibilities towards South Asian dance and dancers. Agrawal, for example, reports approaching an NDA for support and being referred to the local South Asian-specific agency instead (Agrawal 2020). A cursory glance at the relative levels of funding for NDAs and South Asian-specific agencies in the South Asian Dance Alliance suffices to reveal how far such an approach disadvantages South Asian artists.

Comparing the figures in Tables 5.5 and 5.6, the Contemporary Dance Trust as a single entity received more funding per annum than all the South Asian Dance Alliance members combined (their total annual funding figure comes to £1,351,813), with the important proviso that all the SADAA members with the exception of Akademi fund at least two different art disciplines. The new portfolio has brought changes, with the total investment to the same organizations depicted in Table 5.6 increased by 71 per cent for 2023–26 (See Table 5.8).

This is a significant change. Yet while the annual funding allocated to the only South Asian arts agency primarily focused on dance (Akademi) is £218,956

Table 5.5. National dance agency funding, 2018–22. © Magdalen Gorringe.

	Agency name	ACE region	Discipline	Funding/annum in GBP, 2018–22
1	The Place (Contemporary Dance Trust)	London	Dance	1,793,985
2	Dance East	South East	Dance	810,153
3	The Dance Xchange	Midlands	Dance	760,126
4	Dance 4	Midlands	Dance	591,014
5	South East Dance	South East	Dance	570,169
6	Dance City	North	Dance	553,857
7	Pavilion Dance South West	South West	Dance	386,216
8	Yorkshire Dance	North	Dance	325,794

* Figures taken from Arts Council document on NPO funding 2018–22, compiled by M. Gorringe.

Table 5.6. Funding for NPO members of the South Asian Dance Alliance (SADA), 2018–22. © Magdalen Gorringe.

	Company name	ACE region	Discipline	Funding/annum in GBP, 2018–22
1	Milapfest Festival Trust	North	Combined arts	362,908
2	Sampad South Asian Arts	Midlands	Combined arts	243,906
3	Akademi	London	Dance	215,000
4	South Asian Arts UK (SAA Arts)	North	Music	181,000
5	Bharatiya Vidya Bhavan	London	Music	128,999
6	Gem Arts	North	Combined arts	120,000
7	Kala Sangam – The Academy of South Asian Performing Arts	North	Combined arts	100,000

* Figures taken from Arts Council document on NPO funding 2018–22, compiled by M. Gorringe.

per annum, it remains clear that to make a substantive impact, the pursuit of a wider relevance for Indian classical dance forms must necessarily be first accepted as relevant to (and the responsibility of) the wider institutional infrastructure for British dance. Returning to Bazalgette and the Creative Case for Diversity, this is precisely what the Arts Council recognized in 2014: 'There has been an unfair responsibility for diversity conferred on a limited number of organisations. These organisations have often been the more vulnerable ones with relatively small funding grants' (Bazalgette 2014). It is telling that in the experience of both

Table 5.7. National dance agency funding, 2023–26. © Magdalen Gorringe.

	Agency name	ACE region	Discipline	Funding/annum in GBP, 2023–26
1	The Place (Contemporary Dance Trust)	London	Dance	1,826,994
2	Fabric	Midlands	Dance	1,376,001
3	Dance East	South East	Dance	825,060
4	South East Dance	South East	Dance	580,660
5	Dance City	North	Dance	564,048
6	Pavilion Dance South West	South West	Dance	393,322
7	Yorkshire Dance	North	Dance	331,789

* Figures taken from Arts Council document on NPO funding 2023–26, compiled by M. Gorringe.

Table 5.8. Funding for NPO members of the South Asian Dance Alliance (SADA), 2023–26. © Magdalen Gorringe.

	Company name	ACE region	Discipline	Funding/annum in GBP, 2023–26
1	South Asian Arts UK	North	Music	684,330
2	Milapfest Festival Trust	North	Combined arts	477,389
3	Kala Sangam	North	Combined arts	361,840
4	Sampad	Midlands	Combined arts	248,394
5	Akademi	London	Dance	218,956
6	Gem Arts	North	Combined arts	202,208
7	Bharatiya Vidya Bhavan	London	Music	131,373

* Figures taken from Arts Council document on NPO funding 2023–26, compiled by M. Gorringe.

Ray and Agrawal, six years later, this Arts Council intention had yet to have a discernible impact in practice.

To enable such a 'creation' of relevance, and to prevent a return to the superficialities and confusions of multiculturalism, requires first a 'decentring' of the norms and values of 'dominant white culture' to allow space for a fuller expression of humanity and (as part of this project) a wider appreciation of classical Indian dance forms. To develop a possible route towards this, I turn to three distinct yet (in my view) related suggestions. These are philosopher of race George Yancy's (2017) call for 'un-suturing', sociologist Anibal Quijano's (2007) argument for 'de-linking' and Stuart Hall's (1999) proposal for 're-imagining of the post-nation'.

In his powerful study of white racism in America, Yancy cites novelist and activist James Baldwin, who writes,

> White man, hear me! History, as nearly no one seems to know, is not merely something to be read. And it does not refer merely, or even principally, to the past. On the contrary, *the great force of history comes from the fact that we carry it within us, are unconsciously controlled by it in many ways, and history is literally present in all that we do*. It could scarcely be otherwise, since it is to history that we owe our frames of reference, our identities, and our aspirations. (Baldwin, cited in Yancy 2017: 247, my emphasis)

From a different perspective (and rather more poetically) Baldwin makes here a similar argument to Bourdieu, emphasizing the extent to which our acquired habitus determines how we act and how we think, so that we embody our predispositions, our presuppositions – and our unconscious bias. It is the same point that Ahmed, who also draws on the notion of habitus, makes in her argument about 'orientation towards whiteness', building on psychiatrist and philosopher Frantz Fanon's attention to the 'historic-racial schema' (Fanon, cited in Ahmed 2007: 153). Yancy elaborates: 'white gazing is a deeply historical accretion, the result of white historical forces, values, assumptions, circuits of desire, institutional structures, irrational fears, paranoia, and an assemblage of "knowledge"' (Yancy 2017: 243) – resulting in racism.

If Yancy discusses the construction of the 'white gaze', Quijano's argument discusses the way in which, from a broader perspective, not only white people, but people of all races lie subject (since colonialism) to 'hegemonic ideas of what knowledge and understanding are and, consequently, what economy and politics, ethics and philosophy, technology and the organization of society [and, one might add, the nature of professionalism] are and should be' (Mignolo 2007: 459). In both cases, the result is a diminishing of horizons, a narrowness of vision and an inability to really hear or grasp a perspective that derives from alternative 'epistemic and axiological frames of reference' (Yancy 2017: 254).

As a way to escape, overcome and break down the pernicious constraints of such conditioning, Yancy urges that 'white people' must come 'to terms with the vicious history of white supremacy', through 'a practice of un-suturing, . . . a critical distancing from (or disruption of) various hegemonic norms' (2017: 256). This demands not only an acceptance, but an embrace and a pursuit of the process of decentring whiteness. Yancy explains,

> Un-suturing disrupts; it troubles and unsettles; . . . As an aesthetic gesture/site, un-suturing is a form of exposure, an opening, a corporeal style and a dispositional sensibility that troubles the insularity of whiteness . . .

instigating instability, that sense of being thrown off balance, off center [*sic*] and exposing different (and counterhegemonic) ways of being. (ibid.: 259)

Similarly, Quijano argues for the process of 'de-linking' as means to reverse the 'colonisation of the imagination of the dominated', which has served (among other things) 'to impede the cultural production of the dominated' (2007: 169). The process of 'de-linking' works 'to change the terms of the conversation, and above all, of the hegemonic ideas of what knowledge and understanding are' (Mignolo 2007: 459). While 'de-linking' has a wider scope than Yancy's 'un-suturing', the decentring of whiteness remains central to this approach because of colonialism's inextricable intersection with race and its dependence on racial classifications to justify and maintain its existence. The effect of de-linking, like that of un-suturing, results in a widening of the 'horizon of expectations' and thereby a widening of an understanding of the multiple ways in which to be human. This should not rest on 'a total rejection' of the 'Eurocentred paradigm of knowledge', which might result only in the imposition of one 'totality' in place of another. Rather, it is a recognition that 'A world in which many worlds could co-exist can only be made by the shared work and common goals of those who inhabit, dwell in one of the many worlds co-existing in one world and where differences are *not cast in terms of values of plus and minus degree* of humanity' (Mignolo 2007: 499, my emphasis). It is work towards a world of 'pluriversality' in which there will remain no space for a 'deficit' model of cultural capital – because no single version of cultural capital will set the rules.

In his 1999 address, Stuart Hall provides some pointers to what such 'un-suturing' or 'de-linking' might mean in practice, in the specific case of the British 'white nation'. The first step he identifies is 'a redefining' of nation – a 're-imagining of "Englishness" in a more profoundly inclusive manner' (1999: 19). This 're-imagining' of Britain must start not only from an embrace of what Hage points to as the decentring of whiteness through migration, but from a historic 'decentring of whiteness' based on an appreciation that it is only as a result of the use (and exploitation) of the labour, land and resources of the majority world that Britain is where it is today. As Mignolo points out, 'when the industrial revolution took place, race was not a visible issue. The appropriation of land in the colonies was invisible [in Britain]' (2007: 486) – which does not mean that it was not happening. Such a reimagining must start, in other words, from an effort for Britain to 'take seriously its own decolonization' (Mbembe 2010) by fully appreciating colonization 'as a historical phenomenon with historical and contemporary consequences' (ibid.). Such an endeavour, rooted in what Mbembe terms an 'ethics of consequences' (ibid.) necessarily brings with it a profound recognition of the realities of migration, summarized succinctly by anti-racism activist Sivanandan Ambalavaner's aphorism – 'we are here, because you were there' (Ambalavaner 2008). Hall comments that 'The Brits owe this not only to us, but to themselves, for to prepare their people for success in a global and de-centred world by continuing to misrepresent Britain as a closed, embattled, self-sufficient, defensive, tight little island would be to fatally disable them' (Hall 1999: 19). It is not only the British artists who, post-Brexit, are barred from touring Europe without visas, customs waivers and work permits for each individual member state (Snapes 2021) or the Scottish shellfish farmers for whom Brexit has meant the loss of 'centuries old markets' (Holton 2021) who will appreciate the prescience of Hall's words.

Britain's identity, then, must be based on a less myopic understanding of history, which, as with Doreen Massey's understanding of space and place, also understands 'identity' as a process in the making, rather than as an object to be defended and maintained. This must lead, to come to Hall's second point, to an overhaul of the British cultural canon so that it gives 'recognition, exposure and visibility to artists from the South' (Hall 1999: 19), and so that it is no longer the case that 'even when asked directly, white British respondents who identify themselves as cosmopolitan still find it hard to name specific artists, musicians or film-makers from Africa, South America or Asia' (Flemmen and Savage 2017: S239).

Towards a British Natyam?

> What we need is a conservatoire, a youth dance company and a repertory dance company. Let's get on and do it. (Jan de Schynkel, then Dance Relationship Manager, Arts Council England, meeting of the South Asian Dance Alliance, Nehru Centre, London, 29 June 2017, fieldwork notes)

What might such a decentring, such a reimagination of identity and overhaul of the British 'national culture canon', mean for classical Indian dance forms in Britain? A place in the British cultural canon would provide these dance forms with a wider legitimacy, underlining that they take their place in British society as 'common assets', not only as 'ethnic minority art forms' fulfilling 'a specific need of a specific people' (Araeen 1987: 19). This in turn will increase the value of the cultural capital of minority communities, which will also be part of 'the cultural repertoires associated with "national belonging"' (Flemmen and Savage 2017: S238). One practical means towards this might be that selected primary and secondary schools offer students a regular weekly class in a classical Indian dance style, just as the animateur movement enabled Sanjeevini Dutta to provide Katie Ryan and her classmates in the early 1990s (see Chapter 3). A further measure would include the reinstatement of classical Indian dance works as set works (or as making up part of the 'core' dance anthology) for the UK national school examinations in GCSE (General Certificate of Secondary Education) or A

Figure 5.2. Natya Project dancers in rehearsal, Birmingham 2018. © Simon Richardson.

(Advanced) level dance. Such initiatives would help build a wider knowledge and understanding of classical Indian dance forms, while emphasizing their place as an intrinsic part of British culture (rather than as 'enriching' extras).

Such suggestions seem sadly utopian in a context where engagement in the arts of any kind is currently being stripped from the school curriculum. A 2021 government document affirmed that 'music, dance, drama and performing arts; art and design; media studies; and archaeology' are not among its 'strategic priorities' (OFS 2021: 17). On the other hand, the failure to acknowledge the intrinsic interweaving of Indian classical dance forms (among many others) with the 'British' cultural narrative could result in increased problems from a fractured society – and the argument can even be made, if necessary, in terms of economics. Bhikhu Parekh argued in 2000 that 'In an increasingly global yet diverse world, it is societies that know themselves to be internally diverse, and are at ease with their internal differences, which stand the best chance of economic success' (Parekh and Runnymede Trust 2000: 163).

To help develop opportunities for dancers to work (or sustain their livelihood) while staying true to the aesthetics and vocabulary of the classical styles, a repertory company might be established, devoted to the exploration of classical

Indian styles in and of themselves. Such a company would be governed neither by nostalgic demands of 'long-distance nationalism', nor by the extrinsic conventions and values of Euro-American contemporary dance, but could speak to a 'contemporary sensibility', a term used by Akram Khan in a conversation at Darbar 2017 to invoke performing work in a way that asks questions from 'the voice of today'. As Khoo elaborates,

> My example is always – when I am dancing *Yaaro Ivar Yaaro*,[26] my reference point is always Olivia Hussey in the Franco Zeffirelli *Romeo and Juliet*. I always go back to the movie and watch her. I sometimes don't think dancers understand how to look at Anish Kapoor [a British Indian sculptor] and appreciate that work, and then genuinely apply their contemporary sensibility into a *varnam*, thereby making the *varnam* contemporary. Instead, they might think, 'I'll wear jeans and that will contemporize it' – but that's actually very superficial. No! Do the *varnam* properly – but don't be afraid to show who you are within it. I don't go to Chennai and think, 'oh, I'm going to stop being a Londoner now' – not at all. (Khoo 2017)

In other words, a seventeenth-century Tamil *varnam* can be restaged just as a Shakespeare play is restaged today – not as a way of recreating a seventeenth-century experience but as a way of reinterpreting the experience and insight of that particular playwright in that particular century in a way that speaks to our here and now.

Once dancers have a means of securing a livelihood through the practice of (and the value lent to) their particular form of expertise, knowledge and craft, it follows that there will be demand for further training, so that the long-desired vocational school for classical Indian dance forms in Britain might finally prove a realistic proposition.

At this point of meeting the demands of legitimacy, livelihood and expertise, classical Indian dance forms will be able to develop their own autonomous field in Britain, as ballet and Euro-American contemporary dance have done before, creating, as Mira Kaushik proposed at a South Asian Dance Alliance meeting in 2017, 'a British brand of classical Indian dance' (fieldwork notes, 17 February 2017). At this point we will be able to truly claim to have a 'British Natyam', or a 'Natyam' ('dance' or 'drama', as for classical Indian dance forms the concepts are not separate)[27] that has a British inflection, that presents a British *bani*.

The 'National Cultural Canon', *Eudaimonia* and Communities of Practice

How realistic is the pursuit of a 'British Natyam' in the face of the visceral fear of loss arising in response to accelerating cross-global migration, cultural exchange and the 'global forces of postmodernity' (Hall 1997: 36), and a realization that the dominant values of 'whiteness' are being (and must be, for all our sakes) displaced? For Hage, there is an urgent need 'for rethinking a new cultural politics capable of recognizing and dealing with the sense of cultural loss from which neo-fascism is being fed' (Hage 2000: 26). A claim to a 'British Natyam' could evoke such a sense of loss both among certain British nationalists questioning the right of Natyam to make a claim on Britain, and among certain Indian nationalists questioning the right of Britain to make a claim on Natyam.

The nature of global exchange (accelerated in the last century but present throughout human history) means that it can be very difficult to identify where one particular 'national' canon should stop and another begin. How 'national' is a 'national cultural canon' if it embraces and co-opts art forms that originated on the other side of the world? Does the rejection of an unrealistically exclusivist nationalism mean a surrender to the globalization of art forms whereby, as with the versatile body discussed in Chapter 4, the nuance and detail of distinctive dance forms are lost in surrender to a dominant discourse? The alternative approach, however, is no less difficult. In 2019, a colleague and I listened with a mixture of amusement, distress and disbelief as two second-year dance degree undergraduates, seemingly in tune with the zeitgeist, questioned the 'Irishness' of Irish dance given that it had been influenced in the twelfth century by the arrival of the Normans. How should we maintain the striking specificity and precious particularities of art forms on the one hand, while avoiding the perils both of mummification and of dogmatic essentialism on the other?

In a comment on identity, the philosopher Kwame Anthony Appiah reflects, 'each human life begins with many possibilities. Everybody has – or, at least, should have – a great variety of decisions to make in shaping a life. And a philosophical liberal, like me, believes these choices belong, in the end, to the person whose life it is' (Appiah 2006: 18).

Clearly, Appiah says, we all exist within constraints: 'I was born into the wrong family to be a Yoruba Oba and with the wrong body for motherhood; I am too short to be a successful professional basketball player and insufficiently musical to be a concert pianist' (2006: 18) – and there are other social and environmental factors that restrict out choices as well, as I have discussed. Ultimately, however, the decision as to what constitutes their identity should belong 'to the person whose life it is' and should rest on what allows for each person's *eudaimonia* – 'Aristotle's word, perhaps best translated as "flourishing"' (ibid.: 17). Appiah cites John Stuart Mill's *On Liberty*:

> Different persons also require different conditions for their spiritual development . . . The same things which are helps to one person towards the cultivation of his higher nature, are hindrances to another . . . unless there is a corresponding diversity in their modes of life, they neither obtain their fair share of happiness, nor grow up to the mental, moral, and

aesthetic statures of which their nature is capable. (Mill 1963–91: 270, cited in Appiah 2006: 19)

The Arts Council could not ask for a more eloquent articulation of the 'Creative Case for Diversity'. In other words, the choices as to what constitutes a person's identity should not be forced, and should not be dictated by their ethnicity, their gender, their class, their sexuality or anything else, but by what is most likely to allow them to flourish. What this means in terms of the practice of Indian classical dance forms is that their practice should not be determined by class, gender, race or nationality, but by a particular individual's affinity with the dance style, and the sense that it best allows them to express, in Mill's terms, their 'nature'. A bonus of globalization (to counter some of its problems) is that it is not (or should not) be a surprise that Miyako Yoshida (born in Japan) was a Principal Guest Artist of the Royal Ballet; that Sheku Kanneh-Mason (whose parents are from Antigua and Sierra Leone) was 2016 BBC Young Musician of the Year (as a cellist specializing in Western classical music); or that Katie Ryan, born and brought up in Bedford, UK is an odissi dancer.

In September 2019, at the Bhavan in London, bharatanatyam artist Stella Subbiah presented an evening's performance of bharatanatyam entitled *Udal* or *Bodyscapes*. The performance brought together a range of practitioners from a range of different backgrounds – different nationalities, different social classes, different ages. The Italian Marcella Capelletti performed next to the half-Tamil, half-Malayali P.T. Rakesh. The part-Tamil, part-British Australian Chris Gurusamy performed next to a Tamil working mum now living in Wembley, northwest London. In this way *Udal* served to question the dubious and dangerous conflation between culture and genotype and instead insisted on the importance of a 'community of practice' (Wenger 1998), or as dance scholar Judith Hamera (2011) terms it, a 'dancing community'.

Educational theorist Étienne Wenger defines a community of practice as 'a community created over time by the sustained pursuit of a shared enterprise' (Wenger 1998: 45). The value of this notion, as the linguistics scholar Penelope Eckert points out, is 'that it identifies a social grouping not in virtue of shared abstract characteristics (e.g., class, gender) or simple co-presence (e.g., neighborhood, workplace), but in virtue of shared practice' (Eckert 2006: 684). Thus, returning to *Udal*, it is not being born Tamil or being born a Hindu that makes a good bharatanatyam dancer, but the day-to-day commitment, time and work (*sadhana*) given to embodying the art form. A Yorkshire-born, Christian bharatanatyam practitioner sustains the specificity of bharatanatyam; a British, yet East African-born Asian woman now living in Devon turns up at her village hall to sustain the practice of the English folk morris dance. In a globalized world, I suggest, the best chance for the retention of the specificity of art forms is not through the dogmatic and exclusive identification of art with nation but through the patient, creative and generous work of multinational, multifaith and multilingual 'communities of practice'.

This is not a radical suggestion. More radical is what this might suggest, for example, for the practice of bharatanatyam and other classical Indian dance forms in Britain. To truly break the nationalist claim of one nation upon a specific art form demands, in some ways paradoxically, a claim by many nations upon many art forms. A government-funded 'dancing community', such as British school of Natyam, for example, would extend a sense of British national belonging to those familiar with classical Indian dance forms, while making the legitimate claim that these dance forms are now also British. As with the National Ballet of China or the School of Irish Dance in Richmond, Virginia, or, at some point in the future – who can tell – the Mumbai Academy for Morris Dance, such a globalized yet specialized embrace of these specialist yet globalized art forms is not only welcome but necessary for their future.

Returning to the first chapter, the discussion of *BBC Young Dancer* is a vivid demonstration of how the 'expansion of the canon' or of curatorial choices can have a limited impact within the context of wider systemic inequities, where art forms that express and derive from different aesthetic and artistic narratives are nonetheless positioned within the framework of a dominant aesthetic understanding. A meaningful expansion of the canon must rest within what visual arts scholar Ruth Iskin (2017) dubs (drawing on Mignolo) a 'pluriversal canon'. With this understanding a canon is no longer to be valued so much for offering a space of 'consensus' as for offering a space of 'debate'. She cites the acclaimed curator Okwui Enwezor, who declares his interest in the 'exhibition space' as a 'space of encounter, between many contending notions of artistic practice; as a space in which knowledge systems, aesthetic systems and artistic systems converge sometimes in harmony and sometimes in great disharmony' (Enwezor 2008, cited in Iskin 2017: 26). In this light, I suggest, the expansion of the canon plays two fundamental roles.

First, to echo art critic Geeta Kapur (reflecting on the specific instance of the biennials), canons, exhibitions, syllabi, competitions, festivals and other such mechanisms by which artworks are distributed at the interface between state and commerce – while 'never beyond serving vested interests [including] . . . spectacle, cultural hegemony, market interests' – remain 'at the same time a means of creating professional conduits of communication . . . structures [that] erect bridges between the state and private finance, between public spaces and elite enclaves, between artists and other practitioners' (Kapur 2012: 182). These conduits, she argues, are all the more important to those who might not otherwise have the opportunity to engage with the international (or, one might add, the national) art scene. Such conduits, a little like the dance competitions discussed in Chapter 1, offer a means to the expansion of audience that, I argue, is so important for artists to sustain their practice.

Second, the expansion of the canon serves, or should serve, as a reminder of the canon's contingency. The canon, like identity, space, place and nation, cannot be fixed, but must be subject to a permanent process of revision if it is to reflect, in the words of philosopher Cornel West (1987: 201), the 'current crisis in one's society and culture' and thereby hold any meaningful authority. The expansion of the canon should not be perceived as a way to 'include' in the sense of 'tolerate' or 'permit', but rather should form part of an expansive redefinition of citizenship that allows all citizens to say and feel, 'This is my home. I am not an outsider here. I do not have to beg or to apologize to be here. I belong here' (Mbembe 2015). Under this understanding 'the canon' can serve to further, rather than to hinder, the ongoing project of decolonization – within Britain and beyond.

Afterword – the Arts Council Portfolio 2023–26

As an exercise in changing and questioning the established canon, the decisions made for Arts Council England's 2023–26 portfolio merit some reflection. This portfolio investment round was 'the most oversubscribed to date with 1,723 applications requesting over £2 billion' (Arts Council England 2023).

Given the extent of the demand on a limited budget, together with the constraints around the budget uplift assigned to the Arts Council in the Spending Review,[28] ACE was forced to make what its chair, Nicholas Serota, called 'invidious choices' (Arts Council 2022c: 23:41). The criteria informing these choices were based on the Arts Council's ten-year strategy for 2020–30, Let's Create, which commits to a vision of England as a country 'in which the creativity of each of us is valued and given the chance to flourish' and 'where every one of us has access to a remarkable range of high-quality cultural experiences' (Arts Council England 2020). Together with assessing how far each applicant seemed likely to deliver on this strategy, the Arts Council employed a number of 'balancing criteria' that took into account areas of historically low Arts Council investment and low cultural engagement: organizations where 'the leadership and governance ... is more representative of England in relation to disability, race, sex and includes more people from lower socio-economic backgrounds' (Arts Council England 2022a: 67),[29] as well as ensuring a spread of investment across art forms and disciplines, types of organization and types of activity delivered.

The resulting portfolio met with a mixed response, most notably with respect to significant London organizations including the English National Opera (ENO) and the Donmar Warehouse leaving the portfolio.[30] For South Asian dance, however, the new portfolio was a good news story. As Tables 5.9 and 5.10 below illustrate, the number of South Asian dance NPOs in the portfolio almost doubled, and the funding allocated to South Asian dance forms through the portfolio increased by over 66 per cent. Bharatanatyam was brought back into the portfolio for the first time since Jeyasingh's work largely moved away from the form (see discussion in earlier chapters), and with Kala the Arts, the portfolio for the first time ever featured an organization with a focus on odissi. In addition, several organizations that support South Asian dance forms as a significant part of their work (but do not fall under the discipline of dance) also received substantial funding increases. As illustrated in Tables 5.6 and 5.8 above, the organizations in the portfolio that form part of the South Asian Dance Alliance together received a 70 per cent increase in funding. These changes are supported by a shift to increased diverse representation across the portfolio, with the number of organizations led by people from black, Asian and ethnic minority backgrounds increasing from fifty-three in the last portfolio to 143 in 2023–26.[31]

In the debates following the funding decisions, the hereditary peer Valerian Freyburg (Lord Freyburg) spoke in the House of Lords in relation to the ENO, suggesting that with 'the new funding level . . . the Arts Council model is more one of engaging freelancers as and when required, rather than building quality and talent in a maintained opera company'. He went on to argue, 'If the ENO is to be a genuine national opera company, developing talent and creating opera to the highest standards, it is hard to see how it can do that without a permanent company within which to develop and maintain those skills – and that is the case whether or not the Arts Council feels that large-scale grand opera is worthy of support' (Hansard 2022b). As I have argued throughout this book, such permanence, which permits 'the building of quality and talent' and allows for the development and maintenance of skills, is one that is required across art forms – it forms an essential ingredient of 'professionalism' or *virutti*. In this portfolio, for the first time, bharatanatyam dancers working for Seeta Patel Dance, or kathak dancers working for Amina Khayyam Company or Pagrav, are offered some scope for this through the possibility of a contract that extends beyond the precarity of that afforded by project grants.

In some ways, with the demands of this portfolio, the Arts Council can be argued to be a victim of its own success. To tackle the devastation that beset the cultural sector during the Covid-19 pandemic, the Arts Council distributed £1.5 billion in emergency support to more than five thousand cultural organizations across England, many of whom had had little or no relationship with the Arts Council until the pandemic hit. A combination of an increased awareness of the Arts Council and the very possibility of funding, and the strategy of Let's Create, which emphasizes creativity's pluriversality and importance to each and every person, meant that this portfolio, as discussed above, faced unprecedented demand.

How best to apportion limited resources has been a matter for debate since the Arts Council was founded. As Nicholas Serota wrote in the introduction to Let's Create, 'In 1951, the Secretary General of the then Arts Council of Great Britain characterised the Council's mission as growing "few, but roses"', while Let's Create acknowledges 'that the surest way to fill the future with every variety of flower is to recognize that we can all be gardeners' (Arts Council England 2020). Alongside this debate, which can be seen as focused around participation and professionalism, another hereditary peer, the Labour politician Thomas Lyt-

Table 5.9. South Asian dance NPOs 2018–22. © Magdalen Gorringe.

	Company name	ACE region	Discipline	Funding/annum in GBP, 2018–22
1	Akram Khan Company	London	Dance	500,610
2	Leicester Dance Theatre Ltd (Aakash Odedra)	Midlands	Dance	365,000
3	Shobana Jeyasingh Dance Company	London	Dance	258,732
4	Akademi	London	Dance	215,000
5	Balbir Singh Dance Company	North	Dance	150,460
6	Sonia Sabri Company	Midlands	Dance	125,034

* Figures taken from Arts Council document on NPO funding 2023–26, compiled by M. Gorringe.

Table 5.10. South Asian dance NPOs 2023–26. © Magdalen Gorringe.

	Company name	ACE region	Discipline	Funding/annum in GBP, 2023–26
1	Akram Khan Company	London	Dance	509,821
2	Leicester Dance Theatre	Midlands	Dance	371,716
3	Seeta Patel Dance	South West	Dance	310,000
4	Balbir Singh Dance Company	North	Dance	251,728
5	Pagrav Company Ltd.	South East	Dance	250,000
6	Akademi	London	Dance	218,956
7	Sonia Sabri Company	Midlands	Dance	218,135
8	Jaivant Patel Company	Midlands	Dance	195,000
9	Amina Khayyam Dance Company	South East	Dance	135,000
10	Nupur Arts Dance Academy	Midlands	Dance	120,000
11	Kala the Arts	South West	Dance	110,000

* Figures taken from Arts Council document on NPO funding 2023–26, compiled by M. Gorringe.

tleton (Viscount Chandos), argued in the House of Lords that there is a further balance that needs to be struck 'between dynamic change and the preservation and enhancement of what is good and excellent', along with the balance between 'accelerating the provision of arts in underserved parts of the country and the protection . . . of the UK's world-leading position in the creative industries' (Hansard 2022b). Ultimately, fulfilling the various competing demands is, he concedes, 'clearly . . . easier with a larger pie to divide'.

Figure 5.3. Amina Khayyam Dance Company (a new NPO in 2023) in Bird *(Amina Khayyam, 2023). Dancers R-L: Abirami Eswar, Jane Chan, Jalpa Vala, Selene Travaglia © Simon Richardson.*

Let's Create seeks to acknowledge the importance both of participation and professionalism, with the strategy's Outcome 1 (Creative People) focused on the former and its Outcome 3 (a Creative and Cultural Country) focused on the latter. The Arts Council has also tried in this round to expand the canon and to ensure that 'the *diversity* of audiences, leaders, producers and creators of creativity and culture . . . reflect[s] the *diversity of contemporary England*' (Arts Council n.d.c). Any established canon brings with it an inherent inertia, and yet as the Arts Council's Director for Music Claire Mera-Nelson commented in a blog post about the decisions, 'Even though our instincts may be to protect everything we already know to be of value, we can't and shouldn't be making the same choices in perpetuity' (Mera-Nelson 2022: np). Even with the changes made in this portfolio, Mera-Nelson points out, 'opera will still receive £30 million a year from the Arts Council – over 40% of our total investment in music' (ibid.). Conversely, despite the significant increases in investment for South Asian dance, looking solely at NPO funding (without taking into account project grants and grants awarded through the Developing Your Creative Practice award stream), funding for South Asian dance forms stands at 5.7 per cent. As the Arts Council rightly seeks to ensure the representation of previously unrepresented groups with a vari-

Figure 5.4. Seeta Patel Dance Company (another new NPO in 2023) in rehearsal for Patel's interpretation of The Rite of Spring. © *Simon Richardson.*

ety of protected characteristics in terms of gender, race and disability, in addition to social class, against a backdrop of increasing economic pressure, the demands on finite portfolio resources are only likely to increase.

One possible approach could be for the Arts Council to focus its resources on the repertory companies that support the wider development of different art forms, confining artist-led companies that pursue the vision of an individual artists to a 'maximum period' of NPO support. Yet this would arguably deprive us of the support that has led to the success of artists such as Jasmin Vardimon, Matthew Bourne or Akram Khan. Whichever way the 'pie' is divided the only certainty appears to be that the Arts Council's future can only hold yet more 'invidious choices'.

Conclusion

This chapter has considered the challenges that classical Indian dance forms have faced in being incorporated as part of the 'national cultural canon', which I argue is key to the legitimacy and consecration that these forms need in order to establish a professional field within Britain. Comparing the story of the arrival to Britain of these dance forms with those of ballet and contemporary dance, I argue that the most significant factor preventing their more wholescale inclusion in the 'national canon' is the fact that these dance forms, through their techniques, vocabularies, codes and conventions, depart from the norms of whiteness. I suggest that the answer is not to bring classical Indian dance forms into the domains of 'whiteness', but rather to decentre whiteness; to un-suture and de-link our thinking and our imaginations such that the norm we have inherited from colonialism is put in its right place as simply one norm among many equally valid and equally valuable norms. Such decentring will allow for a transformed 'national cultural canon', allowing space for the growth of professional dance fields adhering to many different *doxa* – which need not attempt to shape themselves to the overarching rules of one. Such a recognition of a 'pluriversal' canon, always in the process of being made and remade, will grant each of us space to pursue our individual *eudaimonia* (or flourishing) with a true reflection of the 'diverse modes of life' of which 'our natures are capable'.

Notes

1. Spalding's precise words were: 'They're almost like athletes, dancers, they need to perform' (BBC 2021: 46: 26).
2. In this light it is worth noting that there is no mention of South Asian dance forms at all in the 2021 syllabus and only marginal mention of Shobana Jeyasingh and Akram Khan in the A level syllabus. This is in marked contrast to the years between 1992 and 2007, when works by Jeyasingh, Khan, Pushkala Gopal, Nahid Siddiqui and others featured consistently as set works (Sanders 2006). Thanks to Ann R. David for highlighting this point.
3. See Pulse Dance Club (2021). As noted in the introduction, my investment in South Asian dance in Britain is personal as well as academic. Together with Elena Catalano, I therefore wrote to Sadler's Wells to voice my disappointment. This letter can also be found here (beneath the review). I should note that Spalding subsequently replied to this letter, writing 'With regard to the lack of inclusion of Classical South Asian dance – I can only agree and perhaps in retrospect it's a rich area that we failed to represent on this occasion' (Spalding, personal communication, 4 March 2021), and also expressing the intention of Sadler's to encourage 'younger artists' in the field.
4. Looking solely at NPO funding (without taking into account project grants and grants awarded through the Developing Your Creative Practice award stream), funding for South Asian dance forms stood at 3.8 per cent for the 2018–22 portfolio, including funding for Akram Khan and Shobana Jeyasingh Dance. This increased to 5.7 per cent in the 2023–26 portfolio. NPO funding for ballet stood at 42 per cent for the 2018–22 portfolio and 38 per cent for 2023–26, though this is without the significant funding allocated to ballet through the Royal Opera House. The ROH received the largest allocation of NPO funding in both 2018–22 and 2023–26, with funding recorded at £24,028,840/annum for 2018–22 and £22,268,584/annum for 2023–26. The ROH is classified under

'Music' for 2018–22 and as 'non-discipline-specific' for 2023–26. (All figures calculated by the author on the basis of ACE NPO investment data).
5. Thus Guest records: 'for while the Alhambra corps de ballet was made up of English girls, a foreign background was considered essential in a principal dancer' (1992: 19). See also Carter (1995).
6. Phyllis Bedells is a notable exception. See Genné (1995).
7. This remains the case for the 2023–26 portfolio.
8. The Royal Ballet is not included on these tables as it is not listed on ACE's table of NPOs. The Royal Opera House is listed; see note 4 above.
9. Ninette de Valois was herself an example of a dance artist who felt compelled to change her name to succeed. Christened Edris Stannus, she took the stage name Ninette de Valois 'with its implication of not only French but royal origins' (Genné 1995: 442).
10. This was despite the fact that the founders of neither of the leading ballet companies at the time were themselves British. Ninette de Valois, who founded the Royal Ballet, was originally from Ireland, while Marie Rambert, founder of Ballet Rambert, was an émigrée from Poland.
11. The centrality of Robin Howard's role in the establishment of contemporary dance in Britain through the foundation of the Contemporary Dance Trust (CDT), or the Place, is of such significance that for dance critic Clement Crisp (2004), it is almost impossible to imagine the development of contemporary dance in Britain without him. In this light, the following account from former GLA Dance and Mime officer Lynn Maree is arresting:

> When Robin Howard saw Tara dance, it was probably about 2 weeks after he had fallen in love with Martha Graham. And he once told me that if he had seen Tara before he had seen Martha Graham, he would probably have made a big push behind classical Indian dance – and not contemporary dance. And he meant it.
> (Maree 2017)

It is extraordinary to think about the difference it could have made to the trajectory of classical Indian (and Western contemporary) dance forms in Britain had Howard encountered Rajkumar before Graham. Howard still had a significant role in the development of classical Indian dance forms in Britain, despite the greater part of his largesse going towards contemporary dance. Rajkumar recalls his role in Akademi's very beginning: 'Robin Howard . . . was so generous – he listened and our relationship grew so much that he asked his mum to host a fundraising event at her home. This was amazing and meant that we got access to the arts elite who were able to come and help with the fundraising' (Rajkumar 2017). He was later instrumental in Akademi being given a home for many years within the Contemporary Dance Trust, a location with more than a symbolic significance in allowing Akademi, as Kaushik put it, to become 'engrained within the dance scene' (Kaushik 2017a).

12. Sadly, this is no longer the case. As of 2021, Britain's new blue-black passports are devoid of any images.
13. I attended a performance of *Giselle* at the Mayflower theatre, Southampton in 2016 and overheard a full range of audience responses – from the indignant 'well, it's not really what you would call beautiful is it . . . I expect a ballet to be beautiful', to the enthralled 'well, wasn't that amazing!' (fieldwork notes, 27 October 2016).
14. The choreography was later reworked by Urja Desai Thakore and Amina Khayyam.

15. As I discuss later in the chapter, the 2023–26 portfolio has been a good news story for South Asian dance, with double the number of NPOs in the portfolio, and an organization primarily representing *odissi* joining the portfolio for the first time (the south-west based Kala the Arts).
16. Odedra's work has certainly represented classical *kathak* (in the stunning solo work *Echoes*, for example, choreographed by Aditi Mangaldas, he flies across the stage like a reincarnation of the music legend Prince born to perform *kathak*). His recent ensemble work, however, as I indicate earlier, is work for (Western) contemporary dance artists.
17. Not to mention, of course, that a year after this passport was designed, Britain voted to leave the European Union, deferring to a more parochial vision of Britishness.
18. This is also the title of Paul Gilroy's (2000) excellent book on being black in Britain.
19. Ram Gopal, from the 1989 documentary made on him, *Bandung File: Ram Gopal, Dancing to the Music of Time* (dir. Zoe Hardy, researcher Smita Bhide). Thanks to Ann R. David for sharing this wonderful story.
20. Chapter 1 discussed how an 'artistic' appreciation differs from an 'aesthetic' one, representing a response shaped by a knowledge of the conventions and the narrative of that art form. It is, in other words, an informed response – rather than an immediate or sensual response.
21. In the case of ballet in particular, a deliberate effort was made to 'Britify' the form. Between 1931 and 1946, for example, as ballet historian Tanya Dawn Wetenhall has shown, ballet in Britain was moved consciously away from its Russian incarnation, and ballets such as *Job*, *The Rake's Progress* (Ninette de Valois, 1937) or *Miracle in the Gorbals* (Robert Helpmann, 1944) delivered visual iconographies of Britain – including *Job*, which opened with a front curtain by designer Gwen Raverat on which was painted what appears to be an English oak, based on an engraving by William Blake (Wetenhall, personal communication). The audience was left in no doubt as to the 'take-home' message. Whatever ballet's provenance, these images announced, it was now equally a British art form.
22. In London these are primarily Tamil community-led organizations such as the London Tamil Sangam. David (2008, 2012) has conducted research on these institutions. They remain, however, a largely understudied area, in part possibly because, for the reasons discussed, they do not court such attention.
23. The reviewer erroneously described a dance artist's work as grounded in kathak, when her form is bharatanatyam. To add insult to injury, the institutional response from the Place to the dance artist pointing out this error was to tell her that the onus lay on her to make her form clearer, as the Place 'did not have the time or resources' to do so (Agrawal, personal communication, 2020). The Place, as I highlight below, is in receipt of funding almost equal to all the South Asian companies and agencies put together. For such an institution to put the onus for this work on an individual artist, citing their own lack of resources, would be laughable if it were not so entirely unacceptable. The review in question, with the conceded amendment, could formerly be viewed at the following link, but is no longer available: https://www.theplace.org.uk/blog/resolution-review-2018/tue-23-jan-lydia-touliatouyanaelle-thiranhinged-dance-co (retrieved 12 June 20).
24. Burns, Gallagher and Gamble (2023) explain how dance agencies initially developed in England in the 1980s as a way to provide infrastructure to the dance animateur movement (see Chapter 3, note 36). The national dance agencies developed mostly in the 1990s, with at least one in each Arts Council region. In 2024 there are eight national

dance agencies, all Arts Council NPOs and each with their own buildings: Dance East in Ipswich and South East Dance in Brighton, both in the South East of England; Pavilion Dance South West in Bournemouth, in the South West; the Place (London Contemporary Dance School) in London; Dance City (in Newcastle upon Tyne) and Yorkshire Dance (in Leeds), both in the North; and FABRIC (in Birmingham and Nottingham, an amalgamation of the former Dance Xchange and Dance4, in the Midlands).

25. ADiTi was especially important in the 1990s in creating a directory for South Asian dance in the UK, as well as a regular dance sector magazine (*ADiTi News*), which has now been reincarnated as *Pulse* (see http://kadamdance.org.uk/pulse/, retrieved 24 July 2024). In these days of Google and WhatsApp groups, it is difficult to describe the significance this magazine once held for news, reviews and networking.

26. *Yaaro Ivar Yaaro* ('Who, Oh Who is This?') is a well-known Tamil *padam* (or expressional piece) composed by Arunachala Kaviraya, which captures Rama's emotions on first catching sight of his future wife, Seeta (the song is also interpreted to express the emotions Seeta feels on first sighting Rama).

27. From the Sanskrit word 'nata' – to act or represent.

28. In February 2022, the Arts Council received an instruction from the then Culture Secretary, Nadine Dorries, on how they should use their resources 'in line with the wider objectives of the Government' (Arts Council England 2022b: 3). This instruction made clear that the spending uplift allocated to ACE 'must be invested in order to benefit creativity and culture outside of London' and also required ACE to reduce 'its overall current investment in the National Portfolio in London by £24 million per year by the end of the 2024/25 Financial Year' (approx. 15 per cent of the then London budget) and reinvest that money 'outside of London and, where possible, in ways that benefit Levelling Up for Culture Places' (ibid.). The 'instruction' from the then Culture Secretary raised questions in Parliament and elsewhere about how far this compromised the 'arm's length' principle. For example, Baroness Deborah Bull (principal dancer for the Royal Ballet, 1992–2001; creative director of the Royal Opera House, 2008–12) suggested that the February directive 'gnawed at the fingers of the arm's-length principle' (Hansard 2022a).

29. The guidance explains that 'our Equality Analysis shows that disabled people, women and people from some racial/ethnic groups are currently underrepresented in the leadership and governance of our national portfolio'.

30. These decisions must be understood in the context of the February directive – see note 30 above.

31. Figures quoted by Undersecretary of State Lord Parkinson of Whitley (Hansard 2022a).

Conclusion
Part of the 'British DNA'?

In 2000, Akademi produced *Coming of Age* (directed by Keith Khan), the first spectacle of its kind, through which classical Indian dance forms both claimed and redefined the space of the South Bank.[1] For that performance, after years of, as Chitra Sundaram put it, 'quietly doing our stuff in the Purcell Room',[2] it felt as if South Asian dance had finally found the self-confidence to announce its presence to the wider public (hence *Coming of Age*). The concrete and glass of the Royal Festival Hall, built in 1951 for the Festival of Britain, in part as an 'anniversary monument to the [imperial] 1851 "Great Exhibition"' (Littler 2006: 21), became on those two evenings in 2000 the backdrop for a symbol and expression of a new Britain – diverse and evolving, with, as then Foreign Secretary Robin Cook famously announced, chicken tikka masala as its national dish. At the top of the building, Mavin Khoo launched the show, bare chested and bejewelled, in a deliberate evocation of one of the pioneers of South Asian dance in Britain, Ram Gopal. At the show's close, Gopal himself, still regal and commanding at 88, blessed the occasion with his presence, framed by a ring of lights that echoed both the flames around the dancing Nataraj and the newly opened millennium wheel beyond. This was felt by Richard Blurton, curator at the British Museum, to be 'a defining moment'. For an Asian audience member, it represented 'the reality of how far our community has come in this country' (all quotations taken from Akademi's *Coming of Age* commemorative flyer, 2000), lending a sense, as Mira Kaushik put it, that 'South Asian dance is now part of the British DNA' (Kaushik, in Sundaram 2012). This performance and the optimism surrounding it took place at possibly the peak of 'Asian Kool' under a New Labour government committed equally to the goals of cultural diversity and creative industries (and seeing them both, in business terms, as good investments).[3] In this book I have considered how far Britain has come, and yet how much there remains to be done in terms of establishing the professional practice of classical Indian

Figure 6.1. The author and Kalidasan Chandrasegaram in Akademi's, Coming of Age, *London 2000 Photo © Ali Zaidi. Thanks also to Akademi.*

dance forms in Britain. How far are classical Indian dance forms really part of the 'British DNA'?

The BBC's inclusion of a 'South Asian' dance category in its *Young Dancer* competition brought with it some of the energy and optimism seen in *Coming of Age*. It is an inclusion that in itself highlighted the significance of 'South Asian' dance forms to the world of dance in Britain and, from this perspective, the achievement of South Asian dance artists, choreographers and sector leaders in ensuring their influence and visibility. A closer look at this inclusion, however, shows that this prominent indicator of success masks a hinterland of infrastructural precarity. An analysis using Bourdieu's concept of 'field' shows that an autonomous professional field for classical Indian dance forms in Britain, whereby the standards and conventions are endemic to that field, remains to be established. As yet, dance practitioners and cultural agents have fought to find a place for their dance forms within the field of Euro-American contemporary dance, subject thereby to the 'symbolic violence' of attempting to align themselves with a very different set of conventions and very different sets of expertise.

In the effort to develop such expertise, while the inclusion of the Classical Indian Dance Faculty within the Imperial Society of Teachers of Dancing has been a great step forward and has been welcomed by many practitioners, there remains a significant gap in the provision of professional training for classical Indian dancers in Britain, as there is still nowhere offering immersive, full-time training beyond the days or weeks available as part of summer schools. Training remains largely limited to evening and weekend classes, with practitioners wishing for professional training having to arrange and devise their own training routes, usually through a combination of extra classes, attendance at summer schools, time spent training in India and combining their training in classical Indian dance forms with training in contemporary dance.[4] The South Asian dance Centre for Advanced Training, Yuva Gati, is a significant programme, representing both the only context in which state funding contributes to consistent training in classical Indian dance forms (kathak and bharatanatyam) and the only context in which training is given to a group of students with a professional career in dance in mind. The CATs are clearly intended as pre-vocational training, however, and training is still restricted to a very limited number of days. Several attempts to establish the vocational training dreamed of since the 1970s have failed due to a lack of student numbers. At the same time, the framing of the teaching of Indian classical dance forms in Britain as a means of maintaining links with cultural heritage has prioritized identity with an ancestral 'homeland' over artistic identity. The persistent narrative of 'ethnic' arts, now rechristened 'culturally diverse arts', is that of 'a specific need for a specific people'. This has restricted the potential constituents for the dance forms, both in terms of audience and practitioners, which has in turn led to diminished employment opportunities due to limited audience demand. The lack of clear employment routes has meant the lack of student numbers to make a vocational training course viable, thereby affecting standards of practice.

A vocational school alone, however, merely creates another problem when not accompanied by prospects for employment. On this subject, and considering the overlap between 'livelihood' and 'learning', the demand for the 'versatile' dancer impacts on the way in which classical Indian dancers are trained. In a professional environment that seeks 'versatility', the distinctive aesthetics and bodily *hexes* that characterize classical Indian dance forms are in danger of being lost in favour of the dominant dance vocabulary of Euro-American contemporary dance. While there is no inherent reason that classical Indian dancers trained in Britain should not embody the 'technical habitus' of classical Indian dance forms as fully as dancers trained in India or elsewhere, where there is not the demand for that particular habitus on stage (through choreographic habitus), and where there is not the space that allows the cultivation of that specific habitus (as institutional habitus), training in Britain clearly remains a more difficult proposition. In this light, the demand for the 'versatility' of performers must be replaced by a cultivation of 'versatility' among audiences.

The story of the professionalization of classical Indian dance forms in Britain can be usefully considered here in the light of the comparative cases of Euro-American contemporary dance and ballet, both forms with a presence in Britain not so very much older than that of classical Indian dance forms, and both of which had to work to develop audiences to establish their viability in Britain. The legacy of the post-colonial reconstruction of classical Indian dance forms has undoubtedly contributed to the length of time it has taken for these forms to secure a place in Britain by comparison with ballet and contemporary dance. This legacy both stigmatized performing dance as a profession while at the same time emphasizing the practice of dance as a means to establish an Indian national identity as much if not more than to establish an artistic identity. The more significant obstacle however has been the wider legacy of colonialism – which is that of 'a discursive infrastructure, a symbolic economy, an entire apparatus of knowledge whose violence was epistemic as well as physical' (Mbembe 2021: 68), which manifests in what Hage (2000), Ahmed (2007) and Yancy (2017) variously reveal to be an 'orientation to whiteness'. This is an orientation that allows the practice of ballet and contemporary dance to proceed unmarked by provincialism, while 'classical Indian dance' or 'South Asian dance forms' remain by their very labels geographically tethered. The presumption of the universality of contemporary dance is such that classical Indian dance practitioners are still expected to reflect the artistic narratives of Euro-American contemporary dance in their performance, and to shape their work to the ideals of (Euro-American) contemporary choreographers. Just as Ahmed argues that in the white-orientated institution, 'bodies that might not appear white still have to inhabit whiteness, if they are to get "in"' (2007: 158), so classical Indian dance forms must adapt their technical habitus to that of contemporary dance to attain legitimacy. In this light the moves towards 'cultural diversity' emerge as disappointingly superficial – classical Indian dance forms are welcomed, provided they conform to the codes and conventions of Euro-American contemporary dance. In short, to echo Stuart Hall's observation (about a different context), classical Indian dance forms can be seen as 'stopped short at the frontier by that great unspoken British value – "whiteness"' (1999: 17).

To achieve a genuinely 'diverse' society demands an uncomfortable unseating of the presumed universality of the 'white way of being' to make space for a society that embraces a pluriversal canon – one that encompasses multiple narratives and multiple conventions, aware that each represents a different way of approaching the same tangled and incalculable mystery of life, and that none has greater authority than another. It demands a canon seen not as a site of consensus or stasis, but as an entity necessarily always under revision, premised on an acknowledgement of the necessary failure to master – allowing us thereby to 'become vulnerable to other possibilities for living, for being together in common' (Singh 2018: 21). In a context where 'our very subjectivities have emerged through modern legacies of mastery' (ibid.: 22), Julietta Singh argues for an embrace of what she terms 'vital ambivalence' as a means to subvert colonial fanta-

Figure 6.2. The Natya Project at the Midlands Arts Centre, Birmingham, performing in front of a mural by the black British photographer Vanley Burke, 2018. An illustration of the multiple narratives that interweave in contemporary Britain. © Magdalen Gorringe.

sies of such mastery. Following R. Radhakrishnan, she argues that 'far from being a sign of the instability or weakness of the postcolonial project, ambivalence is its vitality' (ibid.: 21). This aligns with Achille Mbembe's insistence that the project of decolonization must be premised 'on the idea that social worlds are multiple, fractured, contested' (2021: 79), and that it is only through a preparedness to accept and embrace such fracturedness, such 'multivocality' and such 'plurality of narratives from silenced voices and invisible places' that we can 'avoid perpetuating the knowledge/power asymmetries' that more deeply 'fracture global humanity' (ibid.).

Such multiple narratives, I suggest, are essential not only for classical Indian dance forms in Britain to flourish, but for each of us as individuals to attain our own flourishing (*eudaimonia*). Equally, the need for a multiplicity of narratives is not a cause that either can or should be championed from the space of those who have been historically 'excluded' (Desai 2020). It is an endeavour, as acknowledged in the Arts Council's Creative Case for Diversity (2014), that must be led equally, if not more by those who have historically done 'the excluding'. In practical terms this will demand the engagement not only of the South Asian dance but also the national dance agencies – and beyond this, not only of the Arts Council, but of the Department for Education. It will require the establishment of repertory companies for bharatanatyam and kathak devoted to the exploration of these forms in and of themselves, subject neither to the essentialist demands of 'heritage', nor to the changing sensibilities of any single choreographer's artistic journey. It demands a transformation of the 'national cultural canon' that 'takes seriously its own decolonization', accepting an 'ethics of consequences' (Mbembe 2010) that will lead to necessarily uncomfortable transformations in the understanding of British history and nationality. To be truly transformational, this will also require a revision of school education and curricula that incorporates a fuller understanding of the legacies of colonialism and is in line with what scholar of social justice education Megan Boler (1999) terms 'a pedagogy of discomfort'. The aim of such uncomfortable teaching, she explains, is 'for each person, myself included, to explore beliefs and values; to examine when visual "habits" and emotional selectivity have become immune to flexibility; and to identify when and how our habits harm ourselves and others' (ibid.: 185–86). She alerts us, returning to Bourdieu, to the importance of recognizing our habits and our habitus and of seeking to re-evaluate and, where necessary, make changes, through 'awareness and . . . pedagogic effort' (Bourdieu 2005: 45).

Clearly the effort to create a pluriversal canon and to effect a 'pedagogy of discomfort' will need resources, at the mention of which, as Hall puts it, 'the corners of the Government's mouth tends to droop significantly' (1999: 18). At the same time, to propose 'the idea that a major culture-change – nothing short of a cultural revolution – could take place in the way the nation represents the diversity of its "subject-citizens" without a major redirection of resources is to reveal oneself as vacantly trivial about the whole question' (ibid.). It is pointless to deny that the change entailed *will* be uncomfortable, and at times painful. A small glimpse of this discomfort can be seen in the responses to the Arts Council's 2023–26 portfolio discussed in Chapter 5. How, as a society, do we provide the durational stability necessary for the development of professional expertise for one art form without compromising the equally valid and pressing needs of another? It is indisputable, to repeat Viscount Chandos, that fulfilling various competing demands is 'clearly . . . easier with a larger pie to divide' (Hansard 2022b).

Returning to the questions that prompted this study, one remains unresolved, which is the fundamental question, 'why professionalize?' My response to this echoes the rather hackneyed L'Oréal slogan 'because you're worth it'. Professionalization confers, as I have discussed, symbolic capital – and classical Indian dance forms merit such value as much as any other dance form. Additionally, such symbolic capital can lever greater economic capital – which in turn supplies dancers with the means to augment their cultural capital, both through being able to put more time into training (physical capital) and by having more time to develop their work. Classical Indian dance forms can be and indeed are performed by dual-career dancers to an extraordinarily high and creative standard. Such squeezing of the time and space to perform, however, should not be necessary. A recognition of professionalism should help to ensure that classical Indian dance forms are accorded the resources, both in terms of time and money, for their practice as a sole or main career. Professionalization can be damaging where it necessitates the adoption of an artistic narrative, standards and conventions that are outside an occupation's internal frame of reference. This is a problem with the attempt to position classical Indian dance forms within the field of Euro-American contemporary dance. This problem derives, however, not from professionalization so much as from failure to professionalize – or failure to develop an autonomous field assessed on its own terms. Beyond the characteristics of expertise, means of livelihood and legitimacy I suggest that there are no 'professional' qualities that are absolute. Rather, as there are many fields, there are many professionalisms; a pluriversal canon is met by a pluriversal understanding of professionalism.

Returning to the young dancers of *BBC Young Dancer* with whom I started, an autonomous professional field for classical Indian dance forms will not resolve the balancing act that lies at the heart of professionalism – negotiating the dual contracts to one's art form and one's patron or employer. The challenge, as I raise in Chapter 1, to 'present dance that is accessible without being comfortable, that is legible without surrendering to a "vision-bite" stereotype, and that is commercially viable without being driven by a commercial end', and to tread the line between working for 'love' and working for 'money', remains the constant negotiation of any professional artist.

As discussed in Chapter 2, this negotiation is made ever more fraught by the consistent erosion of conditions that allow for 'professionalism' in terms of occupation, both as a sole means of livelihood and a committed way of life (Martin 2012; Harvie 2013; Kedhar 2014, 2020; Kunst 2015), while the neoliberal clamour for the supposed 'professional' grows ever shriller. A closer look at what might be required for this latter form of professionalism reveals a disciplinarian force wherein the primary virtue is conformity. The careers website indeed.com, for example, defines professionalism as including 'standards for behavior [*sic*] and the employee's ability to embody the company's values and do what their employer expects of them' (Herrity 2024:np) Such 'organizational professionalism' (Evetts 2013: 787) has served to substitute for a loyalty to one's profession a loyalty to the 'organization'. This understanding of 'professionalism', to adapt Theodor Adorno's scathing assessment of the 'culture industry', 'lives parasitically . . . without concern for the laws of form [expertise] demanded by aesthetic [professional] autonomy' (1975: 14). An obedience to the organizational understanding of professionalism, or an adherence to a particular ideology, becomes the test for whether or not one can be considered a 'professional' – rather than the commitment to profess, or practice, one's chosen skill or craft. At the same time, this disciplinarian force replicates the violences of colonialism in seeking to elevate one (provincial) understanding of professionalism above others. Subjugation to (or mastery by) a particular notion of 'professionalism' replaces the committed and patient pursuit of a profession that can, and should, never be mastered.

One possible way to invoke the concept of professionalism as referencing both livelihood and expertise without its contemporary or historic Euro-American baggage is, I suggest, to replace the term 'profession' with that of *virutti*, a term that encompasses both way of life and devotion, both regularity and duration. *Virutti*, I argue, both rejects neoliberalism's increasing pressure towards professionalism combined with the decreasing opportunities for its expression, and inherently rejects the very possibility of mastery in its necessary commitment to ongoing process. In the face of the increasing precarity of neoliberalism (marketed disingenuously as 'flexibility'), the funding for arts projects provided by institutions such as the Arts Council becomes all the more necessary and important in helping artists to cultivate a *virutti*. Hence Lord Freyburg's concern, seen in the last chapter, at the loss of funding by the English National Opera, and his suggestion that with 'the new funding level . . . the Arts Council model is more one of engaging freelancers' and that it is hard to see how an organization can sustain 'talent and create opera [or any art form] to the highest standards . . . without a permanent company within which to develop and maintain those skills' (Hansard 2022b). From this perspective it is pertinent to consider the increasing attention being given to the proposal for universal basic income, a non-means-tested unconditional allowance paid to each citizen – an idea that has gained increasing support partly due to the need for widespread government income support as a result of Covid-19. For artists, the guarantee of a living wage could mean the freedom to focus solely on their 'contract' with their art forms, with the possible implication that 'professionalism' might once again lose its economic imperative.

Such visions – of a National Curriculum premised on a 'pedagogy of discomfort'; of a British Royal Natyam; of a pluriversal canon; and of universal basic income – are admittedly utopian. They are especially so against a backdrop of an administration[5] that has clearly stated that its priorities do not include the arts, and that in 2021 authorized a report produced by the Commission on Race and Ethnic Disparities that objects to the use of the term 'white privilege' (Sewell et al. 2021: 36), that attempts to find the silver lining in slavery and that has suggested that focus be shifted away from attention on 'structural' or more 'systemic racism' to discussions with 'more objective foundations' (ibid.).[6]

In the meantime, local authorities, historically an important source of funding for the arts, have had their own funding reduced, meaning a steady decrease in investment in their non-statutory spend on the arts. In 2024 the Midlands-based authorities of Birmingham and Nottingham issued 114 notices, in effect declaring themselves bankrupt. As a result, both authorities have cut their funding to the arts by 100 per cent. Funding for dance has not escaped. Self-proclaimed 'dance veterans' Susanne Burns, Karen Gallagher and June Gamble, who have been involved in dance production, research and consultancy in Britian for over thirty-five years, wrote in 2023 lamenting the reduction to dance infrastructure due to the loss of several of the regional dance agencies, accompanied by 'the loss of dance in schools, the closure of dance programmes in Higher Education and reduced dance programming in some cities and towns' (Burns, Gallagher and Gamble 2023). In their view, 'The dance infrastructure has never been so fractured and we believe this is because of policy decisions that have destroyed what has been built over four decades' (ibid.). Meanwhile, the Campaign for the Arts reports a 47 per cent decline in arts enrolment at GCSE, and a 29 per cent decline at A level (CFTA 2023: np).

Nonetheless, I make these suggestions in the spirit of envisioning a different world, or in the words of Martin Luther King, in the refusal to submit 'the "oughtness" of a new order to the "isness" of an old order' (King 1954). For Singh, 'The desire for utopia is always and already a failed desire, but the real and contextual effects of its failure are precisely where we can find mastery's interstices' (2018: 27–28). Emboldened by these leaders and thinkers, heartened by the presence of such camaraderie, I take courage to urge my words to dance out the 'possibility of a new human relation, a relation to the future of the world that was not available *then* but could be available now' (Kelleher 2009: 53). At least at some point. At least as an idea.

***

I am in the Foyle Studio at the Midlands Arts Centre in Birmingham. It's a studio I know well, but today it feels different. In front of the short set of raked seating, there are rugs and cushions arranged on the floor, on which some audience members are already seated, as if in their front room at home. The performance starts, but the house lights are not entirely dimmed. The soft lighting covering both stage and seating emphasizes a continuum between performer and audience, conjuring again the informal atmosphere of a living room. The performance is by the kathak master Pandit Rajendra Gangani, presented by Sampad together with Sonia Sabri Company and kathak artist Seetal Kaur Dhadyalla. The air of informality is deliberate. The presenters are attempting to recreate the sense of a 'baithak', a word meaning 'parlour' or 'living room' in Urdu, but also referring to a particular kind of intimate performance in which, as Dhadyalla explains, 'you feel the energy of the performers and they are able to feel yours' (field notes, 20 June 2019). The performance that follows is not a display from an isolated stage but involves a constant exchange – between Gangani and the musicians, Gangani and the audience. As he dances, he narrates, he explains, he tells a story to highlight a point he is making. Between anecdotes he performs with a skill and command that is the result of a lifetime of training. He dances a short piece about Krishna stealing the butter from the gopis *– and his* abhinaya *is so effective that he* *transports us into the room where the village woman is making butter. His evocation is so clear that as my friend sitting next to me observes, she can practically 'see' the cupboard into which the* gopi *is placing her churning stick. At another point, he performs footwork so intricate and controlled as to be able to depict at one moment a thunderstorm, at another a swarm of bees, at another a light shower of rain. The audience is utterly engaged – keeping the* taal, *uttering an involuntary 'Wah! Wah!'*[7] *at moments of particular appreciation. Gangani talks to the audience, flitting between Hindi and English. The audience talks back, questions, admires. The evening is an interweaving of discussion, explanation, expert music and dance, and I feel caught up in Gangani's artistry, for a brief time a co-collaborator in creating the experience of kathak.*

This performance, in its informality, in its unchoreographed to and fro between artist and audience, has provided me with an experience qualitatively different to that of most of the other forty odd shows I have attended as part of my fieldwork – in which the exchange between audience and performer, where it exists, is usually confined to a discrete and carefully facilitated Q and A. There are points at which I feel lost – when the conversation slips into Hindi and I struggle to catch the odd word I can make sense of. In the grand scheme of things, however, this is an enviably safe space in which to feel 'lost'. Nothing depends on it except perhaps a greater artistic appreciation of the performance. There is a part of me that notes my own frustrated incomprehension and wonders if the experience isn't good for me. It confronts me very immediately with my limitations and with a whole landscape of meaning that I have yet to discover. The performance both discomfits and unsettles me, but also nudges me to look further and see more. It expands my 'horizon of expectations'.

Slowly, I begin to accept this discomfort as a gift. I start to glimpse the narrowness of what I know, and hence the incalculable excitement of what I don't. I have the same sense of vertigo as when I learn that there are two trillion galaxies in the universe. Gangani's ghunghrus *tumble like stars, each one promising another way of knowing.*

Notes

1. Shorthand for the 'South Bank Centre', a complex of artistic buildings on the south bank of the River Thames in London, including the Royal Festival Hall, the Queen Elizabeth Hall, the National Theatre and the Hayward Gallery, and just a short walk from the Tate Modern. See https://southbank.london/ (retrieved 25 July 2024).
2. An intimate 295-seater venue located within the Queen Elizabeth Hall in the South Bank Centre, immediately next to the Royal Festival Hall.
3. See Kedhar (2020: Chapter 1) for a detailed discussion of South Asian dance during this period of New Labour and 'Cool Britannia'.
4. One unexpected and welcome by-product of the otherwise devastating Covid-19 pandemic has been the rise of professional classes run over Zoom with leading artists based in Britain and elsewhere. The use of the internet has allowed for a critical mass of students to make such classes sustainable in a way that was not previously considered feasible. How far these on-screen classes match the calibre of training provided by direct contact remains an open question.

5. On July 4th 2024, the Labour party, then in opposition, won the general election, unseating the Conservatives as the primary governing party for the first time in fourteen years. The Labour party's approach to the arts departs from the Conservatives, stressing the arts as a 'necessity not a luxury' (Labour leader Keir Starmer in a speech to the Labour Creative conference, 2024) and promising to change the curriculum to ensure a 'creative education for every child' (Labour's plan for the Creative Industries, 2024). This offers grounds for optimism that the arts may be better supported under the new government, and optimism necessarily tempered by the bleak messaging at the time of writing in September 2024 about the £22 billion fiscal black hole and the inevitable pressures on public spending this will entail.
6. While the report concedes that 'different groups are distinguished in part by their different cultural patterns and expectations', it maintains that 'it is hardly shocking to suggest that some of those traditions can help individuals succeed more than others' (Sewell et al. 2021: 234) – without any apparent curiosity or misgivings as to why this might be the case. This report has been widely critiqued by MPs, unions and equality rights campaigners. The UN issued a particularly trenchant condemnation, arguing that the report seeks to 'rationalize' white supremacy (OHCHR 2021:np).
7. 'Wah, wah' is an exclamation of pleasure or admiration.

Appendix 1

List of Judges and Mentors Engaged for *BBC Young Dancer*

Full profiles of these mentors and judges can be found here: https://www.bbc.co.uk/programmes/profiles/1Nv0NN8yTqX8ntCKWWWNvk4/judges (retrieved 14 May 2021).

BBC Young Dancer 2015

Judges
Mira Balchandran Gokul: Bharatanatyam dancer, teacher and choreographer, co-artistic director of Sankalpam Dance.
Pratap Pawar: Leading exponent and guru of kathak dance (students include Akram Khan).
Adjudicator across all categories: **Kenneth Tharp**, choreographer, director and former Chief Executive of the Place.

Mentors
Seeta Patel: Bharatanatyam dancer, teacher and choreographer, founder of Seeta Patel Dance.
Aakash Odedra: Kathak dancer and choreographer, founder of Aakash Odedra Dance Company (Leicester Dance Theatre).

Grand Final Judges
Matthew Bourne: Artistic Director of New Adventures.

Mavin Khoo: Bharatanatyam choreographer, dancer and (then) Artistic Director of ZFin Malta dance ensemble.
Wayne McGregor: Founder of Studio Wayne McGregor and resident choreographer at the Royal Ballet.
Tamara Rojo: Artistic Director of English National Ballet.
Kenrick Sandy: Dancer and choreographer (urban, commercial and theatrical dance).
Alistair Spalding: Chief Executive and Artistic Director of Sadler's Wells.

BBC Young Dancer 2017

Judges
Kajal Sharma: Teacher and leading exponent of kathak.
Chitra Sundaram: Bharatanatyam dance/theatre choreographer, performer and educator.
Adjudicator across all categories: **Shobana Jeyasingh**, choreographer, founder of Shobana Jeyasingh Dance.

Mentors
Mira Balchandran Gokul: Bharatanatyam dancer, teacher and choreographer, co-founder of Sankalpam Dance.
Sonia Sabri: Kathak dancer, teacher and choreographer, co-founder of Sonia Sabri Company.

Grand Final Judges
Kevin O'Hare: Director of the Royal Ballet.
Jasmin Vardimon: Choreographer and Artistic Director of the Jasmin Vardimon Company.
Marc Brew: Artistic Director of Marc Brew Company and choreographer.
Kate Prince: Choreographer and Artistic Director of ZooNation.
Kenneth Tharp: Choreographer, director and former Chief Executive of the Place.
Nahid Siddiqui: Kathak dancer and choreographer.

BBC Young Dancer 2019

Judges
Gauri Sharma Tripathi: Kathak dancer, teacher and choreographer, founder of Ankh Dance.
Seeta Patel: Bharatanatyam dancer, teacher and choreographer, founder of Seeta Patel Dance.

Adjudicator across all categories: **Jonzi D**, founder and Artistic Director of Jonzi D Projects and Breakin' Convention.

Mentors
Geetha Sridhar: Bharatanatyam dancer, tutor, performer and choreographer.
Urja Desai Thakore: Kathak dancer, teacher and choreographer, founder of Pagrav Dance UK.

Grand Final Judges
Emma Gladstone: (Then) Artistic Director and Chief Executive of Dance Umbrella.
Wayne McGregor: Founder of Studio Wayne McGregor and resident choreographer at the Royal Ballet.
Shobana Jeyasingh: Choreographer and founder of Shobana Jeyasingh Dance.
B-Boy Junior/Bosila Banya: Dancer, teacher and member of Wanted Posse crew.
Chitra Sundaram: Bharatanatyam dance/theatre choreographer, performer and educator.
Christopher Hampson: Artistic Director and Chief Executive of Scottish Ballet.

BBC Young Dancer 2022

Judges for Initial Auditions
Annie Hanauer: Independent dance artist.
Geetha Sridhar: Bharatanatyam dancer, tutor, performer and choreographer. Chair of judges for initial auditions and Artistic Director for *BBC Young Dancer* 2022: **Emma Gladstone**, cultural and creative facilitator, former Artistic Director and Chief Executive of Dance Umbrella.

Judges for Initial Auditions and Programme Choreographers and Mentors
Begoña Cao: Former principal ballerina of English National Ballet.
Dickson Mbi: Award-winning hip-hop artist, founder of Dickson Mbi Company.
Gianni Gi: Street, freestyle and commercial dance artist and choreographer.
Ivan Blackstock: Multidisciplinary creative, founder of CRXSS PLATFXRM and the production company ALTRUVIOLET.
Seeta Patel: Bharatanatyam dancer, teacher and choreographer, founder of Seeta Patel Dance.

Additional Choreographers for Programme
Sadé and Kristina Alleyne: Dancers, choreographers, founders of Alleyne Dance.

Workshop Leaders
Julia Cheng: Creative director, founder of House of Absolute, an all-female collective of multidisciplinary dancers.

Theo Clinkard: Dancer, teacher, choreographer, founder of Theo Clinkard Company.

Grand Final Judges

Arthur Pita: Choreographer, director, Artistic Director of Ballo Arthur Pita.
Kate Prince: Choreographer and Artistic Director of ZooNation.
Ryoichi Hirano: Principal dancer, Royal Ballet.
Subathra Subramanian: Bharatanatyam dancer and choreographer, Artistic Director of Akademi, South Asian Dance in the UK.

Appendix 2

Table of South Asian Dance Tuition in British HE Institutions

Courses are only included where classical Indian dance forms are or were taught consistently, not as a one-off, though Bisakha Sarker rightly makes the point that these longer courses have only been made possible on the foundations provided by the many hundreds of one-off classes taught in schools and colleges across Britain over the years – 'it takes so long to prepare the ground' (Sarker, phone conversation, June 2021). Of the courses listed below only the short-lived dance degree at De Montfort University and later at LCDS can be considered to have offered any degree of vocational training in classical Indian dance forms.

Stacey Prickett notes that the presence of South Asian dance in British higher education started much earlier than this with the inclusion of classical Indian dance forms performed by artists such as Uday Shankar and Anjali (Ann Marie Gaston) in teaching at Dartington Hall (Prickett 2009).

Appendix 2.1. 'Chart'-ing the courses teaching South Asian dance in Britain – a Table of South Asian Dance Tuition in British HE Institutions © Magdalen Gorringe.

Dates	Institution	Course
Mid- to late 1980s	Laban Centre	Modules on the Community Dance MA launched by Peter Brinson. Tutor: Pushkala Gopal
2/3 years in the 'late eighties' (Gopal 2018).	University of Surrey	Part of the Dance BA, co-ordinated by Alwyn Marriage. Introduction to Indian dance with overview lectures and practicals in *bharatanatyam*. Tutor: Puskhala Gopal
1992–93	De Montfort University (formerly Leicester Polytechnic)	South Asian Dance combined honours degree. The course grew out of 'detailed and lengthy consultation work between East Midlands Arts, ADiTi and Mike Huxley, Head of Dance at the polytechnic' (David 2003: 7). There was one graduate from this course: Priti Raithathah, who was forced to finish her course with contemporary dance modules due to a lack of tutors.
1993–2002	Middlesex University	15-week module in South Asian dance as part of BA (Hons) in Dance. Replaced in 2002 by a non-South Asian dance-specific module entitled 'Cultural Diversity in Dance' (David 2003: 7). Tutors: Pushkala Gopal
1995–2000	Bretton Halls in partnership with ADiTi and Middlesex University	Certificate for South Asian dance artists working in schools. Course graduates include Nilima Devi and Priti Raithathah (David 2003: 7).
1995–2022	University of Surrey	BA in Dance and Culture (in which training in first kathak and later bharatanatyam was integral). Tutors have included: Nahid Siddiqui, Alpana Sengupta, Alison Turner, Amina Khayyam (kathak). In 2014/15 Stella Uppal Subbiah together with Sabine Sorgel revised the syllabus incorporating bharatanatyam, rather than kathak. Subbiah taught this course until 2018/19. Kamala Devam took over the course from 2019 to 2022.

2002–present (2003 excepted)	Goldsmiths College, University of London	
Autumn 2002 (2002–3 academic year)	Pilot Programme (BA-level)	A pilot programme of workshops and a simple repertoire taught piece in bharatanatyam for Drama Dept BA Year 1 students. 10 weekly sessions per tutor, total 20 hours. Tutors: Chitra Sundaram and Pushkala Gopal
2004–14	BA – Drama Year 1: 'Space/Body/Spectator'	'Bharatanatyam' module – contemporaneous options with Butoh and Contemporary Performance modules as exposure to varied praxis. Bharatanatyam-based training offered holistically yet highlighting the relationship and ethos of bharatanatyam with relation to the 'body', 'space' and 'spectator' through exercises. No repertoire. Each a self-contained week except the last. Weekly, 4 weeks, total 12 hours for about 20–25 students. Mandatory modules – everyone got a taste of all three modules; no prerequisites. Tutor: Chitra Sundaram
2004–present	MA – 'MA Performance Making' [Course title changes: - 'MA Performance Making' - 'MA Performance-Making: Performance Methodologies' - 'MA Performance-Making: Scenography' Module title changes: - 'Bharatanatyam' - South Asian Dance-Theatre Methodologies' - 'Abhinaya'] Module changes reflect shift in desired module outcomes and Sundaram's emphasis on what she wanted to deliver. Increasingly geared to Rasa theory-based actor training and dramaturgy.	Module offered alongside Butoh and Contemporary Dance (previously Contact Improvisation). Students choose* and remain in the module the entire time. No prerequisites. Tailored, progressive focused explorations and exercises. No single complete repertoire piece. Guest artists invited to present during class including Manorama Prasad, R.R. Prathap, Sujata Banerjee, Stella Subbiah, Geetha Sridhar, Shane Shambhu, Anita Ratnam and Richard Schechner. Initially 21 hours over 7 weeks. Then 15 hours over 5 weeks. In addition, some hours delivered as workshops and Performance Research Forum evenings. *Choice is made after the modules are each 'tasted' in an introductory session for all students enrolled in MA Performance Making.
2017–present	MA World Theatres	Theoretical module on Asian theatre. Full term where students explore Rasa theory, some movement, and watch South Asian dance – among other theatres.

2004–9	London Contemporary Dance School	BA in Contemporary Dance with South Asian dance strand (offered in kathak and bharatanatyam). The syllabus was devised by Gauri Sharma Tripathi (kathak) and Stella Uppal Subbiah in partnership with Akademi (bharatanatyam). Tutors included Stella Uppal Subbiah, Geetha Sridhar (bharatanatyam); Gauri Sharma Tripathi (kathak). Graduates include Archana Ballal, Marcella Cappellati, Thalia Mari Papadopoulou (first batch); Katie Ryan, Vipul Bhatti, Shreya Kumar (second batch); Satyajit Raja Verma (third batch).
2005–16	University of Roehampton	MA in South Asian Dance Graduates include Urja Desai Thakore, Divya Kasturi Stella Uppal Subbiah was an Erasmus Scholar at Roehampton for the Erasmus Mundus Choreomundus MA students. Hari Krishnan has also taught for the Erasmus MA.
2006–present	Kingston University	Bharatanatyam, odissi (and for one-year sattriya) taught as part of a BA in Dance. Tutors have included Menaka Bora, Geetha Sridhar (bharatanatyam), Elena Catalano (odissi).
2010–present	University of East London	Bharatanatyam and kalaripayattu taught as part of second years' curriculum in Dance: Urban Practice BA degree programme. Set up and taught by Dr Jyoti Argade, then by Veena Basavarajaiah (2013), Ankur Bahl and Kamala Devam from 2014 to the present (artists covering Devam's classes include Seeta Patel, Ankur Bahl, Shane Shambhu). Seeta Patel took over for Devam's maternity leave during 2020. The module is only offered in the autumn term.
2009–19	University of Chichester	Bharatanatyam taught as a course component to Musical Theatre students. Tutor: Geetha Sridhar.
2015–19	Hope University, Liverpool	Various classes and courses including: Technique, Distillation of Movement, Facial Expressions and Gestural Economy, Post-Colonialism and Bharatanatyam, Influence of World Migration on Dance, and Movement Vocabulary. Courses facilitated by Rachel Sweeney and Declan Patrick (then Senior Lecturers at the Dance Department).
2015–22	E15	Aspects of bharatanatyam taught as part of the course 'non-Western character acting'. Tutor: Shane Shambhu

Appendix 3

Table of Members of the South Asian Dance Alliance

Agencies that have formed or continue to form part of this alliance. (Note: Akademi is the only organization with the sole remit of promoting dance not alongside other art forms. All organizations have been/are in receipt of ACE funding, but not all are NPOs.).

It is important to note here the existence of the organization ADiTi (1989–2001). This organization was launched as the National Organization for South Asian Dancers. In 1990 it became the National Organization for South Asian Dance. It was founded in Bradford and moved to London in 1996. Its founding director was Abha Adams and its closing director was Shanti Nagarajah (other directors included Shreela Ghosh and Nasreen Rehman). It offered an information service, advocacy work and networking and CPD opportunities. It also produced a magazine, *ADiTi News*, which became *ExtraDiTion*. This magazine was taken over by Kadam and became *Pulse* (now an e-resource).

Only three of these organizations own their buildings – the Bhavan Centre, CICD and Kala Sangam.

Table of Members of the South Asian Dance Alliance, UK. © Magdalen Gorringe.

Organization	Location	Start Date	First director	Present director	Current aims/Mission statement	Featured projects/specified areas of work/website	Primary art form as listed for ACE funding	ACE funding investment in GBP/annum 2018–22	ACE funding investment in GBP/annum 2023–26
Akademi https://www.akademi.co.uk/ Started as National Academy of Indian Dance Name changed to the Academy of Indian Dance in 1988 Name changed to Akademi, South Asian Dance in the UK in 1997	London	1979	Tara Rajkumar (1979–82) Bharti Kansara and John Chapman (1982–85) Pushkala Gopal and Naseem Khan (1985–88) Mira Misra Kaushik (1989–2019)	Subathra Subramaniam (Artistic Director) and Kirsten Burrows (Exec. Director)	'Akademi makes vibrant, fascinating, and meaningful South Asian dance. We use the compelling power of storytelling, rhythm and gestures to create deeper connections with each other and our wider world, one mudra at a time'. (Akademi n.d.a.)	Productions Projects Work with artists (including mentoring and showcases) Work with older adults Work with schools Work with Mental health and well being Corporate, community and private events Curated events	Dance	215,000	218,956
Bharatiya Vidya Bhavan https//bhavan.net/ (Has own space, studios and theatre. Gained these premises in 1978) First gained Arts Council funding in 1996/97 (Nandakumara 2017)	London	1972	Mathoor Krishnamurthi (1972–95)	Matrur Nandakumara (1995–present)	'The Bhavan's core activities are the teaching and promotion of classical Indian arts, yoga, languages and culture. It is the only organisation in the UK that provides such a wide variety of traditional Indian cultural activities under one roof.' (Bhavan n.d.)	Power of the Arts ('as a force for both personal fulfilment and social good', Bhavan n.d.) Artist Development Relevance of Tradition Social and Community Impact	Music	128,999	131,373

256 ■ Appendix 3

Organization	Location	Start Date	First director	Present director	Current aims/Mission statement	Featured projects/specified areas of work/website	Primary art form as listed for ACE funding	ACE funding investment in GBP/annum 2018–22	2023–26
Chaturangan http://www.chezfred.org.uk/chat/ (Set up as an unincorporated body, 2002) Emerged out of Chaturang, set up in 1999, directed/co-ordinated by Piali Ray [Will soon be wound up. Bisakha Sarker, personal communication, August 2024.] NOT NPO	Liverpool	2002	Bisakha Sarker	Bisakha Sarker	'Chaturangan believes culturally diverse dance to be an integral part of the social and cultural fabric of 21st century British culture. Chaturangan's initiatives support the development of South Asian dance in particular and other dance forms in general' (Chaturangan n.d.).	'Health and well-being initiatives with particular focus on older people, community and educational projects, cross-arts, dance-theatre productions for touring, specially developed resources to support ongoing activities, international conferences on issues of major contemporary concern.' (Chaturangan n.d.)	N/A	N/A	N/A
Centre for Indian Classical Dance https://www.cicd.org.uk/ (Own centre with archive and rehearsal studio) Gained charitable status in 1997 NOT NPO	Leicester	1981	Nilima Devi	Nilima Devi	The Centre for Indian Classical Dance '(CICD) is a visionary South Asian dance organisation which acts as a specialist dance agency in the East Midlands. It promotes and develops South Asian dance through training at all levels, performances, networking and partnerships at local, regional and national level' (CICD n.d.).	The Centre provides a six-year Diploma Course in *kathak*. Teaching Outreach Production Training for advanced students (Devi, 2017)	N/A	N/A	N/A

Gem Arts https://www.gemarts.org/ Gem Arts is part of the wider organization Gateshead Visible Ethnic Minorities Support Group, which was set up in 1989	Newcastle	2001	Vikas Kumar	Vikas Kumar	'Our Vision: We believe the arts enrich the lives of individuals and communities through celebrating our shared cultural diversity – Raising aspirations, building stronger communities and breaking down barriers. Our Mission: To increase equality of opportunity for everyone to engage with culturally diverse arts – as producers, participants and audiences' (Gem Arts n.d.).	Artist development and commissions Organising concerts, events, festivals, workshops and commissions Learning and outreach work Youth music project	Combined Arts	120,000	202,208
Kadam Dance and Music http://kadamdance.org.uk/ (Also manages *Pulse*, http://www.pulseconnects.com/) NOT NPO	Luton	1995	Sanjeevini Dutta and Sujata Banerjee (Banerjee stepped down in 2000)	Sanjeevini Dutta	'We create high quality South Asian dance and music performances for everyone. Kadam has been in existence since 1995 with the aim of promoting these art forms through training, performances and supporting the creation of new work'. (Kadam n.d.).	Create music and dance performances for everyone Manages the sector resource, *Pulse*	N/A	N/A	N/A

Appendix 3

Organization	Location	Start Date	First director	Present director	Current aims/Mission statement	Featured projects/specified areas of work/website	Primary art form as listed for ACE funding	ACE funding investment in GBP/annum 2018–22	ACE funding investment in GBP/annum 2023–26
Kala Sangam https://www.kalasangam.org/about-us/mission-and-vision/ (Owns Grade II-listed building, theatre space and rehearsal space)	Bradford (First Leeds in 1993. Moved to Bradford in 1996. Gained its own buildings in 2007. Refurbished 'Ganges Hall' in 2011)	1993	Drs Shripathi and Geetha Upadhyaya Geetha Upadhyaya was director/artistic director between 1993 and 2017	Alex Croft (2017–present)	'Kala Sangam is an intercultural arts hub which aims to reflect the diversity of contemporary Britain through the work we present, the artists we support and the communities we engage. Specialising in South Asian arts and culture, most of our work takes place in our Arts Centre in the heart of Bradford... with our outreach activities extending regionally and nationally', (Kala Sangam n.d.)	Bradford Producing Hub Classes Education and community outreach Programme of shows Artist Development and support	Combined Arts	100,000	361,840
Milapfest https://milap.co.uk/ Based since 2010 in Liverpool Hope University campus (with studio and theatre space that Milapfest can use). Started as Milap in 1990, building on informal activity from 1985. 1993: Milap Festival Trust became a registered charity and NPO	Liverpool	1990	Prashanth Nayak	Alok Nayak (2019–present)	'Milapfest is Britain's leading Indian arts development trust, producing world class performances, education and artist development opportunities across the UK. We are a British Art Organisation specialising in Indian Arts with a strong track record of creating and delivering ground breaking artistic projects nationally', (Milap n.d.b).	Performances Education and outreach (including training schools and arts awards) Artist development and support Youth music ensembles	Combined Arts	362,908	477,389

Sampad https://sampad.org.uk/ Sampad also runs the South Asian Dance CAT, Yuva Gati, in partnership with FABRIC.	Birmingham	1991	Piali Ray	Piali Ray	'Sampad South Asian Arts and Heritage exists to support the development of the South Asian arts sector to be strong and resilient, with the freedom to be creative. Sampad connects people and communities to South Asian and British Asian Arts and Heritage by breaking down barriers, raising critical issues and amplifying unheard voices' (Sampad n.d.)	Events Projects Learning and outreach Continuous professional development Yuva Gati	Combined Arts	243,906	248,394
SAA – UK https://www.saa-uk.org/ (Started as Leeds Centre for Indian Music and Dance – LCIMD, became SAA-UK in 2002)	Leeds	1997	Keranjeet Kaur Virdee	Keranjeet Kaur Virdee	'To enrich people's lives through the engagement and participation in traditional and contemporary South Asian music and dance', (SAA-UK n.d.)	Classes Summer schools School workshops Artist development Performances	Music	181,000	684,330

Appendix 4

Project Interlocutors

My heartfelt thanks to all those listed below, variously artists, arts managers and arts advisers working within or together with Natyam in Britain. A few interviewees did not want to be named and therefore do not appear here. My gratitude to them remains the same.

Agrawal, Shivaangee
Balachandran-Gokul, Mira
Ballal, Archana
Banerjee, Sujata
Brown, Ginny
Cove, Sheila
Croft, Alex
De Schynkel, Jan
Deletant Bell, Monique
Devi, Nilima
Dutta, Sanjeevini
Ghosh, Aishani
Gopal, Pushkala
Gurusamy, Christopher
Hackett, Jane
Head, Nina
Henwood, Alexandra
Jeyasingh, Shobana
Kasturi, Divya
Kaur-Virdee, Keranjeet

Kaushik, Mira
Khan, Akram
Khan, Naseem
Khayyam, Amina
Khoo, Mavin
Laws, Helen
Lewis, Claire
Lewis, Veronica
Maree, Lynn
Nandakumara, M.N.
Nayak, Prashanth
Patel, Seeta
Patel, Vidya
Prakash, Akshay
Rai, Hardial
Rajarani, Nina
Rajkumar, Tara
Ralls, Jane
Ray, Piali
Ryan, Katherine (Katie)
Sabri, Sonia
Sarker, Bisakha
Shambhu, Shane
Srivastava, Anita
Subbiah, Stella
Subramanyam, Anusha
Sundaram. Chitra
Venkataraman, Uma
Yadagudde, Prakash

References

Aakash Odedra Company. n.d. 'About Us'. Retrieved 17 August 2024 from http://www.aakashodedra.co.uk/about-us/.
Abbing, Hans. 2008. *Why Are Artists Poor? The Exceptional Economy of the Arts*. Amsterdam: Amsterdam University Press.
Abrahams, Ruth K. 2007. 'Uday Shankar: The Early Years, 1900–1938', *Dance Chronicle* 30(3): 363–426.
Ackroyd, Stephen. 2016. 'Sociological and Organisational Theories of Professions and Professionalism', in Mike Dent, Ivy Lynn Bourgeault, Jean-Louis Denis and Ellen Kuhlmann (eds), *The Routledge Companion to the Professions and Professionalism*. Abingdon: Routledge, pp. 15–30.
Adegoke, Yomi. 2020. 'Why Suicide is Still the Shadow that Hangs over Reality TV', *Guardian*, 27 May. Retrieved 25 July 2024 from https://www.theguardian.com/tv-and-radio/2020/may/27/why-suicide-is-still-the-shadow-that-hangs-over-reality-tv-hana-kimura-terrace-house.
Adewole, 'Funmi. 2017. 'The Construction of the Black Dance/African People's Dance Sector in Britain: Issues Arising for the Conceptualisation of Related Choreographic and Dance Practices', in Christy Adair and Ramsay Burt (eds), *British Dance: Black Routes*. Abingdon: Routledge, pp. 125–48.
Adorno, Theodor. 1975. 'Culture Industry Reconsidered', trans. Anson Rabinbach, *New German Critique* 6: 12–19.
Agarathi Tamil Dictionary. n.d. Retrieved 25 July 2024 from https://agarathi.com/word/%E0%AE%B5%E0%AE%BF%E0%AE%B0%E0%AF%81%E0%AE%A4%E0%AF%8D%E0%AE%A4%E0%AE%BF.
Agrawal, Shivaangee. 2017. 'Classical Indian Dance Shines at BBC Young Dancer 2017'. *Dance* 480: 45. Retrieved 24 August 2024 from https://issuu.com/imperialsocietyofteachersofdancing/docs/dance_480_digital.
———. 2018. Interviewed by Magdalen Gorringe. 9 October. Phone interview.

———. 2019a. 'Dance Dialogues – Dancer Profiles', *Pulse*, 25 February. Retrieved 25 July 2024 from http://www.pulseconnects.com/dance-dialogues-dancer-profiles.

———. 2019b. Interviewed by Magdalen Gorringe. 12 July. Asia House, London.

———. 2019c. 'Provocation: The Technical Standards of Dance Achieved in the UK Do Not Match Those in India', *Pulse*, 10 June. Retrieved 25 July 2024 from http://pulseconnects.com/provocation-technical-standards-dance-achieved-uk-do-not-match-those-india.

———. 2020. Interviewed by Magdalen Gorringe. 11 June. Phone interview.

Agrawal, Shivaangee, Sanjeevini Dutta and Magdalen Gorringe. 2021. 'Pulse: Response to ACE South Asian Dance and Music Mapping Report', *Pulse*, 3 April. Retrieved 25 July 2024 from http://www.pulseconnects.com/pulse-response-ace-south-asian-dance-and-music-mapping-study.

Ahmed, Sara. 2007. 'A Phenomenology of Whiteness', *Feminist Theory* 8(2): 149–68.

Akademi. n.d.a. 'One Mudra at a Time'. Retrieved 24 August 2024 from https://www.akademi.co.uk/

———. n.d.b. 'South Asian Dance Alliance'. Retrieved 17 August 2024 from https://www.akademi.co.uk/akademi-resources/sadaa/.

Akademi. 2006. *Retrospective 1980–2006*. London.

Akram Khan Company. 2019. 'About Us'. Retrieved 1 October 2019 from https://www.akramkhancompany.net.

Allen, Matthew H. 1997. 'Rewriting the Script for South Indian Dance', *Drama Review* 41(3): 63–100.

Allison, Lincoln. 2001. *Amateurism in Sport: An Analysis and a Defence*. London: Frank Cass.

Alter, Judith. 1997. 'Why Dance Students Pursue Dance: Studies of Dance Students from 1953 to 1993', *Dance Research Journal* 29(2): 70–89.

Ambalavaner, Sivanandan. 2008. 'Catching History on the Wing'. Institute for Race Relations, 6 November. Retrieved 25 July 2024 from https://irr.org.uk/article/catching-history-on-the-wing/.

Anderson, Benedict. 1992. *Long-Distance Nationalism, World Capitalism and the Rise of Identity Politics*. Amsterdam: Centre for Asian Studies.

Anderson, Jack. 1993. 'British Success Story', *Dance Chronicle* 16(2): 283–86.

Appadurai, Arjun. 1996. *Modernity at Large: Cultural Dimensions of Globalization*. Minneapolis: University of Minnesota Press.

———. 2000. 'Grassroots Globalization and the Research Imagination', *Public Culture* 12(1): 1–19.

Appiah, Kwame Anthony. 1994. 'Identity, Authenticity, Survival: Multicultural Society and Social Reproduction', in Amy Gutmann (ed.), *Multiculturalism: Examining the Politics of Recognition*. Princeton: Princeton University Press, pp. 149–64.

———. 2006. 'The Politics of Identity', *Daedalus* 135(4): 15–22.

Appignanesi, Richard. 2011. '"Whose Culture?" Exposing the Myth of Cultural Diversity', in Richard Appignanesi (ed.), *Beyond Cultural Diversity: The Case for Creativity*. London: Third Text/Arts Council England, pp. 5–15.

Araeen, Rasheed. 1987. 'From Primitivism to Ethnic Arts', *Third Text* 1(1): 6–25.

———. 2011. 'Ethnic Minorities, Multiculturalism and the Celebration of the Postcolonial Other', in Richard Appignanesi (ed.), *Beyond Cultural Diversity: The Case for Creativity*. London: Third Text/Arts Council England, pp. 37–59.

Arts Council of Great Britain. 1978. *A Year of Achievement: 33rd Annual Report and Accounts*. London.

———.1980. *Progress and Renewal: 35th Annual Report and Accounts*. London.

———. 1985. *40th Annual Reports and Accounts*. London.

———. 1988. *43rd Annual Report and Accounts*. London.

Arts Council England. n.d.a. 'National Portfolio 2018–22', Retrieved 18 August 2024 from https://www.artscouncil.org.uk/npo

———. n.d.b. 2023–26 'Investment Programme', Retrieved 18 August 2024 from https://www.artscouncil.org.uk/how-we-invest-public-money/2023-26-Investment-Programme.

———. n.d.c. 'Diversity data', Retrieved 23 August 2024 from https://www.artscouncil.org.uk/research-and-data/diversity-data

———. 2000. *Annual Review 2000 Accounts and Lottery Report*. London.

———. 2006. *Navigating Difference: Cultural Diversity and Audience Development*. London.

———. 2018. Corporate Plan 2018–2020. Manchester: Arts Council England. Retrieved 23 August 2024 from https://www.artscouncil.org.uk/sites/default/files/download-file/ACE%20Corporate%20Plan%202018-20_0.pdf.

———. 2020. 'Let's Create'. Retrieved 25 July 2024 from https://www.artscouncil.org.uk/lets-create.

———. 2022a. '2023–26 Investment Programme, Guidance for Applicants (For Organisations Applying to Deliver our Outcomes)'. Retrieved 10 February 2023 from https://www.artscouncil.org.uk/investment23/2023-26-investment-programme-making-your-application.

———. 2022b. '2023–26 Investment Programme, Addendum to the Guidance for Applicants'. Retrieved 10 February 2023 from https://www.artscouncil.org.uk/investment23/2023-26-investment-programme-making-your-application.

———. 2022c. 'Announcing our 2023–26 Investment Programme', YouTube, 4 November. Retrieved 25 July 2024 from https://www.youtube.com/watch?v=Jc9AtASGWbU.

———. 2023. 'Joint Statement from Arts Council England and the English National Opera', 17 January. Retrieved 25 July 2024 from https://www.artscouncil.org.uk/news/joint-statement-arts-council-england-and-english-national-opera.

Aujla, Imogen, and Rachel Farrer. 2015. 'The Role of Psychological Factors in the Career of the Independent Dancer', *Frontiers in Psychology* 6: 1688.

Bain, Alison. 2005. 'Constructing an Artistic Identity', *Work, Employment and Society* 19(1): 25–46.

Bakhtin, Mikhail. 1981. *The Dialogic Imagination*. Austin: University of Texas Press.

Balarajan, Brammhi. 2020. 'Professionalism Standards Uphold White Supremacy: Brammhi's Ballot', *The Emory Wheel*, 13 December. Retrieved 25 July 2024 from https://emorywheel.com/professionalism-standards-uphold-white-supremacy/.

Balbir Singh Dance. n.d. About. Retrieved 17 August 2024 from https://www.balbirsinghdance.co.uk/about/

Balchandran-Gokul, Mira. 2017. Interviewed by Magdalen Gorringe. 6 February. Southport.

Bales, Melanie. 2008. 'A Dancing Dialectic', in Melanie Bales and Rebecca Nettl-Fiol (eds), *The Body Eclectic: Evolving Practices in Dance Training*. Urbana: University of Illinois Press, pp. 10–21.

Ballal, Archana. 2017. Interviewed by Magdalen Gorringe. 12 April. Dance Xchange, Birmingham.

Banerjee, Sujata. 2017. Interviewed by Magdalen Gorringe. 8 December. London.

Banerji, Anurima. 2021a. 'The Laws of Movement: The *Natyashastra* as Archive for Indian Classical Dance', *Contemporary Theatre Review* 31(1–2): 132–52.
———. 2021b. 'CSWAC Corner: Anurima Banerji'. Center for the Study of Women, UCLA, 29 July. Retrieved 25 July 2024 from https://csw.ucla.edu/2021/07/29/cswac-corner-anurima-banerji/.
Bannerman, Chris. 2003. 'South Asian Dance in Britain'. South Asian Diaspora Arts Archive. Retrieved 25 July 2024 from http://sadaa.co.uk/studio/files/South-Asian-dance-in-Britain_essay.pdf.
Bashir, Tasawar. 2010. *The Sampad Story*. Sampad South Asian Arts: Birmingham.
Bazalgette, Peter. 2014. 'Arts Council and the Creative Case for Diversity'. Conference paper, 8 December. Retrieved 25 July 2024 from https://www.artscouncil.org.uk/sites/default/files/download-file/Sir_Peter_Bazalgette_Creative_Case_speech_8_Dec_2014.pdf.
BBC. n.d. 'About the Competition'. Retrieved 18 August 2024 from https://www.bbc.co.uk/youngmusician/sites/competition/pages/about.shtml.
———. 2015. *BBC Young Dancer*, Series 1, Episode 3. Dir. Rupert Edwards, BBC Four. 1 May, 20:00.
———. 2017a *BBC Young Dancer*, Series 2, Episode 3. Prod. Ryan Minchin, BBC Four. 7 April, 20:00.
———. 2017b. BBC Young Dancer 2017. [Programme]. BBC: Cardiff.
———. 2019. *BBC Young Dancer*, Series 3, Episode 5. Dir. Rhodri Huw, BBC Two. 18 May, 20:00.
———. 2021. *Dancing Nation*, Part 1: 'Breakin' Convention and Matthew Bourne's Classic Spitfire', BBC Arts. 28 January. Retrieved 25 July 2024 from https://www.bbc.co.uk/iplayer/episode/p097qxkz/dancing-nation-part-one-breakin-convention-and-matthew-bournes-spitfire.
———. 2022a. *BBC Young Dancer*, Series 4, Episode 1. Dir. Rhodri Huw, BBC 4. 17 April, 19:00.
———. 2022b. *BBC Young Dancer*, Series 4, Episode 4. Dir. Rhodri Huw, BBC 2. 7 May, 19:00.
———. 2023. 'BBC Young Dancer 2022: History'. Retrieved 25 July 2024 from https://www.bbc.co.uk/programmes/articles/5Qt0hQdlMx4csFNtZCjvRG/history.
Becker, Howard. 2003 [1974]. 'Art as Collective Action', in Jeremy Tanner (ed.), *The Sociology of Art, A Reader*. London: Routledge, pp. 85–95.
Becker, Howard, and Blanche Geer. 1957. 'Participant Observation and Interviewing: A Comparison', *Human Organisation* 16(3): 28–32.
Best, David. 1982. 'The Aesthetic and the Artistic', *Philosophy* 57(221): 357–72.
Bhabha, Homi.K. 1990. 'The Third Space', in Jonathan Rutherford (ed.), *Identity: Community, Culture, Difference*. London: Lawrence and Wishart, pp. 207–21.
———. 1994. *The Location of Culture*. London: Routledge.
Bhavan. n.d. About. Retrieved 17 August 2024 from https://bhavan.net/about.
Blackwell, Kelsey. 2018. 'Why People of Color Need Spaces without White People', *The Arrow*, 9 August. Retrieved 25 July 2024 from https://www.cambridgema.gov/-/media/Files/officeofthemayor/2019/whypeopleofcolorneedspaceswithoutwhitepeople1.pdf.
Bland, Archie. 2023. 'Inside Arts Council England's Devastating Cuts', *Guardian*, 23 November. Retrieved 25 July 2024 from https://www.theguardian.com/world/2022/nov/23/wednesday-briefing-inside-arts-council-englands-devastating-cuts.
Boler, Megan. 1999. *Feeling Power: Emotions and Education*. New York, Routledge.

Bor, Joep. 2007. 'Mamia, Ammani and Other Bayadères: Europe's Portrayal of India's Temple Dancers', in Martin Clayton and Bennett Zon (eds), *Music and Orientalism in the British Empire 1780s to 1940s: Portrayal of the East*. Aldershot: Ashgate, pp. 39–71.

Bourdieu, Pierre. 1977. *Outline of a Theory of Practice*. Cambridge: Cambridge University Press.

———. 1983. 'The Field of Cultural Production, Or: The Economic World Reversed', *Poetics* 12(4–5): 311–56.

———. 1984. *Distinction: A Social Critique of the Judgement of Taste*, trans. Richard Nice. London: Routledge.

———. 1986. 'Forms of Capital', in John Richardson (ed.), *Handbook of Theory and Research for the Sociology of Education*. Westport, CT: Greenwood Press, pp. 241–58.

———.1988. 'Program for a Sociology of Sport', *Sociology of Sport Journal* 5(2): 153–61.

———. 1990. *The Logic of Practice*. Cambridge: Polity.

———. 1991. *Language and Symbolic Power*, ed. John Thompson. Cambridge: Polity.

———. 1993. *Sociology in Question*. London: Sage.

———. 1998. 'On Male Domination', *Le Monde Diplomatique*, 10 October. Retrieved 24 July 2024 from https://mondediplo.com/1998/10/10bourdieu.

———. 2000. *Pascalian Meditations*. Cambridge: Polity Press.

———. 2001. *Masculine Domination*. Cambridge: Polity Press.

———. 2005. 'Habitus', in Emma Rooksby and Jane Hillier (eds), *Habitus: A Sense of Place*. Abingdon: Routledge, pp. 43–52.

Bourdieu, Pierre, and Loic Wacquant. 1992. *An Invitation to Reflexive Sociology*. Cambridge: Polity Press.

Brante, Thomas. 1988. 'Sociological Approaches to the Professions', *Acta Sociologica* 31(2): 119–42.

Brinson, Peter (ed.). 1993. *Tomorrow's Dancers: The Papers of the 1993 Conference: Training Tomorrow's Professional Dancers*. London: Laban Centre for Movement and Dance in association with Dance UK.

Brooke, Peter. 2007. 'India, Post-Imperialism and the Origins of Enoch Powell's "Rivers of Blood" Speech', *Historical Journal* 50(3): 669–87.

Brown, Cynthia, and Werner Menski. 2012. *Karman – History of South Asian Dance in Leicester and Leicestershire*. Leicester: CICD.

Brown, Ginnie. 2018. Interviewed by Magdalen Gorringe. 12 February. London, ISTD Offices.

Brown, Ismene. 2015. 'Why Dance Needs a Simon Cowell', *Spectator*, 15 May. Retrieved 25 July 2024 from https://www.spectator.co.uk/article/why-dance-needs-a-simon-cowell/.

Buckland, Theresa. 1999. 'All Dances Are Ethnic, but Some Are More Ethnic Than Others: Some Observations on Dance Studies and Anthropology', *Dance Research: The Journal of the Society for Dance Research* 17(1): 3–21.

———. 2007. 'Crompton's Campaign: The Professionalisation of Dance Pedagogy in Late Victorian England', *Dance Research: The Journal of the Society for Dance Research* 25(1): 1–34.

Burns, Susanne, and Sue Harrison. 2009. *Dance Mapping*. London: Arts Council England.

Burns, Susanne, Karen Gallagher and June Gamble. 2023. 'What Do We Do Now? The Deconstruction of Four Decades of Dance Development in England', *Animated*, Summer edition. Retrieved 25 July 2024 from https://www.communitydance.org.uk/DB/animated

-library/what-do-we-do-now-the-deconstruction-of-four-decades-of-dance-development-i.
CFTA (Campaign for the Arts). 2023. 'Huge decline in arts subjects worsens at GCSE and A-Level.' August 24. Retrieved 24 August 2024 from https://www.campaignforthearts.org/huge-decline-in-arts-subjects-worsens-at-gcse-and-a-level/.
Cantle, Ted. 2014. 'National Identity, Plurality and Interculturalism', *Political Quarterly* 85(3): 312–19.
'Capybara'. 2022. 'BBC Young Dancer 2022' [online forum comment], 19 April. Retrieved 25 July 2024 from https://www.balletcoforum.com/topic/25560-bbc-young-dancer-2022/.
Carroll, Noel. 2001 *Beyond Aesthetics: Philosophical Essays*. Cambridge: Cambridge University Press.
Carter, Alexandra. 1995. 'Blonde, Bewigged and Winged with Gold: Ballet Girls in the Music Halls of Late Victorian and Edwardian England', *Dance Research: The Journal of the Society for Dance Research* 13(2): 28–46.
CATS/ National Centres for Advanced Training. n.d. 'What are CATs', Retrieved 23 August 2024 from https://www.nationaldancecats.co.uk/what-are-cats/.
Chacko, Elizabeth, and Rajiv Menon. 2013. 'Longings and Belongings: Indian American Youth Identity, Folk Dance Competitions, and the Construction of "Tradition"', *Ethnic and Racial Studies* 36(1): 97–116.
Chandra, Shefali. 2020. 'Decolonizing the Orgasm: Caste, Whiteness and Knowledge Production at the "End of Empire"', *South Asia: Journal of South Asian Studies* 43(6): 1179–95.
Chakrabortty, Aditya. 2009. 'Dance Brings My Culture Back to Me', *Guardian*, 28 July. Retrieved 25 July 2024 from https://www.theguardian.com/stage/2009/jul/28/indian-dance.
Chatterjea, Ananya. 1996. 'Training in Indian Classical Dance: A Case Study', *Asian Theatre Journal* 13(1): 68–91.
———. 2013. 'On the Value of Mistranslations and Contaminations: The Category of "Contemporary Choreography" in Asian Dance', *Dance Research Journal* 45(1): 7–21.
Chaturangan n.d. 'Welcome to Chaturangan', Retrieved 24 August 2024 from http://www.chezfred.org.uk/chat/index.html.
Chaudhury, Parbati. 2019. 'Strength through Networking: Building Resilience in South Asian Dance', *One Magazine*, Spring edition: 28.
CICD (Centre for Indian Classical Dance). n.d. 'Mission Statement', Retrieved 24 August 2024 from https://www.cicd.org.uk/.
Cohen Bull, Cynthia Jean. 1997. 'Sense, Meaning and Perception in Three Dance Cultures', in Jane Desmond (ed.), *Meaning in Motion: New Cultural Studies of Dance*. Durham, NC: Duke University Press, pp. 269–88.
Conquergood, Lorne Dwight. 2013. 'Performing as a Moral Act: Ethical Dimensions of the Ethnography of Performance' in Lorne Dwight Conquergood and E. Patrick Johnson (ed.). *Cultural Struggles: Performance, Ethnography, Praxis*. Ann Arbor: University of Michigan Press, pp 65-80.
Conquergood, Lorne Dwight, and E. Patrick Johnson. 2013. *Cultural Struggles: Performance, Ethnography, Praxis*. Ann Arbor: University of Michigan Press.
Coorlawala, Uttara Asha. 2004. 'The Sanskritized Body', *Dance Research Journal* 36(2): 50–63.
Courtney Consulting. 2020. *South Asian Dance and Music Mapping Study*. Arts Council England. Retrieved 25 July 2024 from https://www.artscouncil.org.uk/south-asian-dance-music-mapping-study.

Crenshaw, Kimberlé, Neil Gotanda, Gary Peller and Kendall Thomas (eds). 1995. *Critical Race Theory: The Key Writings that Formed the Movement*. New York: New Press.
Crisp, Clement. 2004. 'Robert Cohan', *Dance Research: The Journal of the Society for Dance Research* 22(2): 96–100.
Croft, Alex. 2017. Interviewed by Magdalen Gorringe. 23 October. Kala Sangam, Bradford.
Crossley, Nick. 2001. *The Social Body: Habit, Identity and Desire*. London: Sage.
Daboo, Jerri. 2018. 'The Arts Britain Still Ignores?' *Studies in Theatre and Performance* 38(1): 3–8.
Dance.net. 2019. 'Jazz Professionals'. Dance.net website. Retrieved 30 May 2019 from http://www.dance.net/topic/4351007/1/Jazz-Professionals.
DanceXchange.2009. 'Invitation to Tender. Centre for Advanced Training for South Asian and Contemporary Dance Research Study Consultancy Brief.' [Invitation to Tender]. Birmingham: DanceXchange.
Darst, Lightsey. 2012. 'The Poorest Art: Dance and Money.' *Huffington Post*, 1 August. Retrieved 18 August 2024 from https://www.huffpost.com/entry/dancer-income-wages-lifestyle_b_1556794.
Daugherty, Diane. 2000. 'Fifty Years On: Arts Funding in Kerala Today', *Asian Theatre Journal* 17(2): 237–52.
David, Ann R. 2001. 'Perceptions and Misconceptions: Ram Gopal's Challenge to Orientalism'. MA thesis. Guildford: University of Surrey.
———. 2003. 'Where Have All the Courses Gone?' *Pulse* (Winter): 6.
———. 2005a. 'Negotiating Natyam', *Akademi's One Day Conference at the Linbury Studio, Royal Opera House, London, Held on Sunday October 2005*. Retrieved 25 July 2024 from https://akademi.co.uk/wp-content/uploads/2021/03/Akademis-Negotiating-Natyam-conference-Report-by-Dr-Ann-David.pdf.
———. 2005b. 'Performing Faith: Dance, Identity and Religion in Hindu Communities in Leicester and London'. PhD thesis. Leicester: De Montfort University.
———. 2007. 'Religious Dogma or Political Agenda? Bharatanatyam and its Re-Emergence in British Tamil Temples', *Journal for the Anthropological Study of Human Movement* 14(4).
———. 2008. 'Local Diasporas/Global Trajectories: New Aspects of Religious "Performance" in British Tamil Hindu Practice', *Performance Research* 13(3): 89–99.
———. 2010a. 'Dancing the Diasporic Dream? Embodied Desires and the Changing Audiences for Bollywood Film Dance', *Participants: Journal of Audience and Reception Studies* 7(2): 215–35.
———. 2010b. 'Gendered Orientalism? Gazing on the Male South Asian Dancer', Conference Paper for 24th Symposium of the ICTM Study Group on Ethnochoreology Trest, Czech Republic. Retrieved 17 August 2024 from https://www.academia.edu/1771608/Gendered_Orientalism.
———. 2010c. 'Negotiating Identity: Dance and Religion in British Hindu Communities', in Pallabi Chakravorty and Nilanjana Gupta (eds), *Dance Matters: Performing India*. New Delhi: Routledge, pp. 89–107.
———. 2012. 'Embodied Migration: Performance Practices of Diasporic Sri Lankan Tamil Communities in London', *Journal of Intercultural Studies* 33(4): 375–94.
———. 2013a. 'Practice and Pedagogy as Research Engaging with Theoretical Concerns in Dance', *DANCE* 466: 53–59.

———. 2013b. 'Ways of Moving and Thinking: The Emplaced Body as a Tool for Ethnographic Research', in Peter Harrop and Dunja Njaradi (eds), *Performance and Ethnography: Dance, Drama, Music*. Newcastle upon Tyne: Cambridge Scholars, pp. 45–66.

———. 2014. 'Embodied Traditions: Gujarati (Dance) Practices of Garba and Raas in the UK Context', in Ann R. David and Linda Dankworth (eds), *Dance Ethnography and Global Perspectives: Identity, Embodiment, Culture*. Basingstoke: Palgrave Macmillan, pp. 13–36.

———. 2024. *Ram Gopal: Interweaving Histories of Indian Dance*. London: Bloomsbury.

Deletant Bell, Monique. 2019. Interviewed by Magdalen Gorringe. 30 May. John Lewis, Birmingham.

Delgado, Richard, and Jean Stefancic. 2011. *Critical Race Theory, An Introduction*, 2nd edn. New York: New York University Press.

Desai, Jemma. 2020. *'This Work isn't for us.'* [Paper] Retrieved 23 August 2024 from https://heystacks.com/doc/337/this-work-isnt-for-us--by-jemma-desai.

Devi, Nilima. 2017. Interviewed by Magdalen Gorringe. 13 June. CICD, Leicester.

Devlin, Graham. 1989. *Stepping Forward: Some Suggestions for the Development of Dance in England during the 1990's*. London: Arts Council.

Dodds, Sherril. 2011. *Dancing on the Canon: Embodiments of Value in Popular Dance*. Basingstoke: Palgrave Macmillan.

Dodds, Sherril, and Colleen Hooper. 2014. 'Faces, Close-Ups and Choreography: A Deleuzian Critique of *So You Think You Can Dance*', *International Journal of Screendance* 4: 93–113.

Dubois, Abbé Jean Antoine, and Henry Beauchamp. 1985. *Hindu Manners, Customs and Ceremonies*, 3rd edn. New Delhi: Asian Educational Services.

Dutta, Sanjeevini. 2017. Interviewed by Magdalen Gorringe. 12 October. London.

Eckert, Penelope. 2006. *Communities of Practice*. Oxford: Elsevier.

Edgerton, Jason D., and Lance W. Roberts. 2014. 'Cultural Capital or Habitus? Bourdieu and Beyond in the Explanation of Enduring Educational Inequality', *Theory and Research in Education* 12(2): 193–220.

Elswit, Kate. 2012. '*So You Think You Can Dance* Does Dance Studies', *Drama Review* 56(1): 133–42.

'Emeralds'. 2022. 'BBC Young Dancer 2022' [online forum comment], 5 May. Retrieved 18 August 2024 from https://www.balletcoforum.com/topic/25560-bbc-young-dancer-2022/.

Equity. n.d.a 'Who Can Join Equity?' Retrieved 24 August 2024 from https://www.equity.org.uk/join-us/who-can-join-equity.

———. 2022. 'Equity Insurance Guide 2022'. Equity website. Retrieved 24 August 2024 from https://www.equity.org.uk/advice-and-support/insurance/equity-insurance-guide-2022.

———. 2021. 'Professionally Made Professionally Paid'. Equity website. Retrieved 25 July 2024 from https://www.equity.org.uk/getting-involved/campaigns/professionally-made-professionally-paid/.

Erdman, Joan L. 1983. 'Who Should Speak for the Performing Arts? The Case of the Delhi Dancers', *Pacific Affairs* 56(2): 247–69.

———. 1996. 'Dance Discourses: Rethinking the History of the "Oriental Dance"', in Gay Morris (ed.), *Moving Words: Re-Writing Dance*. London: Routledge, pp. 252–66.

Evetts, Julia. 2013. 'Professionalism: Value and Ideology', *Current Sociology* 61(5–6): 778–96.

———. 2014. 'The Concept of Professionalism: Professional Work, Professional Practice and Learning', in Stephen Billett, Christian Harteis and Hans Gruber (eds), *International

Handbook of Research in Professional and Practice-Based Learning. Dordrecht: Springer Netherlands, pp. 29–56.

Fabian, Johannes. 2014. *Time and the Other: How Anthropology Makes Its Object*. New York: Columbia University Press.

FABRIC. (2012) 'Centre for Advanced Training – Full Film.' YouTube. Retrieved 23 August 2024 from https://www.youtube.com/watch?v=R8bYiDBRAcA.

Farnell, Brenda. 2000. 'Getting out of the Habitus: An Alternative Model of Dynamically Embodied Social Action', *Journal of the Royal Anthropological Institute* 6(3): 397–418.

Fischer-Lichte, Erika, Torsten Jost and Saskya Iris Jain (eds). 2014. *The Politics of Interweaving Performance*. London: Routledge.

Fisher, Michael H., Shompa Lahiri and Sindar Thandi. 2007. *A South Asian History of Britain: Four Centuries of Peoples from the Indian Sub-Continent*. Westport, CT: Greenwood.

Fleming, Rachel C. (2004). 'Resisting Cultural Standardization: Comhaltas Ceoltóirí Éireann and the Revitalization of Traditional Music in Ireland'. *Journal of Folklore Research*, Vol. 41, No. 2/3, Special Double Issue: Advocacy Issues in Folklore (May - Dec., 2004), pp. 227-257.

Flemmen, Magne, and Mike Savage. 2017. 'The Politics of Nationalism and White Racism in the UK', *British Journal of Sociology* 68: S233–S264.

Foster, Susan L. 1997. 'Dancing Bodies', in Jane Desmond (ed.), *Meaning in Motion: New Cultural Studies in Dance*. Durham, NC: Duke University Press, pp. 235–58.

———. 2009. *Worlding Dance*. Basingstoke: Palgrave Macmillan.

———. 2014. 'Performing Authenticity and the Gendered Labor of Dance'. Retrieved 24 August 2024 from https://www.scribd.com/document/260505250/Susan-Foster-Performing-Authenticity-and-the-Gendered-Labor-of-Dance

Foucault, Michel. 1980. *Power/Knowledge: Selected Interviews and Other Writings, 1972–1977*, ed. Colin Gordon. Harlow: Longman.

Fournier, Valérie. 1999. 'The Appeal to "Professionalism" as a Disciplinary Mechanism', *Sociological Review* 47(2): 280–307.

Fox, Kate. 2004. *Watching the English: The Hidden Rules of English Behaviour*. London: Hodder.

Frederickson, Jon, and James F. Rooney. 1990. 'How the Music Occupation Failed to Become a Profession', *International Review of the Aesthetics and Sociology of Music* 21(2): 189–206.

Freidson, Eliot. 2004 [2001]. *Professionalism: The Third Logic*. Cambridge: Polity.

Freire, Paulo. 2017. *Pedagogy of the Oppressed*. St. Ives: Penguin.

Friedman, Sam. 2016a. 'Habitus Clivé and the Emotional Imprint of Social Mobility', *Sociological Review* 64(1): 129–47.

———. 2016b. 'The Limits of Capital Gains – Using Bourdieu to Understand Social Mobility into Elite Occupations', in Jenny Thatcher, Nicole Ingram, Ciaran Burke and Jessie Abrahams (eds), *Bourdieu: The Next Generation: The Development of Bourdieu's Intellectual Heritage in Contemporary UK Sociology*. London: Routledge, pp. 107–22.

Frow, John. 1996. *Cultural Studies and Cultural Value*. Oxford: Oxford University Press.

Garratt, Lindsey. 2016. 'Using Bourdieusian Scholarship to Understand the Body: Habits, Hexes and Embodied Cultural Capital', in Jenny Thatcher, Nicole Ingram, Ciaran Burke and Jessie Abrahams (eds), *Bourdieu: The Next Generation: The Development of Bourdieu's Intellectual Heritage in Contemporary UK Sociology*. London: Routledge, pp. 73–87.

Gaston, Anne-Marie. 1996. *Bharata Natyam: From Temple to Theatre*. New Delhi: Manohar.

Gem Arts. n.d. 'Creating and Profiling Diverse Arts', Retrieved 24 August 2024 from https://www.gemarts.org/.
Genné, Beth. 1995. 'Openly English: Phyllis Bedells and the Birth of British Ballet', *Dance Chronicle* 18(3): 437–51.
Gibson, Rachel. 2016. *Navadisha 2016: Conference Report*. Retrieved 16 June 2021 from http://navadisha2016.co.uk/wp-content/uploads/2017/01/Navadisha-Report-final-lr.pdf.
———. 2017. *SADAA Meeting 17 February*, minutes.
Gilroy, Paul. 2000. *There Ain't No Black in the Union Jack: The Cultural Politics of Race and Nation*, 5th edn. London. Routledge.
———. 2008. 'Multiculturalism and Post-Colonial Theory', in John S. Dryzek, Bonnie Honig and Anne Phillips (eds), *The Oxford Handbook of Political Theory*. Oxford: Oxford University Press, pp. 656-676.
Giurchescu, Anca. 2001. 'The Power of Dance and its Social and Political Uses', *Yearbook for Traditional Music* 33: 109–21.
Glick Schiller, Nina. 2005. 'Long-Distance Nationalism', in Melvin Ember, Carol. R. Ember and Ian Skoggard (eds), *Encyclopedia of Diasporas: Immigrant and Refugee Cultures around the World*. New York: Springer, pp. 570–80.
Glissant, Edouard. 2002. 'The Unforeseeable Diversity of the World', trans. Hans Saussy, in Elisabeth Mudimbe-Boyi (ed.), *Beyond Dichotomies: Histories, Identities, Cultures, and the Challenge of Globalization*. Albany: State University of New York Press, pp. 287–95.
Gopal, Pushkala. 2018. Interviewed by Magdalen Gorringe. 6 March. Zoom.
Gopal, Ram. 1957. *Rhythm in the Heavens*. London: Secker and Warburg.
Gorringe, Magdalen T. 2005. 'Arangetrams and Manufacturing Identity – the Changing Role of a Bharatanatyam Dancer's Solo Debut in the Context of the Diaspora', in Hae-Kyung Um (ed.), *Diasporas and Interculturalism in Asian Performing Arts*. London: Routledge, pp. 91–103.
Gorringe, Magdalen T., Delia Jarrett-Macauley and Anita Srivastava. 2018. *South Asian Dance Feasibility Study 2018 – A Report*. Birmingham: Dance Hub.
Gorringe, Timothy J. 2004. *Furthering Humanity: A Theology of Culture*. Aldershot: Ashgate.
Gottschild, Brenda Dixon. 1997. 'Some Thoughts on Choreographing History', in Jane Desmond (ed.), *Meaning in Motion: New Cultural Studies in Dance*. Durham, NC: Duke University Press, pp. 167–78.
Grau, Andrée. 1997. 'Dance, South Asian Dance and Higher Education', *Choreography and Dance* 4(2): 55–62.
———. 1999. 'Fieldwork, Politics, Power', in Theresa Buckland (ed.), *Dance in the Field: Theory, Methods and Issues in Dance Ethnography*. London. Palgrave Macmillan, pp. 163–74.
———. 2001. *South Asian Dance in Britain – Negotiating Cultural Identity through Dance*. Retrieved 26 July 2024 from https://www.researchgate.net/publication/282019278_Report_South_Asian_Dance_in_Britain_SADiB.
———. 2004. 'A Sheltering Sky? Negotiating Identity through South Asian Dance'. Retrieved 25 July 2024 from https://www.researchgate.net/publication/276935889_A_sheltering_sky_Negotiating_identity_through_South_Asian_dance.
———. 2011. 'The Lure of the East'. Unpublished manuscript.
Graves, Tony. 2006. 'Programming Outside the Comfort Zone', in Heather Maitland (ed.), *Navigating Difference: Cultural Diversity and Audience Development*. London: Arts Council England, pp. 154–57.

Gray, Ann. 2003. *Research Practice for Cultural Studies: Ethnographic Methods and Lived Cultures*. London: Sage.

Gray, Aysa. 2019. 'The Bias of "Professionalism" Standards', *Stanford Social Innovation Review*, 4 June. Retrieved 25 July 2024 from https://ssir.org/articles/entry/the_bias_of_professionalism_standards.

Greenwood, Ernest. 1957. 'Attributes of a Profession', *Social Work* 2(3): 45–55.

Guest, Ivor F. 1992. *Ballet in Leicester Square: The Alhambra and the Empire, 1860–1915*. London: Dance.

Gupta, Uma. 2002. 'In Pursuit of a Different Freedom: Tagore's World University at Santiniketan', *India International Centre Quarterly* 29(3–4): 25–38.

Gurusamy, Chris. 2017. Interviewed by Magdalen Gorringe. 12 April. Dance Xchange, Birmingham.

Hackett, Jane. 2015. 'Bringing BBC Young Dancer 2015 to Life', *About the BBC Blog*, 8 May. Retrieved 25 July 2024 from https://www.bbc.co.uk/blogs/aboutthebbc/entries/02edb45c-678a-456d-90a3-5d4f90b3f4f6.

———. 2017. Interviewed by Magdalen Gorringe. March. Skype.

Hage, Ghassan. 2000. *White Nation: Fantasies of White Supremacy in a Multicultural Society*, 2nd edn. New York: Routledge.

Hall, Stuart. 1973. *Encoding and Decoding in the Television Discourse*. Birmingham: Centre for Cultural Studies, University of Birmingham.

———. 1997. 'The Local and the Global: Globalization and Ethnicity', in Anthony King (ed.), *Culture, Globalisation and the World System*. Minneapolis: University of Minnesota Press, pp. 19–40.

———. 1999. 'Un-Settling "the Heritage": Re-Imagining the Post-Nation', in *Whose Heritage? The Impact of Cultural Diversity on Britain's Living Heritage*. London: Arts Council England, pp. 13–22.

Hamera, Judith. 2011. *Dancing Communities: Performance, Difference and Connection in the Global City*. Basingstoke: Palgrave Macmillan.

Hanna, Judith Lynne. 1988. *Dance, Sex and Gender. Signs of Identity, Dominance, Defiance and Desire*. Chicago: Chicago University Press.

Hanly, Nouska. 2016. 'Dance Training: Dance Artists Are Not Born, but Made', *The Stage*, 15 April. Retrieved 25 July 2024 from https://www.thestage.co.uk/advice/2016/dance-artists-are-not-born-but-made/.

Hansard. 2022a. 'Arts and Creative Industries Strategy: Volume 826: Debated on Thursday 8 December 2022'. Retrieved 25 July 2024 from https://hansard.parliament.uk/lords/2022-12-08/debates/56C94C97-D761-454A-9FFC-5AF5671225E1/ArtsAndCreativeIndustriesStrategy.

———. 2022b. 'Arts Council England: Regional Distribution of Funding: Volume 826: Debated on Thursday 15 December 2022'. Retrieved 25 July 2024 from https://hansard.parliament.uk/Lords/2022-12-15/debates/CEAD4C3A-1DEE-465A-98D4-5BACE016DC74/ArtsCouncilEnglandRegionalDistributionOfFunding.

Harpe, Bill. 2005. 'Surya Kumari: Obituary', *Guardian*, 18 May. Retrieved 25 July 2024 from https://www.theguardian.com/news/2005/may/18/guardianobituaries.artsobituaries.

Harrop, Peter. 2013. 'Introduction by Way of Long Ethnography', in Peter Harrop and Dunja Njaradi (eds), *Performance and Ethnography: Dance, Drama, Music*. Newcastle upon Tyne: Cambridge Scholars, pp. 1–22.

Harvie, Jen. 2013. *Fair Play: Art, Performance and Neoliberalism*. Basingstoke: Palgrave Macmillan.

Hastrup, Kirsten. 1995. *Passage to Anthropology: Between Experience and Theory*. London: Routledge.

Heilbrun, James. 1984. 'Keynes and the Economics of the Arts', *Journal of Cultural Economics* 8(2): 37–49.

Henwood, Alexandra, and Claire Lewis. 2018. Interviewed by Magdalen Gorringe. 16 January. Dance Xchange, Birmingham.

Herrity, Jennifer. 2024. '15 Characteristics of Professionals', *indeed*, 16 August. Retrieved 23 August 2024 from https://www.indeed.com/career-advice/career-development/professional-characteristics.

Higgins, Charlotte. 2015. *This New Noise: The Extraordinary Birth and Troubled Life of the BBC*. London: Guardian/Faber.

Hilgers, Mathieu, and Eric Mangez. 2014. *Bourdieu's Theory of Social Fields: Concepts and Applications*. London: Routledge.

HMPO (Her Majesty's Passport Office). 2015. 'Introducing the New U.K. Passport Design', *HMPO Magazine*, 3 November. Retrieved 25 July 2024 from https://assets.publishing.service.gov.uk/government/uploads/system/uploads/attachment_data/file/473495/HMPO_magazine.pdf.

Holton, Kate. 2021. 'Brexit Red Tape a "Catastrophe" for Scottish Fisheries That Export to EU', *Globe and Mail*, 8 January. Retrieved 25 July 2024 from https://www.theglobeandmail.com/business/international-business/european-business/article-brexit-red-tape-a-catastrophe-for-scottish-fisheries-that-export-to-eu/.

Home Office. n.d. 'What we do.' Retrieved 23 August 2024 from https://www.gov.uk/government/organisations/home-office.

Howse, Justin. 2000. *Dance Technique & Injury Prevention*, 3rd edn. New York: Routledge.

Hughes, Everett C. 1963. 'Professions', *Daedalus* 92(4): 655–68.

Hutchinson, Sydney (ed.). 2015. *Salsa World: A Global Dance in Local Contexts*. Philadelphia: Temple University Press.

Huxley, Aldous. 1979 [1932]. *Brave New World Revisited*. London: Chatto and Windus.

Iskin, Ruth (ed.). 2017. *Re-Envisioning the Contemporary Art Canon: Perspectives in a Global World*. Abingdon: Routledge.

ISTD. n.d.a. 'Quality Assurance'. ISTD website. Retrieved 25 July 2024 from https://www.istd.org/examinations/quality-assurance.

———. n.d.b. 'Faculty Committees'. ISTD website. Retrieved 24 August 2024 from https://www.istd.org/discover/our-governance/faculty-committees/.

———. 2013. 'Classical Indian Dance Faculty News', 9 September. ISTD website. Retrieved 7 December 2017 from https://www.istd.org/about-us/documents/classical-indian-dance-faculty-news-september/.

ISTD South Asian Dance Faculty. 2000. *Bharatanatyam Grade Examinations Specifications*. London.

Iyer, Alessandra. 1997a. *South Asian Dance: Mapping Out Models of Vocational Training and Delivery Mechanisms*. London: Academy of Indian Dance.

———. (ed.). 1997b. *South Asian Dance: The British Experience*. Amsterdam: Harwood Academic.

Jackson, Peter. 1983. 'Principles and Problems of Participant Observation', *Geografiska Annaler: Series B, Human Geography* 65(1): 39–46.

Jenkins, Richard. 2002 [1992]. *Pierre Bourdieu*, rev. edn. London: Routledge.
Jennings, Luke. 2015. 'The Struggle for the Soul of British Dance', *Guardian*, 12 July. Retrieved 25 July 2024 from https://www.theguardian.com/stage/2015/jul/12/contemporary-dance-debate-shechter-khan-newson-laban-students-training.
Jeyasingh, Shobana. 1993. 'Classical and Contemporary Training', in Peter Brinson (ed.), *Tomorrow's Dancers: The Papers of the 1993 Conference: Training Tomorrow's Professional Dancers*. London: Laban Centre for Movement and Dance in association with Dance UK, pp. 55-57.
———. 2010. 'Getting Off the Orient Express', in Alexandra Carter and Janet O'Shea (eds), *The Routledge Dance Studies Reader*, 2nd edn. London: Routledge, pp. 181–87.
———. 2018. Interviewed by Magdalen Gorringe. 9 February. Skype.
Johar, Navtej. 2021. 'The Transient Source' Yuva Gati/BIDF panel discussion '11 June. Zoom.
Joffe, Carole E. 1977. *Friendly Intruders: Childcare Professionals and Family Life*. Berkeley. University of California Press.
Johnson, Terence. 1972. *Professions and Power*. London: Macmillan.
Jones, Demelza. 2014. 'Diaspora Identification and Long-Distance Nationalism among Tamil Migrants of Diverse State Origins in the UK', *Ethnic and Racial Studies* 37(14): 2547–63.
Jordan, Glenn, and Chris Weedon. 1995. *Cultural Politics: Class, Gender, Race and the Postmodern World*. Oxford: Blackwell.
Jordan, Stephanie. 1992. *Striding Out: Aspects of Contemporary and New Dance in Britain*. London: Dance.
Kadam. n.d. 'About', Retrieved 24 August 2024 from http://kadamdance.org.uk/about/.
Kaeppler, Adrienne. 1999. 'The Mystique of Fieldwork', in Theresa Buckland (ed.), *Dance in the Field*. London: Palgrave Macmillan, pp. 13–25.
Kala Sangam. n.d. 'Mission and Vision', Retrieved 24 August 2024 from https://www.kalasangam.org/about-us/mission-and-vision/
Kanakarathnam, Ramakrishnan. 2015. 'Prof. Ashish Mohan Khokar's AttenDANCE – World Dance Day 2015 – Part 2 of 4'. YouTube. Retrieved 25 July 2024 from https://www.youtube.com/watch?v=LUVKwxWaarQ.
Kapur, Geeta. 2012. 'Curating in Heterogenous Worlds', in Alexander Dumbadze and Suzanne Hudson (eds), *Contemporary Art: 1989 to the Present*. Chichester: Wiley, pp. 178–91.
Kasturi, Divya. 2019. 'Bharatanatyam, the Connecting Force between Community and Culture', *The Hindu*, 3 June. Retrieved 25 July 2024 from https://www.thehindu.com/entertainment/dance/connecting-to-community-and-culture/article27327273.ece.
Kaur, Keranjeet. 2017. Interviewed by Magdalen Gorringe. 17 February. Leeds.
Kaushik, Mira. 2017a. Interview 1. Interviewed by Magdalen Gorringe. 22 February. Akademi, London.
———. 2017b. Interview 2. Interviewed by Magdalen Gorringe. 3 March. Phone call.
———. 2017c. Interview 3. Interviewed by Magdalen Gorringe. 14 June. Akademi, London.
Keali'inohomoku, Joann. 2001 [1969]. 'An Anthropologist Looks at Ballet as a Form of Ethnic Dance', in Ann Dils and Ann C. Albright (eds), *Moving History/Dancing Cultures*. Middleton, CT: Wesleyan University Press, pp. 33–43.
Kedhar, Anusha Lakshmi. 2011. 'On the Move: Transnational South Asian Dancers and the "Flexible" Dancing Body'. PhD thesis. Riverside: University of California, Riverside. Retrieved 25 July 2024 from https://escholarship.org/uc/item/6m4475v1.

———. 2014. 'Flexibility and Its Bodily Limits: Transnational South Asian Dancers in an Age of Neoliberalism', *Dance Research Journal* 46(1): 23–40.
———. 2020. *Flexible Bodies: British South Asian Dancers in an Age of Neo-Liberalism*. New York: Oxford University Press.
Kelleher, Joe. 2009. *Theatre and Politics*. Basingstoke: Palgrave Macmillan.
Khan, Akram. 2018. Interviewed by Magdalen Gorringe. 31 January. Ballet Boyz Studio, London.
Khan, Naseem. 1976. *The Arts Britain Ignores: The Arts of the Ethnic Minorities in Britain*. London: Commission for Racial Equality.
———. 1997. 'South Asian Dance in Britain 1960–1995', in Alessandra Iyer (ed.), *South Asian Dance: The British Experience*. Amsterdam: Harwood Academic, pp. 25–30.
———. 2006. 'Arts Council England and Diversity: Striving for Change', in Heather Maitland (ed.), *Navigating Difference: Cultural Diversity and Audience Development*. London: Arts Council England, pp. 21–26.
———. 2017. Interviewed by Magdalen Gorringe. 13 February. London.
Khayyam, Amina. 2018. Interviewed by Magdalen Gorringe. 16 March. Laban Centre, London.
Khilnani, Sunil. 2003. *The Idea of India*, updated edn. London: Penguin.
Khokar, Ashish M. 2012. 'Leadership in the Arts: Rukmini Devi Arundale', *India International Centre Quarterly* 39(3): 186–200.
Khoo, Mavin. 2017. Interviewed by Magdalen Gorringe. 9 November. Sadler's Wells, London.
King, Martin Luther. 1954. 'The Vision of a World Made New'. 9 September. Retrieved 25 July 2024 from https://kinginstitute.stanford.edu/king-papers/documents/vision-world-made-new.
Kolb, Alexandra. 2013. 'The Migration and Globalization of Schuhplattler Dance: A Sociological Analysis', *Cultural Sociology* 7(1): 39–55.
———. 2018. 'Akram Khan, Lloyd Newson, and the Challenges of British Multiculturalism', *Dance Research* 36(2): 224–52.
Kumar, Nish. 2020. 'Akram Khan in conversation with Nish Kumar'. Continental Breakfast, Dance Umbrella. 25 November. Retrieved 18 August 2024 from https://danceumbrella.co.uk/event/continental-breakfast/.
Kunst, Bojana. 2015. *Artist at Work: Proximity of Art and Capitalism*. Winchester: Zero.
Kwan, SanSan. 2017. 'When is Contemporary Dance?' *Dance Research Journal* 49(3): 38–52.
Lal, Swati. 1984. 'Rabindranāth Tagore's Ideals of Aesthetic Education', *Journal of Aesthetic Education* 18(2): 31–39.
Lammy, David. 2019. 'Black, Listed by Jeffrey Boakye Review', *Guardian*, 15 April. Retrieved 25 July 2024 from https://www.theguardian.com/books/2019/apr/15/black-listed-jeffrey-boakye-review-race-identity-power-of-words.
Lancaster, Roger N. 1994. *Life is Hard: Machismo, Danger, and Intimacy of Power in Nicaragua*. Berkeley: University of California Press.
Lepecki, André. 2004. *Of the Presence of the Body: Essays on Dance and Performance Theory*. Hanover, NH: Wesleyan University Press.
Lewis, Veronica. 2018. Interviewed by Magdalen Gorringe. 17 October. London.
Lim, Chai Hong. 2006. 'Quick Steps Win Dance World's Turner Prize', *Guardian*, 1 October. Retrieved 25 July 2024 from https://www.theguardian.com/stage/2006/oct/01/dance2.

Littler, Jo. 2006. '"Festering Britain": The 1951 Festival of Britain, National Identity and the Representation of the Commonwealth', in Anandi Ramamurthy and Simon Faulkner, (eds), *Visual Culture and Decolonisation in Britain*. Aldershot: Ashgate, pp. 21–42.

Lopez y Royo, Alessandra. 2003. 'Classicism, Post-Classicism and Ranjabati Sircar's Work: Re-Defining the Terms of Indian Contemporary Dance Discourses', *South Asia Research* 23(2): 153–69.

———. 2004. 'Dance in the British South Asian Diaspora: Redefining Classicism', *Postcolonial Text*. Retrieved 25 July 2024 from https://www.postcolonial.org/index.php/pct/article/view/367.

Macdonald, John. 2006. 'Think You Can Dance for a Career? Think Again'. Retrieved 23 May 2019 from https://www.bankrate.com/finance/jobs-careers/think-you-can-dance-for-a-career-think-again.aspx.

Mackrell, Judith. 2013. 'When Anna Pavlova Met Uday Shankar and Changed Dance Forever', *Guardian*, 7 October. Retrieved 25 July 2024 from https://www.theguardian.com/stage/2013/oct/07/anna-pavlova-uday-shankar-dance-movetube.

———. 2014. 'Is the BBC Young Dancer a Step Too Far?' *Guardian*, 3 October. Retrieved 25 July 2024 from https://www.theguardian.com/stage/dance-blog/2014/oct/03/bbc-young-dancer-competition-carlos-acosta-tamara-rojo.

Maitland, Heather (ed.). 2006. *Navigating Difference: Cultural Diversity and Audience Development*. London: Arts Council England.

Malone, Justine. 2017. 'Calling Musicians for Twelfth Night/The Tempest – RSC Dell & Oxford Castle'. 29 March. SCUDD [online] Retrieved 20 June 2020 from https://www.jiscmail.ac.uk/.

Manch UK. 2020a. Shaalini Shivashankar on Manch UK. Facebook, 9 May. Retrieved 25 July 2024 from https://www.facebook.com/watch/live/?v=277088933448975&ref=watch_permalink.

———. 2020b. Ashwini Kalsekar on Manch UK. Facebook, 12 May. Retrieved 25 July 2024 from https://www.facebook.com/watch/live/?v=184005266105404&ref=watch_permalink.

———. 2020c. Nina Rajarani on Manch UK. Facebook, 14 May. Retrieved 25 July 2024 from https://www.facebook.com/manchukarts/videos/688298051947506.

———. 2020d. Re-Rooted Collective on Manch UK. Facebook, 18 June. Retrieved 25 July 2024 from https://www.facebook.com/manchukarts/videos/721060731981477.

Maree, Lynn. 2017. Interviewed by Magdalen Gorringe. 28 November. London.

Marglin, Frédérique A. 1985. *Wives of the God-King: The Rituals of the Devadasis of Puri*. Delhi: Oxford University Press.

Marion, Jonathan S. 2008. *Ballroom: Culture and Costume in Competitive Dance*. Oxford: Berg.

Marriott, Bruce. 2015. 'Young Dancer Award 2015 – Some Thoughts', *Dance Tabs*, 18 May. Retrieved 25 July 2024 from https://dancetabs.com/2015/05/bbc-young-dancer-award-2015-some-thoughts/.

Martin, Randy. 2012. 'A Precarious Dance, a Derivative Sociality', *TDR: The Drama Review* 56(4): 62–77.

Martin, Randy, and Toby Miller. 1999. *SportCult*. Minneapolis: University of Minnesota Press.

Marwick, Arthur. 2003. *British Society since 1945*, 4th edn. London: Penguin.

Massey, Doreen. 1991. 'A Global Sense of Place', *Marxism Today* (June): 24–29. Retrieved 25 July 2024 from https://banmarchive.org.uk/marxism-today/june-1991/a-global-sense-of-place/.
———. 1994. *Space, Place, and Gender*. Minneapolis: University of Minnesota Press.
———. 2005. *For Space*. London. Sage.
Massey, Reginald. 1982. 'The Contribution of Indian Dance to British Culture'. Conference report. London: Academy of Indian Dance. Retrieved 24 August 2024 from https://www.vads.ac.uk/digital/collection/SADAA/id/5072/rec/1.
Mbembe, Achille. 2009. 'Figures of Multiplicity – Can France Reinvent its Identity?' In Charles Tshimanga, Didier Gondola and Peter J. Bloom (eds), *Frenchness and the African Diaspora: Identity and Uprising in Contemporary France*. Bloomington: Indiana University Press, pp. 55–69.
———. 2010. 'After Postcolonialism: Transnationalism or Essentialism'. 8 May, Tate Modern, London. Retrieved 24 August 2024 from https://www.tate.org.uk/audio/after-post-colonialism-transnationalism-or-essentialism-audio-recordings.Own transcript.
———. 2015. 'Decolonizing Knowledge and the Question of the Archive'. 29 April, Wits University, Johannesburg. Retrieved 24 August 2024 from https://worldpece.org/content/mbembe-achille-2015-%E2%80%9Cdecolonizing-knowledge-and-question-archive%E2%80%9D-africa-country/.
———. 2021. *Out of the Dark Night: Essays on Decolonization*. New York: Columbia University Press.
McCracken, Grant. 2009. *Chief Culture Officer: How to Create a Living, Breathing Corporation*. New York. Basic Books.
McFee, Graham. 2005. 'The Artistic and the Aesthetic', *British Journal of Aesthetics* 45(4): 368–87.
Meduri, Avanthi. 2001. 'Bharatha natyam – What are You?' in Ann Dils and Ann C. Albright (eds), *Moving History/Dancing Cultures*. Middletown, CT: Wesleyan University Press, pp. 103–13.
———. 2004. 'Bharatanatyam as a Global Dance: Some Issues in Research, Teaching, and Practice', *Dance Research Journal* 36(2): 11–29.
———. 2005. *Rukmini Devi Arundale (1904–1986): A Visionary Architect of Indian Culture and the Performing Arts*. New Delhi: Motilal Banarsidass.
———. 2008a. 'Labels, Histories, Politics: Indian/South Asian Dance on the Global Stage', *Dance Research: The Journal of the Society for Dance Research* 26(2): 223–43.
———. 2008b. 'The Transfiguration of Indian/Asian Dance in the United Kingdom: Contemporary "Bharatanatyam" in Global Contexts', *Asian Theatre Journal* 25(2): 298–328.
———. 2010. 'Global Dance Transmission(s) in London', in Susanne Franco and Marina Nordera (eds), *Ricordanze: Memoria in Movimento e Coreografie della Storia*. Novara: UTET (Tracce di Tersicore), pp.345- 360.
———. 2012. 'Geo-Politics, Dissensus, and Dance Citizenship: The Case of South Asian Dance in Britain', in Gabriele Brandstetter and Gabriele Klein (eds), *Dance [and] Theory*. Bielefeld: Transcript, pp. 177–82.
———. 2019. 'Interweaving Dance Archives: Devadasis, Bayadères and Nautch Girls of 1838', in Gabriele Brandstetter (ed.), *Movements of Interweaving: Dance and Corporeality in Times of Travel and Migration*. New York: Taylor and Francis, pp. 299–320.

———. 2020. 'British Multiculturalism and Interweaving Hybridities in South Asian Dance', *Performance Research* 25(4): 107–15.
Menski, Werner. 2011. *Moving On*. Retrieved 13 June 2017 from www.cicd.org.uk/upcoming_events/-Media?id=ed5e25e0-0d5f-4688-976e.
Mera-Nelson, Claire. 2022. 'Investing in the future of music.' [blog], 10 November. Retrieved 23 August 2024 from https://www.artscouncil.org.uk/blog/investing-future-music.
Mignolo, Walter D. 2002. 'The Enduring Enchantment (Or the Epistemic Privilege of Modernity and Where to Go From Here)', *South Atlantic Quarterly* 101(4): 927–54.
———. 2007. 'Delinking', *Cultural Studies* 21(2–3): 449–514.
Milapfest. n.d.a. 'Our Work'. Retrieved 24 August 2024 from https://oldsite.milapfest.com/#.
Milapfest. n.d.b. 'About'. Retrieved 24 August 2024 from https://milap.co.uk/we-are-milap/about-milap/.
Millerson, Geoffrey. 1964. *The Qualifying Associations*. London: Routledge and Kegan Paul.
Mitra, Royona. 2015. *Akram Khan: Dancing New Interculturalism*. Basingstoke: Palgrave Macmillan.
———. 2017. 'Beyond Fixity: Akram Khan on the Politics of Dancing Heritages', in Larraine Nicholas and Geraldine Morris (eds), *Rethinking Dance History: Issues and Methodologies*. London: Taylor and Francis, pp. 32–43.
Monten, Joshua. 2008. 'Something Old, Something New, Something Borrowed', in Melanie Bales and Rebecca Nettl-Fiol (eds), *The Body Eclectic: Evolving Practices in Dance Training*. Urbana: University of Illinois Press, pp. 52–67.
Moran, Caitlin. 2011. *How to Be a Woman*. Chatham: Ebury.
Morcom, Anna. 2015. 'Terrains of Bollywood Dance: (Neoliberal) Capitalism and the Transformation of Cultural Economies', *Ethnomusicology* 59(2): 288–314.
Morris, Gay. 2001. 'Bourdieu, the Body, and Graham's Post-War Dance', *Dance Research: The Journal of the Society for Dance Research* 19(2): 52–82.
Morris, Geraldine. 2003. 'Problems with Ballet: Steps, Style and Training', *Research in Dance Education* 4(1): 17–30.
———. 2008. 'Artistry or Mere Technique? The Value of the Ballet Competition', *Research in Dance Education* 9(1): 39–54.
Moya, Patricia. 2014. 'Habit and Embodiment in Merleau-Ponty', *Frontiers in Human Neuroscience* 8: 1–3.
Nandakumara, Mattur. 2017. Interviewed by Magdalen Gorringe. 8 December. London, Bharatiya Vidya Bhavan.
Narayan, Kirin. 1993. 'How Native Is a "Native" Anthropologist?' *American Anthropologist* 95(3): 671–86.
Nayak, Prashant. 2017. Interviewed by Magdalen Gorringe. 2 August. Milapfest, Liverpool.
Neal, Mark, and John Morgan. 2000. 'The Professionalization of Everyone? A Comparative Study of the Development of the Professions in the United Kingdom and Germany', *European Sociological Review* 16(1): 9–26.
New Art Exchange. 2019. 'Events'. Retrieved 24 May 2019 from http://www.nae.org.uk/event/subash-viman-and-jyoti-parwana-double/641.
Nilakantha Sastri, Kallidai A. 1939. *Foreign Notices of South India*. Madras: University of Madras.
———. 1955. *A History of South India, from Prehistoric Times to the Fall of Vijayanagar*. London: Oxford University Press.

O'Connor, Barbara. 2013. *The Irish Dancing: Cultural Politics and Identities 1900–2000*. Cork: Cork University Press.

O'Shea, Janet. 1998. '"Traditional" Indian Dance and the Making of Interpretive Communities', *Asian Theatre Journal* 15(1): 45–63.

———. 2003. 'At Home in the World? The Bharatanatyam Dancer as Transnational Interpreter', *TDR* 47(1): 176–86.

———. 2007. *At Home in the World: Bharata Natyam on the Global Stage*. Middletown, CT: Wesleyan University Press.

OFS (Office for Students). 2021. *Consultation on Recurrent Funding for 2021–22*. 26 March. Retrieved 25 July 2024 from https://www.officeforstudents.org.uk/publications/consultation-on-recurrent-funding-for-2021-22/.

OHCHR (The Office for the High Commissioner for Human Rights). 2021. 'UN Experts Condemn UK Commission in Race and Ethnic Disparities Report'. 19 April. Retrieved 23 August 2024 from https://www.ohchr.org/en/press-releases/2021/04/un-experts-condemn-uk-commission-race-and-ethnic-disparities-report?LangID=E&NewsID=27004.

OSCE (Organization for Security and Co-operation in Europe). n.d. *Helsinki Final Act*. Retrieved 18 August 2024 from https://www.osce.org/helsinki-final-act.

Pakes, Anna. 2001. 'Dance Interpretation and the Cultural Institution: Exploring the Condition(s) of British and French Contemporary Dance in the 1990s'. PhD thesis. London: City University. Retrieved 25 July 2024 from https://openaccess.city.ac.uk/id/eprint/11878/.

Parekh, Bhikhu C., and Runnymede Trust. 2000. *The Future of Multi-Ethnic Britain: Report of the Commission on the Future of Multi-Ethnic Britain*. London: Profile.

Patel, Vidya. 2017. Interviewed by Magdalen Gorringe. 7 June. Birmingham.

PEC (Creative Industries Policy and Evidence Centre). 2023. 'A New Deal for Arts Funding in England?' 12 January. [blog]. Retrieved 25 July 2024 from https://pec.ac.uk/blog_entries/a-new-deal-for-arts-funding-in-england/.

Penman, Robert. 1993. 'Ballet and Contemporary Dance on British T.V.', in Stephanie Jordan and Dave Allen (eds), *Parallel Lines: Media Representations of Dance*. London: Arts Council of Great Britain.

Perugini, Mark. 1919. 'Why Not British Ballet?' *Proceedings of the Musical Association* 46: 43–58. Retrieved 25 July 2024 from http://www.jstor.org/stable/765485.

Phelan, Penny. 1993. *Unmarked: The Politics of Performance*. London: Routledge.

Pillai, Shanti. 2002. 'Rethinking Global Indian Dance through Local Eyes: The Contemporary Bharatanatyam Scene in Chennai', *Dance Research Journal* 34(2): 14–29.

Pillai, Nrithya. 2020. 'The Politics of Naming the South Indian Dancer', *Conversations Across the Field of Dance Studies* 40: 13–15.

Polley, Martin. 2000. '"The Amateur Rules": Amateurism and Professionalism in Post-War British Athletics', in Adrian Smith and Dilwyn Porter (eds), *Amateurs and Professionals in Post-War British Sport*. London: Frank Cass, pp. 81–114.

Postman, Neil. 2007 [1985]. *Amusing Ourselves to Death: Public Discourse in the Age of Show Business*. London: Methuen.

Potter, Caroline. 2007. 'Learning to Dance: Sensory Experience in British Contemporary Dance Training'. PhD thesis. Oxford: University of Oxford.

Power, Elaine M. 1999. 'An Introduction to Pierre Bourdieu's Key Theoretical Concepts', *Journal for the Study of Food and Society* 3(1): 48–52.

Prakash, Akshay. 2017. Interviewed by Magdalen Gorringe. 13 February. London.
Prakash, Brahma. 2019. *Cultural Labour: Conceptualizing the 'Folk Performance' in India*. New Delhi: Oxford University Press.
Press Association. 2016. 'Strictly Come Dancing ends most popular ever series on ratings high'. *Guardian*, 18 December. Retrieved 18 August 2024 from https://www.theguardian.com/tv-and-radio/2016/dec/18/strictly-come-dancing-most-popular-series-ratings.
Press Association. 2007. 'Enoch Powell's Rivers of Blood Speech', *Telegraph*, 6 November. Retrieved 19 August 2024 from https://www.telegraph.co.uk/comment/3643823/Enoch-Powells-Rivers-of-Blood-speech.html.
Prickett, Stacey. 2004. 'Techniques and Institutions: The Transformation of British Dance Tradition through South Asian Dance', *Dance Research: The Journal of the Society for Dance Research* 22(1): 1–21.
———. 2007. 'Guru or Teacher? Shishya or Student? Pedagogic Shifts in South Asian Dance Training in India and Britain', *South Asia Research* 27(1): 25–41.
———. 2009. 'Expanding the Canon: South Asian Dance Training in British Universities' in T Randall (ed.), *Global Perspectives on Dance Pedagogy: Research and Practice, Special Conference: Congress on Research in Dance Conference Proceedings*: 188.
———. 2013a. *Embodied Politics: Dancing Protest and Identities*. Alton: Dance.
———. 2013b. 'Hip-Hop Dance Theatre in London: Legitimising an Art Form', *Dance Research* 31(2): 174–90.
Pulse Dance Club. 2021. 'Dancing Nation', Pulse Connects, 24 February. Retrieved 23 August 2024 from http://www.pulseconnects.com/dancing-nation
Puri, Stine S. 2014. 'Dancing for Money, Men and Gods: Temple Women in Historical Perspectives', in Esther Fihl and A.R. Venkatachalapathy (eds), *Beyond Tranquebar: Grappling across Cultural Borders in South India*. New Delhi: Orient Blackswan, pp. 202–26.
Purkayastha, Prarthana. 2012. 'Dancing Otherness: Nationalism, Transnationalism, and the Work of Uday Shankar', *Dance Research Journal* 44(1): 69–92.
———. 2015. 'The Annotation of Skin', *Performance Research* 20(6): 114–21.
———. 2017a. 'Choreographing Gender in Colonial Bengal: The Dance Work of Rabindranath Tagore and Pratima Devi', *Women, Gender, History* 46: 64–83.
———. 2017b. 'Decolonising Dance History', in Larraine Nicholas and Geraldine Morris (eds), *Rethinking Dance History: Issues and Methodologies*. London: Taylor and Francis, pp. 123–35.
———. 2019. 'Dance and Identity', in Sherill Dodds (ed.), *Bloomsbury Companion to Dance Studies*. London: Bloomsbury, pp. 139–55.
———. 2020. 'Decolonising Human Exhibits: Dance, Re-Enactment and Historical Fiction', in Tina K. Ramnarine, *Dance, Music and Cultures of Decolonisation in the Indian Diaspora*. Oxford: Taylor and Francis, pp. 231–60.
Putcha, Ramya S. 2013. 'Between History and Historiography: The Origins of Classical Kuchipudi Dance', *Dance Research Journal* 45(3): 91–110.
Puwar, Nirmal. 2003. *Space Invaders: Race, Gender and Bodies out of Place*. Oxford: Berg.
Quijano, Anibal. 2007. 'Coloniality and Modernity/Rationality', *Cultural Studies* 21(2–3): 168–78.
Quora. 2020. 'Why Are Black People So Good with Rhythm (Music)?' Retrieved 25 July 2024 from https://www.quora.com/Why-are-black-people-so-good-with-rhythm-music.

Radcliffe, Caroline. 2017. 'Calling Musicians for Twelfth Night/The Tempest – RSC Dell & Oxford Castle'. 30 March. SCUDD [online]. Retrieved 20 June 2020 from https://www.jiscmail.ac.uk.

Radnoti, Sandor. 1981. 'Mass Culture', *Telos* 48: 27–47.

Ragaviah Charry, P. 1808 [1806]. 'Account of the Hindoostanee Dancing Girls, Treating Concisely on the General Principles of Dancing and Singing, with Translations of Two Hindoo Songs', in Charles Taylor (ed.), *Literary Panorama* 3: 545–54. Retrieved 25 July 2024 from https://www.google.co.uk/books/edition/The_Literary_Panorama/st0RAAAAYAAJ?hl=en&gbpv=1.

Rai, Hardial. 2021. Interviewed by Magdalen Gorringe. 18 February. Zoom.

Rajarani, Nina. 2018. Interviewed by Magdalen Gorringe. 24 April. Harrow Arts Centre, Middlesex.

Rajkumar, Tara. 2017. Interviewed by Magdalen Gorringe. 11 April. Birmingham. Skype.

Ralls, Jane. 2018. Interviewed by Magdalen Gorringe. 18 February. Phone call.

Ram, Kalpana. 2000. 'Dancing the Past into Life: The *Rasa, Nrtta* and *Rāga* of Immigrant Existence', *Australian Journal of Anthropology* 11: 261–73.

Ramdhanie, Bob. 2017. 'African Dance in England – Spirituality and Choreography', in Christy Adair and Ramsay Burt (eds), *British Dance: Black Routes*. Abingdon: Routledge, pp. 78–98.

Ramphal, Vena, and Olu Alake. 2010. *Developing Progression Routes for Young Kathak and Bharatanatyam Dancers*. Birmingham: Centre for Advanced Training.

Ratnam, Anita. 2000. 'Reflections on Navadisha', *Narthaki*. Retrieved 25 July 2024 from https://narthaki.com/info/articles/article1.html.

Rattansi, Ali. 2011. *Multiculturalism: A Very Short Introduction*. Oxford: Oxford University Press.

Ray, Piali. 2017a. Interview 1. Interviewed by Magdalen Gorringe. 2 June.

———. 2017b. Interview 2. Interviewed by Magdalen Gorringe. 25 November.

Reay, Diane. 2004. '"It's All Becoming a Habitus": Beyond the Habitual Use of Habitus in Educational Research', *British Journal of Sociology of Education* 25(4): 431–44.

Redden, Guy. 2008. 'Making Over the Talent Show', in G. Palmer (ed.), *Exposing Lifestyle Television: The Big Reveal*. Aldershot: Ashgate, pp. 129–44.

———. 2010. 'Learning to Labour on the Reality Talent Show', *Media International Australia* 134(1): 131–40.

Ritzer, George. 1975. 'Professionalization, Bureaucratization and Rationalization: The Views of Max Weber', *Social Forces* 53(4): 627–34.

Robinson, Laura. 2014. 'The Dance Factor: Hip-Hop, Spectacle, and Reality Television', in Melissa Blanco Borelli (ed.), *The Oxford Handbook of Dance and the Popular Screen*. Oxford: Oxford University Press, pp.304-319.

Rueschemeyer, Dietrich. 1983. 'Professional Autonomy and the Social Control of Expertise', in R. Dingwall and P. Lewis (eds), *The Sociology of the Professions*. London: Macmillan, pp. 38–58.

Ryan, Katharine. 2017. Interviewed by Magdalen Gorringe. 30 September. Oxford.

SAA-UK. n.d. 'Mission & History', Retrieved 24 August 2024 from https://www.saa-uk.org/about-us/mission-history/.

Sabri, Sonia. 2018. Interviewed by Magdalen Gorringe. 16 March. Birmingham, Midlands Arts Centre.

SADAA (South Asian Diaspora Arts Archive). 2016. 'Ram Gopal Documentary'. YouTube, 11 July. Retrieved 25 July 2024 from https://www.youtube.com/watch?v=aC32jtTVv9o.

Sadler's Wells. n.d. 'Our Story'. Retrieved 18 August 2024 from https://www.sadlerswells.com/about-us/our-story/.

Sahin-Dikmen, Melahat. 2013. 'A Bourdieusian Lens onto Professions: A Case Study of Architecture'. PhD thesis. York: University of York. Retrieved 25 July 2024 from https://etheses.whiterose.ac.uk/5616/.

Said, Edward W. 1994. *Culture and Imperialism*. London: Vintage.

———. 1995 [1978]. *Orientalism*. Reprinted with a new afterword. London: Penguin.

Sampad. n.d. 'About Sampad', Retrieved 24 August 2024 from https://sampad.org.uk/about-sampad/.

Sanders, Lorna. 2006. 'Dance Education Renewed: A Reconceptualisation of the Subject of Dance in Education in England and Wales with Particular Reference to GCSE and GCE A Level'. PhD thesis. Guildford: University of Surrey. Retrieved 25 July 2024 from http://epubs.surrey.ac.uk/854809/.

Sanjek, Roger. 1990. *Fieldnotes: The Makings of Anthropology*. Ithaca, NY: Cornell University Press.

Sarker, Bisakha. 2017. Interviewed by Magdalen Gorringe. 23 August. Liverpool.

Satkunaratnam, Ahalya. 2013. 'Staging War: Performing Bharata Natyam in Colombo, Sri Lanka', *Dance Research Journal* 45(1): 81–108.

Schama, Simon. 1995. *Landscape and Memory*. London: Harper Perennial.

Schinkel, Willem, and Mirko Noordegraaf. 2011. 'Professionalism as Symbolic Capital: Materials for a Bourdieusian Theory of Professionalism', *Comparative Sociology* 10: 67–96.

Select Committee on Culture Media and Sport. 2004. 'Memorandum Submitted by South Asian Dance Alliance'. Minutes of Evidence. April. Retrieved 25 July 2024 from https://publications.parliament.uk/pa/cm200304/cmselect/cmcumeds/587/4051105.htm.

Sergot, Bertrand, and Anne-Laure Saives. 2016. 'Unplugged – Relating Place to Organization: A Situated Tribute to Doreen Massey', *M@n@gement* 19(4): 335–52. Retrieved 25 July 2024 from https://www.cairn.info/revue-management-2016-4-page-335.htm.

Sewell, Tony, et al. 2021. *Commission on Race and Ethnic Disparities: The Report*. Retrieved 25 July 2024 from https://assets.publishing.service.gov.uk/government/uploads/system/uploads/attachment_data/file/974507/20210331_-_CRED_Report_-_FINAL_-_Web_Accessible.pdf.

Sewell, Robert. 1972. *A Forgotten Empire (Vijayanagar): A Contribution to the History of India*. Shannon/New York: Irish University Press/Barnes & Noble.

Shah, Purnima. 2002. 'Where they danced: Patrons, institutions, spaces: State patronage in India: Appropriation of the "regional" and "national"'. *Dance Chronicle* 25(1):125-141

Shambhu, Shane. 2017. *Confessions of a Cockney Temple Dancer*. Unpublished script.

Shay, Anthony. 2008. *Dancing across Borders: The American Fascination with Exotic Dance Forms*. Jefferson, NC: McFarland.

Shilling, Chris. 1991. 'Educating the Body: Physical Capital and the Production of Social Inequalities', *Sociology* 25(4): 653–72.

———. 2012 [1993]. *The Body and Social Theory*, 3rd edn. Los Angeles: Sage.

Shobana Jeyasingh Dance. n.d. 'About'. Retrieved 3 July 2024 from https://www.shobanajeyasingh.co.uk/about/.

Siddall, Jeanette. 1999. 'The Evolution of Dance Management in Britian', in Linda Jasper and Jeanette Siddall (eds), *Managing Dance: Current Issues and Future Strategies*. Horndon: Northcote House, pp. 5–24.

Singh, Julietta. 2018. *Unthinking Mastery: Dehumanism and Decolonial Entanglements*. Durham, NC: Duke University Press.

Sklar, Deirdre. 2008. 'Remembering Kinaesthesia: An Inquiry into Culturally Embodied Knowledge', in Carrie Noland and Sally Ann Ness (eds), *Migrations of Gesture*. Minneapolis: University of Minnesota Press, pp. 85–111.

Somasundaram, Nisha, and Urbi Basu. 'Editorial: What Does BBC Young Dancer 2015 Mean for South Asian Dance?' *Finding Lila, South Asian Arts UK*, 5 June. Retrieved 11 September 2017 from http://www.findinglila.com/articles/editorial-bbc-young-dancer-south-asian-dance.

Sommerlade, Kristine. 2018. 'Identity, Knowledge and Ownership: Contemporary Theatre Dance Artists in the UK's Creative Economy'. PhD thesis. London: Middlesex University. Retrieved 25 July 2024 from https://repository.mdx.ac.uk/item/88161.

Sonia Sabri Company. n.d. Retrieved 17 August 2024 from https://www.ssco.org.uk/.

Soneji, Devesh. 2010. *Bharatanatyam: A Reader*. New Delhi: Oxford University Press.

———. 2012. *Unfinished Gestures: Devadāsīs, Memory, and Modernity in South India*. Chicago: University of Chicago Press.

Snapes, Laura. 2021. 'UK Government Rejects "Musician Passports" as Stars Attack "Shameful" Touring Deal', *Guardian*, 20 January. Retrieved 25 July 2024 from https://www.theguardian.com/music/2021/jan/20/uk-government-rejects-musician-passports-as-stars-attack-shameful-touring-deal.

Sporton, Gregory. 2004. 'Dance as Cultural Understanding: Ideas, Policy, and Practice', *Dance Research Journal* 36(2): 80–90.

Sreenivas, Mytheli. 2011. 'Creating Conjugal Subjects: Devadasis and the Politics of Marriage in Colonial Madras Presidency', *Feminist Studies* 37(1): 63–92.

Srinivasan, Amrit. 1983. 'The Hindu Temple-Dancer: Prostitute or Nun?' *Cambridge Anthropology* 8(1): 73–99.

———. 1985. 'Reform and Revival: The Devadasi and Her Dance', *Economic and Political Weekly* 20(44): 1869–76.

Srinivasan, Priya. 2009. 'A "Material"-ist Reading of the Bharata Natyam Dancing Body: The Possibility of the "Unruly Spectator"', in Susan L. Foster (ed.), *Worlding Dance*. Basingstoke: Palgrave Macmillan, pp. 53-75.

———. 2012. *Sweating Saris: Indian Dance as Transnational Labor*. Philadelphia, PA: Temple University Press.

Srivastava, Anita. 2017. Interviewed by Magdalen Gorringe. 21 September. Peterborough.

Stebbins, Robert A. 1992. *Amateurs, Professionals, and Serious Leisure*. Montreal: McGill-Queen's University Press.

Stevens, Jayne. 2016/17. 'The bubble that didn't burst: dance animateurs in the 1980s'. Animated. Autumn/Winter edition. Retrieved 23 August 2024 from https://www.communitydance.org.uk/DB/animated-library/the-bubble-that-didnt-burst-dance-animateurs-in-th.

Subbiah, Stella. 2018. Interviewed by Magdalen Gorringe. 7 February. The Place, London.

Subramanyam, Anusha. 2017. Interviewed by Magdalen Gorringe. 31 May. Dance Xchange, Birmingham.

Sundaram, Chitra. 2012. 'South Asian Arts – Changing Landscapes', *Guardian*, 2 March. Retrieved 25 July 2024 from https://www.theguardian.com/culture-professionals-network/culture-professionals-blog/2012/mar/02/south-asian-arts-funding-support.

———. 2014. 'ISTD Histories – the Classical Indian Dance Faculty'. ISTD website. Retrieved 24 August 2024 from https://www.istd.org/dance/dance-genres/classical-indian-dance/history-of-classical-indian-dance/.

———. 2018. Interviewed by Magdalen Gorringe. 20 April. London.

Svensson, Lennart G. 2015. 'Occupations and Professionalism in Art and Culture', *Professions and Professionalism* 5(2): 1–13.

Taylor, Charles. 1994. 'The Politics of Recognition', in A. Gutmann (ed.), *Multiculturalism: Examining the Politics of Recognition*. Princeton: Princeton University Press, pp. 25–74.

'Taxi4ballet'. 2022. 'BBC Young Dancer 2022' [online forum comment], 28 April. Retrieved 25 July 2024 from https://www.balletcoforum.com/topic/25560-bbc-young-dancer-2022/.

Thamarai. 2017. 'Tamil Dancer Competes in BBC Young Dancer 2017'. 24 January. Retrieved 25 July 2024 from https://thamarai.com/dance/tamil-dancer-competes-bbcs-young-dancer-2017.

Tharp, Kenneth. 2016. 'What a Difference a Year Makes'. 30 March. Retrieved 17 March 2017 from http://www.theplace.org.uk/blog/kenneth-tharps-blog/what-difference-year-makes.

Thatcher, Jenny, et al. 2016. *Bourdieu: The Next Generation: The Development of Bourdieu's Intellectual Heritage in Contemporary UK Sociology*. London. Routledge.

Thobani, Sitara. 2017. *Indian Classical Dance and the Making of Postcolonial National Identities: Dancing on Empire's Stage*. London: Routledge.

Todorov, Tsvetan. 2010. 'The Coexistence of Cultures', *Policy Futures in Education* 8(3–4): 419–26.

Tshimanga, Charles. 2009. 'Let the Music Play: The African Diaspora, Popular Culture, and National Identity in Contemporary France', in Charles Tshimanga, Didier Gondola and Peter J. Bloom (eds), *Frenchness and the African Diaspora: Identity and Uprising in Contemporary France*. Bloomington: Indiana University Press, pp. 248-276.

Tucker, Catherine. 1993. *Traditions on the Move*. Conference report. London: Academy of Indian Dance. Retrieved 24 August 2024 from https://www.vads.ac.uk/digital/collection/SADAA/id/4809/rec/2.

Urgo, Ricky. 2019. 'Professionalism or Socialized White Supremacy', *Naspa: Student Affairs Administrator in Higher Education*, 24 September. Retrieved 25 July 2024 from https://www.naspa.org/blog/professionalism-or-socialized-white-supremacy.

Van Assche, Annelies, Katharina Pewny and Rudi Laermans. 2019. 'Mayday, Mayday, Mayday! Moving from European Discourses on the Precarious and Art to the Realities of Contemporary Dance', *Dance Research: The Journal of the Society for Dance Research* 37(2): 129–46.

Varoufakis, Yanis. 2017. *And the Weak Suffer What They Must? Europe, Austerity and the Threat to Global Stability*. London: Vintage.

Vatsyayan, Kapila M. 1972. *Some Aspects of Cultural Policies in India*. Paris: UNESCO.

———. 1982. *Guru-Shishya Parampara: The Master-Disciple Tradition in Classical Indian Dance and Music*. London: Arts Council of Great Britain.

Venkataraman, Uma. 2018. Interviewed by Magdalen Gorringe. 6 March. Skype.

Visram, Rozina. 2002. *Asians in Britain: 400 Years of History*. London: Pluto.

Wacquant, Loic J.D. 1995. 'Pugs at Work: Bodily Capital and Bodily Labour among Professional Boxers', *Body & Society* 1(1): 65–93.
Wagg, Stephen. 2000. '"Time Gentlemen Please": The Decline of Amateur Captaincy in English County Cricket', *Contemporary British History* 14(2): 31–59.
Wahlberg, Ayo. 2007. 'A Quackery with a Difference – New Medical Pluralism and the Problem of "Dangerous Practitioners" in the UK', *Social Science and Medicine* 65: 2307–16.
Wainwright, Steven P., Clare Williams and Bryan S. Turner. 2006. 'Varieties of Habitus and the Embodiment of Ballet', *Qualitative Research* 6(4): 535–58.
———. 2007. 'Globalization, Habitus, and the Balletic Body', *Cultural Studies ↔ Critical Methodologies* 7(3): 308–25.
Wallace, Derron O. 2016. 'Re-Interpreting Bourdieu, Belonging and Black Identities', in Jenny Thatcher, Nicole Ingram, Ciaran Burke and Jessie Abrahams (eds), *Bourdieu: The Next Generation: The Development of Bourdieu's Intellectual Heritage in Contemporary UK Sociology*. London: Routledge, pp. 37–54.
Watts, Graham. 2017. 'BBC Young Dancer Award 2017'. *Dance Tabs*, 23 April. Retrieved 25 July 2024 from https://dancetabs.com/2017/04/bbc-young-dancer-award-2017/.
Weber, Max. 1979 [1922]. *Economy and Society: An Outline of Interpretive Sociology*, ed. Claus Wittich and Guenther Roth. Berkeley: University of California Press.
Weedon, Chris. 2004. *Identity and Culture: Narratives of Difference and Belonging*. Maidenhead: McGraw-Hill International.
Weibye, Hanna. 2015. 'BBC Young Dancer, BBC 4', *Arts Desk*, 18 April. Retrieved 25 July 2024 from https://theartsdesk.com/dance/bbc-young-dancer-2015-bbc-four.
Weickmann, Dorion. 2007. 'Choreography and Narrative: The Ballet d'Action of the Eighteenth Century', in Marion Kant (ed.), *The Cambridge Companion to Ballet*. Cambridge: Cambridge University Press, pp. 51–64.
Weidman, Amanda. 2003. 'Gender and the Politics of Voice: Colonial Modernity and Classical Music in South India', *Cultural Anthropology* 18(2): 194–232.
Weisbrod, Alexis Arnow. 2010. 'Competition Dance: Redefining Dance in the United States'. PhD thesis. Riverside: University of California Riverside. Retrieved 25 July 2024 from https://escholarship.org/uc/item/6924g6c6.
———. 2014. 'Defining Dance, Creating Commodity: The Rhetoric of *So You Think You Can Dance*', in Melissa Blanco Borelli (ed.), *The Oxford Handbook of Dance and the Popular Screen*. Oxford: Oxford University Press, pp.320-336.
Wenger, Étienne. 1998. *Communities of Practice: Learning, Meaning, and Identity*. Cambridge: Cambridge University Press.
West, Cornel. 1987. 'Minority Discourse and the Pitfalls of Canon Formation'. *Yale Journal of Criticism* 1(1): 193-201.
West London Tamil School. 2018. 'Oriental Fine Arts Academy London'. Retrieved 25 July 2024 from http://www.wlts-ofaal.co.uk/ofaal.html.
Whyte, William F. 1979. 'On Making the Most of Participant Observation', *American Sociologist* 14(1): 56–66.
Wilensky, Harold L. 1964. 'The Professionalization of Everyone?' *American Journal of Sociology* 70(2): 137–58.
Williams, Raymond. 1979. 'The Arts Council', *Political Quarterly* 50(2): 157–71.
Winder, Robert. 2005. *Bloody Foreigners: The Story of Immigration to Britain*. London: Abacus.

Winship, Lyndsey. 2018. 'Darbar Festival Review – Akram Khan's Spellbinding Taster of Indian Dance', *Guardian*, 26 November. Retrieved 25 July 2024 from https://www.theguardian.com/stage/2018/nov/26/darbar-festival-review-akram-khan-sadlers-wells-london.

Wolff, Janet. 1993 [1981]. *The Social Production of Art*, 2nd edn. London: Macmillan.

Wong, Sau-ling Cynthia. 2010. 'Dancing in the Diaspora: Cultural Long-Distance Nationalism and the Staging of Chineseness by San Francisco's Chinese Folk-Dance Association', *Journal of Transnational American Studies* 2(1).

Wulff, Helena. 2007. *Dancing at the Crossroads: Memory and Mobility in Ireland*. Oxford: Berghahn.

Yadagudde, Prakash. 2017a. Interviewed by Magdalen Gorringe. 13 February. London.

Yadagudde, Prakash. 2017b. *Anjaneya*. Performed by Akshay Prakash, for the *BBC Young Dancer* category final, the Lowry Theatre, Manchester, 23 January.

Yancy, George. 2017. *Black Bodies, White Gazes: The Continuing Significance of Race in America*, 2nd edn. Lanham, MD: Rowman & Littlefield.

Young, Robert J. 2010. 'Cultural Translation as Hybridization', *Trans-Humanities Journal* 1(5): 155–75.

Younge, Gary. 2020. 'In These Bleak Times, Imagine a World Where You Can Thrive', *Guardian*, 10 January. Retrieved 25 July 2024 from https://www.theguardian.com/commentisfree/2020/jan/10/bleak-times-thrive-last-column-guardian.

Index

Aakash Odedra Dance Company. *See* Leicester Dance Theatre
abhinaya, 5, 50, 58, 71, 170, 172, 186
   definition of, 29n24
Academy of Indian Dance, 11, 13, 54, 145, 198. *See also* Akademi
Adams, Abha, 58
adavus, 17, 118, 145
   nattadavu, 118
   tattadavu, 118
   tat tei ta ha adavu, 184
Adelphi Theatre, 8–9
ADiTi, 29n27, 58, 158n36, 215, 234n25, 254
Adorno, Theodore
   on cultural commodification, 43
   on culture as industry, 43, 241
African dance, 189, 209–10
   parallels with South Asian dance, 22, 208
Africanization, 11
Agrawal, Shivaangee, 142, 185, 215
   on classical Indian dance forms as cultural artefacts, 134
   on standards of dance practice in the UK compared with India, 136
Agudo, Jose, 187
Ahmed, Sara, 16, 218, 238
   on the 'habit of whiteness', 206
   on 'institutionalized whiteness', 204
Akademi (India): Sangeet Natak, Sahitya, Lalita Kala, 97, 98, 125
Akademi (UK), 11, 20–22, 26n4, 81. *See also* Academy of Indian Dance
The Adventures of Mowgli, 13
Bells, 137, 199
and the BA in South Asian Dance, 140
Coming of Age, 235–36
and ISTD, 145–6
Paradiso, 180, 186–87, 199
Sufi:Zen, 199
and Tara Rajkumar, 206, 232n11
The Troth, 199
Akram Khan Company, 199–200, 246. *See also* Khan, Akram
Giselle, 199, 232n23
Mud of Sorrow, 193, 199
in the Opening Ceremony of 2012 London Olympics, 197
as not representative of classical Indian dance, 2–3, 57, 66, 180
Alston, Richard 48, 52, 197
amateurs, 82–83, 85, 105–7. *See also* 'noble hobbyist'
in British sport, 91–92, 103, 115n14
and the practice of bharatanatyam, 94–96
dance training fit for, 143
and fatigue, 103
in the context of the arts, 86–87, 113
Ambalavaner, Sivanandan
   'We are here because you were there', 219–20
Amina Khayyam Dance Company, 228–29. *See also* Khayyam, Amina
Bird, 229
Anderson, Benedict
   on long-distance nationalism, 131
Angika Dance Company, 142
Appadurai, Arjun
   on cultural reproduction, 131
Appiah, Kwasi Anthony

on *eudaimonia*, 223
Appignanesi, Richard
  on the limits of 'cultural diversity',
    133–34
Araeen, Rasheed, 130
aramandi, 161, 168, 184
arangetram, 96, 116n16, 123, 149
art
  and 'art for art's sake', 90–91, 95–96. *See also* 'reversed economy'
  as commodity, 41–43, 94
  and distinctions between high/low/ popular, 21, 40–42
  'fast' art, 43
  funding for, 12–14, 41, 97–98, 227, 242. *See also* Arts Council.
  and narrative, 5, 50, 62, 73–74, 207–8, 238–39, 241
  artistic/ aesthetic, distinction between, 37–40, 49, 67, 73, 176, 207–8
Arts Council
  Creative Case for Diversity, 215–16, 239
  and cultural diversity, 4, 28n20,180,215–17, 239
  and dance funding, 13, 41, 195
  foundation of by Royal Charter, 12
  and the 'national cultural canon', 194
  National Portfolio Organizations (NPO), 3, 13, 195–96, 216–17, 226–30
  and South Asian dance, 8, 13, 29nn26–27, 30n39, 66, 110, 134, 139, 145, 153–54, 197, 199, 200–5, 208–9, 226–30
  South Asian Dance and Music Mapping Study, 203
Arundale, Rukmini Devi. *See* Devi, Rukmini
Ashton, Frederick, 39, 195
Asian Music Circle, 127
ascesis, 176–177. *See also sadhana*
assimilation (cultural), 54–55, 74, 153, 208
Association for Dance of the African Diaspora (ADAD), 22

Bakhtin, Mikhail
  on organic/forced hybridization, 64–65
Balasaraswati, 11
Balasundari, 127
Balbir Singh Dance Company, 3, 228

Balchandran-Gokul, Mira, 57, 94
Ballal, Archana,101, 186
ballet
  and the 'ballet girl', 95
  in the *BBC Young Dancer*, 1–2, 34, 49, 59–60, 67, 71, 73
  as a British dance form, 195, 197–198, 108, 214, 233n21
  competitions, 38–39. *See also* Morris, Geraldine
  as a form of ethnic dance, 168–69
  in the ISTD, 144
  perceived as the 'apogee of performing arts', 67, 72
Banerjee, Sujata, 101, 128, 142, 162
  In Akbar's Palace, 55
Banerji, Anurima, 22–23, 191n4
banis, 64, 145, 168, 222. *See also* bharatanatyam
Bangladesh, 21
bayadères, 8–9, 29n30, 30n31. *See also* hereditary dancers
Bazalgette, Peter, 215–16
Becker, Howard, 207
Bedi, Protima Gauri, 125
Bedford, 137, 173, 224
Best, David
  on the artistic and the aesthetic, 38–39, 67
bhangra, 23
bharatanatyam, 80, 119–20, 155n3, 198, 208. *See also banis*, classical Indian dance forms
  in the Arts Council National Portfolio, 142, 158n38, 226–27
  and the BA in London Contemporary Dance School, 140, 149
  in the *BBC Young Dancer*, 34, 50, 55–57, 64, 69–71, 73, 77n31, 246–49
  and choreography, 62
  classes in the UK, 118–121, 185, 250
  and cultural nationalism, 123, 131
  opportunities for work, 89, 102, 139, 142
  history of – suppression and reconstruction within India, 92–96
  in the ISTD, 141, 145–47
  and the 'noble hobbyist', 79, 123–24

and the need for money, 96–99
as representative of cultural identity, 127, 129–31, 134–35, 162, 169, 170–72, 213
in the work of Shobana Jeyasingh, 2, 27n13
in Yuva Gati, 128, 150, 152, 237
Bhabha, Homi, 155, 199
Bharatiya Vidya Bhavan, London (The Bhavan Centre), 5, 11, 21, 28n21, 53, 66, 79–81, 126, 128, 130, 140–41, 144, 146, 158n35, 189, 211–12, 252
Birmingham, 17, 20, 34, 70, 118–20, 127, 136, 150, 215, 221, 239, 242–43
Birmingham Royal Ballet, 65–66, 174, 195
Birmingham Hippodrome, 119
Blackstock, Ivan, 69–70, 248
Blackwell, Kelsey, 213
Bolar, Anaya, 26n7, 55
Bolar, Chitralekha, 127, 141
Boler, Megan
on 'a pedagogy of discomfort', 240
bollywood, 21, 23, 53, 98
bols, 119
Bourdieu, Pierre, 14. *See also* capital, field of cultural production, habitus, reversed economy
on *ascesis*, 176
on consecration, 26, 89, 194
on *doxa*, 116n24
on field, 109, 112, 236
on the field of production, 87, 90, 95, 115n11
on the formation of taste, 207
on forms of capital, 87, 124, 163, 176, 185
on habitus, 26, 163–66, 171, 187, 191n1, 240
on *hexis*, 173, 187
influence of upbringing on, 14–15
malleability of concepts, 15–16, 167
on profession, 25, 82, 11, 113
on rational action theory (RAT), 15, 166
and relevance to decolonization, 15–16
on the 'reversed economy', 7, 41, 90, 95–96, 115n11
on 'symbolic violence', 111
Bourne, Matthew, 48, 60, 230, 246

Bradford, 128, 185, 215, 252
Brante, Thomas, 24
on Cynical and Naïve understandings of professions, 83–84. *See also* Freidman, Eliot; professions, professional, professionalism
Britain
and the Commonwealth, 11, 129, 205. *See also* British Nationality Act 1948
and Empire, 11, 53
and the National Health Service, 12
British Broadcasting Corporation (BBC)
as iconic institution, 26n3, 56–57, 194
and *Dancing Nation*, 193–94
and John Reith, 50
BBC Young Dancer (*BBCYD*), 21, 35–36, 188, 225, 246–49
BBCYD 2015, 1–2, 35, 50–52, 55
BBCYD 2017, 2, 33, 37, 47, 51, 54, 60–61
BBCYD 2022, 34–35, 68–73
as a contrast to other televised dance competitions, 47–51, 58, 66
and dialogic representation, 53–56
as framed by the ideology of Euro-American dance, 60–65, 67, 69–74
and the myth of meritocracy, 68, 74
and professional dance, 1, 2, 34, 36, 47–49, 50, 57, 73–74
and the understanding of 'contemporary dance', 61–65
and the visibility of South Asian dance, 51–53, 67
BBC Young Musician, 1, 35, 47, 77n27
British dance
as 'defined by its diversity', 188–90. *See also* McGregor, Wayne
British Home Office, 133, 134
British Nationality Act 1948, 11, 205
British Natyam, 26, 220–23
Brixton riots, 132, 157n29
Brown, Ginnie, 144. *See also* ISTD
Brown, Ismene, 59, 66
Buckland, Theresa,
All Dances Are Ethnic, but Some Are More Ethnic Than Others, 65, 133
Crompton's Campaign, 86, 144
Bussell, Darcey, 48

Cabaret of Angels, 42
Cao, Begoña, 69, 248
canon
   British and place of classical Indian dance forms, 24, 26, 202, 205–7, 214, 220–31, 238–240
   national cultural canon, 14, 26, 194, 223–26. *See also* capital, national cultural capital
   pluriversal canon, 58, 225–26, 238–240. *See also* Mignolo, Walter
capital, forms of, 15. *See also* Bourdieu, Pierre
   cultural capital, 163, 173, 185,
   embodied capital, 163, 167–68
   physical capital, 163. See also, Shilling, Chris.
   national cultural capital, 26, 194–95, 220. *See also* Hage, Ghassan
   relation between different forms, 41, 87, 95–96, 167–68, 240
Carnatic music, 3, 5, 125
carnival, 200. *See also mela*, Hage, Ghassan
Centres for Advanced Training (CATs), 25, 70–71, 150, 159n48, 237. *See also* Yuva Gati
Centre for Indian Classical Dance (CICD), 58, 144, 252
Centre for Indian Performing Arts, 127
Chandra, Shefali
   on re:colonization, 24
Chang-Clarke, Olivia, 71
Charry, Ragaviah, P., 92, 122–23
Chatterjea, Ananya
   on conformity on the global stage, 188
   on dance training routes in India, 125
Chaudhury, Parbati, 81
Cheng, Julia, 69, 71, 248
Chennai, 96, 97, 169, 172, 174, 222
Chidambaram temple, 175
chowka talam, 167
classical Indian dance forms. *See also*, South Asian dance in Britain
   in the Arts Council national portfolio, 3, 199, 226–30
   and a 'contemporary sensibility', 222. *See also* Khan, Akram
   and cultural nationalism, 110, 123, 129, 134, 202
   demographic of practitioners in the UK, 18, 120–21,137, 158n34
   engagement in within Britain, 4, 127–28, 141, 146, 194
   and framing as minority art forms in the UK, 25, 132, 206, 220
   as instruments of marginalization, 23–24
   and ISTD. *See* ISTD
   and lack of work opportunities, 2–3,27n14, 100–103, 139, 142, 179–81
   as 'not wanted in Britain', 4, 198
   as 'part of the British DNA', 236
   shift from importance of economic to symbolic capital in practice of, 99, 124, 135
   training in. *See* training
   as an unsatisfactory collective grouping, 20–23
Clinkard, Theo, 69
colonialism, 8, 16, 25, 124, 131, 133–34, 154, 213, 218–19, 231, 238, 240, 242
   and 'invisible violence', 134. *See also* Purkayastha, Prarthana
   professionalism as a manifestation of, 109
colonization, 14, 111, 220
   of the imagination, 61. *See also* Quijana, Anibal
Commonwealth Immigrants Act (1962 and 1968), 205
competition dance, 36–38
   and manufactured identity, 45–46
   and networking, 37, 53, 225
   and the privileging of display, 37–40
   televised competition dance, 24, 36–37
   and accessibility, 37
   and the escape from the ordinary, 44–45
   and extended choreography, 37, 46. *See also* Elswit, Kate
   and the Toyotaist model of labour, 44–45, 47
communities of practice, 224–25.
consecration, 26, 89, 194, 230. *See also* legitimacy

contemporary dance
  British, 195, 197, 214
  equation with Euro-American contemporary dance, 63, 74
  presumption of universality of, 238
Contemporary Dance Trust, 65, 197, 215, 232n11. *See also* London Contemporary Dance School, The Place
Conquergood, Dwight, 55
Coming of Age. See Akademi.
Cook, Robin, 235
Council for the Encouragement of Music and Arts (CEMA), 13. *See also* Arts Council
critical race theory, 75
Croft, Alex, 185
Crompton, Robert, 86
  and the formation of the ISTD, 143–44
assimilation, 54–55, 74, 153, 208
cultural diversity, 4, 137–38, 189, 200, 205, 235, 238
  limitations of, 132–134
cultural education, 99, 129, 169
  and the tuition of heritage, 127–29
cultural homogenization, 7. *See also* assimilation
cultural long-distance nationalism, 25, 129, 130–31
Cunningham, Merce, 11, 64, 149, 197
de Cahusac, Louis, 51

Daboo, Jerri, 7
Dalit, 23, 32n57
dance animateur movement, 17, 23, 31n48, 137, 147, 157n33, 220, 233n24
Dance Hub Birmingham, 20, 136, 188
Dance Umbrella, 35, 58, 89, 215, 248
Dance UK. *See* One Dance UK
Dance Xchange (now FABRIC), 119, 120, 150, 152, 215
Dancing Nation. See BBC
Darbar, 153, 177, 212, 222
dasi attam, 122, 123, 155n3
Dartington School of Arts, 69, 250
Dattani, Shyam, 2, 27n11, 60, 146, 147
David, Ann R., 10, 52, 96

decolonization, 14, 16, 20, 24, 26, 53, 67, 111, 220, 226, 239–40
Deletant Bell, Monique, 136
de-linking, 214, 217, 219. *See also* Quijano, Anibal
De Montfort University, 140, 184, 250
Department for Culture, Media and Sport (DCMS), 6, 13
devadasis. *See* hereditary dancers
de Valois, Ninette, 195
  Job, 197
Devam, Kamala, 187, 192n19
Devi, Chandrabhaga, 124, 127
Devi, Nilima, 147
Devi, Rukmini, 93–94, 124–25
Devlin, Graham
  Stepping Forward, 215
Dhadyalla, Seetal Kaur, 243
dialogical performance, 55, 66. *See also* Conquergood, Dwight
dialogic representation, 51, 53, 56
diaspora, 131
  Indian subcontinental/ South Asian, 121–22, 129, 132–33, 135, 169
Dodds, Sherril
  on high/low/ popular art, 40–43
doxa, 100, 110–11, 116n24, 153, 166, 202, 206, 231
dual-career dancer, 100–101, 103, 105, 184, 241
Dutta, Sanjeevini, 137, 153, 157n33, 173, 201, 203, 220

Edinburgh Festival
  early performers of classical Indian dance at, 11
  and expectations of an 'Indian' dancer, 19
Elswit, Kate
  on 'extended choreography', 37
Emmanus, Brenda, 193
English National Ballet, 65, 195, 199, 247–48
engram, 182
Equity, 88, 107, 112
'ethnic arts'
  as a form of policing, 132–34. See also Jordan, Glenn, Weedon, Chris

as a 'specific need for a specific people', 220, 237. *See also* Araeen, Rasheed
ethnography, 16–20
and the 'insider-outsider', 18–19
long ethnography, 17–19. *See also* Harrop, Peter
eudaimonia, 223, 231, 239
examinations, 4, 129, 142, 144
ISTD, 144, 148
limitations of, 148, 154
exotic, exoticism, 9, 11, 132, 153, 174, 190, 208

FABRIC, 215. *See also* DanceXchange
Fanon, Frantz, 218
Farnell, Brenda
on habitus, 164–65
'fast art', 43, 66
Festival of Britain 1951, 235
field of cultural production, 41, 87, 90, 95, 115n11,219. *See also* Bourdieu, Pierre
Flaubert, Gustave, 41
Fordist model of labour, 44
Foster, Susan Leigh, 177
on habitus, 163
on the 'hired body', 4, 15, 150, 183, 187
on *So You Think You Can Dance*, 44
Freidson, Eliot
on professionalism and an ideology of service, 83
Freire, Paulo, 61, 68
and cultural inauthenticity, 61
'fusion' dance, 64, 151, 152, 160, 208

Gangani, Rajendra, 243–44
Garratt, Lindsay
on habitus as a 'somatised lens', 163
Gautier, Theophile, 41
Gem Arts, 66
geographical tethering, 178–9, 190
gharanas, 145, 168
Ghosh, Aishani, 28, 185
Ghosh, Sushmita, 145, 147
Gi, Gianni, 69
Cantarea Romaniei, 46
Gladstone, Emma, 69–70, 75n4
Glasstone, Richard, 38
globalization, 224

and erasure of difference, 172–73, 188, 223
Golvala, Sunita, 127. *See also* Navakala
Gopal, Pushkala, 146, 178, 182
Gopal, Ram, 10–12, 38, 124, 126–27, 206, 235
and early classes in classical Indian dance forms in Britain, 126–27
as putting classical Indian dance on the British radar, 10
legendary status of, 10–12
Gorania, Subhash Viman, 55
Govind, Priyadarshini, 102
Graham, Martha, 64, 149
Grau, Andrée, 17
on institutions, 56–57
Graves, Tony, 138
Great Exhibition 1851
grhastha, 94, 112
gunghrus, 119
Gurusamy, Chris, 97, 105
guru-shishya. *See* training

habit of whiteness, 206. *See also* institutionalized whiteness; Ahmed, Sara
habitus, 16, 26, 163–66, 173, 181, 182, 184, 187, 188, 190, 218, 237, 240. *See also* Bourdieu, Pierre, Turner, Bryan S., Wainwright, Steven, Williams, Claire
choreographic, 167, 168, 179–80, 237
individual, 167, 169–70, 175, 176, 177, 190
institutional, 167–68, 171, 177, 237
technical, 167, 168–69, 171, 176, 177–79, 180, 182, 186–87, 190, 193, 237, 238
and Farnell, Brenda, 26, 164–65
as a 'somatised lens', 163. *See also*, Garrett, Lindsay
Hackett, Jane, 35, 50–52, 56, 58–59, 61–62, 65, 71, 75n5, 203–4
Hage, Ghassan, 16, 26, 194, 214, 219, 223, 238. *See also* white nation
on carnival, 200
on repertoires of 'national cultural capital', 26, 194
White Nation, 26

Hall, Stuart, 40, 46, 189, 217, 219–20, 238, 240
  on meaning of art made together with audience, 40
  on reimagining the post-nation, 219–20
Hanauer, Annie, 69, 248
Harrop, Peter, 17. *See also* ethnography
Harrow Tamil School, 54
Helsinki Declaration, 1975, 132
Henwood, Alexandra, 151
hereditary dancers, 8–10, 25, 29, 92–94, 111, 115n15, 124, 207. *See also bayadères*
  training of, 123
hexis, 16, 172–73, 182, 187, 190, 191n10. *See also* Bourdieu, Pierre
hip hop, 1, 46, 57, 209
Hirano, Ryoichi, 70, 249
Howard, Robin, 197, 232n11
Hughes, Everett, 84–85
Hutchinson, Sydney, 121
Huxley, Alduous, 44
  Brave New World, 44
hybridization
  organic/ forced, 64–65. *See also* Bakhtin, Mikhail

immigration, 11–12, 129
  of East African Asians, 130
  of Sri Lankan Tamils, 130, 157n28
  post Second World War, 12
Imperial Society for Training in Dance (ISTD), 4, 21–23, 25, 128, 135, 141, 143–48, 154, 197
  Classical Indian Dance Faculty (CIDF), 21, 25, 29n27, 128, 141, 143–47, 153–54, 197, 236–37
India, 9, 10, 11–12, 14, 17–19, 21, 53, 80, 92, 94, 96–99, 108, 110, 123–34, 128, 131, 137, 144, 154, 160, 170–72, 175–79, 189–90
  and the dual-career dancer, 82, 113
  influence on South Asian dance sector in Britain, 99–100, 122, 133, 136, 144, 154, 160, 162
India Dance Wales, 128
'industry-ready dancer'. *See* Yuva Gati
Iyal, Isai, Natakam, 135, 157n30

Iyer, E. Krishna, 93

Jaivant Patel Dance, 142
Jardine, Debbie, 152. *See also* Dance Xchange
Jawaharlal Nehru Manipuri Dance Academy, 125
Jayant, Ananda Shankar, 99, 106
Johnson, Terence
  on professions as occupational control, 84
Jeyasingh, Shobana, 48, 57, 60, 68, 79, 82, 84, 104, 108, 132, 134, 136, 143, 149, 180, 183, 189, 193, 213, 226, 247–48. *See also* Shobana Jeyasingh Dance Company
  on the 'noble hobbyist', 94, 115n13
  on professionalism, 208–9
Johar, Navtej Singh, 134
Jonzi D, 188, 248
Jordan, Glenn, 133, 138

Kadam, 17, 29, 100, 137, 153, 215
Kalakshetra, 93, 99, 125–27, 140
  dancers, 76n17, 110, 117n30, 168
  rejection of commercialism, 94–95
Kalamandalam, 124–25
Kala Sangam, 66, 128, 185, 252
Kala, the Arts, 226, 233n15
Kali Khautvom, 72
Kalsekar, Ashwini, 177–78, 182
Kanneh-Mason, Sheku, 224
kapitha, 33
kartarimukah, 120
Kasturi, Divya, 129
kathak, 2, 3, 17, 21–23, 50, 53, 55–57, 60, 61, 64, 67, 70, 81, 102, 119–20, 122–23, 125–26, 128, 130, 135, 137, 13, 140–42, 145–47, 149, 151– 52, 155, 160, 162, 176–79, 181, 184–86, 193–94, 197, 199, 209, 212, 227, 237, 240, 243–44, 246–48
kathakali, 22, 64, 94, 125
kudiyattam, 125
Kathak Kendra, 31n49, 125
Kaur, Keranjeet, 147–48
Kaushik, Mira, 1, 11, 17, 99, 136, 222, 235
  on the BBC Young Dancer 1, 34, 56–57, 60, 81

and the Classical Indian Dance Faculty in
  ISTD (Kaushik's campaign), 143–45,
  148–49
 on the 'professional', 88
Kayani-Skeef, Tulani, 40
Keali'inohomoku, Joann, 67, 174
 and ballet as a form of 'ethnic' dance, 168
Kedhar, Anusha, 9, 12, 49, 54, 110, 200,
  208
 on 'hyperflexibility', 113
Kesavan, Piriyanga, 53
Keynes, John Maynard, 13
Khan, Akram, 3, 50, 55, 59, 102, 130,139–
  40, 148–49, 160, 162, 177, 184, 189,
  193, 197–99, 222, 230, 246
 on being of Bangladeshi heritage, 18,
  31n49
 on professionalism, 79, 83
 on 'South Asian dance', 20
Khan, Naseem, 6–7, 11, 126–27, 143, 202
 and *The Arts Britain Ignores,* 4
Khayyam, Amina, 17, 142, 209–10, 227,
  229
Khokar, Ashish, 95, 99, 107
Khoo, Mavin, 17, 110, 184, 222, 235
 on the classical Indian dance sector in
  Britian as uncertain of its identity, 110
 on professionalism, 90, 108
King, Martin Luther, 243
Kuchipudi, 22–23, 26, 50, 126, 128,
  197–98, 212
Kumar, Archita, 186
Kunst, Bojana
 and the performer as the ideal worker
  within capitalism, 44
 on 'projective temporality', 113

Lakhia, Kumudhini, 102, 199
legitimacy, 26, 56, 73, 86, 88, 111–14, 131,
  134, 139, 181, 194, 197, 210, 220,
  222, 230, 238, 241
Leeds, 128, 147
Leicester, 58, 144, 250, 254
Leicester Dance Theatre (Aakash Odedra
  Dance Company), 3, 27n14, 246
 #JeSuis, 3
Let's Create, 226–27, 229. *See also* Arts
  Council

Lewis, Claire, 152
Lewis, Veronica, 140, 149, 157n33
Liberace, 42–43, 46
Limon, José, 64, 197
livelihood, 25, 84, 91, 93, 100, 106, 111–
  14, 121–24, 202, 222, 237, 241–42
Liverpool, 21, 128
London, 1, 5, 8–12, 17, 20, 52–53, 64–65,
  69, 79–81, 89, 105, 118–120, 126–28,
  130, 141, 145, 161–62, 170, 173, 180,
  187, 189, 193, 195, 197, 199, 201,
  206, 210–12, 214–15, 222, 224, 226,
  234n28, 236, 250, 254
London Contemporary Dance School
  (The Place), 25, 29n27, 51, 54, 71,
  77n29,116n20, 140, 154, 185, 197,
  211
 and BA in South Asian Dance,25, 29n27,
  140, 149–50, 186, 211
London Contemporary Dance Theatre, 71,
  140, 149, 197
London Olympics 2012, 197
London Tamil School, 135, 156
Lowry, The, 33, 78
Luton, 17

Mbembe, Achille, 219, 239
McCracken, Grant,
 on 'fast culture', 43
McGregor, Wayne, 28, 183, 188, 197,
  247–48
Mackrell, Judith, 47, 70
Macmillan, Harold, 205
Madras Prevention of the Dedication of
  Devadasis Act 1947, 93–94
Manchester, 33, 52, 60
manipuri, 125
Maree, Lynn, 189
Martin, Randy, 114
Massey, Doreen
 and a relational understanding of space,
  171, 220
mastery, 117
 as repeating patterns of colonialism, 109,
  114, 238–39, 242–43. *See also* Singh,
  Julietta
Mbi, Dickson, 69, 248
McFee, Graham, 38–39, 49, 62, 67

mela, 200, 202. *See also* carnival
Menon, Vallathol Narayan, 125
meritocracy
   myth of, 15, 44–45
Mignolo, Walter, 58, 65, 219
   on the 'horizon of expectations', 58, 73
   on pluriversality, 58, 67
   on the 'rhetoric of modernity', 63, 74
migration, 11, 131, 173, 219, 222
Milapfest, 21, 66, 126, 128, 214
Mill, John Stuart, 223–24
Mitra, Royona
   on danced/dancing heritage, 134
   on Akram Khan, 198–99
Modasia, Jaina, 54–55, 60–62, 146
mohiniattam, 125–26, 186
money
   and classical Indian dance forms, 94–100, 103, 113, 153
   and professionalism, 79, 83–86, 90–91, 105, 112, 114
   reluctance of dancers to discuss, 41–42, 91
Moran, Caitlin, 175
   The 'Moran' test, 175, 189
Morris, Geraldine, 36, 182
   on competitions in ballet, 38–39
mudra, 184
muzhamandi, 118
multiculturalism
   as replicating the hierarchies of colonialism, 133–34, 153, 202, 205, 217

namaskaram, 168
Nandakumara, M.N., 128, 140–41, 212
narrative
   importance of own to understanding an artform, 34, 38–39, 50, 52, 71, 202, 207, 238
Natesa Khautvom, 120
national cultural canon. *See* canon
National Dance Agency, 150, 215–217
National Portfolio Organizations. *See* Arts Council
nattuvanar, 123
nattuvangam, 117
natyarambhe, 168
Natyam

British, 222–23, 225, 242
   as possible collective grouping, 23
Navadal, 146
Navadisha 2000, 174, 191n11
Navadisha 2016, 8, 16, 20, 27, 79, 102, 127, 129
Navakala, 127, 130
Nayak, Prashanth
   on 'making relevance', 214
neo-guru, 125–26
   term coined by Stacey Prickett, 156n11
New Dimensions Arts Management, 8, 63. *See also* Srivastava, Anita
'noble hobbyist', 94. *See also* Jeyasingh, Shobana, amateur
Northern School of Contemporary Dance, 184, 197
nritta, 55, 207
Nrityagram, 125

O'Shea, Janet, 62, 97, 131, 172
Odedra, Aakash, 3, 146, 199, 246. *See also* Leicester Dance Theatre
odissi, 23, 50, 123, 126, 128, 137–38, 173, 186, 194, 212, 224, 226, 233
One Dance UK (formerly Dance UK), 81, 88, 136
Organization for Security and Co-operation in Europe (OSCE), 132
Oriental, Orientalia
   European preoccupation with, 9–11
Orientalism, 54, 134
Oriental Fine Arts Academy of London (OFAAL), 129

padam, 19, 234
Pagrav Dance, 142
Pakistan, 11, 21
Paradiso. *See* Akademi
Parekh, Bhikhu, 57, 221
Paris, 8, 10–11, 168, 175
participant observer, 16, 19. *See also* ethnography
Patel, Saijal, 129
Patel, Seeta, 50, 63, 69, 246–48. *See also* Seeta Patel Dance
Patel, Vidya, 2–3, 146
Pavlova, Anna, 10

Perugini, 195
Pita, Arthur, 70, 249
Place, The, 3, 51, 192, 212. See also London Contemporary Dance School
pluriversality, 26, 58, 67, 219, 227
portfolio career, 101–2
Postman, Neil
Amusing Ourselves to Death, 44
Powell, Enoch, 12, 130
Prakash, Akshay, 5
  and *BBC Young Dancer*, 33–34, 52–53, 62, 64, 67
precarity, 27, 34, 99–101, 105–6, 113–14, 131, 202, 204, 227, 236, 242. See also Martin, Randy
Prince, Kate, 70, 247, 249
profession, 82, 84, 109, 111–12
  as Anglo-American concept, 81, 113
  as a concept linked to value and prestige, 81, 83, 85, 88–89. See also Hughes, Everett
  as a commitment to 'love' and 'money', 83, 107, 111, 114, 241
  dance as a, 114, 135, 141, 144, 162, 238
  necessity and, 105. See also Stebbins, Roger
  parallels with a religious order, 84, 91, 177
  training fit for dance as a, 136, 143, 189
professional
  as independent gentleman, 84, 91
  concept in British sport, 91–92
  as a 'jobber', 92
  as defined by 'being paid', 82–83, 88, 91–92, 96, 107–108
professionalism
  and the arts, 86–91
  and trait theory, 85
  Cynical and Naïve understandings of, 83–84, 86
  as a disciplinary mechanism, 108
  many professionalisms, 14, 241
  multiple theories of, 81–85, 90
  as a preoccupation for South Asian dancers in Britain, 81, 85
professionalization
  and symbolic capital, 240

Purkayastha, Prarthana, 124, 206
  and invisible violence, 134

Quijano, Anibal, 61
  on de-linking, 217–19
  on European culture as provincialism cast as universalism, 66

race, 12, 16, 46, 74, 174–75, 204–6, 219
  riots in Britain, 12, 157. See also Brixton riots
racism, 19, 132, 174, 203, 206, 218–19
Rai, Hardial, 59, 105–6, 213–14
Raghavan, V., 94
Rajarani, Nina, 18, 100, 105, 128, 138, 141, 160, 162, 170–72, 178, 201
  winner of Place prize, 3
  and Srishti, 128
Rajkumar, Tara, 94, 206. See also Akademi
Ram, Kalpana, 131, 133–34
Rambert Dance Company, 66
Random Dance Company
  Polar Sequences, 183
rangmanchpravesh, 123, 149
Rational Action Theory, 66
Ratna, Kiran, 128
Ray, Piali, 34, 215
Rao, U.S Krishna, 124, 127
Redden, Guy, 37
  on televised competitions and 'rupture', 44–45
Reddy, Muthulakshmi, 93
Reith, John. See BBC
reversed economy. See Bourdieu, Pierre
riyaaz, 176–78
Roundhouse, London, 69
Royal Ballet, 65, 120, 154, 168, 178, 182, 193, 195, 202, 224, 247–49
Royal Ballet School, 154, 195
Royal Festival Hall, 187, 235
Ryan, Katherine (Katie), 137–38, 173, 179, 220, 224
Russ, Paul, 58

St. Denis, Ruth, 9–10
Sabri, Sonia, 102, 139, 160, 170, 243, 247. See also Sonia Sabri Dance Company

sadhana, 177–78, 224
sadir, 123, 155n3
Sadler's Wells Theatre, 1, 35, 75n6, 153, 193–94, 212, 247
Sampad Arts, 17, 20, 34, 66, 100, 150, 215, 243
and Navadisha 2016, 8
Sarukkai, Malavika, 102
Sarker, Bisakha, 17, 68, 213, 250
Sartre, Jean Paul
on the 'original project', 15
Savani, Shree, 71
Maa, 72
Scarman Report, 132, 157n29
Scanlan, Kai, 69–70
Second World War, 130–31
Seeta Patel Dance Company, 142, 227, 230. See also Patel, Seeta
Something Then, Something Now, 63
The Rite of Spring, 28n17, 230
Serota, Nicholas, 226–37
Shambhu, Shane, 17
Confessions of a Cockney Temple Dancer, 207, 211
Shankar, Uday, 10–11, 250
A Hindu Wedding, 10
Krishna and Radha, 10
Sharma, Kajal, 135, 247
Shastry, Adhya, 69–73
Shaw, George Bernard
on professions as a conspiracy against laity, 83
Shechter, Hofesh, 40, 142
Shilling, Chris,
on physical capital, 163
shikara, 33, 118, 171–72
Shimakawa, Karen
on 'abject bodies', 132
Shivashankar, Shaalini, 160
Shobana Jeyasingh Dance Company, 17, 142, 199
Contagion, 193
Duets with Automobiles, 57
as not representative of classical Indian dance, 2, 27n13
Siddiqui, Nahid, 48
Singh, Julietta

on mastery, 114
on 'vital ambivalence', 214
Sonia Sabri Dance Company, 3, 27n14, 243, 247
South Asian Arts (SAA) UK, 66, 128, 147, 159
South Asian dance in Britain
and choreography, 180, 209–10
and 'community' dance, 1–2, 57, 81, 139, 153, 181
and deficit-based reading of, 181, 209–10, 219
as part of the British DNA, 235–36
as part of the national cultural capital, 194–5, 202
and the racialization of culture, 204–6
sector in Britain as divided, 7, 58–59, 203–4
as signifying 'contemporary South Asian dance', 23
as an unsatisfactory collective grouping, 20–23
South Asian Dance Alliance (SADAA), 6, 17, 29n26, 66, 81, 140, 215–17, 222, 227, 254–259
So You Think You Can Dance, 1, 36, 41–42, 45–46, 48–49
space, a relational understanding of. See Massey, Doreen
Spalding, Alistair, 35
on Arts Council policy, 153, 201
and *BBC Young Dancer*, 48
and *Dancing Nation*, 193
Sri Lanka, 21, 157
Sri Lankan Tamils, 130, 157n28
Sridhar, Geetha, 69, 248
Srinivasan, Priya,129,132
and the 'unruly' spectator, 40
Srishti (Nina Rajarani Dance Creations), 128
Srivastava, Anita, 63–64, 141, 201
Stebbins, Roger,
on professional artists, 87, 103
on necessity and profession, 105
Strictly Come Dancing, 36, 51
Subbiah, Stella Uppal, 135–36
Udal, 224

Subramaniam, Subathra, 69
Subramanyam, Anusha, 89, 151–52
Summer schools, 143, 212
   importance to dance training of, 100, 126, 179, 237
Sundaram, Chitra, 62, 149, 201, 208, 211, 235, 247–48
Suryakumari, 127
Suzuki, Ai, 71
symbolic violence, 111, 211, 236. *See also* Bourdieu, Pierre

tal/talam, 5, 119, 167
tarana, 133
tattikumbattu, 161, 168
Thanjavur temple, 170, 172, 175–76
Tharp, Kenneth, 48, 51, 246–47
The Arts Britain Ignores. *See* Khan, Naseem
Thobani, Sitara, 139, 180
Todorov, Tsvetan, 133, 205
Toyotaist model of labour, 44–45, 47
tradition
   bharatanatyam choreography seen as representative of, 62–63
   reifying of, 46
   positioned against modernity, 67, 74
training in classical Indian dance forms. *See also* profession
   in Britain, 2–4, 59–60, 125–29, 139–41, 142–54, 178, 181, 185, 237, 250–51
   in evening and weekend dance schools, 103, 126, 128, 137, 143, 153–54, 178, 189, 237
   and the *guru-shishya* model, 123–26
   importance of immersion for, 160, 178–79, 190
   in India, 122–25, 178–79
   and the versatile dancer, 150–52, 181–82, 184, 237
Trinity Laban, 140, 197
tripataka, 184
tuition of heritage, 127–129
Turner, Bryan S., 167–68. *See also* habitus

unconscious bias, 165–66, 218
un-suturing, 217–18. *See also* Yancy, George
Universal Basic Income, 41, 242

University of Surrey, 126

Vardimon, Jasmin, 48, 142, 230, 247
varnam, 5–6, 222
Vatsyayan, Kapila, 98
Vazhavur style, 168
Venkataraman, Uma, 29, 210–11
Verma, Piya, 71
versatile dancer, 25, 73, 77, 110, 122, 162, 181–84, 187, 204
   impact on training, 126, 150–52, 54. *See also* training
versatility
   as not a neutral entity, 182–83, 186
vocational school. *See* training
virutti, 25, 111–114, 117, 135, 227, 242
'visionbite', 66

Wallace, Derron, 16
Wainwright, Steven, 167–68. *See also* habitus
Ward, Kaine, 55
Watts, Graham, 67–68
Weber, Max
   and professional closure, 83–84
Weedon, Chris, 133, 138
Weisbrod, Alexis, 41, 43
   and the normative v. the transgressive in competition dance, 37–40, 49
   on *So You Think You Can Dance*, 45–46, 52
West London Tamil School, 129, 144
white gaze, 207, 218
white nation, 200, 204, 219. *See also* Hage, Ghassan
Wignakumar, Anjelli, 53
Wilensky, Harold, 85
Williams, Clare, 167–68. *See also* habitus
Wilson, Harold, 85
Wong, Sau-Ling, 130–31. *See also* cultural long-distance nationalism

Yadagudde, Prakash, 17, 103–4, 120, 148–49
   on *BBC Young Dancer*, 34
   Kadiragama Kuravanji, 78
   Shivoham, 5–6
   on staying within the *bani*, 64

on training in India, 171
Yancy, George, 26, 217–19, 238. *See also* un-suturing
Yuva Gati, 23, 25, 89, 128–29, 135, 139, 147, 149–52, 154, 156–57, 162, 180–81, 185, 237. *See also* Centres for Advanced Training
and creating an 'industry-ready dancer', 70, 122,151

www.ingramcontent.com/pod-product-compliance
Lightning Source LLC
LaVergne TN
LVHW020248020825
817679LV00004B/221